Jiffy
Phrasebook
SPANISH

Langenscheidt
NEW YORK

Phonetic Transcriptions: Walter Glanze Word Books
(The Glanze Intersound System)

Jiffy Phrasebooks are also available for many other languages.

Jiffy Travel Packs combine the Jiffy Phrasebooks with a travel-oriented 60-minute cassette. Each can be used independently of the other.
(Jiffy Travel Pack Spanish ISBN 0-88729-975-x)

For detailed information please contact
Langenscheidt Publishers, Inc.
46-35 54th Road, Maspeth, NY 11378
(718) 784-0055

INFORMATION

GUIDE TO THE USE OF THE PHRASEBOOK

This Spanish phrasebook offers you all the important words and phrases you may need on a visit to Spain. The phonetic transcriptions which follow the Spanish expressions are designed as an aid to correct pronunciation, and the systematic arrangement of the phrasebook will help you to find what you are looking for in the shortest possible time.

Structure of the phrasebook

The phrasebook is divided into 20 chapters. It begins with general words and phrases, followed by sections on transportation, accommodations, food and drink, and many other important aspects of travel abroad. There are chapters on shopping, health, cultural activities, and entertainment; the appendix gives you lists of common signs and abbreviations, weights and measures, and colors. For easy reference, English words and phrases are printed in heavy black type, while the Spanish translations are in blue. Following these are the phonetic transcriptions of the Spanish phrases in normal black type.

Occasionally two or more phrases have been combined and the interchangeable elements given in italics. For example, the sentence "Is it going to *rain (snow)?*" corresponds to the Spanish "¿Va a *llover (nevar)*?" Thus "Is it going to rain?" is translated "¿Va a llover?" and "Is it going to snow?" becomes "¿Va a nevar?"

In the boxes you will find help on certain language difficulties, tips on general etiquette, and information on travel, eating out, using the telephone, etc., which will help you get by in everyday situations you may encounter while traveling abroad.

An asterisk at the beginning of a sentence indicates that this is something someone else might say to you.

Spanish pronunciation

On pp. 8–11 you will find a detailed guide to Spanish pronunciation. Most of the symbols used in the phonetic system are taken from the Latin alphabet, so you should have no difficulty getting accustomed to the transcriptions.

Spanish grammar

If you would like to get to know some important aspects of Spanish grammar, the brief survey on pp. 195–203 will give you a basic grounding. Apart from offering you an insight into the structure of the Spanish language and helping you to understand the expressions in the phrasebook, this grammatical survey will also enable you to form simple sentences of your own.

Traveler's Dictionary and Index

The glossary at the end of the book is 53 pages long and is for quick reference to words and phrases. The translations are followed by phonetic transcriptions and page references, so that this glossary serves as an index as well.

Carry this phrasebook with you all the time to make the most of your stay.

CONTENTS

Guide to the Phrasebook 3
Pronunciation Guide 8

General Words and Phrases . 12

Greetings 12
Forms of Address; Letters .. 13
Introductions 14
A Visit 15
Farewells 17
General Questions 18
Wishes, Requests 20
Thanks; Yes and No 21
Pardon; Regrets; Congratu-
    lations and Condolences .. 22
Complaints 23
Communication 24
Weather 25
Numbers 28
Time 30
Times of the Day 31
Days of the Week; Months;
    Seasons; Holidays 33
The Date; Age 34
Family 35
Occupations 36
Education 38

On the Road again 40

Asking the Way; Vehicles .. 40
Renting a Car 41
On a Drive 42
Garage, Parking Lot 44
Gas Station, Car Repair 45
Oil; Tires 46
Car Wash 47
Breakdown, Accident 48
Repair Workshop 50
Car Parts, Repairs 51

Tools 57
Traffic Signs 58

On the Bus 59

By Train 60

At the Station; Time Table . 60
Information 61
Tickets 62
Baggage 63
Porter; On the Platform 64
On the Train 65

By Plane 68

Information and Reserva-
    tions 68
At the Airport 69
On the Plane; By Plane –
    Vocabulary 70

By Ship 72

Information, Tickets 72
In the Harbor 73
On Board 74
By Ship – Vocabulary 75

At the Border 78

Passport Control 78
Customs Control 80

Accommodations 81

Checking it out 81
Checking in 82
Price 83
Registration, Luggage 84
Reception, Desk Clerk 85

6 Contents

Maid 87
Complaints 88
Checking out 89
Accommodations – Vocabulary 90
Camping, Youth Hostels ... 95

Eating and Drinking 98

Ordering 98
Table Service 99
Breakfast 100
Lunch and Dinner 101
Cooking; Ingredients 102

The Menu 104

Appetizers 104
Soups 105
Some Typical Spanish Dishes 106
Fish and Shellfish 106
Poultry 107
Meat 108
Some Typical Mexican
  Dishes 109
Vegetables 109
Cheese 110
Bread; Fruit 111
Desserts 112

Beverages 113

Wine; Beer; Liquor 113
Other 114
Complaints, Paying the
  Check 115

Downtown 116

On the Street 116
Bus, Taxi 117
Sightseeing and Excursions . 118
Downtown – Vocabulary ... 120

Religion, Churches 123

Let's go Shopping 126

General Words and Phrases 126
Stores 128
Flowers; Bookshop 130
Photo Shop 131
Jeweler; Clothing 133
Dry Goods; Fabrics 136
Cleaning, Alterations, Repairs 137
Optician; Stationery 138
Shoes 139
Cigar Store; Toiletries 140
Watchmaker 142
Sundries 143

The Post Office 145

Telegrams; Telephone 147
Code Alphabet; Post
  Office – Vocabulary 149

Bank, Currency Exchange .. 151

Police Station 153

Reporting 153
Police – Vocabulary 154

Beauty Shop, Barber Shop .. 155

Beauty Shop 155
Barber Shop 157
Vocabulary 158

Health 159

Pharmacy 159
Medication and Bandages .. 160
The doctor is in 162
Parts of the Body and
  their Functions 166

What's wrong? 169

In the Hospital 172

At the Dentist's 173

Taking a Cure 175

Concert, Theatre, Movies ... 176

Box Office 176

Movies 179

Pastimes 180

Fun and Games 180

Getting acquainted 182

On the Beach 185

Sports 186

Appendix 191

Signs 191

Abbreviations 192

Weights and Measures 193

Colors 194

Important Grammar Rules ... 195

English-Spanish Dictionary .. 204

SPANISH PRONUNCIATION

The sounds of a foreign language have to be learned by hearing and imitating a native or near-native speaker of that language. No amount of written information will teach you the true pronunciation of a foreign word or phrase. Many transcription systems have been devised toward this purpose; but all of them use either unfamiliar combinations of letters or odd-looking new characters—combinations or characters that have to be learned in addition to learning the foreign language.

The pronunciation system that was developed for the Langenscheidt Jiffy Phrasebooks* is entirely different: The symbols you find here are the ones you are likely to be familiar with from your use of high-school, college, or desk dictionaries of the English language. (That is, the symbols are the same ordinary letters of the alphabet with the same markings, such as [ē] for the vowel sound in *he*.)

This new pronunciation system is meant to be an approximation, serving practical needs, as encountered by the traveler. But, then, even those complicated systems remain an approximation. The true sounds, as we have said, must be learned by listening.

The basic symbols you see in the table are the same that you will find in other Langenscheidt Jiffy Phrasebooks for speakers of English. Therefore, when using these Phrasebooks in traveling from country to country, you don't have to shift from one set of symbols to another.

For Spanish, words of more than one syllable are shown with an accent mark, and occasionally with two equal accent marks: *general* [henerä l'], *norteamericano* [nōr′te·ämerēkä′nō].

To avoid ambiguity, two neighboring vowel symbols (and occasionally two consonant symbols) are separated by a raised dot [·]. This separation is meant to be a convenience to the eye and usually does not mean a break in pronunciation: *ahora* [ä·ō′rä], *sangria* [säng·grē′ä].

The transcription is that of individual words, even in a sentence. The rhythm of a sentence or phrase has to be learned by ear.

The pronunciation of this Jiffy Phrasebook reflects the Spanish of the Americas, rather than classical or Castillian Spanish. (See also the remarks on regional Spanish beneath the table.)

---

* The Glanze Intersound System

Symbol	Approximate Sound	Examples
	Vowels	
[ä]	The a of father or watch; the o of doll or box.	*casa* [kä′sä]
[e]	The e of met (but tending towards the a of fate).	*meses* [me′ses]
[ē]	The e of he.	*camino* [kämē′nō] *ir* [ēr]
[ī]	The i of time.	*hay* [ī] *mosáico* [mōsī′kō]
[ō]	The o of nose (but without the "upglide").	*como* [kō′mō] *norte* [nōr′te]
[oi]	The oi of voice.	*estoy* [estoi′]
[o͞o]	The u of rule.	*agudo* [äg͞oo′dō]
[ou]	The ou of house.	*causa* [kou′sa]
	Consonants	
[b]	A Spanish sound that has to be learned by listening. Until you have learned this sound, use the b of bed. See also [v].	*hablar* [äblär′]
[d]	The d of door.	*rendir* [rendēr′]
[f]	The f of fat.	*efecto* [efek′tō]
[g]	The g of go.	*gato* [gä′tō]

Symbol	Approximate Sound	Examples
[h]	A sound that has to be learned by listening. (This "guttural" sound resembles the ch in Scottish *loch* and German *Bach* and, more remotely, the *r* in French *Paris*.) Until you have learned this sound, use the *h* of *hot*.	*Juan* [hoo·än′] *gente* [hen′te]
[k]	The c of can.	*cubo* [koo′bō]
[l]	The l in love. (Not the l in old.) (See also the combination [ly] below.)	*lado* [lä′dō]
[m]	The m of more.	*mesa* [me′sä]
[n]	The n of nest. (See also the combination [ny] next page.)	*andar* [ändär′]
[ng]	The ng of sing.	*banco* [bäng′kō]
[p]	The p of pen.	*poco* [pō′kō]
[r]	The r of run, but stronger "trilled" in many words, especially all words with rr.	*rico* [rē′kō] *grande* [grän′de] *perro* [pe′rrō]
[s]	The s of sun. (See also [z].)	*servir* [servēr′]
[t]	The t of tea.	*tiempo* [tyem′pō]
[tsh]	The ch of much.	*muchacha* [mootshä′tshä]
[v]	A Spanish sound that is usually identical to the [b] above. But this pronunciation varies greatly, and for the sake of simplicity, the letter *v* is represented by the symbol [v].	*vida* [vē′dä] *huevo* [oo·e′vō]

Symbol	Approximate Sound	Examples
[y]	The y of year. (See also the combinations [ly] and [ny] below.)	*yo* [yō] *hielo* [ye'lō]
[z]	The z of zeal. (Note: Spanish s is pronounced [z] before the "voiced" consonants b, d, g, l, m, n, and r.)	*mismo* [mēz'mō] *desde* [dez'de]

Note also these combinations:

[ly] as in *caballo* [käbä'lyō], *julio* [hoo'lyō]

[ny] as in *año* [ä'nyō], *junio* [hoo'nyō]

[oo·e] as in *bueno* [boo·e'nō]

[oo·ä] as in *cuanto* [koo·än'tō]

[oo·ē] as in *muy* [moo·ē']

[oo·ō] as in *cuota* [koo·ō'tä]

[e'ē] as in *rey* [re'ē]

[e·oo] as in *neumático* [ne·oomä'tēkō]

[ä·ē] as in *caída* [kä·ē'dä]

(Each of these combinations should be pronounced as almost one "gliding" sound.)

Among other aspects of Spanish that may be learned through listening and practice are:

- The great regional differences in pronunciation (and vocabulary) not only between the "Castillian" Spanish of Spain and the Spanish of the Americas, but also generally among the speech habits of the twenty countries where Spanish is spoken.

- The typical pronunciation of many letters: the *b* and *v*, the final *d*, the *c* and *z*, the *r*, *rr*, *l*, *y*, and *h*, and other letters and their combinations.

The Spanish Alphabet

A a	B b	C c	Ch ch	D d	E e	F f	G g	H h	I i	J j
ä	be	se	tshe	de	e	e'fe	he	ä'tshe	ē	hō'tä

K k	L l	Ll ll	M m	N n	Ñ ñ	O o	P p	Q q	R r	S s
kä	e'le	e'lye	e'me	e'ne	e'nye	ō	pe	koo	e're	e'se

T t	U u	V v	W w	X x	Y y	Z z
te	oo	be	dō'blebe	e'kēs	ēgrē·egä	se'tä

GENERAL WORDS AND PHRASES

`Greetings`

Good morning!
¡Buenos días!
bōō·e'nōs dē'äs

Good afternoon!
¡Buenas tardes!
bōō·e'näs tär'des

Good evening!
¡Buenas noches!
bōō·e'näs nō'tshes

"Buenos días" *is used in the morning until lunchtime, and* "buenas tardes" *from lunchtime until dark.*

Welcome! (Pleased to see you!)
¡Bienvenido! (Encantado/Encantada de verlo/*Sp* verle)
(*fam* verte)
byenbene'dō (enkäntä'dō/enkäntä'dä de ver'lō/ver'le)
(ver'te)

Hi!
¡Hola!
ō'lä

Did you have a good trip?
¿Tuvo/*Sp* a tenido/un buen viaje?
tōō'vō/ä tene'dō/ōōm bōō·em' byä'*he*

I'm delighted to see you!
Me alegro mucho de verlo/*Sp* verle.
me äle'grō mōō'tshō de ver'lō/ver'le

How are you?
¿Cómo está usted?
kō'mō estä' ōōste'

How're you doing?
¿Qué tal?
ke täl

How's it going?
¿Cómo le va?
kō'mō le vä

Thanks, just fine.
Muy bien, gracias.
mōō'ē byen, grä'syäs

And you?
¿Y usted?
ē ōōste'

How's the family?
¿Cómo está la familia?
kō'mō estä' lä fäme'lyä

My . . . is sick.
Mi . . . está enfermo/enferma.
mē . . . estä' emfer'mō/em-
fer'mä

Did you sleep well?
¿Descansó?/*Sp* ¿Ha dormido bien?
deskänsō'/ä dōrme'dō byen

We're feeling fine.
Nos encontramos bien.
nōs enkonträ'mōs byen

Thanks for your cordial welcome.
Gracias por la cordial acogida.
grä'syäs pōr lä kōrdyäl' äkō*hē*'dä

Forms of Address

Mr. *(name)*	Señor	senyōr'
Mrs. *(name)*	Señora	senyō'rä
Madam/Sir	señora/señor	senyō'rä/senyōr'
Miss	señorita	senyōrē'tä
Ladies and	¡Señoras y	senyō'räs ē
Gentlemen!	Señores!/¡Damas y	senyō'res/dä'mäs ē
	caballeros!	käbälye'rōs
your wife	su esposa (su mujer) ..	sōō espō'sä (sōō mōōher')
your husband	su esposo (su marido) .	sōō espō'sō (sōō märē'do)
Doctor *(when addressing him or her)*	doctor/doctora	dōktōr', dōktō'rä
Professor	profesor/profesora	prōfesōr', prōfesō'rä

Don *and* Doña + *first name is a form of affectionate respect used for older men and women.*

Letters

The "double" last name in Spanish speaking countries consists of both the father's and the mother's paternal surnames: Fernando Rivera García.

Dear Mr. López	Distinguido	dēstēngē'dō
	Sr. López	senyōr' lō'pes
Dear Mrs. López	Distinguida	dēstēngē'dä
	Sra. López	senyō'rä lō'pes
Dear Miss López	Distinguida	dēstēngē'dä
	Srta. López	senyōrē'tä lō'pes
Dear Sirs, Gentlemen	Muy Sres. míos	mōō'ē senyō'res mē'ōs
Dear Mr. Cook *(to a respected friend)* ...	Estimado Sr. Cook	estēmä'dō senyōr' ...
Dear Mrs. Cook	Estimada Sra. Cook ...	estēmä'dä senyō'rä
Dear Peter	Querido Pedro	kerē'dō pe'drō
Yours sincerely, **Cordially yours,** ...	Con un saludo cordial	kōn ōōn sälōō'dō kōrdyäl'

Introductions

My name is ...
Me llamo ...
me lyä'mō ...

Let me introduce	Le presento a	le presen'tō ä
my son	mi hijo	mē ē'hō
my daughter	mi hija	mē ē'hä
my friend *(male)*	mi amigo	mē ämē'gō
my friend *(female)* ..	mi amiga	mē ämē'gä
my friends	mis amigos	mēs ämē'gōs
my boyfriend	mi novio	mē nō'vyō
my girlfriend	mi novia	mē nō'vyä
my fiancé	mi prometido /	mē prōmetē'dō,
	mi novio	mē nō'vyō
my fiancée	mi prometida /	mē prōmetē'dä,
	mi novia	mē nō'vyä

> Novio/novia *mean both boyfriend/girlfriend and fiancé/fiancée. At a wedding, the bride and groom are* "los novios."

Glad to meet you (How do you do?)
¡Encantado! / ¡Encantada!
enkäntä'dō/enkäntä'dä

Haven't we seen each other before?
¿No nos conocemos ya de vista?
nō nōs kōnōse'mōs yä de vēs'tä

Do you live here?
¿Vive usted aquí?
vē've ōoste' äkē'

Are you *Mr. (Mrs., Miss)* Smith?
¿Es usted *el señor (la señora, la señorita)* Smith?
es ōoste' el senyōr' (lä senyō'rä, lä senyōrē'tä) Smith

What is your name, please?
¿Cómo se llama usted, por favor?
kō'mō se lyä'mä ōoste', pōr fävōr'

Where are you from?
¿De dónde es usted?
de dōn'de es ōoste'

We've been here for a week.
Llevamos aquí una semana.
lyevä'mōs äkē' ōo'nä semä'nä

Do you like it here?
¿Le gusta aquí?
le gōos'tä äkē'

Are you here alone?
¿Está usted aquí solo/sola?
estä' ōoste' äkē' sō'lō/sō'lä

Where do you work?
¿Dónde trabaja usted?
dōn'de träbä'hä ōoste'

What do you do for a living?
¿Cuál es su profesión?
kōo·äl' es sōo prōfesyōn'

What are you studying? (What's your major?)
¿Qué estudia usted?
ke estōo'dyä ōoste'

Got some time?
¿Tiene tiempo?
tye'ne tyem'pō

Shall we go to the . . .?
¿Vamos al (a la) . . .?
vä'mōs äl (ä lä) . . .

What time shall we meet?
¿A qué horas / Sp a qué hora /
nos encontramos?
ä ke ō'räs / ä ke ō'rä /
nōs enkōnträ'mōs

May I pick you up?
¿Quiere que lo / Sp le / (la) recoja?
kye're ke lō / le / (lä) rekō'hä

Please leave me alone!
¡Por favor, déjeme en paz!
pōr fävōr', de'heme em päs

Get lost! (Buzz off!)
¡Váyase ya!
vä'yäse yä

A Visit

Is Mr. (Mrs., Miss) . . . at home?
¿Está en casa el señor (la señora, la señorita) . . .?
estä' en kä'sä el senyōr' (lä senyō'rä, lä senyōrē'tä) . . .

Could I speak to Mr. (Mrs., Miss) . . .?
¿Podría hablar con el señor (la señora, la señorita) . . .?
pōdrē'ä äblär' kōn el senyōr' (lä senyō'rä, lä senyōrē'tä) . . .

Does Mr. (Mrs., Miss) . . . live here?
¿Vive aquí el señor (la señora, la señorita) . . .?
vē've äkē' el senyōr' (lä senyō'rä, lä senyōrē'tä) . . .

I'm looking for . . .
Busco . . .
bōos'kō . . .

When will he (she) be home?
¿A qué hora estará en casa?
ä ke ō'rä estärä' en kä'sä

I'll drop by again later.
Volveré más tarde.
vōlvere' mäs tär'de

When can I (shall we) come?
¿A qué hora puedo (debemos) venir?
ä ke ō'rä pōo·e'dō (debe'mōs) venēr'

I'd (We'd) love to come.
Voy (Vamos) encantado(s).
voi (vä′mōs) enkäntä′dō(s)

*Come in!
¡Adelante! / ¡Pase!
ädelän′te / pä′se

*Please have a seat.
Siéntese, por favor.
syen′tese, pōr fävōr′

*Just a minute, please.
Un momento, por favor.
ōōn mōmen′tō, pōr fävōr′

Thanks so much for the invitation.
Muchísimas gracias por la invitación.
mōōtshē′sēmäs grä′syäs pōr lä ēmbētäsyōn′

Am I bothering you?
¿Lo / *Sp* le / molesto?
lō / le / mōles′tō

Please don't go to a lot of trouble.
No se moleste, por favor.
nō se mōles′te, pōr fävōr′

*What'll you have?
¿Desea tomar algo?
dese′ä tōmär′ äl′gō

What may I offer you?
¿Puedo ofrecerle algo?
pōō·e′dō ōfreser′le äl′gō

Mr. (Mrs.) Smith sends you *his (her)* regards (love).
Muchos saludos de parte *del señor (de la señora)* Smith.
mōō′tshōs sälōō′dōs de pär′te del senyōr′ (de lä senyō′rä) Smith

I'm afraid I've got to go now.
Lo siento, ahora tengo que marcharme.
lō syen′tō, ä·ō′rä ten′gō ke märtshär′me

Thanks so much for *a lovely evening (coming)*.
Muchas gracias por *esta agradable velada (su visita)*.
mōō′tshäs grä′syäs pōr es′tä ägrädä′ble velä′dä (sōō vēsē′tä)

Please give Mr. (Mrs.) ... my best regards.
Salude por favor *al señor (a la señora)* ... de mi parte.
sälōō′de pōr fävōr′ äl senyōr′ (ä lä senyō′rä) ... de mē pär′te

I'll tell him (her) you said hello.
Le daré un saludo de su parte con mucho gusto.
le däre′ ōōn sälōō′dō de sōō pär′te kōn mōō′tshō gōōs′tō

I hope we'll meet again soon.
Espero que volveremos a vernos pronto.
espe′rō ke vōlvere′mōs ä ver′nōs prōn′tō

Farewells

Good-bye!
¡Adiós!
ädyōs´

See you soon!
¡Hasta luego!
äs´tä lōō•e´gō

Good night!
¡Buenas noches!
bōō•e´näs nōtshes

See you tomorrow!
¡Hasta mañana!
äs´tä mänyä´nä

All the best!
¡Que le / te *(fam)* / vaya
bien!
ke le / te / vä´yä byen

Have a good trip!
¡Buen viaje!
bōō•em´ byä´*he*

I'd like to say good-bye!
Quisiera despedirme.
kēsye´rä despedēr´me

I'm afraid we have to go.
Lo siento, ahora tenemos que irnos.
lō syen´tō, ä•ō´rä tene´mōs ke ēr´nōs

Thanks so much for coming.
Muchas gracias por venir.
mōō´tshäs grä´syäs pōr venēr´

Come again soon!
Vuelva / vuelve *(fam)* / pronto.
vōō•el´vä / vōō•el´ve / prōn´tō

When can we get together again?
¿Cuándo nos veremos?
kōō•än´dō nōs vere´mōs

I'll give you a call tomorrow.
Lo / *Sp* le / te *fam* / llamo mañana.
lō / le / te / lyä´mō mänyä´nä

Can I give you a lift home?
¿Quiere que lo / *Sp* le / te *fam* / lleve a su / tu *fam* /
casa?
kye´re ke lō / le / te / lye´ve ä sōō / tōō / kä´sä

It's pretty late.
Ya es tarde.
yä es tär´de

Give ... my best!
¡Saludos a ...!
sälōō´dōs ä ...

Thanks very much.
¡Muchísimas gracias!
mōōtshē´sēmäs
grä´syäs

I had a lovely time.
Ha sido muy agradable.
ä sē´dō mōō´e ägrä-
dä´ble

I enjoyed myself very much.
Me ha gustado mucho.
me ä gōōstä´dō mōō´tshō

Till next time.
Hasta la próxima.
äs´tä lä prō´ksēmä

I'll *take you to (give you a lift to)* the ...
Le / te *(fam)* / acompaño (llevo / *Mex* doy un aventón) a ...
le / te / äkōmpä´nyō (lye´vō / doi ōōn äventōn´) ä ...

---

*In Spanish-speaking countries, "Adiós" (good-bye) is also used as a
greeting in passing when you have no time to stop and chat.*

General Questions

When?	Why?	What?	What kind of ...?
¿Cuándo?	¿Por qué?	¿Qué?	¿Qué clase de ...?
koo·än'dō	pōr ke	ke	ke klä'se de ...

Which?	To whom?	With whom?	Whose?
¿Cuál?	¿A quién?	¿Con quién?	¿De quién?
koo·äl'	ä kyen	kōn kyen	de kyen

Who?	How?	How long?
¿Quién?	¿Cómo?	¿Cuánto tiempo?
kyen	kō'mō	koo·än'tō tyem'pō

How *much (many)*?	Where?	Where from?
¿*Cuánto*? (¿*Cuántos*?)	¿Dónde?	¿De dónde?
koo·än'tō (koo·än'tōs)	dōn'de	de dōn'de

Where to?	What for?	Can I ...?
¿Adónde?	¿Para qué?	¿Puedo ...?
ädōn'de	pä'rä ke	poo·e'dō ...

Is ... allowed here?	Do you need ...?
¿Se puede ... aquí?	¿Necesita / necesitas *(fam)* ...?
se poo·e'de ... äkē'	nesesē'tä / nesesē'täs ...

Have you got ...?	When can I get ...?
¿Tiene/tienes *(fam)* ...?	¿Cuándo puedo tener ...?
tye'ne/tye'nes ...	koo·än'dō poo·e'dō tener' ...

What time do you *open (close)*?	What would you like? (What can I do for you? May I help you?)
¿A qué hora *abren (cierran)*?	¿Qué desea? (¿En qué puedo servirle?)
ä ke ō'rä ä'bren (sye'rrän)	ke dese'ä (en ke poo·e'dō servēr'le)

What's *this/that*?	What happened?	What does that mean?
¿Qué es *esto/eso*?	¿Qué pasó?	¿Qué significa eso?
ke es es'tō/e'sō	ke päsō'	ke sēgnēfē'kä e'sō

How much does that cost?	What are you looking for?
¿Cuánto cuesta? (¿Cuánto vale?)	¿Qué busca usted?
koo·än'tō koo·es'tä (koo·än'tō vä'le)	ke boos'kä ooste'

Whose is that?	*Whom do you wish to see?
¿De quién es?	¿A quién quiere ver?
de kyen es	ä kyen kye're ver

Who's there?
¿Quién es?
kyen es

Who can (Can anyone) ...?
¿Quién puede ...?
kyen poo·e'de ...

What's your name?
¿Cómo se llama/te llamas *(fam)*?
kō'mō se lyä'mä / te lyä'mäs

How do you say ... in Spanish?
¿Cómo se dice ... en español?
kō'mō se dē'se ... en espänyōl'

How do I get to ...?
¿Por favor, cómo se va a ...?
pōr fävōr, kō'mō se vä ä ...

How does that work?
¿Cómo funciona eso?
kō'mō foonsyō'nä e'sō

How long does it take?
¿Cuánto tiempo tarda?
koo·än'tō tyem'pō tär'dä

How much do I get?
¿Cuánto recibo?
koo·än'tō resē'bō

How much is it?
¿Cuánto vale?
koo·än'tō vä'le

Where can I find ... (is ... located)?
¿Dónde se encuentra ...?
dōn'de se enkoo·en'trä ...

Where *is (are)* ...?
¿Dónde está *(están)* ...?
dōn'de estä' (estän') ...

Where's the nearest ...?
¿Dónde está el/la ... más cercana?
dōn'de estä' el / lä ... mäs serkä'nä

Where can I ...?
¿Dónde puedo ...?
dōn'de poo·e'dō ...

Where can I get (find) ...?
¿Dónde puedo conseguir ...?
dōn'de poo·e'dō konsegēr' ...

Where is (are) there ...?
¿Dónde hay ...?
dōn'de ī ...

Where do you live?
¿Dónde vive/vives *(fam)*?
dōn'de vē've / vē'ves

Where are we?
¿Dónde estamos?
dōn'de estä'mōs

Where do you come from?
¿De dónde viene/vienes *(fam)*?
de dōn'de vye'ne / vye'nes

Where are you going?
¿Adónde va/vas *(fam)*?
ädōn'de vä / väs

Where does *this road (street)* lead?
¿Adónde conduce *este camino (esta calle)*?
ädōn'de kōndoo'se es'te kämē'nō (es'tä kä'lye)

Wishes, Requests

> *As in any language, the liberal use of polite expressions – such as por favor, gracias, con permiso, perdón, etc., – not only reflects well on you, the speaker, but helps in getting things done, solving problems, making friends and, in general, having a more enjoyable trip.*

Would you please *bring (give, show) me* ...?
¿Por favor, *tráigame (déme, enséñeme)* ...?
pōr fävōr', trī'gäme (de'me, ense'nyme) ...

Would you please tell me ...?
¿Por favor, podría/podrías *(fam)* / decirme ...?
pōr fävōr', pōdrē'ä / pōdrē'äs / desēr'me ...

Beg your pardon?
¿Perdón? (¿Cómo?/*Mex* ¿Mande?)
perdōn' (kō'mō / män'de)

What can I do for you?
¿En qué puedo servirle?
en ke pōō·e'dō servēr'le?

May I help you?
¿Puedo ayudarle?
pōō·e'dō äyōōdär'le

I'd like (We'd like) ...
Quisiera (Quisiéramos) ...
kēsye'rä(kēsyer'ämōs)...

I need ...
Necesito ...
nesesē'tō ...

I'd rather have ...
Prefiero ...
prefye'rō ...

Could I *have (get)* ...?
¿Podría *tener (conseguir)* ...?
pōdrē'ä tener' (kōnsegēr') ...

Please help me!
¡Ayúdeme!/¡Ayúdame! *(fam)*,
por favor.
äyōō'deme/äyōō'däme/pōr fävōr'

Certainly! (Sure!)
¡Cómo no!
kō'mō nō

Allow me? (Excuse me?)
¿Permiso?
permē'sō

Get well soon!
¡Que se mejore / te mejores *(fam)*!
ke se me*h*ō're / te me*h*ō'res

All the best!
¡Que le / te *(fam)* / vaya bien!
ke le / te / vä'yä byen

Have a good time!
¡Diviértase! / ¡Diviértete! *(fam)*
dēvyer'täse / dēvyer'tete

I wish you ...
Le / te *(fam)* / deseo ...
le / te / dese'ō ...

Thanks

Thanks (Thank you) very much!
Gracias!, ¡Muchísimas gracias!
grä´syäs, mōōtshē´sēmäs grä´syäs

Thanks a lot!
¡Muchas gracias!
mōō´tshäs grä´syäs

Thank you too!
Gracias a usted/a ti *(fam)*!
grä´syäs ä ōōste´/ä tē/

No, thanks.
No, gracias.
nō, grä´syäs

I'm very grateful to you.
.e/te *(fam)*/estoy muy agradecido.
e/te/estoi´ mōō´ē ägrädese´dō

You're welcome.
De nada.
de nä´dä

Thanks very much for *your help (all your trouble)*!
Muchas gracias por *su/tu (fam)/ayuda (sus/tus (fam)/gestiones)*.
mōō´tshäs grä´syäs pōr sōō/tōō/äyōō´dä (sōōs/tōōs/hestyō´nes)

(We) thank you so much for ...
.e/te *(fam)/agradezco (agradecemos)* mucho por ...
e/te/ägrädes´kō (ägrädese´mōs) mōō´tshō pōr ...

Thanks a million!
Mil gracias!
mēl grä´syäs

Don't mention it.
No hay de qué.
nō ī de ke

Glad to do it.
Con mucho gusto.
kōn mōō´tshō gōōs´tō

Yes and No

Yes.
Sí.
sē

Certainly.
Desde luego.
des´de lōō•e´gō

Of course.
Por supuesto.
pōr sōōpōō•es´tō

Good! (Fine!)
¡Muy bien!
mōō´ē byen

I'd be glad to.
Con mucho gusto.
kōn mōō´tshō gōōs´tō

Right!
¡Eso es!
e´sō es

Terrific!
¡Estupendo!
estōōpen´dō

With pleasure!
Con mucho gusto.
kōn mōō´tshō gōōs´tō

No.
No.
nō

Never.
Nunca.
nōōng´kä

Nothing.
Nada.
nä´dä

Out of the question!
¡Ni hablar!
nē äblär´

Certainly not! (No way!)
De ninguna manera!
de nēngōō´nä mäne´rä

I'd rather not!
Más bien no quiero hacerlo.
mäs byen nō kye´rō äser´lō

I don't want to (can't).
No *quiero (puedo)*.
nō kye´rō (pōō•e´dō)

Perhaps (Maybe).
Quizá(s).
kēsä(s)´

Probably.
Probablemente.
prōbäblemen´te

Pardon

Excuse me!
¡Discúlpeme!/¡Discúlpame! *(fam)*
dēskō͞ol'peme/dēskō͞ol'päme

I beg your pardon!
¡Perdón!
perdōn'

Please excuse me!
¡Discúlpeme/discúlpame *(fam)*/, por favor!
dēskō͞ol'peme/dēskō͞ol'päme/, pōr fävōr'

I'm very sorry.
Lo siento mucho.
lō syen'tō mō͞o'tshō

I'm extremely sorry.
Lo siento muchísimo.
lō syen'tō mō͞otshē'sēmō

I must apologize to you.
Tengo que pedirle/pedirte *(fam)*/
perdón.
ten'gō ke pedēr'le/pedēr'te/perdōn'

Please don't be angry.
Por favor, no se enfade/no te enfades *(fam)*/*Mex* no se enoje/no te enojes *(fam)*.
pōr fävōr', nō se enfä'de/no te enfä'des/nō se enō'he/nō te enō'hes

Regrets

What a pity! (Too bad!)
¡Qué lástima! ¡Qué pena!
ke läs'tēmä, ke pe'nä

What a shame that ...
Es una lástima que ...
es ō͞o'nä läs'tēmä ke ...

To my (great) regret ...
Con (gran) pesar mío ...
kōn (grän) pesär' mē'ō ...

I'm afraid that isn't possible.
Lo siento, pero no es posible.
lō syen'tō, pe'rō nō es posē'ble

Congratulations and Condolences

> *The* "día del santo" *(patron saint's day) is an important day and is widely celebrated.*

Congratulations!
¡Felicitaciones!
felēsētäsyō'nes

I congratulate you ...
Quiero felicitarle/te *(fam)* ...
kyē'rō felēsētär'le/te/ ...

on your birthday	por su/tu *(fam)*/ cumpleaños	pōr sō͞o/tō͞o/ kō͞omple·ä'nyōs
on your marriage	por su/tu *(fam)*/boda .	pōr sō͞o/tō͞o/bō'dä

All the best! (Best wishes!)
¡Muchas felicidades!
mōō'tshäs felēsēdä'des

Happy birthday!
¡Feliz cumpleaños!
felēs' kōōmple·ä'nyōs

Merry Christmas!
¡Feliz Navidad!
felēs' nävēdäd'

Happy New Year!
¡Próspero Año Nuevo!
prōs'perō ä'nyō nōō·e'vō

The Christmas season itself extends from about Dec. 16 to Jan. 6,
"día de los reyes magos". In most families children receive presents
both *on Christmas* and *on Epiphany, (from the* reyes magos, *3*
kings).

I (We) wish you ...
Le/te *(fam)/deseo (deseamos)* ...
le/te/dese'ō (dese·ä'mōs) ...

Good luck!
¡Mucha suerte!
mōō'tshä sōō·er'te

Success!
¡Mucho éxito!
mōō'tshō e'ksētō

All the best!
¡Qué le/te *(fam)/vaya bien!
ke le/te/vä'yä byen

My sincerest condolences.
¡Le/te *(fam)*/acompaño en el
sentimiento!/¡Mi sentido pésame!
le/te/äkōmpä'nyō en el sentē-
myen'tō/mē sentē'dō pe'säme

Our warmest sympathy.
¡Le/te *(fam)*/acompañamos en el
sentimiento!
le/te/äkōmpänyä'mōs en el sen-
tēmyen'tō

Complaints

I'd like to register a complaint.
Quisiera hacer una reclamación/
un reclamo.
kēsye'rä äser' ōō'nä reklämäsyōn'/ōōn reklä'mō

I'd like to speak to the *manager*
(owner).
Quisiera hablar con el *director or*
gerente (dueño).
kēsye'rä äblär' kōn el dērektōr'
(heren'te) (dōō·e'nyo)

I'm afraid I'll have to make a complaint about ...
Tengo que hacer una reclamación/un reclamo/por ...
ten'gō ke äser' ōō'nä reklämäsyōn'/ōōn reklä'mō/pōr ...

... *is (are)* missing.
Falta (faltan) ...
fäl'tä (fäl'tän) ...

... doesn't work.
... no funciona.
... nō fōōnsyō'nä

... is not in order.
... no está *or* no va bien.
... nō estä' (nō vä byen)

Communication

Do you speak English? **German?** **French?**
¿Habla/hablas *(fam)*/inglés? ¿Alemán? ¿Francés?
äb'lä/äb'läs/ēngles' älemän' fränses'

Can you understand me? **I understand.**
¿Me entiende/entiendes *(fam)*? Entiendo.
me entyen'de/entyen'des entyen'dō

I can't understand a thing.
No entiendo nada.
nō entyen'dō nä'dä

Would you please speak a little slower?
Por favor, hable/habla *(fam)*/más despacio.
pōr fävōr, äb'le/äb'lä/mäs despä'syō

How do you say ... in Spanish?
¿Cómo se dice ... en español?
kō'mō se dē'se ... en espänyōl'

How do you say that in Spanish?
¿Cómo se dice eso en español?
kō'mō se dē'se e'sō en espänyōl'

What does that mean? **I beg your pardon?**
¿Qué significa eso? ¿Perdón? ¿Cómo?/*Mex* ¿Mande?
ke sēgnēfē'kä e'sō perdōn' kō'mō/män'de

How do you pronounce this word?
¿Cómo se pronuncia esta palabra?
kō'mō se prōnoon'syä es'tä pälä'brä

Would you please translate this for me?
¿Podría/podrías *(fam)*/traducírmelo?
pōdrē'ä/pōdrē'äs/trädoosēr'melō

Would you please write that down for me?
¿Podría/podrías *(fam)*/escribírmelo?
pōdrē'ä/pōdrē'äs/eskrēbēr'melō

Would you spell that, please?
¿Podría/podrías *(fam)*/deletrearlo, por favor?
pōdrē'ä/pōdrē'äs/deletre·är'lō, pōr favōr'

Weather

How's the weather going to be?
¿Qué tiempo hará?
ke tyem'pō ärä'

What's the weather report?
¿Qué anuncia el parte meteorológico?
ke änōōn'syä el pär'te mete·ōrō-
lō'hēkō

The barometer's *rising (falling)*.
El barómetro está *subiendo (bajando)*.
el bärō'metrō estä' sōōbyen'dō (bähän'dō)

We're going to have ...
Va a hacer ...
vä ä äser' ...

good weather	buen tiempo	bōō·en tyem'pō
bad weather	mal tiempo	mal tyem'pō
changeable weather ..	tiempo variable	tyem'pō värē·ä'ble

It's going to stay nice.
El tiempo sigue bueno.
el tyem'pō sē'ge bōō·e'nō

Is it going to *rain (snow)*?
¿Va a *llover (nevar)*?
vä ä lyōver' (nevär')

How are the road conditions between here and ...?
¿Qué tal está la carretera entre ... y ...?
ke täl estä' lä kärrete'rä en'tre ... ē ...

It's very slippery.
Está resbaladizo/
resbaloso.
estä' resbäläde'sō/
resbälō'sō

– very hot.
Hace mucho calor.
ä'se mōō'tshō kälōr'

– foggy (misty).
Hay niebla (neblina).
ī nye'blä (neblē'nä)

– very muggy.
Hace bochorno.
ä'se bōtshōr'nō

– very windy.
Hace viento/aire.
ä'se vyen'tō/ī're

– stormy.
El viento es muy fuerte.
el vyen'tō es mōō'ē fōō·er'te

What's the temperature?
¿A cuántos grados estamos?
ä kōō·än'tōs grä'dōs estä'mōs

It's ... *above (below)* zero.
Tenemos ... grados *sobre (bajo)* cero.
tene'mōs ... grä'dōs sō'bre (bä'hō) se'rō

It's *cold (hot)*.
Hace frío. (Hace calor.)
ä'se frē'ō (ä'se kälōr')

I'm *cold (hot)*.
Tengo frío. (Tengo calor.)
ten'gō frē'ō (ten'gō kälōr')

Is the weather going to stay nice?
¿Sigue el buen tiempo?
sē'ge el bōō·en tyem'pō

The weather's going to change.
El tiempo va a cambiar.
el tyem'pō vä ä kämbyär'

It'll be nice again.
Ya vuelve a hacer buen tiempo.
yä vōō·el've ä äser' bōō·en tyem'pō

The wind has dropped.
El viento ha amainado.
el vyen'tō ä ämīnä'dō

The wind has changed.
El viento ha cambiado (de rumbo).
el vyen'tō ä kämbyä'dō (de rōōm'bō)

We're going to have a thunderstorm.
Va a haber tormenta.
vä ä äber' tōrmen'tä

There's going to be a storm.
Habrá tempestad.
äbrä' tempestäd'

Is the fog going to lift?
¿Se disipará la niebla?
se dēsēpärä' lä nye'blä

It's stopped raining.
Ha dejado de llover.
ä de*h*ä'dō de lyōver'

The sun is shining.
Hace sol.
ä'se sōl

The sun is burning hot.
El sol quema.
el sōl ke'mä

The sky is clear.
El cielo está despejado.
el sye'lō estä' despe*h*ä'dō

In Spanish-speaking countries, temperatures are measured in degrees Centigrade. To convert
Fahrenheit to Centigrade: $°F - 32 \times 55 = °C$
Centigrade to Fahrenheit: $°C + 17.8 \times 1.8 = °F$

---

air	aire *m*	ī're
atmospheric pressure	presión *f* atmosférica	presyōn' ätmōs-fe'rēkä
barometer	barómetro *m*	bärō'metrō
blizzard	ventisca *f*	ventēs'kä
climate	clima *m*	klē'mä
cloud	nube *f*	nōō'be
cloudburst	chaparrón *m*	tshäpärrōn'
cloud cover, cloudy skies, cloudy	nuboso, nublado	nōōbō'sō, nōōblä'dō
dew	rocío *m*	rōsē'ō
dusk	crepúsculo *m*	krepōōs'kōōlō
earthquake	terremoto *m*, temblor *m*	terremō'tō, temblōr'

fog	niebla *f*	nye'blä
frost	helada *f*	elä'dä
heat	calor *m*	kälör'
high pressure (system)	anticiclón *m*	äntēsēklōn'
hurricane	ciclón *m*, huracán *m*	sēklōn', ōōrräkän'
ice	hielo *m*	ye'lō
icy road	carretera *f* helada	kärrete'rä elä'dä
it's freezing	está helando	estä' elän'dō
it's hailing	cae granizo	kä'e gränē'sō
it's raining	está lloviendo	estä' lyōvyen'dō
it's snowing	está nevando	estä' nevän'dō
it's thawing	deshiela	desye'lä
it's windy	hace viento	ä'se vyen'tō
lightning	relámpago *m*	reläm'pägō
low pressure (system)	de baja presión	de bä'*h*ä presyōn'
mist	neblina *f*	neblē'nä
moon	luna *f*	lōō'nä
north (east) wind	viento *m* del *norte (este)*	vyen'tō del nōr'te (es'te)
precipitation	precipitaciones *fpl*	presēpētäsyō'nes
road conditions	estado *m* de las carreteras	estä'dō de läs kärrete'räs
shower	chubasco *m*	tshōōbäs'kō
snow	nieve *f*	nye've
snow flurries	copos *mpl* de nieve	kō'pōs de nye've
south (west) wind	viento *m* del *sur (oeste)*	vyen'tō del sōōr (ō·es'te)
star	estrella *f*	estre'lyä
storm	tormenta *f*	tōrmen'tä
sun	sol *m*	sōl
sunrise	salida *f* del sol	sälē'dä del sōl
sunset	puesta *f* del sol	pōō·es'tä del sōl
temperature	temperatura *f*	temperätōō'rä
thaw	deshielo *m*	desye'lō
thunder	trueno *m*	trōō·e'nō
thunderstorm	tempestad *f*	tempestäd'
weather	tiempo *m*	tyem'pō
weather prediction	pronóstico *m*	prōnōs'tēkō
weather report	parte *m* meteorológico	pär'te mete·ōrō-lō'*h*ēkō
wind	viento *m*	vyen'tō

Numbers

Cardinal Numbers

0	cero	se′rō			
1	un, uno	ōn, ōō′nō	6	seis	se′ēs
2	dos	dōs	7	siete	sye′te
3	tres	tres	8	ocho	ō′tshō
4	cuatro	kōō·ä′trō	9	nueve	nōō·e′ve
5	cinco	sēng′kō	10	diez	dyes

11	once	ōn′se
12	doce	dō′se
13	trece	tre′se
14	catorce	kätōr′se
15	quince	kēn′se
16	dieciséis	dyesēse′ēs
17	diecisiete	dyesēsye′te
18	dieciocho	dyesē·ō′tshō
19	diecinueve	dyesēnōō·e′ve
20	veinte	ve′ēnte
21	veintiuno, -a	ve′ēntē·ōō′nō, -ä
22	veintidós	ve′ēntēdōs′
23	veintitrés	ve′ēntētres′
30	treinta	tre′ēntä
40	cuarenta	kōō·ären′tä
50	cincuenta	sēngkōō·en′tä
60	sesenta	sesen′tä
70	setenta	seten′tä
80	ochenta	ōtshen′tä
90	noventa	nōven′tä
100	cien, ciento	syen, syen′tō
200	doscientos, -as	dōsyen′tōs, -äs
1,000	mil	mēl
1,000,000	un millón	ōōn mēlyōn′
1,000,000,000	mil millones	mēl mēlyō′nes

When writing numbers, the use of commas and periods in Spanish is the opposite of their use in English. For example:

8,700 *people* = 8.700 *personas*   35.7% = 35,7%
4,500 *pesetas* = 4.500 *pesetas* $ 10.50 = 10,50 $

Ordinal Numbers

> The ordinal numbers between 1 and 10 are commonly used, those
> between 11 and 20 are seldom used and from 21 on are occasionally
> used in writing (never in speech), being replaced by the cardinal
> numbers.
>
> Ordinals are abbreviated by a period and an upraised "°":
>   *primero* = 1.°; *segundo* = 2.°; *tercero* = 3.° etc.

1st	.....	primero	prēme′rō
2nd	.....	segundo	segōōn′dō
3rd	.....	tercero	terse′rō
4th	.....	cuarto	kōō·är′tō
5th	.....	quinto	kēn′tō
6th	.....	sexto	seks′tō
7th	.....	séptimo	sep′tēmō
8th	.....	octavo	ōktä′vō
9th	.....	noveno/nono	nōve′nō/nō′nō
10th	.....	décimo	de′sēmō
11th	.....	undécimo	ōōnde′sēmō
12th	.....	duodécimo	dōō·ōde′sēmō
13th	.....	décimo tercero	de′sēmō terse′rō
14th	.....	décimo cuarto	de′sēmō kōō·är′tō
20th	.....	vigésimo	vēhe′sēmō
21st	.....	vigésimo primero	vēhe′sēmō prēme′rō
22nd	.....	vigésimo segundo	vēhe′sēmō segōōn′dō
30th	.....	trigésimo	trēhe′sēmō
40th	.....	cuadragésimo	kōō·ädrähe′sēmō
50th	.....	quincuagésimo	kēnkōō·ähe′sēmō
60th	.....	sexagésimo	seksähe′sēmō
70th	.....	septuagésimo	septōō·ähe′sēmō
80th	.....	octogésimo	ōktōhe′sēmō
90th	.....	nonagésimo	nōnähe′sēmō
100th	.....	centésimo	sente′sēmō
1,000th	.....	milésimo	mēle′sēmō

> *The 100 year anniversary of an event is the* centenario; *the 1,000 year
> anniversary is the* milenario.

Time

What time is it?	**Have you got the exact time?**
¿Qué hora es?	¿Tiene/tienes (fam)/la hora exacta?
ke ō'rä es	tye'ne/tye'nes/lä ō'rä eksäk'tä
It's one o'clock.	**It's about two o'clock.**
Es la una.	Son las dos aproximadamente.
es lä ōō'nä	sōn läs dōs äprōksēmädämen'te
It's exactly three o'clock.	**It's quarter past five.**
Son las tres en punto.	Son las cinco y cuarto.
sōn läs tres em pōōn'tō	sōn läs sēng'kō ē kōō·är'tō
It's half past six.	**It's quarter to nine.**
Son las seis y media.	Son las nueve menos cuarto.
sōn läs se'ēs ē me'dyä	sōn läs nōō·e've me'nōs kōō·är'tō
It's five (minutes) past four.	**It's ten (minutes) to eight.**
Son las cuatro y cinco.	Son las ocho menos diez.
sōn läs kōō·ä'trō ē sēng'kō	sōn läs ō'tshō me'nōs dyes

The time of day is expressed by the cardinal numbers preceded by la
or las: *It's one o'clock* = Es *la una.*
       It's two o'clock = Son *las dos.*   *etc.*

When?	**At ten o'clock (10:00).**	**At eleven sharp.**
¿Cuándo?	A las diez.	A las once en punto.
kōō·än'dō	ä läs dyes	ä läs ōn'se em pōōn'tō

At *four (eight-fifteen)* **p.m.**
A las *cuatro de la tarde (ocho y cuarto de la noche).*
ä läs kōō·ä'trō de lä tär'de (ō'tshō ē kōō·är'tō de lä nō'tshe)

From eight to nine a.m.	**Between ten and twelve a.m.**
De las ocho a las nueve	Entre las diez y las once
de la mañana.	de la mañana.
de läs ō'tshō ä läs nōō·e've	en'tre läs dyes ē läs ōn'se
de lä mänyä'nä	de lä mänyä'nä

---

*The 24 hour clock is used in written Spanish in general. In spoken
Spanish, however, you can use the 12 hour clock, adding* de la
mañana, de la tarde, *or* de la noche *to the time if there is any doubt.*

In half an hour.
Dentro de media hora.
den'trō de me'dyä ō'rä

In two hours.
Dentro de dos horas.
den'trō de dōs ō'räs

Not before seven.
No antes de las siete.
nō än'tes de läs sye'te

Shortly after eight.
Poco después de las ocho.
pō'kō despoo·es' de läs ō'tshō

It's (too) late.
Es (demasiado) tarde.
es (demäsyä'dō) tär'de

It's still too early.
Es aún temprano.
es ä·ōon' temprä'nō

Is this clock right?
¿Va bien este reloj?
vä byen es'te relōh'

It's too *fast (slow)*.
Va *adelantado (retrasado)*.
vä ädeläntä'dō (reträsä'dō)

Times of the Day

During the day.
De día.
de dē'ä

In the morning.
Por la mañana.
pōr lä mänyä'nä

In the afternoon.
Por la tarde.
pōr lä tär'de

At noon.
A mediodía.
ä medyōdē'ä

Yesterday.
Ayer.
äyer'

Today.
Hoy.
oi

Tomorrow.
Mañana.
mänyä'nä

In the evening.
Por la tarde *or* noche.
pōr lä tär'de (nō'tshe)

At night.
Por la noche.
pōr lä nō'tshe

Tonight.
Esta noche.
es'tä nō'tshe

At midnight.
A medianoche.
ä medyänō'tshe

Daily (every day).
Todos los días.
tō'dōs lōs dē'äs

Hourly (every hour).
Cada hora.
kä'dä ō'rä

The day before yesterday.
Anteayer.
änte·äyer'

The day after tomorrow.
Pasado mañana.
päsä'dō mänyä'nä

A week from now.
De hoy en ocho días.
de ōi en ō'tshō dē'äs

A week from Wednesday.
Del miércoles en ocho días.
del myer'kōles en ō'tshō dē'äs

Two weeks from now.
De hoy en quince días.
de ōi en kēn'se dē'äs

This *morning (afternoon, evening)*.
Esta *mañana (tarde)*.
es'tä mänyä'nä (tär'de)

This noon.	**A month ago.**	**For the last ten days.**
Hoy al mediodía.	Hace un mes.	Desde hace diez días.
oi äl medyōdē'ä	ä'se ōōn mes	des'de ä'se dyes dē'äs

During this time (meanwhile).	**Within a week.**
Mientras tanto.	Dentro de una semana.
myen'träs tän'tō	den'trō de ōō'nä semä'nä

This coming week.	*Last (next)* **year.**
La semana que viene.	El año *pasado (que viene)*.
lä semä'nä ke vye'ne	el ä'nyō päsä'dō (ke vye'ne)

Every year (annually).	**Every week (weekly).**
Todos los años.	Cada semana.
tōdōs lōs ä'nyōs	kä'dä semä'nä

From time to time.	**Now and then.**	**At the moment.**
De vez en cuando.	A veces.	De momento.
de ves en kōō·än'dō	ä veses	de mōmen'tō

a little while ago	hace poco	ä'se pō'kō
any time now	de un momento a otro	de ōōn mōmen'tō ä ō'trō
earlier	antes	än'tes
later	más tarde	mäs tär'de
now	ahora	ä·ō'rä
on time	a la hora, a tiempo	ä lä ō'rä, ä tyem'pō
previously (before)	antes	än'tes
recently	recientemente	resyentemen'te
since	desde	des'de
sometimes	a veces	ä ve'ses
soon	pronto	prōn'tō
temporarily (for the time being)	por el momento	pōr el mōmen'tō
until	hasta	äs'tä
second	segundo *m*	segōōn'dō
minute	minuto *m*	mēnōō'tō
hour	hora *f*	ō'rä
day	día *m*	dē'ä
week	semana *f*	semä'nä
month	mes *m*	mes
year	año *m*	ä'nyō
half year	medio año *m*	me'dyō ä'nyō
quarter, three months	trimestre *m*	trēmes'tre

Days of the Week

Monday	lunes *m*	loo'nes
Tuesday	martes *m*	mär'tes
Wednesday	miércoles *m*	myer'kōles
Thursday	jueves *m*	hoo·e'ves
Friday	viernes *m*	vyer'nes
Saturday	sábado *m*	sä'bädō
Sunday	domingo *m*	dōmēn'gō

Months of the Year

January	enero *m*	ene'rō
February	febrero *m*	febre'rō
March	marzo *m*	mär'sō
April	abril *m*	äbrēl'
May	mayo *m*	mä'yō
June	junio *m*	hoo'nyō
July	julio *m*	hoo'lyō
August	agosto *m*	ägōs'tō
September	se(p)tiembre *m*	se(p)tyem'bre
October	octubre *m*	ōktoo'bre
November	noviembre *m*	novyem'bre
December	diciembre *m*	dēsyem'bre

Seasons

Spring	primavera *f*	prēmäve'rä
Summer	verano *m*	verä'nō
Autumn	otoño *m*	ōtō'nyō
Winter	invierno *m*	ēmbyer'nō

Holidays

New Year's Eve	Año Viejo	ä'nyō vye'hō
New Year's Day	Año Nuevo	ä'nyō noo·e'vō
Good Friday	Viernes Santo	vyer'nes sän'tō
Easter	Pascua	päs'koo·ä
Christmas Eve	Nochebuena	nōtsheboo·e'nä
Christmas	Navidad	nävēdäd'

The Date

What's the date today?	**It's the second of July.**
¿A cuántos estamos?	Hoy es el dos de julio.
ä kōō·än'tōs estä'mōs	ōi es el dōs de hōō'lyō

On the twenty ninth of August, 19 …
El veintinueve de agosto de mil novecientos …
el ve·ēntēnōō·e've de ägōs'tō de mēl nōvesyen'tōs …

On the fifteenth *of this (next)* **month**
El quince *de este (del próximo)* mes.
el kēn'se de es'te (del prō'ksēmō) mes

Until the twenty fourth of April.
Hasta el veinticuatro de abril.
äs'tä el ve'ēntēkōō·ä'trō de äbrēl'

On June first *of this (last)* **year.**
El primero de junio *de este año (del año pasado)*.
el prēme'rō de hōō'nyō de es'te ä'nyō (del ä'nyō päsä'dō)

We leave on the nineteenth of September.
Salimos el diecinueve de se(p)tiembre.
sälē'mōs el dyesēnōō·e've de se(p)tyem'bre

We arrived on the twelfth of January.
Llegamos el doce de enero.
lyegä'mōs el dō'se de ene'rō

The letter was mailed on the ninth of October.
La carta fue expedida el nueve de octubre.
lä kär'tä fōō·e' ekspedē'dä el nōō·e've de ōktōō'bre

Thank you for your letter of February 2nd.
Le agradecemos su carta del dos de febrero.
le ägrädese'mōs sōō kär'tä del dōs de febre'rō

Age

How old are you?	**I'm twenty years old.**
¿Cuántos años tiene/tienes *(fam)*?	Tengo veinte años.
kōō·än'tōs ä'nyōs tye'ne/tye'nes/	ten'gō ve'ēnte ä'nyōs
I'm over 18.	**Children under 14.**
Soy mayor de edad.	Niños menores de 14 años.
sōi mäyōr' de edäd'	nē'nyōs menō'res de kätōr'se ä'nyōs

I was born on the ...	He's *younger (older).*	– under age.
Nací el ...	El es *más joven (mayor).*	menor de edad.
näsē' el ...	el eś mäs hō'ven (mäyōr')	menōr' de edäd'

– grown up.	At the age of ...	At my age.
adulto.	A la edad de ...	A mi edad.
ädōōl'tō	ä lä edäd' de ...	ä mē edäd'

Family

aunt	tía *f*	tē'ä
boy	niño *m*, muchacho *m*	nē'nyō, mōōtshä'tshō
brother	hermano *m*	ermä'nō
brother-in-law	cuñado *m*	kōōnyä'dō
cousin *(female)*	prima *f*	prē'mä
cousin *(male)*	primo *m*	prē'mō
daughter	hija *f*	ē'*h*ä
family	familia *f*	fämē'lyä
father	padre *m/Mex* papá *m*	pä'dre/päpä'
father-in-law	suegro *m*	sōō·e'grō
girl	niña *f*, muchacha *f*	nē'nyä, mōōtshä'tshä
grandchild	nieto *m*	nye'tō
granddaughter	nieta *f*	nye'tä
grandfather	abuelo *m*	äbōō·e'lō
grandmother	abuela *f*	äbōō·e'lä
grandparents	abuelos *mpl*	äbōō·e'lōs
grandson	nieto *m*	nye'tō
husband	esposo *m*, marido *m*	espō'sō, märē'dō
mother	madre *f/Mex* mamá *f*	mä'dre/mämä'
mother-in-law	suegra *f*	sōō·e'grä
nephew	sobrino *m*	sōbrē'nō
niece	sobrina *f*	sōbrē'nä
parents	padres *mpl*	pä'dres
sister	hermana *f*	ermä'nä
sister-in-law	cuñada *f*	kōōnyä'dä
son	hijo *m*	ē'*h*ō
uncle	tío *m*	tē'ō
wife	esposa *f*, mujer *f*	espō'sä, mōō*h*er'

Occupations

apprentice	aprendiz *m*	äprendēs'
artist	artista *m + f*	ärtēs'tä
auto mechanic	mecánico *m* de carros/	mekä'nēkō de
	Sp de coches	kä'rrōs/de kō'tshes
baker	panadero *m*	pänäde'rō
bank teller	cajero *m*	kä*h*e'rō
bookkeeper	tenedor *m* de libros	tenedōr' de lē'brōs
bookseller	librero *m*	lēbre'rō
bricklayer	albañil *m*	älbänyēl'
butcher	carnicero *m*	kärnēse'rō
cabinetmaker	ebanista *m*	ebänēs'tä
carpenter	carpintero *m*	kärpēnte'rō
chef	jefe *m* de cocina	*h*e'fe de kōsē'nä
civil servant	funcionario *m*	fōōnsyōnär'yō
clergyman	clérigo *m*	kle'rēgō
confectioner	pastelero *m*	pästele'rō
cook	cocinero *m*	kōsēne'rō
dentist	dentista *m + f*	dentēs'tä
doctor	médico *m + f*	me'dēkō
dressmaker	costurera *f*	kōstōōre'rä
driver	conductor *m*,	kōndōōktōr',
	chófer *m*	tshō'fer
driving instructor	profesor *m*	prōfesōr'
	de auto-escuela	de outōeskōō·e'lä
electrician	electricista *m*	elektrēsēs'tä
engineer *(scientific)*	ingeniero *m*	ēn*h*enye'rō
engineer *(railroad)*	maquinista *m*	mäkēnēs'tä
farmer	agricultor *m*	ägrēkōōltōr'
fisherman	pescador *m*	peskädōr'
forest ranger	guarda *m* forestal	gōō·är'dä fōrestäl'
gardener	jardinero *m*	*h*ärdēne'rō
glazier	vidriero *m*	vēdrē·e'rō
hairdresser	peluquero *m*	pelōōke'rō
interpreter (translator)	intérprete *m + f*	ēnter'prete
journalist	periodista *m + f*	peryōdēs'tä
judge	juez *m + f*	*h*ōō·es'
kindergarten teacher	maestra *f* de párvulos,	mä·es'trä de pär'vōōlōs,

	maestra f de preescolar	mä·es'trä de pre·es-kōlär'
lawyer	abogado m + f	äbōgä'dō
librarian	bibliotecario m	bēblē·ōtekär'yō
locksmith	cerrajero m	serrä*h*e'rō
mailman	cartero m	kärte'rō
metalworker	metalúrgico m	metälōōr'*h*ēkō
midwife	comadrona f, partera f	kōmädrō'nä, pärte'rä
miner	minero m	mēne'rō
musician	músico m + f	mōō'sēkō
notary	notario m	nōtär'yō
nurse (female)	enfermera f	emferme'rä
nurse (male)	enfermero m	emferme'rō
optician	óptico m	ōp'tēkō
painter	pintor m	pēntōr'
pastry chef	pastelero m	pästele'rō
pharmacist	farmacéutico m	färmäse'·ōōtēkō
plumber	plomero m/Sp. fonta-nero m	plōme'rō/fōntäne'-rō
postal clerk	empleado m de correos	emple·ä'dō de kōrre'ōs
pupil	alumno m	älōōm'nō
railroad man	ferroviario m	ferrōvyär'yō
retailer	comerciante m	kōmersyän'te
retiree	pensionista m + f	pensyōnēs'tä
salesperson	dependiente m	dependyen'te
scholar	erudito m	erōōdē'tō
scientist	científico m	syentē'fēkō
sculptor	escultor m	eskōōltōr'
secretary	secretaria f	sekretär'yä
shoemaker	zapatero m	säpäte'rō
storekeeper	tendero m	tende'rō
student	estudiante m + f	estōōdyän'te
tailor	sastre m	säs'tre
teacher	profesor m, maestro m	prōfesōr', mä·es'trō
technician	técnico m	tek'nēkō
trainee	aprendiz m	äprendēs'
translator	traductor m	trädōōktōr'
truck driver	chófer m, camionero m	tshō'fer, kämyō-ne'rō

veterinarian	veterinario *m*	veterēnär′yō
waiter	camarero *m*/*Mex* mesero *m*	kämäre′rō/mese′rō
waitress	camarera *f*/*Mex* mesera *f*	kämäre′rä/mese′rä
watchmaker	relojero *m*	relōhe′rō
wholesaler	mayorista *m + f*	mäyōrēs′tä
worker	obrero *m*	ōbre′rō
writer	escritor *m*	eskrētōr′

To form the feminine form of the occupations given above, change the -*o* ending to -*a* (for example: *el peluquero, la peluquera*) or, for endings other than -*o*, simply add an -*a* (for example: *el aprendiz, la aprendiza*). In cases where the same noun is used for men and women, only the article is changed from *el* to *la* (for example: *el médico, la médico*). These are designated by *m + f*.

Education

Where are you studying? (What college or university do you attend?)
¿Dónde estudia/estudias *(fam)*?
dōn′de estoo′dyä/estoo′dyäs

I'm at ... college (university).	**I'm studying (majoring in) ...**
Estudio en ...	Estudio ...
estoo′dyō en ...	estoo′dyō ...

I got to (am attending) the ... school.
Voy a la escuela ...
vōi ä lä eskoo•e′lä ...

class	clase *f*	klä′se
major	asignatura *f* principal ..	äsēgnätoo′rä prēnsēpäl′
school	escuela *f*	eskoo•e′lä
– **boarding school** ...	internado *m*	ēnternä′dō
– **business school**	escuela *f* de comercio ..	eskoo•e′lä de kōmer′syō
– **grammar school** ...	escuela *f* primaria, colegio *m*	eskoo•e′lä prēmär′yä, kōle′hyō
– **high school**	instituto *m* de bachillerato	ēnstētoo′tō de bätshēlyerä′tō

– vocational school	escuela f de formación profesional	eskōō·e'lä de fōrmä-syōn' prōfesyōnäl'
subject	asignatura f	äsēgnätōō'rä
– American studies	estudios mpl americanos	estōō'dyōs ämerē-kä'nōs
– archaeology	arqueología f	ärke·ōlōhē'ä
– architecture	arquitectura f	ärkētektōō'rä
– art history	historia f de arte	ēstōr'yä de är'te
– biology	biología f	bē·ōlōhē'ä
– business administration	economía f de empresas	ekōnōmē'ä de empre'säs
– chemistry	química f	kē'mēkä
– dentistry	odontología f	ōdōntōlōhē'ä
– economics	ciencias fpl económicas	syen'syäs ekōnō'-mēkäs
– education	pedagogía f	pedägōhē'ä
– English	filología f inglesa	fēlōlōhē'ä ēngle'sä
– geology	geología f	he·ōlōhē'ä
– German	filología f germánica	fēlōlōhē'ä hermä'-nēkä
– history	historia f	ēstōr'yä
– journalism	periodismo m	peryōdēz'mō
– law	derecho m	dere'tshō
– mathematics	matemáticas fpl	mätemä'tēkäs
– mechanical engineering	construcción f mecánica	kōnstrōōksyōn' mekä'nēkä
– medicine	medicina f	medēsē'nä
– musicology	música f	mōō'sēkä
– painting	pintura f	pēntōō'rä
– pharmacy	farmacia f	färmä'syä
– physics	física f	fē'sēkä
– political science	ciencias fpl políticas	syen'syäs pōlē'tēkäs
– psychology	psicología f	sēkōlōhē'ä
– Romance languages	filología f románica	fēlōlōhē'ä rōmä'nēkä
– Slavic languages	eslavística f	eslävēs'tēkä
– sociology	sociología f	sōsyōlōhē'ä
– veterinary medicine	veterinaria f	veterēnär'yä
– zoology	zoología f	sō·ōlōhē'ä
technical college	escuela f superior técnica	eskōō·e'lä sōōpe-ryōr' tek'nēkä
university	universidad f	ōōnēversēdäd'

ON THE ROAD AGAIN

Asking the Way

Where *is (are)* ...?
¿Dónde está *(están)* ...?
dōn'de estä' (estän') ...

How do I get to ...?
¿Cómo se va a ...?
kō'mō se vä ä ...

How many kilometers is it to the next town?
¿A cuántos kilómetros está la ciudad más cerca?
ä kōō·än'tōs kēlō'metrōs estä' lä syōōdäd' mäs ser'kä

> 8 kilometers = 5 miles

Is this the road to ...?
¿Es ésta la carretera a ...?
es es'tä lä kärrete'rä ä ...

Is this the right way to ...?
¿Voy bien a ...?
vōi byen ä ...

Would you please show me that on the map?
Por favor, enséñemelo en el mapa.
pōr fävōr', ense'nyemelo en el mä'pä

Do I have to go ...?
¿Tengo que ir ...?
ten'gō ke ēr ...

Right.	**Left.**	**Straight ahead.**	**Turn around.**
A la derecha.	A la izquierda.	Todo derecho.	Dar la vuelta.
ä lä dere'tshä	ä lä ēskyer'dä	tō'dō dere'tshō	där lä vōō·el'tä

Here.	**There.**	**This way.**	**As far as ...**
Aquí.	Allá.	Por allí.	Hasta ...
äkē'	älyä'	pōr älyē'	äs'tä ...

How long?	**Where (to)?**	**How far is it to ...?**
¿Cuánto tiempo?	¿A dónde?	¿A qué distancia está ...?
kōō·än'tō tyem'pō	ä dōn'de	ä ke dēstän'syä estä' ...

Vehicles

camping trailer	caravana *f*/*Mex* trayler *m*	kärävä'nä/trīler
camper vehicle	cámper *m*	käm'per
car	automóvil *m*	outōmō'vēl
– delivery truck, van .	furgoneta *f*, camioneta *f*	fōōrgōne'tä, kä-myōne'tä
– passenger car	carro *m*/*Sp* coche *m* ...	kä'rrō/kō'tshe
– ranch station wagon	camioneta *f*/*Mex* combi *f*	kämyōne'tä/kōm'bē
– truck	camión *m*	kämyōn'

bicycle	bicicleta *f*	bēsēkle′tä
horse cart	carro *m/Mex* carreta *f* .	kä′rrō/kärre′tä
moped, motorbike ...	ciclomotor *m*	sēklōmōtōr′
motorcycle	motocicleta *f*, moto *f* ..	mōtōsēkle′tä, mō′tō
motor home	casa rodante *f*,	kä′sä rōdän′te,
	coche-vivienda *m*	kō′tshe-vēvyen′dä
motor scooter	escúter *m*	eskōō′ter
trailer	remolque *m*	remōl′ke
vehicle	vehículo *m*	ve·ē′kōōlō

Renting a Car

Where can I rent a car?
¿Dónde puedo alquilar/*Mex* rentar/un carro/*Sp* un coche?
dōn′de pōō·e′dō älkēlär′/rentär′/ōōn kä′rrō/ōōn kō′tshe

I'd like to rent a car.
Quisiera alquilar/*Mex* rentar/un carro/*Sp* un coche.
kēsye′rä älkēlär′/rentär′/ōōn kä′rrō/ōōn kō′tshe

... with chauffeur.
... con chófer.
... kōn tshō′fer

... for 2 (6) people.
... para *dos (seis)* personas.
... pä′rä dōs (se′ēs) persō′näs

... for *one day (one week, two weeks)*.
... por *un día (una semana (8 días), dos semanas (15 días))*.
... pōr ōōn dē′ä (ōō′nä semä′nä (ō′tshō dē′äs), dōs semä′näs (kēn′se dē′äs))

How much will it cost?
¿Cuánto cuesta?
kōō·än′tō kōō·es′tä

... including full coverage insurance?
... con seguro incluido?
... kōn segōō′rō ēnklōō·ē′dō

Will I have to pay for the gasoline myself?
¿Tengo que pagar yo la gasolina?
ten′gō ke pägär′ yō lä gäsōlē′nä

How much will I have to deposit?
¿Cuánto debo depositar?
kōō·än′tō de′bō depōsētär′

When (Where) can I pick up the car?
¿*Cuándo (Dónde)* puedo recoger el carro/*Sp* el coche?
kōō·än′dō (dōn′de) pōō·e′dō rekōher′ el kä′rrō/el kō′tshe

Will somebody be there when I bring the car back?
¿Habrá alguien cuando devuelva el carro/*Sp* el coche?
äbrä′ äl′gyen kōō·än′dō devōō·el′vä el kä′rrō/el kō′tshe

On a Drive

I'm *going (driving)* to ...
Voy *(en carro)* a ...
vōi (en kä'rrō) ä ...

Are you going to ...?
¿Va/vas *(fam)*/a ...?
vä/väs/ä ...

To go by *car (motorcycle, bicycle)*.
Ir en *carro*/*Sp coche*/*(motocicleta, bicicleta)*.
ēr en kä'rrō/kō'tshe (mōtōsēkle'tä, bēsēkle'tä)

Fast.	Slow.
Rápido.	Despacio.
rä'pēdō	despä'syō

access road	acceso *m*	äkse'sō
bike lane	pista *f* de bicicletas	pēs'tä de bēsēkle'täs
bridge	puente *m*	pōō·en'te
curve	curva *f*	kōōr'vä
detour	desviación *f*	desvē·äsyōn'
direction sign	indicador *m* de camino ...	ēndēkädōr' de kämē'nō
driver's license	carnet *m* de conducir/ *Mex* licencia *f* de manejar	kärnet' de kōndōō-sēr'/lēsen'syä de mänehär'
driveway	calzada *f*	kälsä'dä
exit	salida *f*	sälē'dä
falling rocks	desprendimiento *m* de piedras/*Mex* zona *f* de derrumbes	desprendēmyen'tō de pye'dräs/sō'nä de derrōōm'bes
highway	autopista *f*	outōpēs'tä
intersection	cruce *m*/*Mex* crucero *m*	krōō'se/krōōse'rō
lane	carril *m*	kärrēl'
limited parking zone	zona *f* de estaciona- miento limitado	sō'nä de estäsyōnä- myen'tō lēmētä'dō
maximum speed ...	velocidad *f* máxima ...	velōsēdäd' mä'ksē-mä
no parking	estacionamiento *m* prohibido	estäsyōnämyen'tō prō-ēbē'dō
no passing	prohibido adelantar/ *Mex* no rebase........	prō-ēbē'dō ädelän-tär'/nō rebä'se
no stopping	prohibido detenerse ...	prō-ēbē'dō dete-ner'se
parking disc	disco *m* de estaciona- miento...............	dēs'kō de estäsyō-nämyen'tō
parking lot	aparcamiento *m*	äpärkämyen'tō
parking meter	parquímetro *m*	pärkē'metrō

path (footpath)	camino *m* (senda *f*) ...	kämē'nō (sen'dä)
railroad crossing ...	paso *m* a nivel/*Mex* cruce *m* de F.C.	pä'sō ä nēvel'/ krōō'se de e'fe se
registration	papeles *mpl* del carro/*Sp* coche	päpe'les del kä'rrō/ kō'tshe
right of way	preferencia *f* de paso .	preferens'yä de pä'sō
road	carretera *f*, camino *m* .	kärrete'rä, kämē'nō
– **country road**	camino *m* vecinal	kämē'no vesēnäl'
– **cross road**	travesía *f*	trävesē'ä
– **main road (street)**	carretera *f* (calle *f*) principal	kärrete'rä (kä'lye) prēnsēpäl'
road sign	señal *f* de circulación .	senyäl' de sērkōōläsyōn'
road under construction	obras *fpl*/*Mex* hombres *mpl* trabajando	ō'bräs/ōm'bres träbähän'dō
route	ruta *f*	rōō'tä
side wind	viento *m* de costado ..	vyen'tō de kōstä'dō
slippery road	piso *m* resbaloso/*Sp* resbaladizo	pē'sō resbälō'sō/ resbäládē'sō
speed limit	límite *m* de velocidad .	lē'mēte de velōsēdäd'
steep downgrade ...	bajada *f* (peligrosa) ...	bähä'dä (pelēgrō'sä)
steep upgrade	cuesta *f*, subida *f*	kōō·es'tä, sōōbē'dä
toll	peaje *m*/*Mex* cuota *f* .	pe·ä'*he*/kōō·ō'tä
traffic	circulación *f*, tráfico *m*	sērkōōläsyōn', trä'fēkō
traffic circle	glorieta *f*	glōrye'tä
traffic light	semáforo *m*, disco *m* .	semä'fōrō, dēs'ko
trip (journey)	viaje *m*	vyä'*he*
– **brake**	frenar	frenär'
– **drive**	conducir, manejar	kōndōōsēr', mäne*h*är'
– **get in lane (merge)**	tomar fila	tōmär' fē'lä
– **get out (of car)** ...	bajar (del carro/*Sp* coche)	bä'*h*är (del kä'rrō/ kō'tshe)
– **park**	estacionar/*Sp* aparcar	estäsyōnär'/äpärkär'
– **stop**	parar	pärär'
– **turn (the car)**	dar la vuelta, virar	där lä vōō·el'tä, vērär'
– **turn (into a road)** .	entrar en	enträr' en
– **turn off (a road)** ..	doblar/*Sp* torcer	dōblär'/tōrser'
winding road	camino *m* sinuoso ...	kämē'nō sēnōō·ō'sō
zebra crossing	paso *m* de peatones, paso *m* cebra	pä'sō de pe·ätō'nes, pä'sō se'brä

Garage, Parking Lot

Where can I leave my car (for safekeeping)?
¿Dónde hay un estacionamiento/*Sp* aparcamiento/(vigilado) por aquí?
dōn'de ī ōōn estäsyōnämyen'tō/(äpärkämyen'tō)/(*vēhē*lä'dō) pōr äkē'

Is there a garage near here?
¿Hay un garaje cerca de aquí?
ī ōōn gärä'*he* ser'kä de äkē'

Have you still got *a vacant garage (parking space)?*
¿Tiene todavía un garaje (un sitio) libre?
tye'ne tōdävē'ä ōōn gärä'*he* (ōōn sē'tyō) lē'bre

Where can I leave the car?
¿Dónde puedo dejar el carro/*Sp* el coche?
dōn'de pōō·e'dō de*här*' el kä'rrō/el kō'tshe

Can I leave it here?
¿Puedo dejarlo aquí?
pōō·e'dō de*här*'lō äkē'

Can I park here?
¿Puedo aparcar/estacionar/aquí?
pōō·e'dō äpärkär'/estäsyōnär'/äkē'

Is this parking lot guarded?
¿Está vigilado el parqueadero/*Sp*
vigilado el aparcamiento?
estä' *vēhē*lä'dō el pärke·äde'rō/
*vēhē*lä'dō el äpärkämyen'tō

Is there a space free?
¿Queda todavía un sitio libre?
ke'dä tōdävē'ä ōōn sē'tyō lē'bre

How long can I park here?
¿Cuánto tiempo puedo aparcar/estacionar/aquí?
kōō·än'tō tyem'pō pōō·e'dō äpärkär'/estäsyōnär'/äkē'

How much does it cost to park here *overnight (until …)?*
¿Cuál es el precio del estacionamiento *por una noche (hasta …)*?
kōō·äl' es el pre'syō del estäsyōnämyen'tō pōr ōō'nä nō'tshe (äs'tä …)

Is the garage open all night?
¿Está abierto toda la noche?
estä' äbyer'tō tō'dä lä nō'tshe

When do you close?
¿A qué hora cierran?
ä ke ō'rä sye'rrän

I'll be leaving *this evening (tomorrow morning at eight).*
Me voy *esta noche (mañana a las ocho).*
me vōi es'tä nō'tshe (mänyä'nä ä läs ō'tshō)

I'd like to take my car out of the garage.
Quisiera sacar mi carro/*Sp* mi coche/del garaje.
kēsye'rä säkär' mē kä'rrō/mē kō'tshe/del gärä'*he*

Gas Station, Car Repair

Where's the nearest gas station?
¿Dónde está la bomba de gasolina (*or*
estación de servicio) más próxima?
dōn'de estä' lä bōm'bä de gäsōlē'nä (estäsyōn' de servē'syō) mäs prō'ksēmä

How far is it?
¿A qué distancia está?
ä ke dēstän'syä estä'

Fifteen liters of *regular (high test)* please.
Quince litros de gasolina *normal (extra)*, por favor.
kēn'se lē'trōs de gäsōlē'nä nōrmäl' (eks'trä), pōr fävōr'

> *1 gallon* = *3.8 liters*

I'd like 20 liters of diesel, please.
Quisiera veinte litros de gasóleo/*Mex* diesel/
por favor.
kēsye'rä ve'ēnte lē'trōs de gäsō'le·ō/
dyesel'/pōr fävōr'

Fill it up, please.
Lleno, por favor.
lye'nō, pōr fävōr'

I need water (coolant).
Necesito agua para el radiador.
nesesē'tō ä'gōō·ä pä'rä el rädyädōr'

A road map, please.
Un mapa de carreteras, por favor.
ōōn mä'pä de kärrete'räs, pōr
fävōr'

Would you please fill up the radiator?
Póngame agua en el radiador, por favor.
pōn'gäme ä'gōō·ä en el rädyädōr', pōr fävōr'

Would you please check the brake fluid?
Revise el líquido de frenos, por favor.
revē'se el lē'kēdō de fre'nōs, pōr fävōr'

brake fluid	líquido *m* de frenos	lē'kēdō de fre'nōs
car repair service	taller *m* mecánico	tälyer' mekä'nēkō
coolant	agua *f* para el radiador	ä'gōō·ä pä'rä el rä-dyädōr'
gasoline	gasolina *f*	gäsōlē'nä
gasoline can	bidón *m* de gasolina ...	bēdōn'de gäsōlē'nä
gas station	gasolinera *f*, estación *f* de servicio	gäsōlēne'rä, estä-syōn' de servē'syō
oil	aceite *m*	äse'ēte
spark plug	bujía *f*	bōō*h*ē'ä
water	agua *f*	ä'gōō·ä
– distilled water	agua *f* destilada	ä'gōō·ä destēlä'dä

Oil

Please check the oil.
Por favor, revise el nivel de aceite.
pōr fävōr′, revē′se el nēvel′
de äse′ēte

Please change the oil.
Cambie el aceite, por favor.
käm′bye el äse′ēte, pōr fävōr′

Please fill up the oil tank.
Ponga el aceite que falta, por favor.
pōn′gä el äse′ēte ke fäl′tä, pōr fävōr′

... liters of oil, please.
... litros de aceite, por favor.
... lē′trōs de äse′ēte, pōr fävōr′

> *1 liter = approx. 2 pints*

gear oil	aceite *m* lubricante	äse′ēte lōōbrēkän′te
lubrication	lubricación *f*	lōōbrēkäsyōn′
motor oil	aceite *m* para el motor	äse′ēte pä′rä el mō-tōr′
oil	aceite *m*	äse′ēte
– special/standard	especial/normal	espesyäl′/nōrmäl′
oil can	aceitera *f*	äse·ēte′rä
oil change	cambio *m* de aceite	käm′byō de äse′ēte
oil level	nivel *m* de aceite	nēvel′ de äse′ēte

Tires

Can you *repair (retread)* this tire?
¿Se puede *arreglar (recauchutar)* este neumático/*Mex* esta llanta?
se pōō·e′de ärreglär′ (rekoutshōōtär′) es′te ne·ōōmä′tēkō/es′tä
lyän′tä

Can this inner tube be patched?
¿Se puede poner un parche a esta cámara/*Mex* tubo/de aire?
se pōō·e′de pōner′ ōōn pär′tshe ä es′tä kä′märä/tōō′bō/de ī′re

Please change this tire.
Por favor, cámbieme el
neumático/*Mex* la llanta.
pōr fävōr′, käm′byeme el ne·ōō-
mä′tēkō/lä lyän′tä

A new inner tube, please.
Una nueva cámara/*Mex* tubo/
de aire, por favor.
ōō′nä nōō·e′vä kä′märä/tōō′bō/
de ī′re, pōr fävōr′

One of my tires had a blow-out.
He tenido un reventón (*or* pinchazo).
e tenē′dō ōōn reventōn′ (pēntshä′sō)

Would you please check the tire pressure?
Revise la presión de los neumáticos/*Mex* las llantas/por favor.
revē'se lä presyon' de los ne·oomä'tēkos/läs lyän'täs/por fävor'

The front tires are 22.7 and the rear ones are 28.4.
Los de delante necesitan 22.7 y los de atrás 28.4.
los de delän'te nesesē'tän ve'ēntēdos' poon'to sye'te ē los de äträs'
ve'ēntē·o'tsho poon'to koo·ä'tro

blow-out	pinchazo *m*, reventón *m*	pēntshä'so, reventon'
inner tube	cámara *f*/*Mex* tubo *m*/	kä'märä/too'bo/
	de aire	de ī're
jack	gato *m*	gä'to
puncture	pinchazo *m*	pēntshä'so
tires *(in general)* .	neumáticos *mpl*/*Mex*	ne·oomä'tēkos/
	llantas *fpl*	lyän'täs
tire	neumático *m*/*Mex*	ne·oomä'tēko/
	llanta *f*	lyän'tä
tire change	cambio *m* de neu-	käm'byo de ne·oo-
	mático/*Mex* de llanta ..	mä'tēko/de lyän'tä
tire pressure	presión *f* de los neu-	presyon' de los ne·oo-
	máticos/*Mex* las llantas	mä'tēkos/läs lyän'täs
valve	válvula *f*	väl'voolä
wheel...........	rueda *f*	roo·e'dä
– back wheel	rueda *f* trasera	roo·e'dä träse'rä
– front wheel ...	rueda *f* delantera	roo·e'dä delänte'rä
– reserve wheel ..	rueda *f* de repuesto/	roo·e'dä de repoo·es'to/
	Sp de recambio	de rekäm'byo
– wheels	ruedas *fpl*	roo·e'däs

Car Wash

Please wash *the windshield (the windows)*.
Por favor, limpie *el parabrisas (los cristales)*.
por fävor', lēm'pye el päräbrē'säs (los krēstä'les)

I'd like my car washed, please.
Por favor, láveme el carro/*Sp* el coche.
por fävor', lä'veme el kä'rro/el ko'tshe

Please clean out the inside, too.
Por favor, limpie el carro/*Sp* el coche/también por dentro.
por fävor', lēm'pye el kä'rro/el ko'tshe/tämbyen' por den'tro

Breakdown, Accident

I've (We've) **had a breakdown.**
Tengo (Tenemos) una falla mecánica/Sp una avería.
ten'gō (tene'mōs) ōō'nä fä'lyä mekä'nēkä/ōō'nä ävererē'ä

I've had an accident.
He tenido un accidente.
e tenē'dō ōōn äksēden'te

May I use your phone?
¿Puedo telefonear?
pōō·e'dō telefōne·är'

Would you please call the police?
¿Por favor, avise a la policía.
pōr favōr', ävē'se ä lä pōlēsē'ä

Could you lend me ...?
¿Podría prestarme ...?
pōdrē'ä prestär'me ...

Call an ambulance quickly!
¡Llame en seguida una ambulancia!
lyä'me en segē'dä ōō'nä ämbōōlän'syä

Get a doctor!
¡Llame a un médico!
lyä'me ä ōōn me'dēkō

Please help me!
¡Ayúdeme, por favor!
äyōō'deme, pōr favōr'

I need bandages.
Necesito vendajes/*Mex* vendas.
nesesē'tō vendä*hes*/ven'däs

Could you ...?
¿Podría ...?
pōdrē'ä ...

– **look after the injured?**
– cuidar de los heridos?
– kōō·ēdär' de lōs erē'dōs

– **give me a lift?**
– llevarme en carro/*Sp* coche/
   Mex darme un aventón?
– lyevär'me en kä'rrō/kō'tshe/
   där'me ōōn äventōn'

– **tow my car?**
– remolcar el carro/*Sp* el coche?
– remōlkär' el kä'rrō/el kō'tshe

– **get me *a mechanic (a tow truck)*?**
– enviarme *un mecánico (una grúa)/Sp un coche grúa)?*
– embyär'me ōōn mekä'nēkō (ōō'nä grōō'ä/ōōn kō'tshe grōō'ä)

Where is there *a service station (repair shop)*?
¿Dónde hay *una gasolinera (un taller mecánico)*?
dōn'de ī ōō'nä gäsōlēne'rä (ōōn tälyer' mekä'nēkō)

Would you please give me your name and address?
Déme su nombre y dirección, por favor.
de'me sōō nōm'bre ē dēreksyōn', pōr favōr'

It's your fault.
Usted tiene la culpa.
ōōste' tye'ne lä kōōl'pä

I had the right of way.
Yo tenía preferencia.
yō tenē'ä preferen'syä

Nobody's hurt.
Nadie está herido.
nä'dye estä' erē'dō

Where is your car insured?
¿En qué compañía tiene asegurado su carro/*Sp* coche?
en ke kōmpänyē'ä tye'ne äsegōōrä'dō sōō kä'rrō/kō'tshe

You've damaged ...
Ha dañado/*Sp* estropeado ...
ä dänyä'dō/estrōpe·ä'dō ...

... is (badly) injured.
... está (gravemente) herido.
... estä' (grävemen'te) erē'dō

Will you be my witness?
¿Puede servirme de testigo?
pōō·e'de servēr'me de testē'gō

ambulance	ambulancia *f*	ämbōōlän'syä
bandages	vendajes *mpl*/*Mex*	vendä*hes*/
	vendas *fpl*	ven'däs
body and fender damage	daños *mpl* en la carrocería	dä'nyōs en lä kärrōserē'ä
breakdown	avería *f*/*Mex* falla *f* mecánica	äverē'ä/fä'lyä mekä'nēkä
collision	choque *m*	tshō'ke
damage	daños *mpl*	dä'nyōs
danger!	¡peligro!	pelē'grō
dealership garage	taller *m* concesionario	tälyer' kōnsesyōnär'yō
emergency ward	sala *f* de emergencias	sä'lä de emer*h*en'syäs
fire department	bomberos *mpl*	bōmbe'rōs
first aid station	puesto *m* de socorro/ *Mex* primeros auxilios	pōō·es'tō de sōkō'rrō/ prēme'rōs oukse'lyōs
head-on collision	choque *m* de frente	tshō'ke de fren'te
help	ayuda *f*	äyōō'dä
hospital	hospital *m*	ōspētäl'
injury	herida *f*	erē'dä
insurance	seguro *m*	segōō'rō
mechanic	mecánico *m*	mekä'nēkō
police	policía *f*	pōlesē'ä
rear-end collision	accidente *m* en cadena	äksēden'te en käde'nä
service station	gasolinera *f*, estación *f* de servicio	gäsōlēne'rä, estäsyōn' de serve'syō
towing service	servicio *m* de remolque	serve'syō de remōl'ke
tow line	cable *m* de remolque	kä'ble de remōl'ke
tow truck	grúa *f*/*Sp* coche *m* grúa	grōō'ä/kō'tshe grōō'ä

Repair Workshop

Where's the nearest *garage (. . . garage)*?
¿Dónde está el *taller mecánico (taller concesionario de . . .)* más cercano?
dōn'de estä' el tälyer' mekä'nēkō (tälyer' kōnsesyōnär'yō de . . .) mäs serkä'nō

. . . isn't working right.
. . . no funciona bien.
. . . nō fōōnsyō'nä byen

. . . is out of order (isn't working).
. . . está estropeado/dañado.
. . . estä' estrōpe·ä'dō/dänyä'dō

Can you fix it?
¿Puede arreglarlo?
pōō·e'de arreglär'lō

Where can I have this fixed?
¿Dónde se puede arreglarlo?
dōn'de se pōō·e'de ärreglär'lō

Would you please check the . . . ?
¿Podría revisar el/la . . . ?
pōdrē'ä revēsär' el (lä) . . .

Would you please give me . . . ?
¿Podría darme . . . ?
pōdrē'ä där'me . . .

Would you please fix this?
¿Podría arreglar eso?
pōōdrē'ä ärreglär e'sō

Have you got manufacturer's spare parts for . . . ?
¿Tiene piezas de repuesto originales de . . . ?
tye'ne pye'säs de repōō·es'tō ōrēhēnä'les de . . .

How soon can you get the spare parts?
¿Cuándo recibirá las piezas de repuesto?
kōō·än'dō resēbērä' läs pye'säs de repōō·es'tō

I need a new . . .
Necesito un nuevo . . .
nesesē'tō ōōn nōō·e'vō . . .

Can I still drive it?
¿Puedo seguir circulando con esto?
pōō·e'dō segēr' sērkōōlän'dō kōn es'tō

Just do the essentials, please.
Haga sólo lo más necesario, por favor.
ä'gä sō'lō lō mäs nesesär'yō, pōr fävōr'

When will it be ready?
¿Cuándo estará listo?
kōō·än'dō estärä' lēs'tō

How much *does (will)* it cost?
¿Cuánto *cuesta (va a costar)*?
kōō·än'tō kōō·es'tä (vä ä kōstär')

Car Parts, Repairs

accelerator	acelerador *m*	äselerädōr'
air filter	filtro *m* de aire	fēl'trō de ī're
automatic transmission	dispositivo *m* automático	dēspōsētē'vō outō-mä'tēkō
axle	eje *m*	e'*h*e
backfire	petardeo *m*	petärde'ō
ball bearings	cojinete *m* de bolas/*Mex* baleros *mpl*	kō*h*ēne'te de bō'läs/ bäle'rōs
battery	batería *f*/*Mex* a acumulador *m*	bäterē'ä/ äkōōmōōlädōr'
blinker	intermitente *m*/*Mex* direccionales	ēntermēten'te/ dēreksyōnä'les
body	carrocería *f*	kärrōserē'ä
bolt	tornillo *m*	tōrnē'lyō
– nut	tuerca *f*	tōō·er'kä
brake drum	tambor *m* de freno	tämbōr' de fre'nō
brake fluid	líquido *m* de frenos	lē'kēdō de fre'nōs
brake lights	luces *fpl* de freno	lōō'ses de fre'nō
brake lining	guarnición *f* de freno/*Mex* balata *f*	gōō·ärnēsyōn' de fre'nō/bälä'tä
brake pedal	pedal *m* de freno	pedäl' de fre'nō
brakes	frenos *mpl*	fre'nōs
– disc brake	freno *m* de disco	fre'nō de dēs'kō
– foot brake	freno *m* de pedal	fre'nō de pedäl'
– hand brake	freno *m* de mano	fre'nō de mä'nō
bulb	bombilla *f*	bōmbē'lyä
– change the bulb	cambiar la bombilla	kämbyär' lä bōmbē'lyä
bumper	parachoques *m*, defensa *f*	pärätshō'kes/ defen'sä

The battery *has run down (needs charging)*.
La batería *está descargada (debe cargarse)*.
lä bäterē'ä estä' deskärgä'dä (de'be kärgär'se)

The brakes aren't working right.   **They're *slack (too tight)*.**
Los frenos no funcionan bien.   Están *flojos (demasiado tensos)*.
lōs fre'nōs nō fōōnsyō'nän byen   estän' flō'*h*ōs (demäsyä'dō ten'sōs)

The brake drums are getting too hot.
Los tambores de freno se calientan demasiado.
lōs tämbō'res de fre'nō se kälyen'tän demäsyä'dō

cable	cable *m*	kä′ble
camshaft	árbol *m* de levas	är′bōl de le′väs
carburetor	carburador *m*	kärbōōrädōr′
carburetor jet	esprea *f*	espre′ä
car door	puerta *f* del carro/*Sp*	pōō·er′tä del kä′rrō/
	del coche	del kō′tshe
car keys	llaves *fpl* del carro/*Sp*	lyä′ves del kä′rrō/
	del coche	del kō′tshe
chains	cadenas *fpl*	käde′näs
– snow chains	cadenas *fpl* antidesli-	käde′näs äntēdezlē-
	zantes	sän′tes
chassis	chasís *m*/*Sp* chasis *m*	tshäsēs′/tshä′sēs
clutch	cloche *m*/*Sp* embrague *m*	klō′tshe/embrä′ge
compression	compresión *f*	kōmpresyōn′
condenser	condensador *m*	kōndensädōr′
connecting rod	biela *f*	bye′lä
– connecting rod	cojinete *m* de biela/*Mex*	kō*h*ēne′te de bye′lä/
bearing	metales *mpl* de bielas	metä′les de bye′läs
contact	contacto *m*	kōntäk′tō
crankshaft	cigüeñal *m*	sēgōō·enyäl′
cylinder	cilindro *m*	sēlēn′drō
– cylinder head	culata *f*/*Mex* cabeza *f*	kōōlä′tä/käbe′sä/
	del cilindro	del sēlēn′drō
– cylinder head	junta *f* de la culata/*Mex*	*h*ōōn′tä de lä kōōlä′tä/
gasket	empaque *m* de cabeza	empä′ke de käbe′sä
diesel nozzle	tobera *f*	tōbe′rä
differential	diferencial *m*	dēferensyäl′
dip stick	varilla *f* del nivel de	värē′lyä del nēvel′
	aceite	de äse′ēte
distributor	distribuidor *m*	dēstrēbōō·ēdōr′
door lock	cerradura *f*, chapa *f*	serrädōō′rä/tshä′pä
drive shaft	árbol *m* del cardán	är′bōl del kärdän′
dynamo	dínamo *m* + *f*/*Sp f*	dē′nämō
exhaust	escape *m*	eskä′pe

The dynamo isn't charging.   There's oil leaking out of the gear-box.

La dínamo no da corriente.   Gotea aceite de la caja de cambios.

lä dē′nämō nō dä kōrryen′te   gōte′ä äse′ēte de lä kä′*h*ä de käm′byōs

It won't stay in … gear.

La … marcha no agarra/el cambio no entra.

lä … mär′tshä nō ägä′rrä/el käm′byō no en′trä

fan	ventilador *m*	ventēlädōr'
fan belt	correa *f* de ventilador/ *Mex* banda *f* de ventilador	kōrre'ä de ventēlädōr'/bän'dä de ventēlädōr'
fender	guardabarros *m*	gōō·ärdäbä'rrōs
fire extinguisher	extintor *m*, extinguidor *m*	ekstēntōr', ekstēngēdōr'
fuel injector	bomba *f* de inyección	bōm'bä de ēnyeksyōn'
fuel lines	conducto *m* de gasolina	kōndōōk'tō de gäsōlē'nä
fuel pump	bomba *f* de gasolina	bōm'bä de gäsōlē'nä
fuse	fusible *m*	fōōsē'ble
gas	gasolina *f*	gäsōlē'nä
gasket	junta *f*, empaque *m*	hōōn'tä, empä'ke
gear	marcha *f*/*Mex* engrane *m*	mär'tshä/engrä'ne
– neutral	punto *m* muerto	pōōn'tō mōō·er'tō
– reverse	marcha *f* atrás	mär'tshä äträs'
– to put in gear	meter la marcha	meter' lä mär'tshä
gear box	caja *f* de cambios	kä'hä de käm'byōs
gear lever, gear shift	palanca *f* de cambios	pälän'kä de käm'byōs
handle	manecilla *f*, manija *f*	mänese'lyä, mänē'hä
headlight	faro *m*/*Mex* focos *mpl*	fä'rō/fō'kōs
– dipped headlights	luz *f* de cruce	lōōs de krōō'se
– full beam	luz *f* de carretera	lōōs de kärrete'rä
– parking lights	luz *f* de población	lōōs de pōbläsyōn'
– rear lights	luz *f* trasera	lōōs träse'rä
heating system	calefacción *f*	kälefäksyōn'
hood	capó *m*, capota *f*	käpō', käpō'tä
horn	bocina *f*, claxon *m*, pito *m*	bōsē'nä, klä'ksōn, pē'tō
hub	cubo *m*	kōō'bō
hub cap	tapacubos *m*, copa *f*	täpäkōō'bōs, kō'pä

The heating doesn't work.
La calefacción no funciona.
lä kälefäksyōn' nō fōōnsyō'nä

The radiator has sprung a leak.
Se escapa agua del radiador.
se eskä'pä ä'gōō·ä del rädyädōr'

The clutch *slips (won't disengage).*
El cloche/*Sp* el embrague/*patina (no se suelta).*
el klō'tshe/el embrä'ge/pätē'nä (nō se sōō·el'tä)

ignition	encendido *m*	ensendē′dō
– ignition cable ...	cable *m* (del encendido)	kä′ble (del ensen-dē′dō)
– ignition key	llave *f* de contacto	lyä′ve de kōntäk′tō
– ignition lock	interruptor *m* (del encendido)	ēnterrōōptōr′ (del ensendē′dō)
insulation	aislamiento *m*	īzlämyen′tō
interrupter	ruptor *m*	rōōptōr′
lamp	lámpara *f*	läm′pärä
license plate	matrícula *f*, placa *f*	mätrē′kōōlä, plä′kä
lighting system	alumbrado *m*, luces *fpl*	älōōmbrä′dō, lōō′ses
lubricant	lubricante *m*	lōōbrēkän′te
mileage indicator ..	cuentakilómetros *m* ...	kōō·entäkēlō′metrōs
motor	motor *m*	mōtōr′
– diesel motor	motor *m* diesel	mōtōr′ dyesel′
– rear motor	motor *m* trasero	mōtōr′ träse′rō
– two-stroke motor	motor *m* de dos tiempos	mōtōr′ de dōs tyem′pōs
nationality plate ..	placa *f* de nacionalidad	plä′kä de näsyōnä-lēdäd′
oil filter	filtro *m* de aceite	fēl′trō de äse′ēte
oil pump	bomba *f* de aceite	bōm′bä de äse′ēte
paint job	pintura *f*/*Sp* barniz *m* .	pēntōō′rä/bärnēs′
pedal	pedal *m*	pedäl′
piston	émbolo *m*, pistón *m* ...	em′bōlō, pēstōn′
– piston ring	segmento *m* de émbolo (de pistón)	segmen′tō de em′-bōlō (de pēstōn′)
pipe	tubo *m*	tōō′bō
power brake	servofreno *m*	servōfre′nō
power steering	servodirección *f*	servōdēreksyōn′
radiator	radiador *m*	rädyädōr′
– radiator grill	rejilla *f* del radiador ...	rehē′lyä del rädyädōr′

The motor lacks power.   **– is overheating.**
El motor no tira/no tiene fuerza.   – se calienta.
el mōtōr′ nō tē′rä/ nō tye′ne fōō·er′sä   – se kälyen′tä

– knocks.   **– suddenly stalls.**   **– misses.**
– golpea, pica/*Mex* suena.   – se cala/se apaga.   – da sacudidas
– gōlpe′ä, pē′kä/sōō·e′nä   – se kä′lä/se äpä′gä   – dä säkōōdē′däs

rear view mirror	espejo *m* retrovisor	espe'hō retrōvēsōr'
repair	reparación *f*	repäräsyōn'
reserve fuel can	tarro *m* de reserva/*Sp*	tä'rrō de reser'vä/
	bidón *m* de reserva	bēdōn' de reser'vä
roof	capota *f*	käpō'tä
screw	tornillo *m*	tōrnē'lyō
seat belt	cinturón *m* de seguridad	sēntoōrōn' de
		segoōrēdäd'
shock absorber	amortiguador *m*	ämōrtēgoō·ädōr'
short circuit	cortocircuito *m*	kōrtōsērkoō·ē'tō
sliding sun roof	techo *m* corredizo	te'tshō kōrredē'sō
solder	soldar	sōldär'
speedometer	taquímetro *m*	täkē'metrō
spoke	rayo *m* (de rueda)	rä'yō (de roō·e'dä)
seat	asiento *m*	äsyen'tō
– back seat	asiento *m* trasero	äsyen'tō träse'rō
– driver's seat	asiento *m* del conductor	äsyen'tō del
		kōndoōktōr'
– front seat	asiento *m* delantero	äsyen'tō delänte'rō
– front passenger seat	asiento *m* delantero del	äsyen'tō delänte'rō
	pasajero	del päsähe'rō
spare part	pieza *f* de recambio, de	pye'sä de rekäm'-
	repuesto	byō, de repoō·e'stō
spare wheel	rueda *f* de recambio, de	roō·e'dä de rekäm'-
	repuesto	byō, de repoō·e'stō
spark	chispa *f*	tshēs'pä
spark plug	bujía *f*	boōhē'ä
spring	ballesta *f*	bälyes'tä
starter	arranque *m*/*Mex*	ärrän'ke, mär'tshä
	marcha *f*	

The windshield wiper *smears (is broken off)*.
El limpiaparabrisas *ensucia el vidrio*/*Sp* el cristal *(está roto)*.
el lēmpyäpäräbrē'säs ensoō'syä el vē'drē·ō/el krēstäl' (estä' rō'tō)

This screw needs *tightening (loosening)*.
Hay que *apretar (aflojar)* este tornillo.
ī ke äpretär' (äflōhär') es'te tōrnē'lyō

The fuse has blown.
Los fusibles están fundidos.
lōs foōsē'bles estän' foōndē'dōs

steering	dirección *f*	dĕreksyōn′
– steering wheel	volante *m*	võlän′te
switch	interruptor *m*	ēnterrōōoptōr′
thermostat	termostato *m*/*Mex* toma *f* de agua	termōstä′tō/tō′mä de ä′gōō·ä
(screw) thread	rosca *f*	rōs′kä
top	capota *f*	käpō′tä
transmission	transmisión *f*	tränsmēsyōn′
trunk	portamaletas *m*, maletero *m*/*Mex* cajuela *f*	pōrtämäle′täs, mälete′rō/kähōō·e′lä
turn signal flasher	intermitente *m*/*Mex* destallador *m*	ēntermēten′te/ destälyädōr′
valve	válvula *f*	väl′vōolä
warning triangle	triángulo *m* de peligro	trē·än′gōolō de pelē′grō
washer	arandela *f*	ärände′lä
wheel	rueda *f*	rōō·e′dä
windshield	parabrisas *m*	päräbrē′säs
windshield washer	lavaparabrisas *m*	läväpäräbrē′säs
windshield wiper	limpiaparabrisas *m*	lēmpyäpäräbrē′säs

Would you please straighten out my bumper?
Por favor, enderece el parachoques, la defensa.
pōr fävōr′, endere′se el pärätshō′kes, lä defen′sä

Would you please *check (clean)* the carburetor?
Por favor, *revise (limpie)* el carburador.
pōr fävōr′, revē′se (lēm′pye) el kärbōōrädōr′

Would you please change the spark plugs?
Por favor, cámbieme las bujías.
pōr fävōr′, käm′byeme läs bōo*h*ē′äs

Tools

Can you loan me ...?
¿Puede/puedes *(fam)*/prestarme ...?
poo·e'de/poo·e'des/prestär'me ...

I need ...
Necesito ...
nesesē'tō ...

air pump	bomba *f* de aire	bōm'bä de ī're
bolt	tornillo *m*	tōrnē'lyō
– nut	tuerca *f*	too·er'kä
cable	cable *m*	kä'ble
chisel	cincel *m*	sēnsel'
cloth	paño *m*	pä'nyō
drill	taladro *m*	tälä'drō
file	lima *f*	lē'mä
funnel	embudo *m*	emboo'dō
hammer	martillo *m*	märtē'lyō
inspection light	lámpara *f* piloto *or* de prueba	läm'pärä pēlō'tō (de proo·e'bä)
jack	gato *m*	gä'tō
nail	clavo *m*	klä'vō
pincers	tenazas *fpl*	tenä'säs
pliers	alicates *mpl*, pinzas *fpl*	älēkä'tes, pēn'säs
rag	trapo *m*	trä'pō
sandpaper	papel *m* de lija	päpel' de lē'hä
screw	tornillo *m*	tōrnē'lyō
screwdriver	destornillador *m*/*Mex* desarmador *m*	destōrnēlyädōr'/ desärmädōr'
socket wrench	llave *f* de dado	lyä've de dä'dō
string	cordel *m*, cuerda *f*	kōrdel', koo·er'dä
tools	herramientas *fpl*	errämyen'täs
– tool *box (kit)*	caja *f* de herramientas	kä'hä de errämyen'täs
wire	alambre *m*	äläm'bre
– a piece of wire	un trozo de alambre	oon trō'sō de äläm'bre
wrench	llave *f* inglesa	lyä've ēngle'sä

TRAFFIC SIGNS

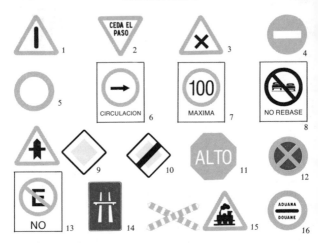

1 DANGER Peligro · 2 YIELD RIGHT OF WAY Ceda el paso ·
3 INTERSECTION Cruce · 4 DO NOT ENTER Acceso prohibido · 5
NO VEHICLES ALLOWED Circulación prohibida a todos los
vehículos · 6 ONE WAY STREET Calle de dirección única · 7 SPEED
LIMIT Velocidad máxima · 8 NO PASSING Prohibido adelantar ·
9 PRIORITY ROAD Cruce con prioridad · 10 END OF PRIORITY
ROAD Fin de prioridad · 11 STOP Alto, Pare · 12 NO STOPPING
Prohibida la parada · 13 NO PARKING Estacionamiento prohibido ·
14 EXPRESSWAY/FREEWAY Autopista · 15 RAILROAD CROSS-
ING NO GATES Paso a nivel sin barreras · 16 CUSTOMS Aduana

Road signs are color and shape-coded. Triangular signs with a red
rim are *warning signs*; round blue signs are *regulatory signs*; round
signs with a red rim are *prohibit movement signs*; rectangular
yellow signs with a black rim are *destination signs*; rectangular
blue signs with white letters are *destination signs* on highways.

ON THE BUS

Where do the buses to … stop?
¿Dónde paran los buses/*Mex* camiones/para …?
dōn'de pä'rän lōs bōō'ses/kämyō'nes/pärä …

Is that far?
¿Está lejos?
estä' le'*h*ōs

When does *a (the first, the last)* bus leave for …?
¿A qué hora sale *un (el primer, el último)* autobús/*Mex* camión/para …?
ä ke ō'rä sä'le ōōn (el prēmer', el ōōl'tēmō) outōbōōs'/kämyōn'/
pä'rä …

Which bus goes to …?
¿Qué bus/*Mex* camión/va a …?
ke bōōs/kämyōn'/vä ä …

Where does the bus go?
¿A dónde va el bus/*Mex* camión?
ä dōn'de vä el bōōs/kämyōn'

Is there a bus (Does this bus go) to …?
¿Hay un autobús (Va este autobús) a …?
ī ōōn outōbōōs' (vä es'te outōbōōs') ä …

When do we get to …?
¿Cuándo llegamos a …?
kōō·än'dō lyegä'mōs ä …

Do I have to change buses for …?
¿Tengo que cambiar para …?
ten'gō ke kämbyär' pä'rä …

Where do I have to change?
¿Dónde tengo que cambiar?
dōn'de ten'gō ke kämbyär'

One (two) round-trip ticket(s), please.
Un (dos) boleto(s)/*Sp* billete(s)/de ida y
vuelta para …
ōōn (dōs) bōle'tō(s)/bēlye'te(s)/de ē'dä
ē vōō·el'tä pä'rä …

bus …………	bus *m*, autobús *m*/*Mex* camión *m* …………	bōōs, outōbōōs'/kämyōn'
bus terminal ….	estación *f* de autobuses	estäsyōn' de outōbōō'ses
direction ……..	dirección *f* …………	dēreksyōn'
driver ……..	conductor *m*, chófer *m*	kōndōōktōr', tshō'fer
last stop ……..	terminal *f or m* …….	termēnäl'
luggage ………	equipaje *m* …………	ekēpä'*h*e
route ……..	línea *f* ……………	lē'ne·ä
stop …………	parada *f* ……………	pärä'dä
ticket ………	boleto *m*/*Sp* billete *m* ..	bōle'tō/bēlye'te
ticket checker …	cobrador *m* …………	kōbrädōr'
transfer ……..	correspondencia *f* …..	kōrrespōnden'syä

BY TRAIN

At the Station

Where is the *station (main station)?*	Where *is (are)* …?
¿Dónde está *la estación (central)* de ferrocarril?	¿Dónde *está (están)* …?
dōn'de estä' lä estäsyōn' (senträl') de ferrōkärrēl'	dōn'de estä' (estän') …

the information office …	información *f* …	ēnfōrmäsyōn'
the money exchange	oficina *f* de cambio …	ōfēsē'nä de käm'byō
the rest room …	lavabos *mpl*/servicios *mpl*/*Mex* baños *mpl* …	lävä'bōs/servē'syōs/bä'nyōs
the ticket window ..	despacho *m* de billetes, taquilla *f* …	despä'tshō de bē-lye'tes, täkē'lyä
a time table …	horario *m* …	ōrär'yō
the waiting room ..	sala *f* de espera …	sä'lä de espe'rä

Time Table

arrival/departure ..	llegada *f*/salida *f* …	lyegä'dä/sälē'dä
connection …	combinación *f*/*Sp* enlace *m* …	kōmbēnäsyōn'/enlä'se
couchette sleeper ..	coche-literas *m*/*Mex* cama *f* alta, baja …	kō'tshe-lēte'räs/kä'mä äl'tä, bä'hä
dining bar …	coche-restaurante *m* …	kō'tshe restourän'te
express train …	expreso *m* …	ekspre'sō
fast train …	tren *m* rápido …	tren rä'pēdō
long distance express	expreso *m* de largo recorrido …	ekspre'sō de lär'gō rekōrrē'dō
motorail service …	autotrén *m* …	outōtren'
platform …	andén *m* …	änden'
railroad car …	coche *m* …	kō'tshe
sleeper/sleeping car	coche-cama *m*/*Mex* camarín *m*, alcoba *f* …	kō'tshe-kä'mä/kämärēn', älkō'bä

A couchette car provides overnight travelers with a simple bench or a berth to stretch out on during the night. A sleeping car contains little bedrooms complete with private washing facilities.

supplemental fare .	suplemento *m*	sōōplemen'tō
system time table ..	guía *f* de ferrocarriles .	gē'ä de ferrōkärrē'les
through car	coche *m* directo	kō'tshe dērek'tō
track	vía *f*	vē'ä

Information

When is there a *fast (express)* train to ...?

¿Cuándo sale un tren *rápido (expreso)* para ...?

kōō·än'dō sä'le ōōn tren rä'pēdō (ekspre'sō) pä'rä ...

Where is the train to ...?

¿Dónde está el tren para ...?

dōn'de estä' el tren pä'rä ...

Is this the train to ...?

¿Es éste el tren para ...?

es es'te el tren pä'rä ...

Does this train stop in ...?

¿Para este tren en ...?

pä'rä es'te tren en ...

Is the train from ... late?

¿Tiene retraso el tren de ...?

tye'ne reträ'sō el tren de ...

Can we make a connection to ...?

¿Tenemos conección para ...?

tene'mōs kōneksyōn' pä'rä ...

When does it get to ...?

¿Cuándo llega a ...?

kōō·än'dō lye'gä ä ...

Do we have to change trains?

¿Tenemos que hacer transbordo?

tene'mōs ke äser' tränsbōr'dō

Where?

¿Dónde?

dōn'de

Is there a dining car (are there sleepers) on the train?

¿Hay *un coche-restaurante (coche-camas/Mex camarines, alcobas)* en el tren?

ī ōōn kō'tshe-restourän'te (kō'tshe-kä'mäs/kämärē'nes, älkō'bäs) en el tren

Can I interrupt the trip in ...?

¿Puedo interrumpir el viaje en ...?

pōō·e'dō ēnterrōōmpēr' el vyä'*he* en ...

What platform does the train from ... come in on?

¿En qué andén entra el tren de ...?

en ke änden' en'trä el tren de ...

What platform does the train for ... leave from?

¿De qué andén sale el tren para ...?

de ke änden' sä'le el tren pä'rä ...

Tickets

One ticket (two full fares and two reduced fares) to ..., please.
Un boleto/Sp billete/(dos boletos/Sp billetes/a precio normal y dos a precio reducido) a ..., por favor.
ōōn bōle'tō/bēlye'te/(dōs bōle'tōs/bēlye'tes/ä pre'syō normäl ē dōs ä pre'syō redōōsē'dō) ä ... pōr fävōr'

– round trip.	– one way.	– first class.	– second class.
– de ida y vuelta.	– de ida solo.	– de primera clase.	– de segunda clase.
– de ē'dä ē vōō·el'tä	– de ē'dä sō'lō	– de prēme'rä klä'se	– de segōōn'dä klä'se

I'd like to reserve a seat on the twelve o'clock train to ...
Quisiera reservar un asiento para el tren de las doce a ...
kēsye'rä reservär' ōōn äsyen'tō pä'rä el tren de läs dō'se ä ...

How long is the ticket valid?
¿Cuánto tiempo es válido este boleto/Sp billete?
kōō·än'tō tyem'pō es vä'lēdō es'te bōle'tō/bēlye'te

I'd like to interrupt the trip in ...
Quiero interrumpir el viaje en ...
kye'rō ēnterrōōmpēr' el vyä*he* en ...

How much is the fare to ...?
¿Cuánto cuesta el boleto/Sp billete/a ...?
kōō·än'tō kōō·es'tä el bōle'tō/bēlye'te/ä ...

I'd like to reserve ...
Quisiera reservar ...
kēsye'rä reservär' ...

fare	precio *m* del boleto/Sp billete *m*	pre'syō del bōle'tō/bēlye'te
group fare ticket	boleto *m* colectivo	bōle'to kōlektē'vō
half fare	boleto *m* de media tarifa	bōle'tō de me'dyä tärē'fä
reduced fare	boleto *m* a precio reducido	bōle'tō ä pre'syō redōōsē'dō
seat reservation	reserva *f* de asiento	reser'vä de äsyen'tō
sleeper reservation	boleto *m*/Sp billete *m*/ de coche-cama/Mex de camarín, de alcoba	bōle'tō/bēlye'te/de kō'tshe-kä'mä/de kämärēn', de älkō'bä
supplemental fare ticket	suplemento *m*	sōōplemen'tō
ticket	boleto *m*/Sp billete *m*	bōle'tō/bēlye'te

Baggage

I'd like to ...	– send this luggage on to ...
Quisiera ...	– facturar este equipaje para ...
kēsye′rä ...	– fäktōōrär′ es′te ekēpä′he pä′rä ...

– leave this luggage here.	– *insure (claim) my luggage.*
– dejar aquí este equipaje.	– *asegurar (recoger) mi equipaje.*
– dehär′ äkē′ es′te ekēpä′he	– äsegōōrär′ (rekōher′) mē ekēpä′he

Here's my claim check.
Aquí tiene el talón/recibo/resguardo.
äkē′ tye′ne el tälōn′/resē′bō/rezgōō·är′dō

There are two suitcases and a traveling bag.
Son dos maletas y un bolso/una bolsa/de viaje.
sōn dōs mäle′täs ē ōon bōl′sō/ōō′nä bōl′sä/de vyä′he

Will my baggage be on the same train?	**When does it get to ...?**
¿Sale el equipaje en el mismo tren?	¿Cuándo llegará a ...?
sä′le el ekēpä′he en el mēz′mō tren	kōō·än′dō lyegärä′ ä ...

These aren't mine.	**One suitcase is missing.**
No son míos.	Falta una maleta.
nō sōn mē′ōs	fäl′tä ōo′nä mäle′tä

baggage	equipaje *m*	ekēpä′he
baggage check area	depósito *m*/Mex "guarda equipaje"	depō′sētō/gōō·är′dä ekēpä′he
baggage claim area	entrega *f* de equipaje/Mex andenes *mpl* de equipaje	entre′gä de ekēpä′he/ände′nes de ekēpä′he
baggage room	despacho *m* de equipaje	despä′tshō de ekēpä′he
claim check	talón *m*/recibo *m*/resguardo *m*	tälōn′/resē′bō/rezgōō·är′dō
hand luggage	bultos *mpl* de mano	bōōl′tōs de mä′nō
luggage	equipaje *m*	ekēpä′he
luggage locker	consigna *f* automática	kōnsēg′nä outōmä′tēkä
suitcase	maleta *f*	mäle′tä
traveling bag	bolso *m*/bolsa *f*/de viaje	bōl′sō/bōl′sä/de vyä′he

Porter

porter . . . .   mozo *m* . . . .   mō′sō

Please bring *this luggage (suitcase)* ...
Por favor, *estos bultos (esta maleta)* ...
pōr fävŏr′ es′tōs bōol′tōs (es′tä mäle′tä)

– to the ... train.
– al tren de ...
– äl tren de ...

– to Platform 2
– al andén 2.
– äl änden′ dōs ...

– to the baggage check area.
– a la consigna/*Mex* guarda equipaje.
– ä lä kōnsēg′nä/gōo·är′dä ekēpä′*he*

– to the exit.
– a la salida.
– ä lä sälē′dä

– to a taxi.
– al taxi.
– äl tä′ksē

– to the ... bus.
– al autobús/*Mex* al camión/para ...
– äl outōbōos′/äl kämyōn′/pä′rä ...

On the Platform

Is this the train *to (from)* ...?
¿Es éste el tren *para (procedente de)* ...?
es es′te el tren pä′rä (prōseden′te de) ...

Where is ...?
¿Dónde está ...?
dōn′de estä′ ...

– first class?
– la primera clase?
– lä prēme′rä klä′se

– the through car to ...?
– el coche directo para ...?
– el kō′tshe dērek′tō pä′rä

– the couchette car?
– el coche literas/*Mex* las camas?
– el kō′tshe lēte′räs/läs kä′mäs

– the sleeping car?
– el coche-cama/*Mex* los camarines, las alcobas?
– el kō′tshe-kä′mä/lōs kämärē′nes, läs älkō′bäs

– the dining car?
– el coche-restaurante?
– el kō′tshe-restourän′te

– the luggage car?
– el furgón?
– el fōorgōn′

– car number ...?
– el coche número ...?
– el kō′tshe nōo′merō ...

There.	Up front.	In the middle.
Allí.	En la cabeza.	En el centro.
älyē′	en lä käbe′sä	en el sen′trō

At the rear.	What time does the train arrive?
En la cola.	¿A qué hora llega el tren?
en lä kō′lä	ä ke ō′rä lye′gä el tren

INSPECCION	INFORMACION	SALIDA
Station Master	**Information**	**Exit**

PASO A LOS ANDENES	REFRESCOS
To trains	**Refreshments**

ENTREGA DE EQUIPAJES	VIA
Luggage Checking	**Platform (Track)**

PUESTO DE SOCORRO *Mex* PRIMEROS AUXILIOS	AGUA POTABLE
First Aid	**Drinking Water**

SERVICIOS *Am* BAÑOS	CABALLEROS	SEÑORAS
Rest Rooms	**Men**	**Ladies**

SALA DE ESPERA
Waiting Room

On the Train

Is this seat taken?	That's my seat.
¿Está libre este asiento?	Este es mi asiento.
estä′ lē′bre es′te äsyen′tō	es′te es mē äsyen′tō

Mind if I *open (close)* the window?	Allow me (to get past you)?
¿Puedo *abrir (cerrar)* la ventanilla?	¿Me permite?
pōō·e′dō äbrēr′ (serrär′) lä ventänē′lyä	me permē′te

Could you please help me?
¿Puede ayudarme, por favor?
pŏŏ·e'de äyōōdär'me, pōr fävōr'

Would you mind changing places?
¿Le importaría cambiar el asiento conmigo?
le ēmpōrtärē'ä kämbyär' el äsyen'tō kōnmē'gō

I don't like riding backwards.
No me gusta viajar de espaldas.
nō me gōōs'tä vyähär' de espäl'däs

***Tickets, please.**
Boletos/*Sp* billetes/por favor.
bōle'tōs/bēlye'tes/pōr fävōr'

I'd like to *pay the excess fare (pay the supplement, pay now)*.
Quisiera *pagar la diferencia (el suplemento, ahora)*.
kēsye'rä pägär' lä dēferen'syä (el sōōplemen'tō, ä·ō'rä)

How many stations before ...?
¿Cuántas estaciones hasta ...?
kōō·än'täs estäsyō'nes äs'tä ...

Where are we now?
¿Dónde estamos ahora?
dōn'de estä'mōs ä·ō'rä

Will we get to ... on time?
¿Llegaremos sin retraso a ...?
lyegäre'mōs sēn reträ'sō ä ...

How long do we stop here?
¿Cuánto tiempo paramos aquí?
kōō·än'tō tyem'pō pärä'mōs äkē'

***All change, please!**
¡Cambio de tren!
käm'byō de tren

***Passengers for ... change at ...**
Pasajeros con destino a ... cambian en ...
päsähe'rōs kōn destē'nō ä ... käm'byän en ...

***Passengers for ... get on in the *front (rear)* of the train.**
Pasajeros con destino a ... suben por las portezuelas/puertas/*delanteras (de atrás)*.
päsähe'rōs kōn destē'nō ä ... sōō'ben pōr läs pōrtesōō·e'läs/pōō·er'täs/delänte'räs (de äträs')

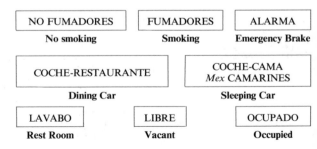

NO FUMADORES	FUMADORES	ALARMA
No smoking	Smoking	Emergency Brake

COCHE-RESTAURANTE	COCHE-CAMA *Mex* CAMARINES
Dining Car	Sleeping Car

LAVABO	LIBRE	OCUPADO
Rest Room	Vacant	Occupied

*all aboard!	¡Señores pasajeros, al tren!	senyō′res päsä-*he*′rōs, äl tren
arrival	llegada *f*	lyegä′dä
arrive	llegar	lyegär′
baggage	equipaje *m*	ekēpä′*he*
barrier	barrera *f*	bärre′rä
car	coche *m*, vagón *m*	kō′tshe, vägōn′
car door	portezuela *f*, puerta *f*	pōrtesoo·e′lä, poo·er′tä
change trains	hacer transbordo	äser′ tränsbōr′dō
compartment	departamento *m*, compartim(i)ento *m*	depärtämen′tō, kōmpärtēm(y)en′tō
conductor	conductor *m*	kōndooktōr′
connection	enlace *m*, corresponden-cia *f*	enlä′se, kōrrespōn-den′syä
depart	salir	sälēr′
departure	salida *f*	sälē′dä
entrance	entrada *f*	enträ′dä
exit	salida *f*	sälē′dä
fare	precio *m* del boleto	pre′syō del bōle′tō
– discount	tarifa *f* reducida	tärē′fä redoosē′dä
get *in (aboard)*	subir (a)	soobēr′ (ä)
get off	bajar (de)	bä*h*är′ (de)
heating	calefacción *f*	kälefäksyōn′
– cold	frío	frē′ō
– hot	caliente	kälyen′te
locomotive	locomotora *f*	lōkōmōtō′rä
luggage rack	rejilla *f*	re*h*ē′lyä
passenger	pasajero *m*	päsä*he*′rō
platform	andén *m*	änden′
railroad	ferrocarril *m*	ferrōkärrēl′
route	línea *f*	lē′ne·ä
station	estación *f*	estäsyōn′
station master	jefe *m* de estación	*he*′fe de estäsyōn′
stop	parada *f*	pärä′dä
system time table	guía *f* de ferrocarriles	gē′ä de ferrōkä-rrē′les
ticket	boleto *m*/*Sp* billete *m*	bōle′tō/bēlye′te
train	tren *m*	tren
window seat	asiento *m* de ventanilla	äsyen′tō de ventä-nē′lyä

BY PLANE

Information and Reservations

Is there a (direct) flight to ...?
¿Hay un vuelo (directo) para ...?
ī ōōn vōō·e′lō (dērek′tō) pä′rä

Is there a connection to ...?
¿Hay conexión para ...?
ī kōneksyōn′ pä′rä ...

When is there a plane *today (tomorrow)* to ...?
¿A qué hora sale *hoy (mañana)* un avión para ...?
ä ke ō′rä sä′le oi (mänyä′nä) ōōn ävyōn′ pä′rä ...

When is the next plane to ...?
¿Cuándo sale el próximo avión para ...?
kōō·än′dō sä′le el prō′ksēmō ävyōn′ pä′rä ...

Does the plane make a stopover in ...?
¿Hace escala en ...?
ä′se eskä′lä en ...

When do we get to ...?
¿Cuándo llegaremos a ...?
kōō·än′dō lyegäre′mōs ä ...

Are there still seats available?
¿Hay todavía plazas libres?
ī tōdävē′ä plä′säs lē′bres

How much is a (round-trip) flight to ...?
¿Cuánto cuesta un pasaje (de ida y vuelta) para ...?
kōō·än′tō kōō·es′tä ōōn päsä′he (de ē′dä ē vōō·el′tä) pä′rä ...

What's the luggage allowance?
¿Cuántos kilos de equipaje se pueden llevar?
kōō·än′tōs kē′lōs de ekēpä′he se pōō·e′den lyevär′

How much does excess baggage cost?
¿Cuánto cuesta el exceso de equipaje?
kōō·än′tō kōō·es′tä el ekse′sō de ekēpä′he

How much is the airport service charge?
¿Cuánto cuesta la tasa del aeropuerto?
kōō·än′tō kōō·es′tä lä tä′sä del ä·erōpōō·er′tō

How do I get to the airport?
¿Cómo se va al aeropuerto?
kō′mō se vä äl ä·erōpōō·er′tō

When is check-in time?
¿A qué hora tengo que estar allí?
ä ke ō′rä ten′gō ke estär′ älyē′

I'd like to reserve a seat on the Friday flight to ...
Quisiera hacer una reserva para el vuelo del viernes a ...
kēsye'rä äser' ōō'nä reser'vä pä'rä el vōō·e'lō del vyer'nes ä ...

I'd like to reserve a round-trip ticket to ... on the 2nd of July.
Quisiera reservar, para el dos de julio, un boleto/*Sp* billete/de ida y
vuelta a ...
kēsye'rä reservär', pä'rä el dōs de *hōō*'lyō, ōon bōle'tō/bēlye'tē/de
ē'dä ē vōō·el'tä ä ...

– First Class.	**– Economy Class.**
– primera clase.	– clase turista.
– prēme'rä klä'se	– klä'se tōōrēs'tä

How long is the ticket valid?
¿Por cuánto tiempo es válido el pasaje?
pōr kōō·än'tō tyem'pō es vä'lēdō el päsä'he

I have to *cancel (change)* my reservation.
Tengo que *anular/cancelar (cambiar)* mi vuelo.
ten'gō ke änōōlär'/känselär' (käm'byär') mē vōō·e'lō

What is the cancellation fee?
¿Cuánto cuesta la cancelación/*Sp* anulación/del pasaje?
kōō·än'tō kōō·es'tä lä känseläsyōn'/änōōläsyōn'/del päsä'he

At the Airport

Can I take this along as hand luggage?
¿Puedo llevar esto como equipaje de
mano?
pōō·e'dō lyevär' es'tō kō'mō ekēpä'he
de mä'nō

How much does it cost?
¿Cuánto cuesta?
kōō·än'tō kōō·es'tä

Where is *the waiting room (Exit B, Gate B)*?
¿Dónde está *la sala de espera (salida B, puerta B)*?
dōn'de estä' lä sä'lä de espe'rä (sälē'dä be, pōō·er'tä be)

Where's the duty-free shop?
¿Dónde se venden mercancías libres de impuestos de aduana?
dōn'de se ven'den merkänse'äs lē'bres de ēmpōō·es'tōs de ädōō·ä'nä

Is the plane to ... late?	**Has the plane from ... landed already?**
¿Tiene retraso el avión a ...?	¿Ha aterrizado ya el avión de ...?
tye'ne reträ'sō el ävyōn' ä ...	ä äterrēsä'dō yä el ävyōn' de ...

On the Plane

*Kindly refrain from smoking.
No fumen, por favor.
nō foo'men, pōr fävōr'

*Please fasten your seat belts.
Abróchense los cinturones
de seguridad, por favor.
äbrō'tshense lōs sēntoorō'nes de
segoorēdäd, pōr fävōr'

How high are we flying?
¿A qué altura volamos?
ä ke ältoo'rä vōlä'mōs

Where are we now?
¿Dónde estamos ahora?
dōn'de estä'mōs ä·ō'rä

What _mountains are those (river is that)_?
¿Qué _montaña es ésta (río es éste)_?
ke mōntä'nyä es es'tä (rē'ō es es'te)

I feel sick.
Me siento mal.
me syen'tō mäl

Have you got an air-sickness remedy?
¿Tiene un medicamento contra el mareo?
tye'ne oon medēkämen'tō kōn'trä el märe'ō

Can I have ...?
¿Me puede dar ...?
me poo·e'de där ...

When do we land?
¿Cuándo aterrizamos?
koo·än'dō äterrēsä'mōs

How's the weather in ...?
¿Qué tiempo hace en ...?
ke tyem'pō ä'se en ...

aircraft	avión _m_	ävyōn'
air jet _(over seat)_	tobera _f_ de aire fresco	tōbe'rä de ī're fres'kō
airline	compañía _f_ aérea	kōmpänyē'ä ä·e're·ä
airport	aeropuerto _m_	ä·erōpoo·er'tō
air sickness	mareo _m_	märe'ō
approach	vuelo _m_ de aproximación	voo·e'lō de äprōksēmä·syōn'
arrival	llegada _f_	lyegä'dä
charter plane	avión _m_ chárter	ävyōn' tshär'ter
climb	ganar altura, subir	gänär' ältoo'rä, soobēr'
crew	tripulación _f_	trēpoo läsyōn'
destination	destino _m_	destē'nō
duty-free goods	mercancías _fpl_ libres de impuestos de aduana	merkänse'äs lē'bres de empoo·es'tōs de ädoo·ä'nä
emergency chute	rampa _f_ de emergencia	räm'pä de emerhen'syä
emergency exit	salida _f_ de emergencia	säle'dä de emerhen'syä
emergency landing	aterrizaje _m_ forzoso	äterēsä'he fōrsō'sō
engine	motor _m_, propulsor _m_	mōtōr', prōpoolsōr'

excess baggage	exceso *m* de equipaje ..	ekse'sō de ekēpä'*he*
exit	salida *f*	sälē'dä
flight	vuelo *m*	vōō·e'lō
flight attendant	azafata *f*/aeromoza *f*, cabinera *f*	äsäfä'tä/ä·erō-mō'sä, käbēne'rä
fly	volar	vōlär'
flying time	duración *f* de vuelo ...	dōōräsyōn' de vōō·e'lō
fog	niebla *f*	nye'blä
gate	puerta *f*	pōō·er'tä
hand luggage	equipaje *m* de mano ...	ekēpä'*he* de mä'nō
helicopter	helicóptero *m*	elēkōp'terō
information	información *f*	ēnfōrmäsyōn'
information counter .	mostrador *m* de información	mōsträdōr' de ēnfōrmäsyōn'
jet plane	jet *m/Sp* avión *m* a reacción	*h*et/ävyōn' ä re·äk-syōn'
land	aterrizar	äterrēsär'
landing	aterrizaje *m*	äterrēsä'*he*
landing gear	tren *m* de aterrizaje ...	tren de äterrēsä'*he*
life jacket	chaleco *m* salvavidas ..	tshäle'kō sälvä-vē'däs
pilot	piloto *m*	pēlō'tō
plane	avión *m*	ävyōn'
reservation	reserva *f*	reser'vä
return flight	vuelo *m* de regreso	vōō·e'lō de regre'sō
scheduled flight	avión *m* de línea	ävyōn' de lē'ne·ä
seat belt	cinturón *m* de seguridad	sēntōōrōn' de segōōrēdäd'
– fasten seat belts ...	abróchense los cinturones de seguridad	äbrō'tshense lōs sēntōōrō'nes de segōōrēdäd'
stopover	escala *f*	eskä'lä
system time table ...	horario *m* de vuelos ...	ōrär'yō de vōō·e'lōs
take off	despegue *m*/descolaje *m*	despe'ge deskōlä'*he*
thunderstorm	tormenta *f*	tormen'tä
ticket	billete *m*, pasaje *m*	bēlye'te, päsä'*he*
waiting room	sala *f* de espera	sä'lä de espe'rä
weather	tiempo *m*	tyem'pō
wing	ala *f*	ä'lä

BY SHIP

Information, Tickets

When does *a ship (the ferry)* leave for …?   **Where?**
¿Cuándo sale *un barco (el transbordador, el*   ¿Dónde?
ferry) para …?   dōn'de
koo·än'dō sä'le ōon bär'kō (el tränsbōrdädōr', el
fe'rē) pä'rä …

How often does the car ferry go to …?
¿Cuántas veces sale un transbordador para …?
koo·än'täs ve'ses sä'le ōon tränsbōrdädōr' pä'rä …

How long does the crossing from … to … take?
¿Cuánto tiempo dura la travesía de … a …?
koo·än'tō tyem'pō doo'rä lä trävesē'ä de … ä …

How far is the railroad station from the harbor?
¿A qué distancia del puerto queda la estación?
ä ke dēstän'syä del poo·er'tō ke'dä lä estäsyōn'

What are the ports of call?   **Where can we get tickets?**
¿En qué puertos hacemos escala?   ¿Dónde se sacan los pasajes?
en ke poo·er'tōs äse'mōs eskä'lä   dōn'de se sä'kän lōs päsä'hes

When do we *dock (land)* at …?
¿Cuándo *atracamos (desembarcamos)* en …?
koo·än'dō äträkä'mōs (desembärkä'mōs) en …

Can I get a connection to …?
¿Hay conexión *or* empalme para …?
ī kōneksyōn' (empäl'me) pä'rä …

Can we go ashore at …?   **For how long?**
¿Es posible desembarcar en …?   ¿Por cuánto tiempo?
es pōsē'ble desembärkär' en …   pōr koo·än'tō tyem'pō

Will there be any land excursions?
¿Se organizan excursiones a tierra?
se ōrgänē'sän ekskoorsyō'nes ä tye'rrä

When do we have to be back on board?
¿Cuándo tenemos que estar a bordo?
koo·än'dō tene'mōs ke estär' ä bōr'dō

I'd like ...
Quisiera ...
kēsye'rä ...

– to book passage to ...
– un pasaje para ...
– ōon päsä'*he* pä'rä ...

– two tickets on the ... to ... tomorrow.
– para mañana dos pasajes en el ... para ...
– pä'rä mänyä'nä dōs päsä'*he*s en el ... pä'rä ...

– a round-trip ticket from ... to ...
– un pasaje de ... a ..., ida y vuelta.
– ōon päsä'*he* de ... ä ..., ē'dä ē vōo·el'tä

– a ticket for a car.
– un billete de transporte para un carro/*Sp* un coche.
– ōon bēlye'te de tränspōr'te pä'rä ōon kä'rrō/ōon kō'tshe

– a single cabin.
– un camarote/*Mex* una cabina/
individual.
– ōon kämärō'te/ōo'nä käbē'nä/
ēndēvēdōo·äl'

– an *outside (inside)* cabin.
– un camarote/*Mex* una cabina/
exterior (interior).
– ōon kämärō'te/ōo'nä käbē'nä/
eksteryōr' (ēnteryōr')

– a double cabin.
– un camarote/*Mex* una
cabina/doble.
– ōon kämärō'te/ōo'nä
käbē'nä/dō'ble

– First Class
– Primera clase
– prēme'rä klä'se

– Tourist class
– Clase turista
– klä'se tōorēs'tä

In the Harbor

Where is the "..." docked?
¿Dónde está atracado el "..."?
dōn'de estä' äträkä'dō el ...

Where does the "..." dock?
¿Dónde atraca el "..."?
dōn'de äträ'kä el ...

Does this ship sail to ...?
¿Va este barco a ...?
vä es'te bär'kō ä ...

When does it sail?
¿Cuándo zarpa? ¿Cuándo sale?
kōo·än'dō sär'pä, kōo'ändō sä'le

Where is the *shipping company's office (harbor police station, customs office)*?
¿Dónde está *la oficina de la compañía naviera (de la policía del puerto, de la administración de aduanas)*?
dōn'de estä' lä ōfēsē'nä de lä kōmpänyē'ä nävye'rä (de lä pōlēsē'ä del pōo·er'tō, de lä ädmēnēsträsyōn' de ädōo·ä'näs)

On Board

I'm looking for cabin nº ...
Busco el camarote/*Mex* la cabina/
número ...
bōōs′kō el kämärō′te/lä käbē′nä/
nōō′merō ...

Where's my baggage?
¿Dónde está mi equipaje?
dōn′de estä′ mē ekēpä/*he*

Have you got ... on board?
¿Tienen ... a bordo?
tye′nen ... ä bōr′dō

Please, where is ...?
¿Por favor, dónde está ...?
pōr fävōr′, dōn′de estä′ ...

the bar	el bar	el bär
the barber shop, beauty parlor	la peluquería	lä pelōōkerē′ä
the dining room	el comedor	el kōmedōr′
the lounge	el salón	el sälōn′
the purser's office	la oficina del contador	lä ōfēsē′nä del kōntädōr′
the radio room	la cabina de radio	lä käbē′nä de rä′dyō
the reading room	la sala de lectura	lä sä′lä de lektōō′rä
the ship's photographer	el fotógrafo (de a bordo)	el fōtō′gräfō (de ä bōr′dō)
the sick bay	el hospital	el ōspētäl′
the swimming pool	la piscina	lä pēsē′nä
the tour guide's office	la dirección del crucero.	lä dēreksyōn′ del krōōse′rō

I'd like to speak to the ...
Quisiera hablar con el ...
kēsye′rä äblär′ kōn el ...

– **captain**	capitán *m*	käpētän′
– **chief steward**	jefe *m* de camareros	*he*′fe de kämäre′rōs
– **deck officer**	oficial *m* de guardia	ōfēsyäl′ de gōō·är′dyä
– **luggage master**	oficial *m* encargado de equipajes	ōfēsyäl′ enkärgä′dō de ekēpä/*he*s
– **purser**	contador *m*	kōntädōr′
– **ship's doctor**	médico *m* de a bordo	me′dēkō de ä bōr′dō
– **tour guide**	guía *m*	gē′ä

Steward, please bring me ...
Camarero/*Mex* mesero/tráigame ..., por favor.
kämäre′rō/mese′rō/trī′gäme ..., pōr fàvōr′

Please call the ship's doctor. **What is the voltage here?**
Llame al médico, por favor. ¿Qué voltaje hay aquí?
lyä′me äl me′dēkō, pōr fàvōr′ ke vōltä′he ī äkē′

Have you got anything for seasickness?
¿Tiene un medicamento contra el mareo?
tye′ne ōōn medēkämen′tō kōn′trä el märe′ō

air conditioning	aire *m* acondicionado	ī′re äkōndēsyōnä′dō
anchor	ancla *f*	äng′klä
bank	orilla *f*	ōrē′lyä
barge	barcaza *f*/*Mex* chalana *f*	bärkä′sä/tshälä′nä
bay	bahía *f*	bä·ē′ä
blanket	manta *f*/cobija *f*	män′tä/kōbē′hä
board (to)	ir a bordo	ēr ä bōr′dō
– on board	a bordo	ä bōr′dō
boat	barco *m*, lancha *f*	bär′kō, län′tshä
– fishing trawler	barco *m* pesquero	bär′kō peske′rō
– launch	lancha *f*	län′tshä
– lifeboat	bote *m* salvavidas	bō′te sälvävē′däs
– motorboat	lancha *f* motora/voladora *f*/*Mex* motonauta *f*	län′tshä mōtō′rä/vōlädō′rä/mōtōnou′tä
– sailboat	barco *m* de vela, velero *m*	bär′kō de ve′lä, vele′rō
bow	proa *f*	prō′ä
breeze	brisa *f*	brē′sä
bridge	puente *m* de mando	pōō·en′te de män′dō
buoy	boya *m*	bō′yä
cabin	camarote *m*/*Mex* cabina *f*	kämärō′te/käbē′nä
cable	cable *m*	kä′ble
call *(at port)*	hacer escala	äser′ eskä′lä
canal	canal *m*	känäl′
captain	capitán *m*	käpētän′
captain's table	mesa *f* del capitán	me′sä del käpētän′
coast	costa *f*	kōs′tä
course	rumbo *m*	rōōm′bō
crew	tripulación *f*	trēpōōläsyōn′
crossing	travesía *f*	trävesē′ä
cruise	crucero *m*	krōōse′rō

deck	cubierta *f*	kōōbyer′tä
– boat deck	cubierta *f* de botes	kōōbyer′tä de bō′tes
– foredeck	cubierta *f* de proa	kōōbyer′tä de prō′ä
– main deck	cubierta *f* principal	kōōbyer′tä prēnsēpäl′
– poop deck	cubierta *f* de popa	kōōbyer′tä de pō′pä
– promenade deck	cubierta *f* de paseo	kōōbyer′tä de päse′ō
– steerage	entrepuente *m*	entrepōō•en′te
– sun deck	cubierta *f* del sol	kōōbyer′tä del sōl
– upper deck	cubierta *f* superior	kōōbyer′tä sōōperyōr′
deck chair	silla *f* de cubierta, tumbona *f*, hamaca *f*	sē′lyä de kōōbyer′tä, tōōmbō′nä, ämä′kä
disembark	desembarcar	desembärkär′
dock *(noun)*	muelle *m*, embarcadero *m*	mōō•e′lye, embärkäde′rō
dock *(verb)*	atracar	äträkär′
excursion	excursión *f*	ekskōōrsyōn′
excursion program	programa *m* de la excursión	prōgrä′mä de lä ekskōōrsyōn′
farewell dinner	comida *f* de despedida	kōmē′dä de despedē′dä
ferry	transbordador *m*, ferry *m*	tränsbōrdädōr′, fe′rrē
– car ferry	transbordador *m*, ferry *m*	tränsbōrdädōr′, fe′rrē
– train ferry	transbordador *m* de trenes	tränsbōrdädōr′ de tre′nes
first officer	segundo comandante *m*	segōōn′dō kōmändän′te
gangway	plancha *f*	plän′tshä
harbor	puerto *m*	pōō•er′tō
harbor police	policía *f* del puerto	pōlēsē′ä del pōō•er′tō
helm	timón *m*	tēmōn′
helmsman	timonel *m*	tēmōnel′
island	isla *f*	ēz′lä
jetty	malecón *m*, muelle *m*	mälekōn′, mōō•e′lye
knot	nudo *m*	nōō′dō
lake	lago *m*	lä′gō
land *(noun)*	tierra *f*	tye′rrä
land *(verb)*	tomar tierra	tōmär′ tye′rrä
landing stage	embarcadero *m*	embärkäde′rō
life belt	salvavidas *m*	sälvävē′däs
life jacket	chaleco *m* salvavidas	tshäle′kō sälvävē′däs

lighthouse	faro *m*	fä'rō
mast	mástil *m*	mäs'tēl
mole	malecón *m*, muelle *m*	mälekōn', mōō·e'lye
ocean	océano *m*	ōse'änō
passenger	pasajero *m*	päsä*he*'rō
pier	embarcadero *m*	embärkäde'rō
playroom	cuarto *m* de niños	kōō·är'tō de nē'nyōs
port *(land)*	puerto *m*	pōō·er'tō
port *(side)*	babor *m*	bäbōr'
port fees	tasa *f* portuaria	tä'sä pōrtōō·är'yä
quay	muelle *m*	mōō·e'lye
railing	baranda *f*	bärän'dä
river	río *m*	rē'ō
rope	cuerda *m*, cabo *m*	kōō·er'dä, kä'bō
rough seas	marejada *f*	märe*h*ä'dä
rudder	timón *m*	tēmōn'
sail	navegar	nävegär'
sailor	marinero *m*	märēne'rō
sea	mar *m*	mär
– on the high seas	en alta mar	en äl'tä mär
seasickness	mareo *m*	märe'ō
ship	barco *m*, buque *m*	bär'kō, bōō'ke
– freighter	carguero *m*	kärge'rō
– passenger ship	barco *m* de pasajeros	bär'kō de päsä*he*'rōs
– warship	buque *m* de guerra	bōō'ke de ge'rrä
ship's doctor	médico *m* de a bordo	me'dēkō de ä bōr'dō
shipboard party	fiesta *f* de a bordo	fyes'tä de ä bōr'dō
shipping agency	agencia *f* marítima	ä*h*en'syä märē'tēmä
shipping company	compañía *f* naviera	kōmpänyē'ä nävye'rä
shore (on)	en tierra	en tye'rrä
starboard	estribor *m*	estrēbōr'
steamer	vapor *m*	väpōr'
stern	popa *f*	pō'pä
steward	camarero *m*/*Mex* mesero *m*	kämäre'rō/mese'rō
strait	estrecho *m*	estre'tshō
tourist class	clase *f* turista	klä'se tōōrēs'tä
tug	remolcador *m*	remōlkädōr'
voyage	viaje *m* (por mar)	vyä'*he* (pōr mär)
wave	ola *f*	ō'lä
yacht	yate *m*	yä'te

AT THE BORDER

Passport Control

When do we get to the border?
¿Cuándo llegamos a la frontera?
kōō·än'dō lyegä'mōs ä lä frōnte'rä

*Your passport, please.
Su pasaporte, por favor.
sōō päsäpōr'te, pōr fävōr'

*Your papers, please.
La documentación, por favor.
lä dōkōōmentäsyōn', pōr fävōr'

Here they are.
Tenga usted.
ten'gä ōōste'

I'll be staying *a week (two weeks, until the ...).*
Me quedaré *una semana (dos semanas, hasta el ...).*
me kedäre' ōō'nä semä'nä (dōs semä'näs, äs'tä el ...)

I'm here *on business (on vacation).*
Hago un viaje de negocios (Estoy de vacaciones).
ä'gō ōōn vyä'he de negō'syōs (estoi' de väkäsyō'nes)

***I am visiting (We are visiting)* ...**
Visito ... (Visitamos ...)
vēsē'tō ... (vēsētä'mōs ...)

Do I have to fill in this form?
¿Tengo que (re)llenar el formulario?
ten'gō ke (re)lyenär' el fōrmōōlär'yō

I haven't got a vaccination certificate.
No tengo un certificado de vacunación.
nō ten'gō ōōn sertēfēkä'dō de väkōōnäsyōn'

What should I do?
¿Qué debo hacer?
ke de'bō äser'

I *have (haven't)* had a *smallpox (cholera)* vaccination.
(No) estoy vacunado contra *la viruela (el cólera).*
(nō) estoi' väkōōnä'dō kōn'trä lä vērōō·e'lä (el kō'lerä)

I'm traveling with the ... group.
Pertenezco al grupo del ...
pertenes'kō äl grōō'pō del ...

The children are entered in my passport.
Los niños figuran en mi pasaporte.
lōs nē'nyōs fēgōō'rän en mē päsäpōr'te

Can I get my visa here?
¿Puedo conseguir la visa/*Sp* el visado/aquí?
pōō·e'dō kōnsegēr' lä vē'sä/el vēsä'dō/äkē'

May I please phone my consulate?
¿Puedo telefonear al consulado?
pōō·e'dō telefōne·är' äl kōnsōōlä'dō

border	frontera *f*	frōnte′rä
date of birth	fecha *f* de nacimiento	fe′tshä de näsē-myen′tō
departure	salida *f*	sälē′dä
driver's license	carnet *m* de conducir	kärnet′ de kōndōōsēr′
entry	entrada *f*	enträ′dä
entry visa	visa *f*/*Sp* visado *m*/de entrada	vē′sä/vēsä′dō/de enträ′dä
exit visa	visa *f*/*Sp* visado *m*/de salida	vē′sä/vēsä′dō/de sälē′dä
identity card	documento *m*/*Sp* carnet *m*/de identidad	dōkōōmen′tō/kärnet′/de ēdentēdäd′
insurance certificate	tarjeta *f* de seguro	tär*h*e′tä de segōō′rō
international vaccination certificate	certificado *m* internacional de vacunación	sertēfēkä′dō ēnternäsyōnäl′ de väkōōnäsyōn′
maiden name	nombre *m* de soltera	nōm′bre de sōlte′rä
marital status	estado *m* civil	estä′dō sēvēl′
– single	soltero (-a)	sōlte′rō (-ä)
– married	casado (-a)	käsä′dō (-ä)
– widowed	viudo (-a)	vyōō′dō (-ä)
– divorced	divorciado (-a)	dēvōrsyä′dō (-ä)
name	nombre *m*	nōm′bre
– first name	nombre *m* de pila	nōm′bre de pē′lä
– middle name	nombre *m* segundo	nōm′bre segōōn′dō
– last name	apellido *m*	äpelyē′dō
nationality	nacionalidad *f*	näsyōnälēdäd′
nationality plate	placa *f* de nacionalidad	plä′kä de näsyōnälēdäd′
number	número *m*	nōō′merō
occupation	profesión *f*	prōfesyōn′
passport	pasaporte *m*	päsäpōr′te
passport control	control *m* de pasaportes	kōntrōl′ de päsäpōr′tes
place of birth	lugar *m* de nacimiento	lōōgär′ de näsēmyen′tō
place of residence	lugar *m* de residencia	lōōgär′ de resēden′syä
renew	renovar	renōvär′
signature	firma *f*	fēr′mä
valid	válido	vä′lēdō

Customs Control

*Do you have anything to declare?
¿Tiene algo que declarar?
tye'ne äl'gō ke deklärär'

I only have articles for my personal use.
Sólo tengo objetos de uso personal.
sō'lō ten'gō ōb*h*e'tōs de ōō'sō persōnäl'

*Please open.
Abra, por favor.
äb'rä, pōr fävōr'

This is a *present (souvenir).*
Es un regalo *(recuerdo).*
es ōōn regä'lō (rekōō·er'dō)

That's my suitcase.
Esa es mi maleta.
e'sä es mē mäle'tä

That isn't mine.
No es mío.
nō es mē'ō

I have ... *cigarettes (a bottle of perfume).*
Tengo ... *cigarrillos/Mex cigarros/(una botella de perfume).*
ten'gō ... sēgärrē'lyōs/sēgä'rrōs/(ōō'nä bōte'lyä de perfōō'me)

*What's in here?
¿Qué hay dentro?
ke ī den'trō

That's all.
Es todo.
es tō'dō

*All right!
¡Está bien!
estä' byen

I'd like to declare this.
Quiesiera declarar esto.
kēsye'rä deklärär' es'tō

Do I have to pay duty on this?
¿Tengo que pagar derechos de aduana?
ten'gō ke pägär' dere'tshōs de ädōō·ä'nä

How much can I bring in duty free?
¿Qué cantidad está libre de aduanas?
ke käntēdäd' estä' lē'bre de ädōō·ä'näs

What do I have to pay for it?
¿Cuánto tengo que pagar
por esto?
kōō·än'tō ten'gō ke pägär'
pōr es'tō

border	frontera *f*	frōnte'rä
border crossing	paso *m* de la frontera	pä'sō de lä frōnte'rä
customs	aduana *f*	ädōō·ä'nä
customs control	control *m* aduanero	kōntrōl' ädōō·äne'rō
customs declaration	declaración *f* de aduana	dekläräsyōn' de ädōō·ä'nä
customs office	edificio *m* de aduanas	edēfē'syō de ädōō·ä'näs
customs officer	aduanero *m*	ädōō·äne'rō
duty	derechos *mpl* de aduana	dere'tshōs de ädōō·ä'nä
– export duty	derechos *mpl* de salida	dere'tshōs de sälē'dä
– import duty	derechos *mpl* de entrada	dere'tshōs de enträ'dä

ACCOMMODATIONS

Checking it out

Where is *the ... hotel (pension)*?
¿Dónde está *el hotel (la pensión) ...*?
dōn'de estä' el ōtel (lä pensyōn')

Is (Are) there ... near here?
¿Hay ... por aquí?
ī ... pōr äkē'

Can you recommend a good hotel?
¿Puede recomendarme un buen hotel?
pōō·e'de rekōmendär'me ōōn bōō·en' ōtel'

accommodations	alojamiento *m*	älō*h*änyen'tō
apartments	apartamentos *mpl*	äpärtämen'tōs
a boarding house	una casa de huéspedes .	ōō'nä kä'sä de ōō·es'pedes
bungalows	bungalows *mpl/Mex* bungalos *mpl*, cabañas *fpl*	bōōngä'lōs/ bōōngä'lōs, käbä'nyäs
a camping site	un camping/*Mex* un campamento	ōōn kämpēn'/ōōn kämpämen'tō
a hotel	un hotel	ōōn ōtel'
an inn	una posada, un hostal .	ōō'nä pōsä'dä, ōōn ōstäl'
a motel	un motel	ōōn mōtel'
a pension	una pensión	ōō'nä pensyōn'
a room in private homes	una habitación/*Mex* un cuarto/en casa particular	ōō'nä äbētäsyōn'/ ōōn kōō·är'tō/en kä'sä pärtēkōōlär'
a youth hostel	un albergue juvenil	ōōn älber'ge *h*ōōvenēl'

– near the beach	**– in a quiet place (centrally located).**
– cerca de la playa.	– tranquilo (céntrico).
– ser'kä de lä plä'yä	– trängkē'lō (sen'trēkō)

How *are the prices (is the food)* there?
¿Qué tal *son los precios (es la comida)*?
ke täl sōn lōs pre'syōs (es lä kōmē'dä)

In Spain and Mexico, only first class and luxury hotels have complete bathrooms attached to every room. Most economical hotels have a sink in each room (sometimes a shower), but usually all showering, bathing and toilet facilities are located down the hall.

Checking in

I reserved a room here.	... six weeks ago.
He reservado aquí una habitación/	... hace seis semanas.
Mex un cuarto.	... ä'se se'ēs semä'näs
e reservä'dō äkē' ōo'nä äbētäsyōn'/	
ōon kōo·är'tō	

The ... travel agency reserved a room for *me (us)*.
La agencia de viajes ... ha reservado una habitación/*Mex* un cuarto/*para mí (para nosotros)*.
lä ä*h*en'syä de vyä'*h*es ... ä reservä'dō ōo'nä äbētäsyōn'/ōon kōo·är'tō/pä'rä mē (pä'rä nōsō'trōs)

Have you got a single room available?
¿Tiene una habitación individual/*Mex* un cuarto sencillo/libre?
tye'ne ōo'nä äbētäsyōn' ēndēvēdōo·äl'/ōon kōo·är'tō sensē'lyō/lē'bre

I'd like to have ...
Quisiera ...
kēsye'rä ...

– **an apartment** ..	un apartamento	ōon äpärtämen'tō
– **a double room** .	una habitación/*Mex* un cuarto/doble	ōo'nä äbētäsyōn'/ōon kōo·är'tō/dō'ble
– **a quiet room** ..	una habitación/*Mex* un cuarto/tranquilo (-a) ..	ōo'nä äbētäsyōn'/ōon kōo·är'tō/trängkē'lō (-ä)
– **a room**	una habitación/*Mex* un cuarto	ōo'nä äbētäsyōn'/ōo'n kōo·är'tō
– **for ... persons** .	para ... personas	pä'rä ... persō'näs
– **on the second floor**	en el segundo piso	en el segōon'dō pē'sō
– **with balcony** ...	con balcón	kōn bälkōn'
– **with bath**	con baño completo	kōn bä'nyō kōmple'tō
– **with running water**	con agua corriente	kōn ä'gōo·ä kōrryen'te
– **with shower** ...	con ducha/*Mex* con regadera	kōn dōo'tshä/kōn regäde'rä
– **with terrace** ...	con terraza	kōn terrä'sä
– **with toilet**	con wáter, con lavabo/ *Mex* con excusado	kōn ōo·ä'ter, kōn lävä'bō/kōn ekskōosä'dō

... **for *one night (two nights, one week, four weeks)*.**
... para *una noche (dos días, ocho días, cuatro semanas).*
... pä′rä ōō′nä nō′tshe (dōs dē′äs, ō′tshō dē′äs, kōō·ä′trō semä′näs)

Can I have a look at the room?
¿Podría ver la habitación/*Mex* el cuarto?
pōdrē′ä ver lä äbētäsyōn′/el kōō·är′tō

I like it.	***I′ll (We′ll)* take it.**
Me gusta.	*Me quedo (Nos quedamos)* con ella.
me gōōs′tä	me ke′dō (nōs kedä′mōs) kōn e′lyä

Could you show me another room?
¿Podría mostrarme/*Sp* enseñarme/otra habitación/*Mex* otro cuarto?
pōdrē′ä mōsträr′me/ensenyär′me/ōt′rä äbētäsyōn′/ōt′rō kōō·är′tō

Could you put in *an extra bed (a crib)*?
¿Podría poner *una cama adicional (una cuna)*?
pōdrē′ä pōner′ ōō′nä kä′mä ädēsyōnäl′ (ōō′nä kōō′nä)

Price

How much is the room *per day (week)*?
¿Cuánto cuesta la habitación/*Mex* el cuarto/*por día (por semana)*?
kōō·än′tō kōō·es′tä lä äbētäsyōn′/el kōō·är′tō/pōr dē′ä (pōr semä′nä)

– with breakfast.	**– with two meals a day.**	**– American plan.**
– con desayuno.	– con media pensión.	– con pensión completa.
– kōn desäyōō′nō	– kōn me′dyä pensyōn′	– kōn pensyōn′kōmple′tä

Is *everything (service)* included?
¿Está *todo* incluido? ¿*Va* incluido *el servicio*?
estä′ tō′dō ēnklōō·ē′dō/vä ēnklōō·ē′dō el servē′syō

What's the *single room surcharge (seasonal surcharge)*?
¿Cuánto es el suplemento *por habitación individual*/*Mex por cuarto sencillo*/*(por temporada)*?
kōō·än′tō es el sōōplemen′tō pōr äbētäsyōn′ ēndēvēdōō·äl′/pōr
kōō·är′tō sensē′lyō/(pōr tempōrä′dä)

Are there reduced rates for children?
¿Hay una rebaja (*or* un descuento) para niños?
ī ōō′nä rebä′h′a (ōōn deskōō·en′tō) pä′rä nē′nyōs

How much deposit do I have to pay?	**How much is that altogether?**
¿Cuánto debo pagar a cuenta?	¿Cuánto es en total?
kōō·än′tō de′bō pägär′ ä kōō·en′tä	kōō·än′tō es en tōtäl′

Registration, Luggage

I'd like to register (check in).
Quisiera inscribirme.
kēsye′rä enskrēbēr′me

Do you need our passports?
¿Necesitan los pasaportes?
nesesē′tän lōs päsäpōr′tes

When do you want back the registration form?
¿Cuándo debo devolver la ficha?
kōō·än′dō de′bō devōlver′ lä fē′tshä

What do I have to fill out here?
¿Qué tengo que (re)llenar?
ke ten′gō ke (re)lyenär′

*I just need your signature.
Basta con la firma.
bäs′tä kōn lä fēr′mä

Would you have my luggage picked up?
¿Podrían recoger mi equipaje?
pōdrē′än rekōher′ mē ekēpä′he

It's still _at the station (airport)_.
Está todavía _en la estación (en el aeropuerto)_.
estä′ tōdävē′ä en lä estäsyōn′ (en el ä·erōpōō·er′tō)

Here's the baggage check.
Aquí el resguardo/_Sp_ el talón.
äkē′ el rezgōō·är′dō/el tälōn′

Where's my luggage?
¿Dónde está mi equipaje?
dōn′de estä′ mē ekēpä′he

Is my baggage already up in the room?
¿Está mi equipaje ya en la habitación/_Mex_ el cuarto?
estä′ mē ekēpä′he yä en lä äbētäsyōn′/el kōō·är′tō

Can I leave my luggage here?
¿Puedo dejar aquí mi equipaje?
pōō·e′dō dehär′ äkē′ mē ekēpä′he

Would you put these valuables in the safe?
¿Podría guardar estos objetos de valor en la caja?
pōdrē′ä gōō·ärdär′ es′tōs ōbhe′tōs de välōr′ en lä kä′hä

Do you have a _garage (parking lot)_?
¿Tiene _garaje (estacionamiento/Sp aparcamiento)_?
tye′ne gärä′he (estäsyōnämyen′tō/äpärkämyen′tō)

Reception, Desk Clerk

Where is room 308?
¿Dónde está la habitación/*Mex* el cuarto/número trescientos ocho?
dōn'de estä' lä äbētäsyōn'/el kōō·är'tō/nōō'merō tresyen'tōs ō'tshō

The key, please.
La llave, por favor.
lä lyä've, pōr fävōr'

Number …, please.
El número …, por favor.
el nōō'merō …, pōr fävōr'

Has anyone asked for me?
¿Ha preguntado alguien por mí?
ä pregōōntä'dō äl'gyen pōr mē

Is there any mail for me?
¿Hay correo para mí?
ī kōrre'ō pä'rä mē

What time does the mail come?
¿A qué hora llega el correo?
ä ke ō'rä lye'gä el kōrre'ō

Do you have any *stamps (picture postcards)*?
¿Tiene *estampillas/Sp sellos/Mex timbres/(postales)*?
tye'ne estämpē'lyäs/se'lyōs/tēm'bres/(pōstä'les)

What's the postage on *a letter (postcard)* to the United States?
¿Cuánto cuesta *una carta (una postal)* a los Estados Unidos?
kōō·än'tō kōō·es'tä ōō'nä kär'tä (ōō'nä pōstäl') ä lōs estä'dōs ōōnē'dōs

Where can I *get (rent)* …?
¿Dónde se puede *conseguir (alquilar/Mex rentar)* …?
dōn'de se pōō·e'de kōnsegēr' (älkēlär'/rentär') …

Where do I sign up for the excursion to …?
¿Dónde puedo inscribirme para la excursión a …?
dōn'de pōō·e'dō ēnskrēbēr'me pä'rä lä ekskōōrsyōn' ä …

Where can I *make a phone call (change some money)*?
¿Dónde puedo *telefonear (cambiar dinero)*?
dōn'de pōō·e'dō telefōne·är' (kämbyär' dēne'rō)

I'd like to place a long distance call to …
Quisiera pedir una llamada a larga distancia/*Sp* una conferencia/con …
kēsye'rä pedēr' ōō'nä lyämä'dä ä lär'gä dēstän'syä/ōō'nä kōnferen'syä/kōn …

I'm expecting a long distance call from the United States.
Estoy esperando una llamada de los Estados Unidos.
estoi' esperän'dō ōō'nä lyämä'dä de lōs estä'dōs ōōnē'dōs

Where can I get an American newspaper?
¿Dónde se venden periódicos norteamericanos?
dōn′de se ven′den perē·ō′dēkōs nōr′te·ämerēkä′nōs

Where is (are) …?	**Could you get me …?**
¿Dónde está (están) …?	¿Puede conseguirme …?
dōn′de estä′ (estän′) …	poo·e′de kōnsegēr′me …

What's the voltage here?
¿Qué voltaje hay aquí?
ke vōltä′he ī äkē′

I'll be back in ten minutes (a couple of hours, right away).
Vuelvo en 10 minutos (en dos horas, en seguida).
voo·el′vō en dyes mēnoo′tōs (en dōs ō′räs, en segē′dä)

We're going down to the beach (into town).
Vamos a la playa (a la ciudad).
vä′mōs ä lä plä′yä (ä lä syoo däd′)

I'll be in the lounge (bar).
Estaré en el salón (en el bar).
estäre′ en el sälōn′ (en el bär)

I lost my key (left my key in the room).
He perdido la llave (He dejado la llave en la habitación/Mex el cuarto).
e perdē′dō lä lyä′ve (e dehä′dō lä lyä′ve en lä äbētäsyōn′/el koo·är′tō)

What time are meals served?	**Where's the dining room?**
¿A qué hora son las comidas?	¿Dónde está el comedor?
ä ke ō′rä sōn läs kōmē′däs	dōn′de estä′ el kōmedōr′

Can we have breakfast in the room?
¿Se puede desayunar en la habitación/Mex el cuarto?
se poo·e′de desäyoonär′ en lä äbētäsyōn′/el koo·är′tō

Could we have breakfast at seven tomorrow morning, please?
¿Podríamos desayunar mañana a las siete, por favor?
pōdrē′ämōs desäyoonär′ mänyä′nä ä läs sye′te, pōr fävōr′

I'd like a box lunch tomorrow morning, please.
Quisiera una bolsa de merienda para mañana por la mañana, por favor.
kēsye′rä oo′nä bōl′sä de meryen′dä pä′rä mänyä′nä pōr lä mänyä′nä,
pōr fävōr′

Please wake me at 7:30 tomorrow.
Despiérteme/Sp llámeme/mañana a las siete y media, por favor.
despyer′teme/lyä′meme/mänyä′nä ä läs sye′te ē me′dyä, pōr fävōr′

Maid

Come in!	**Just a moment, please!**
¡Adelante!	¡Un momento, por favor!
ädelän'te	ōōn mōmen'tō, pōr fävōr'

Could you wait another *five (ten)* minutes?
¿Puede esperar unos *cinco (diez)* minutos?
pōō·e'de esperär' ōō'nōs sēng'kō (dyes) mēnōō'tōs

We'll be going out *in another quarter hour (half hour)*.
Nos vamos dentro de *un cuarto de hora (una media hora)*.
nōs vä'mōs den'trō de ōōn kōō·är'tō de ō'rä (ōō'nä me'dyä ō'rä)

Please *bring me (us)* ...
Por favor, *tráigame (tráiganos)* ...
pōr fävōr', trī'gäme (trī'gänōs) ...

another blanket	otra cobija, otra fra-	ōt'rä kōbē'hä, ōt'rä
	zada/*Sp* otra manta .	fräsä'dä/ōt'rä män'tä
another pillow	otra almohada	ōt'rä älmō·ä'dä
another towel	otra toalla	ōt'rä tō·ä'lyä
an ash tray	un cenicero	ōōn senēse'rō
a blanket	una cobija, una fra-	ōō'nä kōbē'hä,
	zada/*Sp* una manta ..	ōō'nä fräsä'dä/
		ōō'nä män'tä
breakfast	el desayuno	el desäyōō'nō
a cake of soap	una pastilla de jabón	ōō'nä pästē'lyä de
		häbōn'
a couple of clothes	algunas perchas/	älgōō'näs per'tshäs/
hangers	algunos ganchos	älgōō'nōs gän'tshōs

How does this thing work?	**Is our room ready?**
¿Cómo funciona esto?	¿Está ya arreglada (-o) nuestra (-o)
kō'mō fōōnsyō'nä es'tō	habitación/*Mex* cuarto?
	estä' yä ärreglä'dä (-ō) nōō·es'trä (-ō)
	äbētäsyōn'/kōō·är'tō

Would you have these things laundered for me?
¿Puede mandar a lavar esta ropa?
pōō·e'de mändär' ä lävär' es'tä rō'pä

Thanks very much!	**This is for you.**
¡Muchas gracias!	Es para usted.
mōō'tshäs grä'syäs	es pä'rä ōōste'

Complaints

I'd like to speak to the manager, please.
Quisiera hablar con el gerente (director del hotel), por favor.
kēsye'rä äblär' kōn el *h*eren'te (dērektōr' del ōtel'), pōr fävōr'

There's no ...	There are no ...	... doesn't work.
Falta ...	Faltan ...	... no funciona.
fäl'tä ...	fäl'tän ...	... nō fo͞onsyō'nä

There's no light in my room.
En mi habitación/*Mex* cuarto/
no hay luz.
en mē äbētäsyōn'/ko͞o·är'tō/nō ī
lo͞os

The bulb has burned out.
Esta bombilla/*Mex* este foco/
está fundida (-o).
es'tä bōmbē'lyä/es'te fō'kō/
estä fo͞ondē'dä (-ō)

The socket is broken.
El enchufe/*Mex* el soquet, el dado/
está estropeado/roto.
el entsho͞o'fe/el sōket', el dä'dō/
estä' estrōpe·ä'dō/rō'tō

The fuse has blown.
El fusible se ha fundido.
el fo͞osē'ble se ä fo͞ondē'dō

The bell (heating) doesn't work.
El timbre (La calefacción) no funciona.
el tēm'bre (lä kälefäksyōn') nō fo͞onsyō'nä

The key doesn't fit.
La llave no entra en la cerradura.
lä lyä've nō en'trä en lä serrädo͞o'rä

The rain comes in.
Aquí entra la lluvia.
äkē' en'trä lä lyo͞o'vyä

This window *won't shut properly (won't open)*.
La ventana *no cierra bien (no abre)*.
lä ventä'nä nō sye'rrä byen (nō äb're)

There's no (hot) water.	The faucet drips.
No hay agua (caliente).	El grifo gotea.
nō ī ä'go͞o·ä (kälyen'te)	el grē'fō gōte'ä

The toilet won't flush.	There's a leak in this pipe.
El sifón no funciona.	La tubería tiene fugas/escape.
el sēfōn' nō fo͞onsyō'nä	lä to͞oberē'ä tye'ne fo͞o·gäs/eskä'pe

The drain is stopped up.
El desagüe está tapado/*Sp* atascado.
el desä'go͞o·e estä' täpä'dō/ätäskä'dō

Checking out

I'll be leaving tomorrow.
Me marcho mañana.
me mär′tshō mänyä′nä

We're continuing on tomorrow.
Seguiremos el viaje mañana.
segēre′mōs el vyä′he mänyä′nä

Would you please make up my bill?
Prepáreme la cuenta, por favor.
prepä′reme lä koo·en′tä, pōr fävōr′

Could I please have *my (our)* bill?
¿Me puede dar *mi (nuestra)* cuenta?
me poo·e′de där mē (noo·es′trä) koo·en′tä

Please wake me early tomorrow morning.
Despiérteme/*Sp* llámeme/mañana temprano.
despyer′teme/lyä′meme/mänyä′nä temprä′nō

Please order a taxi for me tomorrow morning at 8.
Pídame un taxi para mañana a las ocho.
pē′däme oon tä′ksē pä′rä mänyä′nä ä läs ō′tshō

Would you have my luggage taken *to the station (airport)*?
¿Puede mandarme el equipaje *a la estación (al aeropuerto)*?
poo·e′de mändär′me el ekēpä′he ä lä estäsyōn′ (äl ä·erōpoo·er′tō)

When does *the bus (train)* leave?
¿Cuándo sale *el autobús/Mex el camión/(el tren)* para ...?
koo·än′dō sä′le el outōboos′/el kämyōn′/(el tren) pä′rä ...

Please forward my mail.
Remita mi correo a esta dirección, por favor.
remē′tä mē kōrre′ō ä es′tä dēreksyōn′, pōr fävōr′

Thanks for everything!
¡Gracias por todo!
grä′syäs pōr tō′dō

We had a very good time here.
Hemos tenido una estancia (estadía) muy agradable.
e′mōs tenē′dō oo′nä estän′syä (estädē′ä) moo′ē ägrädä′ble

accommodations ..	alojamiento *m*	älō*h*ämyen'tō
adapter plug	enchufe *m* intermedio .	entshōō'fe ēnter-me'dyō
air conditioning ...	aire *m* acondicionado .	ī're äkōndēsyönä'dō
alternating current	corriente *f* alterna	kōrryen'te älter'nä
American plan	pensión *f* completa	pensyōn' kōmple'tä
apartment	apartamento *m*	äpärtämen'tō
apartment building	casa *f* de pisos	kä'sä de pē'sōs
armchair	butaca *f*, sillón *m*	bōōtä'kä, sē'lyōn
arrival	llegada *f*	lyegä'dä
ash tray	cenicero *m*	senēse'rō
balcony	balcón *m* ··········	bälkōn'
basement	sótano *m* ··········	sō'tänō
bathroom	cuarto *m* de baño	kōō·är'tō de bä'nyō
bed	cama *f*	kä'mä
– **bedspread**	colcha *f*, cubrecama *m*, sobrecama *m*	kōl'tshä, kōōbre-kä'mä, sōbrekä'mä
– **blanket**	cobija *f*, frazada *f*/*Sp* manta *f*	kōbē'*h*ä, fräsä'dä/män'tä
– **crib**	cuna *f*	kōō'nä
– **mattress**	colchón *m*	kōltshōn'
– **pillow**	almohada *f*··········	älmō·ä'dä
bed and two meals .	media pensión *f*	me'dyä pensyōn'
bed linen	ropa *f* de cama	rō'pä de kä'mä
– **cover**	sábana *f*	sä'bänä
– **pillowcase**	funda *f*	fōōn'dä
– **sheets**	sábanas *fpl*	sä'bänäs
bed rug	alfombrilla *f*, pie *m* de cama	älfōmbrē'lyä, pye de kä'mä
bedside table	mesita *f* de noche	mesē'tä de nō'tshe
bell	timbre *m* ··········	tēm'bre
bill	cuenta *f* ··········	kōō·en'tä
breakfast	desayuno *m*	desäyōō'nō
– **eat breakfast**	desayunar ··········	desäyōōnär'
breakfast room	sala *f* de desayuno ...	sä'lä de desäyōō'nō
bucket	cubo *m*, balde *m*	kōō'bō, bäl'de
carpet	moqueta *f*/*Mex* tapete *m*	mōke'tä/täpe'te
category	categoría *f*	kätegōrē'ä
ceiling	techo *m* ··········	te'tshō
cellar	sótano *m* ··········	sō'tänō
central heating	calefacción *f* central ...	kälefäksyōn' senträl'

chair	silla *f*	sē'lyä
check in *(verb)*	inscribirse	ēnskrēbēr'se
check-in *(noun)*	inscripción	ēnskrēpsyōn'
chimney	chimenea *f*	tshēmene'ä
closet	armario *f*	ärmär'yō
clothes hanger	percha *f*, gancho *m*	per'tshä, gän'tshō
complaint	reclamación *f*, reclamo *m*	reklämäsyōn', reklä'mō
concierge	conserje *m*	kōnser'*he*
corridor	pasillo *m*, corredor *m*	päsē'lyō, kōrredōr'
curtain	cortina *f*	kōrtē'nä
day bed	sofá-cama *m*	sōfä'-kä'mä
deck chair	silla *f* de cubierta, hamaca *f*, tumbona *f*	sē'lyä de kōōbyer'tä, ämä'kä, tōōmbō'nä
departure	salida *f*	sälē'dä
deposit	pago *m* a cuenta	pä'gō ä kōō·en'tä
dining room	comedor *m*	kōmedōr'
dinner	cena *f*	se'nä
door	puerta *f*	pōō·er'tä
door handle	picaporte *m*	pēkäpōr'te
drawer	cajón *m*, gaveta *f*	kä*h*ōn', gäve'tä
elevator	ascensor *m*/*Mex* elevador *m*	äsensōr'/elevädōr'
entrance	entrada *f*	enträ'dä
exit	salida *f*	sälē'dä
extension cord	cordón *m*, cable *m* de empalme/*Mex* cable *m* de extensión	kōrdōn', kä'ble de empäl'me/kä'ble de ekstensyōn'
extra week	semana *f* suplementaria	semä'nä sōōplementär'yä
fan	ventilador *m*	ventēlädōr'
faucet	grifo *m*	grē'fō
fireplace	chimenea *f*	tshēmene'ä
floor	piso *m*	pē'sō
front desk	recepción *f*	resepsyōn'
front door	puerta *f* de entrada	pōō·er'tä de enträ'dä
fuse	fusible *m*	fōōsē'ble
garden umbrella	sombrilla *f*, parasol *m*	sōmbrē'lyä, päräsōl'
grill room	parrilla *f*	pärrē'lyä
guest house	casa *f* de huéspedes	kä'sä de ōō·es'pedes

hall	hall *m*, vestíbulo *m*	äl, vestē′bōōlō
head clerk	jefe *m* de recepción	he′fe de resepsyōn′
heating	calefacción *f*	kälefäksyōn′
hotel	hotel *m*	ōtel′
– beach hotel	hotel *m* de playa	ōtel′ de plä′yä
hotel restaurant	restaurante *m* del hotel	restourän′te del ōtel′
house	casa *f*	kä′sä
house key	llave *f* de la casa	lyä′ve de lä kä′sä
inquiry	informe *m*	ēnfōr′me
key	llave *f*	lyä′ve
kitchen	cocina *f*	kōsē′nä
kitchenette	rincón-cocina *m*, cocineta *f*	rēnkōn′-kōsē′nä, kōsēne′tä
lamp	lámpara *f*	läm′pärä
laundry	lavandería *f*	lävänderē′ä
– do laundry	lavar	lävär′
– dry	secar	sekär′
– iron	planchar	pläntshär′
light bulb	bombillo *m*/*Sp* bombilla *f*/*Mex* foco *m*	bōmbē′lyō/bōmbē′lyä/fō′kō
lights	luces *fpl*	lōō′ses
lobby	vestíbulo *m*	vestē′bōōlō
lock	cerrar con llave	serrär′ kōn lyä′ve
– lock up	encerrar	enserrär′
– unlock	abrir con llave	äbrēr′ kōn lyä′ve
lunch	almuerzo *m*, comida *f*	älmōō·er′sō, kōmē′dä
maid	camarera *f*/*Mex* recamarera *f*	kämäre′rä/rekämäre′rä
mirror	espejo *m*	espe′hō
move	mudarse	mōōdär′se
move in	instalarse	ēnstälär′se
move out	abandonar	äbändōnär′
night's lodging	alojamiento *m* para una noche	älo*h*ämyen′tō pä′rä ōō′nä nō′tshe
pail	balde *m*/*Sp* cubo *m*/*Mex* a cubeta *f*	bäl′de/kōō′bō/kōōbe′tä
patio	patio *m*	pä′tyō
pension	pensión *f*	pensyōn′
plug	clavija *f* de enchufe	klävē′*h*ä de entshōō′fe
pot	olla *f*, puchero *m*	ō′lyä, pōōtshe′rō

price	precio *m*	pre′syō
private beach	playa *f* privada	plä′yä prēvä′dä
radiator	radiador *m*	rädyädōr′
reading lamp	lámpara *f* para leer	läm′pärä pä′rä le·er′
reception desk	recepción *f*	resepsyōn′
refrigerator	frigorífico *m*/*Mex* refrigerador *m*	frēgōrē′fēkō/refrēherädōr′
registration	inscripción *f*	ēnskrēpsyōn′
rent *(noun)*	alquiler *m*/arriendo *m* .	älkēler′/ärryen′dō
rent *(verb)*	alquilar, rentar	älkēlär′, rentär′
rest room	baños *mpl*/*Sp* servicios *mpl*	bä′nyōs/servē′syōs
– ladies' room	Señoras	senyō′räs
– men's room	Caballeros	käbälye′rōs
room	cuarto *m*	ko͞o·är′tō
– bedroom	dormitorio *m*, alcoba *f*/*Mex* recámara *f*	dōrmētōr′yō, älkō′bä/rekä′märä
– living room	salón *m*, sala *f* de estar	sälōn′, sä′lä de estär′
– nursery	cuarto *m* de niños	ko͞o·är′tō de nē′nyōs
season	temporada *f*	tempōrä′dä
service	servicio *m*	servē′syō
shower	ducha *f*/*Mex* regadera *f*	do͞o′tshä/regäde′rä
sink	lavabo *m*, lavatorio *m* .	lävä′bō, lävätōr′yō
socket	enchufe *m*/*Mex* soquet *m*, dado *m*	entsho͞o′fe/sōket′, dä′dō
staircase	escalera *f*	eskäle′rä
stairwell	hueco *m* de escalera ...	o͞o·e′kō de eskäle′rä
stove	estufa *f*/*Sp* cocina *f* ...	esto͞o′fä/kōsē′nä
swimming pool	piscina *f*/*Mex* alberca *f*	pēsē′nä/älber′kä
switch *(light)*	interruptor *m*	ēnterro͞optōr′
table	mesa *f*	me′sä
tablecloth	mantel *m*	mäntel′
telephone	teléfono *m*	tele′fōnō
terrace	terraza *f*	terrä′sä
toilet paper	papel *m* higiénico *or* sanitario	päpel′ ēhē·e′nēkō (sänētär′yō)

tour guide	guía *m*	gē'ä
travel agency	agencia *f* de viajes	ä*h*en'syä de vyä'*h*es
vacate the room ...	dejar libre la habitación/	dehär' lē'bre lä
	Mex vencer el cuarto ..	äbētäsyōn'/venser' el
		koo·är'tō
ventilation	ventilación *f*	ventēläsyōn'
voltage	voltaje *m*	vōltä'*h*e
wall	pared *f*, tabique *m*	päred', täbē'ke
water	agua *f*	ä'goo·ä
– cold water	agua *f* fría	ä'goo·ä frē'ä
– hot water	agua *f* caliente	ä'goo·ä kälyen'te
water glass	vaso *m* para agua	vä'sō pä'rä ä'goo·ä
window	ventana *f*	ventä'nä
windowpane	vidrio *m*/*Sp* cristal *m* ..	vē'drē·o/krēstäl'

Camping, Youth Hostels

Is there a *camping site (youth hostel)* near here?
¿Hay un *camping/Mex campamento/(albergue juvenil)* cerca de aquí?
ī ōon kämpēn'/kämpämen'tō/(älber'ge *h*ōōvenēl') ser'kä de äkē'

Can we camp here?	**Is the site guarded at night?**
¿Podemos acampar aquí?	¿Está vigilado durante la noche?
pōde'mōs äkämpär' äkē'	estä' vē*h*ēlä'dō dōōrän'te lä nō'tshe

Do you have room for another tent?
¿Hay sitio para montar otra carpa/*Sp* tienda, *Mex a* casita/de campaña?
ī sē'tyō pä'rä mōntär' ōt'rä kär'pä/tyen'dä, käsē'tä/de kämpä'nyä

How much does it cost to stay overnight?
¿Cuánto cuesta una noche?
kōō·än'tō kōō·es'tä ōō'nä nō'tshe

How much is it for *the car (trailer)*?
¿Cuál es el precio por *el carro/Sp el coche/(el remolque)*?
kōō·äl' es el pre'syō pōr el kä'rrō/el kōtshe/(el remōl'ke)

I'll be staying ... *days (weeks)*.	**Can we ... here?**
Me quedo ... *días (semanas)*.	¿Podemos ... aquí?
me ke'dō ... dē'äs (semä'näs)	pōde'mōs ... äkē'

Is there a grocery store near here?
¿Hay por aquí una tienda de comestibles/*Mex* tienda de abarrotes?
ī pōr äkē' ōō'nä tyen'dä de kōmestē'bles/tyen'dä de äbärrō'tes

Can I rent *bottles gas (exchange gas bottles)* here?
¿Se *alquilan (cambian)* aquí *botellas/cilindros/de gas*?
se älkē'län (käm'byän) äkē' bōte'lyäs/sēlēn'drōs/de gäs

Where are *the rest rooms (wash rooms)*?
¿Dónde están *los baños/Sp los servicios (los lavabos)*?
dōn'de estän lōs bä'nyōs/lōs servē'syōs (lōs lävä'bōs)

Are there any electrical connections here?
¿Hay enchufes/*Mex* soquetes, dados/aquí?
ī entshōō'fes/sōke'tes, dä'dōs/äkē'

Can we drink the water?
¿Se puede tomar el agua?
se po͞o·e'de tōmär' el ä'go͞o·ä

Can I rent ...?	**Where can I ...?**
¿Puedo rentar/*Sp* alquilar ...?	¿Dónde se puede ...?
po͞o·e'dō rentär'/älkēlär' ...	dōn'de se po͞o·e'de ...

advance reservation .	reserva *f* de plaza	reser'vä de plä'sä
camp bed	cama *f* de campaña ...	kä'mä de käm- pä'nyä
camping	camping *m*/*Mex* cam- pismo *m*	kämpēn'/käm- pēz'mō
camping ID	tarjeta *f* de camping ...	tär*h*e'tä de käm- pēn'
camp out	acampar	äkämpär'
camp site ...?	camping *m*/*Mex* campa- mento *m*	kämpēn'/kämpä- men'tō
canteen	cantimplora *f*	käntēmplō'rä
check-in	inscripción *f*	ēnskrēpsyōn'
check-out	aviso *m* de salida	ävē'sō de sälē'dä
cook	cocinar	kōsēnär'
cooking utensils	batería *f* de cocina	bäterē'ä de kōse'nä
day room	sala *f* de estar	sä'lä de estär'
dishes	vajilla *f*	vä*h*ē'lyä
dormitory	dormitorio *m*	dōrmētōr'yō
drinking water	agua *f* potable	ä'go͞o·ä pōtä'ble
get	conseguir	kōnsegēr'
go swimming	ir a nadar, ir a bañarse	ēr ä nädär', ēr ä bänyär'se
hostel parents	encargados *mpl* del albergue	enkärgä'dōs del älber'ge
– hostel mother	encargada *f* del albergue	enkärgä'dä del älber'ge
– hostel father	encargado *m* del alber- gue	enkärgä'dō del älber'ge
iron	planchar	pläntshär'
membership card	tarjeta *f*/*Sp* carnet *m* / de miembro	tär*h*e'tä/kärnet'/de myem'brō
park	parque *m*	pär'ke
playground	parque *m* infantil	pär'ke ēnfäntēl'
recreation room	salón *m* de recreo	sälōn' de rekre'ō

rent	rentar/*Sp* alquilar	rentär'/älkēlär'
rental fee	tarifa *f* de alquiler	tärē'fä de älkēler'
sleeping bag	saco *m*/*Mex* bolsa *f*/de dormir	sä'kō/bōl'sä/de dōrmēr'
take a bath	bañarse	bänyär'se
tent	carpa *f*/*Sp* tienda *f*, *Mex* casita *f*/de campaña	kär'pä/tyen'dä, kä-sē'tä/de kämpä'nyä
trailer	caravana *f*/*Mex* remolque *m*, trayler *m*	kärävä'nä/remōl'ke, trīler'
wash	lavar	lävär'
youth group	grupo *m* juvenil	grōō'pō hōōvenēl'
youth hostel	albergue *m* juvenil	älber'ge hōōvenēl'
youth hostel card	carnet *m* de alberguista/ *Mex* tarjeta *f* para albergues	kärnet' de älber-gēs'tä/tärhe'tä pä'rä älber'ges

Youth Hostels

Although youth hostels are primarily for those under 26 in possession of a youth hostel card, there are also rates for those over 26, families and groups. In Spain there are 122 youth hostels which offer various lodging and eating arrangements from 375 to 950 pesetas a day (1985 rates). Information: Instituto de la Juventud, Calle José Ortega y Gasset 71, 28006 Madrid. For information on youth hosteling in Mexico: Asociación Mexicana de Albergues de la Juventud, Calle Madero 6, México 1, Distrito Federal.

EATING AND DRINKING

Ordering

Is there a *good (economical) restaurant (with regional specialities)*?
¿Hay por aquí *un buen restaurante (un restaurante económico, un restaurante con especialidades de la región)*?
ī pōr äkē' ōon boo·en' restourän'te (ōon restourän'te ekōnō'mēkō, ōon restourän'te kōn espesyälēdä'des de lä rehyōn')

Would you please reserve a table for four at eight p.m.?
¿Nos reserva una mesa para cuatro personas para las ocho de la noche, por favor?
nōs reser'vä ōo'nä me'sä pä'rä kōo·ät'rō persō'näs pä'rä läs ō'tshō de lä nō'tshe, pōr fävōr'

Is *this table (seat)* taken?
¿Está libre *esta mesa (este asiento)*?
estä' lē'bre es'tä me'sä (es'te äsyen'tō)

Waiter!	**Waitress!**	**We'd like a drink.**
¡Camarero!/*Mex* ¡Mesero!	¡Señorita!	Quisiéramos tomar algo.
kämäre'rō/mese'rō	senyōrē'tä	kēsye'rämōs tōmär' äl'gō

Is this your table?	**I'd like a meal.**
¿Sirve usted en esta mesa?	Quisiera comer algo.
sēr've ōoste' en es'tä me'sä	kēsye'rä kōmer' äl'gō

Could I see *the menu (wine list)* please?
¿Me trae *la carta/Am el menú/(la lista de vinos)*, por favor?
me trä'e lä kär'tä/el menōo'/(lä lēs'tä de vē'nōs), pōr fävōr'

What can we have right away?	**Do you have …?**
¿Qué plato nos puede servir en seguida?	¿Hay …?
ke plä'tō nōs pōo·e'de servēr' en segē'dä	ī …

Do you have *vegetarian (diet)* food, too?
¿Tienen también platos *vegetarianos (de régimen)*?
tye'nen tämbyen' plä'tōs vehetäryä'nōs (de re'hēmen)

Please bring us *one portion (two portions)* of …
Por favor, *una ración (dos raciones)* de …
pōr fävōr', ōo'nä räsyōn' (dōs räsyō'nes) de …

***A cup (glass, bottle)* of …, please.**
Por favor, *una taza (un vaso, una botella)* de …
pōr fävōr', ōo'nä tä'sä (ōom bä'sō, ōo'nä bōte'lyä) de …

Table Service

English	Spanish	Pronunciation
ash tray	cenicero *m*	senēse'rō
bottle	botella *f*/*Mex* a frasco *m*	bōte'lyä/fräs'kō
bowl	tazón *m*	täsōn'
bread basket	cestilla *f*/canasta *f*/del pan	sestē'lyä/känäs'tä/del pän
carafe	garrafa *f*	gärrä'fä
cup	taza *f*	tä'sä
– saucer	platillo *m*	plätē'lyō
cutlery	cubiertos *mpl*	kōōbyer'tōs
decanter	jarra *f*	hä'rrä
egg cup	huevera *f*	ōō·eve'rä
fork	tenedor *m*	tenedōr'
glass	vaso *m*	vä'sō
– water glass	vaso *m* para agua	vä'sō pä'rä ä'gōo·ä
– wine glass	vaso *m* para vino	vä'sō pä'rä vē'nō
knife	cuchillo *m*	kōōtshē'lyō
napkin	servilleta *f*	servēlye'tä
pepper mill	molinillo *m* de pimienta	mōlēnē'lyō de pēmyen'tä
pepper shaker	pimentero *m*	pēmente'rō
pitcher	jarra *f*	hä'rrä
– cream pitcher	jarra *f* para leche	hä'rrä pä'rä le'tshe
place setting	cubierto *m*	kōōbyer'tō
plate	plato *m*	plä'tō
– bread plate	platillo *m*	plätē'lyō
– soup plate	plato *m* sopero	plä'tō sōpe'rō
pot	olla *f*	ō'lyä
– coffee pot	cafetera *f*	käfete'rä
– tea pot	tetera *f*	tete'rä
salt shaker	salero *m*	säle'rō
serving dish	fuente *m*	fōo·en'te
spoon	cuchara *f*	kōōtshä'rä
– soup spoon	cuchara *f* sopera	kōōtshä'rä sōpe'rä
– teaspoon	cucharita *f*	kōōtshärē'tä
sugar bowl	azucarera *f*/*Sp* azucarero *m*	äsōōkäre'rä/äsōōkäre'rō
tablecloth	mantel *m*	mäntel'
toothpick	palillo *m*	pälē'lyō
tray	charola *f*/*Sp* bandeja *f*	tshärō'lä/bände'hä

Breakfast

bread	pan *m*	pän
– whole wheat bread	pan *m* de trigo integral	pän de trē'gō ēntegräl'
breakfast	desayuno *m*	desäyōō'nō
– eat breakfast	desayunar	desäyōōnär'
butter	mantequilla *f*	mäntekē'lyä
cereal	cereales *mpl*	sere·ä'les
coffee	café *m*	käfe'
– black (espresso)	solo *m*/*Mex* expreso	sō'lō/espre'sō
– decaffeinated	descafeinado	deskäfe·ēnä'dō
– and milk	con leche	kōn le'tshe
cold cuts	fiambres *mpl*/*Mex* carnes *fpl* frías	fyäm'bres/kär'nes frē'äs
croissant	croissant *m*	krō·äsänt'
egg	huevo *m*/*Mex* blanquillo *m*	ōō·e'vō/blängkē'lyō
– soft-boiled	pasado por agua/*Mex* tibio	päsä'dō pōr ä'gōō·ä/tē'byō
– ham and eggs	huevos *mpl* con jamón	ōō·e'vōs kōn *h*ämōn'
– fried eggs	fritos/*Mex* estrellados	frē'tōs/estrelyä'dōs
– scrambled eggs	revueltos	revōō·el'tōs
fruit juice	jugo *m*/*Sp* zumo *m*	*h*ōō'gō/sōō'mō
– grapefruit juice	jugo *m*/*Sp* zumo *m*/de pomelo/*Mex* de toronja	*h*ōō'gō/sōō'mō/de pōme'lō/de tōrōn'*h*ä
– orange juice	jugo *m*/*Sp* zumo *m*/de naranja	*h*ōō'gō/sōō'mō/de närän'*h*ä
honey	miel *f*	myel
hot chocolate	chocolate *m*	tshōkōlä'te
jam	mermelada *f*	mermelä'dä
milk	leche *f*	le'tshe
– condensed milk	leche *f* evaporada	le'tshe eväpōrä'dä
roll	panecillo *m*/*Mex* bolillo *m*	pänesē'lyō/bōlē'lyō
sausage	salchicha *f*	sältshē'tshä
sugar	azúcar *m*	äsōō'kär
tea	té *m*	te
– camomile tea	té *m* de manzanilla	te de mänsänē'lyä
– mint tea	té *m* de menta/*Mex* de hierba buena	te de men'tä/de yer'bä bōō·e'nä
toast	pan *m* tostado	pän tōstä'dō

> *Breakfast in Latin America and Spain is not as large as in the U.S. It usually consists of coffee, tea or hot chocolate, some sort of bread or pastry, and perhaps butter and jam.*

Lunch and Dinner

I'd (We'd) like to have ...
Quisiera (Quisiéramos) ...
kēsye'rä (kēsye'rämōs) ...

Would you bring us ...?
¿Nos trae ...?
nōs trä'e ...

Please pass ...
Páseme/Pásame *(fam)/ ...*, por favor.
pä'seme/pä'säme/ ..., pōr fävōr'

What's the name of this dish?
¿Cómo se llama este plato?
kō'mō se lyä'mä es'te plä'tō

*Would you like seconds on anything?
¿Desean algo más?
dese'än äl'gō mäs

Yes, please.
Sí, por favor.
sē, pōr fävōr'

Yes, indeed.
Con mucho gusto.
kōn mōō'tshō gōōs'tō

Just a little.
Un poquito, nada más.
ōōn pōkē'tō, nä'dä mäs

Thanks, that's enough.
Gracias, nada más.
grä'syäs, nä'dä mäs

No, thanks.
No, gracias.
nō grä'syäs

I've had enough.
Estoy bien.
estoi' byen

Nothing more, thanks.
Nada más, gracias.
nä'dä mäs, grä'syäs

*Did you like it?
¿Le/te *(fam)* ha gustado?
le/te/ä gōōstä'dō

Delicious!
¡Muy rico!
mōō'ē rē'kō

Cheers!
¡Salud!
sälōōd'

This dish (The wine) is delicious!
Este plato (El vino) es excelente.
es'te plä'tō (el vē'nō) es ekselen'te

I'm not allowed to have any alcohol.
No debo beber alcohol.
nō de'bō beber' älkō·ōl'

> *To wish others at the table an enjoyable meal, say "¡Que aproveche!" or "¡Buen provecho!", which, freely translated, means "make the most of it!"*

Cooking

baked	asado, horneado	äsä′dō, ōrne·ä′dō
barbecue	barbacoa *f*	bärbäkō′ä
boiled	cocido	kōsē′dō
breaded	empanado	empänä′dō
cold	frío	frē′ō
fat	grasa *f*	grä′sä
fresh	fresco	fres′kō
fried	frito	frē′tō
grilled	asado a la parrilla	äsä′dō ä lä pärrē′lyä
hard	duro	dōō′rō
hot	caliente	kälyen′te
hot *(spicy)*	picante	pēkän′te
juicy	jugoso	hōōgō′sō
lean	magro/*Mex a* macizo	mäg′rō/mäsē′sō
medium *(done)*	medio cocido/*Sp* medio asado	me′dyō kōsē′dō/ me′dyō äsä′dō
pickled	escabechado	eskäbetshä′dō
rare	casi crudo/*Sp* a la inglesa	kä′sē krōō′dō/ä lä ēngle′sä
raw	crudo	krōō′dō
roasted	asado, horneado	äsä′dō, ōrne·ä′dō
salted	salado	sälä′dō
seasoned	condimentado	kōndēmentä′dō
smoked	ahumado	ä-ōōmä′dō
soft	blando	blän′dō
steamed	cocido al vapor	kōsē′dō äl väpōr′
stewed	estofado, guisado	estōfä′dō, gēsä′dō
stuffed	relleno	relye′nō
tender	tierno	tyer′nō
tough	duro	dōō′rō
well done	bien hecho, bien asado, bien cocido	byen e′tshō, byen äsä′dō, byen kōsē′dō

Ingredients

bacon	tocino *m*	tōsē′nō
butter	mantequilla *f*	mäntekē′lyä
capers	alcaparras *fpl*	älkäpä′rräs

caraway	semillas *fpl* de Alcaravea	semē′lyäs de älkä-räve′ä
chives	cebollino *m*	sebōlyē′nō
cinnamon	canela *f*	käne′lä
cloves	clavos *mpl* de especia	klä′vōs de espe′syä
cumin seeds	cominos *mpl*	kōmē′nōs
dill	eneldo *m*	enel′dō
garlic	ajo *m*	ä′hō
ginger	jengibre *m*	hen*h*ē′bre
herbs	hierbas *fpl*	yer′bäs
honey	miel *f*	myel
horseradish	rábano *m* picante	rä′bänō pēkän′te
jelly *(fruit)*	jalea *f*, gelatina *f*	*h*äle′ä, helätē′nä
ketchup	salsa *f* de tomate	säl′sä de tōmä′te
lard	manteca *f* (de cerdo)	mänte′kä (de ser′dō)
lemon	limón *m*/*Mex* lima *f*	lēmōn′/lē′mä
lime	lima *f*/*Mex* limón *m*	lē′mä/lēmōn′
margarine	margarina *f*	märgärē′nä
mayonnaise	mayonesa *f*	mäyōne′sä
mushrooms	champiñones *mpl*, hongos *mpl*, setas *fpl*	tshämpēnyō′nes, ōn′gōs, se′täs
mustard	mostaza *f*	mōstä′sä
nutmeg powder	nuez *f* moscada	nōo·es′ mōskä′dä
oil	aceite *m*	äse′ēte
olives	aceitunas *fpl*	äse·ētōō′näs
onion	cebolla *f*	sebō′lyä
paprika (cayenne pepper)	pimentón *m*	pēmentōn′
parsley	perejil *m*	pere*h*ēl′
pepper *(spice)*	pimienta *f* (negra)	pēmyen′tä (ne′grä)
pickles	pepinillos *mpl*	pepēnē′lyōs
raisins	pasas *fpl*	pä′säs
rosemary	romero *m*	rōme′rō
salt	sal *f*	säl
sauce	salsa *f*	säl′sä
– gravy	salsa *f* de asado	säl′sä de äsä′dō
seasoning *(spice)*	especias *fpl*	espe′syäs
thyme	tomillo *m*	tōmē′lyō
vanilla	vainilla *f*	vīnē′lyä
vinegar	vinagre *m*	vēnä′gre

THE MENU

Appetizers

aceitunas *fpl*	äse·ētōō'näs	olives
alcachofas *fpl*	älkätshō'fäs	artichokes
almejas *fpl*	älme'häs	clams
anchoas *fpl*	äntshō'äs	anchovies
boquerones *mpl*	bōkerō'nes	type of anchovy
– fritos	frē'tōs	fried
calamares *mpl*	kälämä'res	squid
– a la romana	ä lä rōmä'nä	breaded and fried
– en su tinta	en sōō tēn'tä	in their own ink
cangrejos *mpl*	kängre'hōs	snails
ceviche *m*	sevē'tshe	raw fish, marinated
croquetas *fpl*	krōke'täs	croquettes
empanadas	empänä'däs	stuffed savory pastries
fiambres *mpl*/*Mex*	fyäm'bres/kär'nes	cold cuts
carnes *fpl* frias	frē'äs	
gambas *fpl*/*Mex*	gäm'bäs/kämärō'nes	shrimp
camarones *mpl*		
– al ajillo	äl ähē'lyō	in garlic
jamón	*h*ämōn'	ham
mejillones *mpl*	me*h*ēlyō'nes	mussels
– en salsa vinagreta	en säl'sä vēnägre'tä	in vinaigrette sauce
ostras *fpl*/*Mex*	ōs'träs/	oysters
ostiones *fpl*	ōstyō'nes	
salchichón *m*	sältshētshōn'	salami
sardinas *fpl*	särdē'näs	sardines
– en escabeche	– en eskäbe'tshe	pickled

Salads

ensalada *f*	ensälä'dä	salad
– de lechuga	– de letshōō'gä	lettuce salad
– de lechuga y tomate	– de letshōō'gä ē tōmä'te	lettuce and tomato salad
– mixta	mē'kstä	mixed salad
ensaladilla *f* rusa	ensälädē'lyä rōō'sä	vegetable salad in mayonnaise dressing

Soups

caldo *m*	käl′dō	broth, bouillon
– de gallina	de gälyē′nä	chicken broth
consomé *m*	kōnsōme′	clear soup
crema *f*	kre′mä	cream soup
potaje *m*	potä′he	stew
pote *m* gallego *(Sp)*	pō′te gälye′gō	stew with beans, meat, potatoes, greens
puré *m*	poore′	purée
sopa *f*	sō′pä	soup
– de ajo	de ä′hō	garlic soup
– de fideos	de fēde′ōs	noodle soup
– de lentejas	de lente′häs	lentil soup
– de pescado	de peskä′dō	fish soup
– de tomate	de tōmä′te	tomato soup
– de verduras	de verdoo′räs	vegetable soup
juliana	hoolyä′nä	vegetable soup

Rice

arroz *m*	ärrōs′	rice
– a la marinera	ä lä märēne′rä	rice with fish
– a la cubana	ä lä koobä′nä	rice with egg and banana
– blanco	bläng′kō	plain white rice

Eggs

huevos *mpl*/*Mex a* blanquillos *mpl*	oo·e′vōs/blänkē′lyōs	eggs
– a la andaluza	ä lä ändäloo′sä	with ham and eggplant
– al plato	äl plä′tō	sunny side up
– rancheros *(Mex)*	räntshe′rōs	in chile sauce
– rellenos	relye′nōs	stuffed eggs, deviled eggs
omelet *m (Mex)*	ōmelet′	omelette
tortilla *f* francesa *(Sp)*	tōrtē′lyä fränse′sä	omelette
– paisana *(Sp)*	pīsä′nä	Spanish tortilla with beans, ham and tomatoes

Some Typical Spanish Dishes

bacalao a la vizcaína	bäkälä′ō ä lä vēs-kä·ē′nä	cod with tomato-onion sauce
callos a la madrileña	kä′lyōs ä lä mädrēle′-nyä	tripe with sausage and spices
cochinillo	kōtshēnē′lyō	roasted baby pig
cocido madrileño . . .	kōsē′dō mädrēle′nyō	stewed chick peas, cabbage, sausages, bacon
fabada asturiana	fäbä′dä ästōōryä′nä .	stew of beans, ham, bacon
gazpacho	gäspä′tshō	cold tomato soup with garnish of cucumbers peppers and onions
paella valenciana	pä·e′lyä välensyä′nä .	saffron rice with seafood, chicken and vegetables
pisto manchego	pēs′tō mäntshe′gō . . .	fried vegetables, usually eggplant, pepper, onion, in spicy tomato sauce
sopa de ajo	sō′pä de ä′hō	garlic soup topped with an egg
tapas	tä′päs	Spanish appetizers
tortilla española	tōrtē′lyä espänyō′lä	round, cake-shaped potato omelette

Fish and Shellfish

abulón m (Mex)	äbōōlōn′	abalone
almeja f	älme′hä	clam
anguila f	ängē′lä	eel
arenque m	ären′ke	herring
atún m	ätōōn′	tuna
bacalao m	bäkälä′ō	(dried) cod
besugo m	besōō′gō	sea bream
bogavante m	bōgävän′te	lobster
bonito m	bōnē′tō	striped tuna
caballa f	käbä′lyä	mackerel
cabrilla f (Mex)	käbrē′lyä	rock fish
camarón m (Mex) . .	kämärōn′	shrimp

cangrejo *m*	kängre'hō	large crab
carpa *f*	kär'pä	carp
esturión *m*	estōōryōn'	sturgeon
gambas *fpl (Sp)*	gäm'bäs	shrimp
huachinango *m (Mex)*	ōō·ätshēnän'gō	red snapper
langosta *f*	läng·gōs'tä	spiny lobster
langostinos *mpl*	läng·gōstē'nōs	crayfish
lenguado *m*	leng·gōō·ä'dō	sole
lucio *m*	lōō'syō	pike
mariscos *mpl*	märēs'kōs	shellfish
mejillones *mpl*	mehēlyō'nes	mussels
merluza *f*	merlōō'sä	hake
mero *m*	me'rō	grouper
pargo *m (Mex)*	pär'gō	sea bass or snapper
perca *f*	per'kä	perch
pescado *m*	peskä'dō	fish
pulpo *m*	pōōl'pō	octopus
rodaballo *m*	rōdäbä'lyō	turbot
roballo *(Mex)*	rōbä'lyō	snook
salmón *m*	sälmōn'	salmon
salmonete *m*	sälmōne'te	red mullet
sierra *f (Mex)*	sye'rrä	Spanish mackerel
trucha *f*	trōō'tshä	trout

Poultry

codornices *fpl*	kōdōrnē'ses	quails
capón *m*	käpōn'	capon
faisán *m*	fīsän'	pheasant
gallina *f*	gälyē'nä	hen, fowl
ganso *m*	gän'sō	goose
guajolote *m (Mex)*	gōō·ähōlō'te	turkey
menudillos *mpl*	menōōdē'lyōs	giblets
pata *f (Sp)*	pä'tä	thigh, drumstick
pato *m*	pä'tō	duck
pierna *f (Mex)*	pyer'nä	thigh, drumstick
pavo *m (Sp)*	pä'vō	turkey
pechuga *f*	petshōō'gä	breast
perdigón *m*	perdēgōn'	young partridge
perdiz *f*	perdēs'	partridge
pichón *m*	pētshōn'	young pigeon
pollo *m*	pō'lyō	chicken

Meat

albóndigas *fpl*	älbōn'dēgäs	meatballs
horneado/*Sp* asado	ōrne·ä'dō/äsä'dō	roasted
bistec *m*	bēstek'	steak
buey *m*	boo·e'ē	ox
carne *f*	kär'ne	meat
– molida/*Sp* picada	mōlē'dä/pēkä'dä	ground meat
callos *mpl*	kä'lyōs	tripe
carnero *m*	kärne'rō	mutton
cerdo *m*/puerco *m*	ser'dō/poo·er'kō	pork
cochinillo *m*, lechón *m*	kōtshēnē'lyō, letshōn'	baby pig
conejo *m*	kōne'hō	rabbit
cordero *m*	kōrde'rō	lamb
– lechal	letshäl'	baby lamb
costillas *fpl*	kōstē'lyäs	ribs
chuleta *f*	tshoole'tä	chop
escalope *m*	eskälō'pe	scallops
filete *m*	fēle'te	fillet
hígado *m*	ē'gädō	liver
jabalí *m*	häbälē'	wild boar
jamón *m*	hämōn'	ham
lacón *m*	läkōn'	shoulder of pork
liebre *f*	lye'bre	hare
lomo *m*	lō'mō	loin
pierna *f* de ternera, pernil *m*	pyer'nä de terne'rä, pernēl'	veal leg shank
riñones *mpl*	rēnyō'nes	kidneys
rosbif *m*	rōsbēf'	roast beef
salchicha *f*	sältshē'tshä	sausage
solomillo *m*	sōlōmē'lyō	sirloin
ternera *f*/*Mex* ternero *m*	terne'rä/terne'rō	veal

Some Typical Mexican Dishes

antojitos	äntōhē'tōs	Mexican hors d'oeuvres
burritos	boorrē'tōs	filled flour tortillas
chicharrones	tshētshärrō'nes	pig cracklings

chile	tshĕ′le	generic name of various types of peppers (mild to hot) used extensively in Mexican cuisine
chile relleno	tshĕ′le relye′nō	mild *Poblano* chiles stuffed with cheese and deep fried
enchiladas	entshēlä′däs	rolled, stuffed tortillas in hot sauce
– suizas	sōō·ē′säs	with sour cream and cheese
frijoles refritos	frēhō′les refrē′tōs	beans refried in lard
gorditas	gōrdē′täs	round stuffed tortilla dough, fried
guacamole	gōō·äkämō′le	spicy avocado dip
mole	mō′le	sauce of chocolate, chile, spices, nuts and herbs
taco	tä′kō	folded, fried tortilla with filling
tamales	tämä′les	steamed, filled corn dough in banana leaf or corn husk
tostada	tōstä′dä	crisp corn tortillas stacked with beans, meat, cheese, etc.
tortilla	tōrtē′lyä	thin pancake-shaped staple of Mexican diet, made of unleavened corn meal or flour
quesadillas	kesädē′lyäs	cheese and chile fried in tortilla dough

Vegetables

acelgas *fpl*	äsel′gäs	Swiss chard
aguacate *m*	ägōō·äkä′te	avocado
alcachofa *f*	älkätshō′fä	artichoke
alubias *fpl (Sp)*	älōō′byäs	white beans
apio *m*	ä′pyō	celery

batatas *fpl*/ camotes *mpl*	bätä'täs/kämō'tes	sweet potatoes
berenjena *f*	beren*he*'nä	eggplant
berza *f* lombarda	ber'sä lōmbär'dä	red cabbage
brécol *m*, brócoli *m*	bre'kōl, brō'kōlē	broccoli
cacahuates *mpl* (*Mex*)	käkä·ōō·ä'tes	peanuts
cacahuetes *mpl* (*Sp*)	käkä·ōō·e'tes	peanuts
calabacines *mpl*	käläbäsē'nes	zucchini
calabaza *f*	käläbä'sä	pumpkin
coles *fpl* de Bruselas	kō'les de brōōse'läs	Brussel sprouts
coliflor *f*	kōlēflōr'	cauliflower
champiñones *mpl*	tshämpēnyō'nes	mushrooms
chícharos *mpl* (*Mex*)	tshē'tshärōs	peas
ejotes *mpl* (*Mex*)	e*h*ō'tes	green beans
elotes *mpl* (*Mex*)	elō'tes	green corn
escarola *f*	eskärō'lä	endive
espárragos *mpl*	espä'rrägōs	asparagus
espinacas *fpl*	espēnä'käs	spinach
frijoles *mpl*	frē*h*ō'les	beans
garbanzos *mpl*	gärbän'sōs	chick peas
guisantes *mpl* (*Sp*)	gēsän'tes	peas
jitomate *m* (*Mex*)	*h*ētōmä'te	red tomato
judías *fpl* verdes (*Sp*)	*h*ōōdē'äs ver'des	green beans
lechuga *f*	letshōō'gä	lettuce
lentejas *fpl*	lente'*h*äs	lentils
maíz *m*	mīs	corn
nabo *m*	nä'bō	turnip
papas *fpl*	pä'päs	potatoes
patatas *fpl* (*Sp*)	pätä'täs	potatoes
remolachas *fpl* (*Sp*)	remōlä'tshäs	beets
repollo *m*	repō'lyō	cabbage (white)
tomate *m* (*Sp*)	tōmä'te	red tomato
tomate *m* (*Mex*)	tōmä'te	green tomato
zanahorias *fpl*	sänä·ōr'yäs	carrots

Cheese

queso *m*	ke'sō	cheese
– ahumado	ä·ōōmä'dō	smoked cheese
– blanco	bläng'kō	white cheese
– de cabra	de kä'brä	goat cheese

– fundido	fōōndē′dō	melted cheese
– rallado	rälyä′dō	grated cheese
– suizo	sōō·ē′sō	Swiss cheese
requesón *m*	rekesōn′	(type of) cottage cheese

Bread

barra *f* de pan	bä′rrä de pän	loaf of bread, baguette
bocadillo *m* *(Sp)*	bōkädē′lyō	sandwich on French bread
bolillo *m* *(Mex)*	bōlē′lyō	French roll
bollos *mpl*	bō′lyōs	sweet rolls, Danish
pan *m*	pän	bread
– dulce *(Mex)*	dōōl′se	sweet bread
– tostado	tōstä′dō	toast
panecillo *m* *(Sp)*	pänesē′lyō	roll
torta *f* *(Mex)*	tōr′tä	sandwich on French roll
tostada *f* *(Sp)*	tōstä′dä	sliced white bread, buttered and grilled

Fruit

albaricoque *m* *(Sp)*	älbärēkō′ke	apricot
almendra *f*	älmen′drä	almond
avellana *f*	ävelyä′nä	hazelnut
cereza *f*	sere′sä	cherry
ciruela *f*	sērōō·e′lä	plum
– pasa	pä′sä	prune
coco *m*	kō′kō	coconut
chabacano *m* *(Mex)*	tshäbäkä′nō	apricot
damasco *m*	dämäs′kō	apricot
dátiles *mpl*	dä′tēles	dates
durazno *m*	dōōräz′nō	peach
fresa *f*	fre′sä	strawberry
granada *f*	gränä′dä	pomegranate
guayaba *f*	gōō·äyä′bä	guava
higo *m*	ē′gō	fig
mandarina *f*	mändärē′nä	tangerine
manzana *f*	mänsä′nä	apple

melocotón *m* (*Sp*)	melōkōtōn'	peach
melón *m*	melōn'	melon
membrillo *m*	membrē'lyō	quince
naranja *f*	närän'hä	orange
nuez *f*	nōō·es'	nut
pera *f*	pe'rä	pear
piña *f*	pē'nyä	pineapple
plátano *m*	plä'tänō	banana
pomelo *m*	pōme'lō	grapefruit
toronja *f* (*Mex*)	tōrōn'hä	grapefruit
sandía *f*	sändē'ä	watermelon
uva *f*	ōō'vä	grape

Baby Food

baby bottle	biberón *m*	bēberōn'
baby cereal	papilla *f*	päpē'lyä
baby food	alimentos *mpl* infantiles	älēmen'tōs ēnfäntē'les
baby formula	leches *fpl* infantiles	le'tshes ēnfäntē'les

---

Desserts

arroz *m* con leche	ärrōs' kōn le'tshe ..	rice pudding
budín *m*	bōōdēn'	pudding
buñuelos *mpl* (*Mex*) ..	bōōnyōō·e'lōs	fried dough with sugar and honey
buñuelos *mpl* (*Sp*) de viento	bōōnyōō·e'lōs de vyen'tō	(type of) cream puff
bizcocho *m* (*Sp*)	bēskō'tshō	pound cake
churros *mpl*	tshōō'rrōs	crunchy, deep fried dough
compota *f*	kōmpō'tä	compote
coctel *m* de frutas (*Mex*)	kōktel' de frōō'täs .	fruit cocktail
crema *f* batida (*Mex*) .	kre'mä bätē'dä	whipped cream
flan *m* (de caramelo) ..	flän (de käräme'lō)	caramel custard
galletas *fpl*	gälye'täs	plain cookies, biscuits
helado *m*	elä'dō	ice cream
– de chocolate	de tshōkōlä'te	chocolate ice cream
– de fresa	de fre'sä	strawberry ice cream
– de vainilla	de vīnē'lyä	vanilla ice cream

macedonia *f* de frutas *(Sp)*	mäsedō'nyä de frōo'täs	**fruit cocktail**
nata *f (Sp)*	nä'tä	**whipped cream**
natillas *fpl*	nätē'lyäs	**egg custard**
paleta *f (Mex)*	päle'tä	**flavored ice on a stick**
pastas *fpl (Sp)*	päs'täs	**cookies**
rosquilla *f (Sp)*	rōskē'lyä	**(type of) donut**
tarta *f*/torta *f*	tär'tä/tōr'tä	**cake**

BEVERAGES

Wine

champán *m*	tshämpän'	**champagne**
jerez *m*	*h*eres'	**sherry**
– fino	fē'nō	**pale, dry**
– amontillado	ämōntēlyä'dō	**full-bodied**
– oloroso	ōlōrō'sō	**sweet**
sangría *f*	säng·grē'ä	**wine punch with fruit**
vino *m*	vē'nō	**wine**
– añejo	änye'hō	**vintage**
– blanco	bläng'kō	**white**
– de la casa	de lä kä'sä	**house wine**
– dulce	dōol'se	**sweet**
– nuevo	nōo·e'vō	**new**
– rosado	rōsä'dō	**rosé**
– seco	se'kō	**dry**
– tinto	tēn'tō	**red**

Beer

caña *f (Sp)*	kä'nyä	**glass of beer**
cerveza *f*	serve'sä	**beer**
– de barril	de bärrēl'	**draft beer**
– de botella	de bōte'lyä	**bottled beer**
– negra	ne'grä	**dark beer**
– clara/*Sp* rubia	klä'rä, rōo'byä	**light beer**

Liquor

aguardiente *m*	ägōō·ärdyen'te	clear liquor
anís *m*	änēs'	anisette liqueur
aperitivo *m*	äperētē'vō	apéritif
coñac *m*	kōnyäk'	cognac, brandy
ginebra *f*	*h*ēne'brä	gin
Kahlúa *f (Mex)*	kälōō'ä	coffee liqueur
mezcal *m (Mex)*	mes'käl	mescal
pulque *m (Mex)*	pōōl'ke	fermented sap of maguey cactus
sidra *f*	sē'drä	cider
tequila *f*	tekē'lä	tequila
vodka *f*	vōd'kä	vodka
whisk(e)y *m*	ōō·ēs'kē	whisk(e)y

Other

agua *f*	ä'gōō·ä	water
– dulce	dōōl'se	fresh water
– mineral	mēneräl'	mineral water
– potable	pōtä'ble	drink water
– purificada	pōōrēfēkä'dä	bottled water
atole *m (Mex)*	ätō'le	drinking of ground corn, sugar and water
batidos *mpl (Sp)*	bätē'dōs	shakes
granizado *m*	gränēsä'dō	iced beverage
– de café	de käfe'	iced coffee
– de limón	de lēmōn'	lemon juice and ice
horchata *f (Mex)*	ōrtshä'tä	ground melon seeds and water
horchata *f (Sp)*	ōrtshä'tä	almond milk
jugo *m (Mex)*	hōō'gō	juice
licuado *m (Mex)*	lēkōō·ä'dō	shake
limonada *f*	lēmōnä'dä	lemonade
naranjada *f*	närän*h*ä'dä	orangeade
refresco *m*	refres'kō	drink, soft drink
tónica *f*	tō'nēkä	tonic water
zumo *m (Sp)*	sōō'mō	juice

Complaints, Paying the Check

We need another *portion (set of silverware, glass)*.
Falta otra *porción/Sp ración (un cubierto, un vaso)*.
fäl'tä ō'trä pōrsyōn'/räsyōn' (ōon kōobyer'tō, ōom bä'sō)

This isn't what I ordered.
Esto no es lo que pedía.
es'tō nō es lō ke pedē'ä

I wanted ...
Quería ...
kerē'ä ...

This is ...
Está ...
estä' ...

too fatty	demasiado grasiento ..	demäsyä'dō gräsyen'tō
too hard	demasiado duro	demäsyä'dō dōo'rō
too hot *(temperature)*	demasiado caliente	demäsyä'dō kälyen'te
too spicy	demasiado picante	demäsyä'dō pēkän'te
too cold	demasiado frío	demäsyä'dō frē'ō
too salty	demasiado salado	demäsyä'dō sälä'dō
too sour	demasiado agrio	demäsyä'dō ä'grē·ō
too tough	demasiado duro	demäsyä'dō dōo'rō

The check, please!
¡La cuenta, por favor!
lä kōo·en'tä, pōr fävōr'

All together, please.
Todo junto, por favor.
tō'dō hōon'tō, pōr fävōr'

Separate checks, please.
Cuentas separadas, por favor.
kōo·en'täs sepärä'däs, pōr fävōr'

I don't think this is correct.
Me parece que aquí hay un error.
me päre'se ke äkē' ī ōon errōr'

We didn't have that.
Esto no nos lo han servido.
es'tō nō nōs lō än servē'dō

Thanks very much.
Muchas gracias.
mōo'tshäs grä'syäs

Keep the change.
Para usted.
pä'rä ōoste'

DOWNTOWN

On the Street

Where is ...?
¿Dónde está ...?
dōn'de estä'

the bus stop	la parada de autobuses/ *Mex* de camiones	lä pärä'dä de outōbōo'ses/de kämyō'nes
the Catholic Church .	la iglesia católica	lä ēgle'syä kätō'lēkä
city hall	el ayuntamiento/la alcaldía	el äyōōntämyen'tō/ lä älkäldē'ä
the harbor	el puerto	el pōo·er'tō
the ... Hotel	el hotel	el ōtel'
the museum	el museo	el mōose'ō
the police station	la comisaría	lä kōmēsärē'ä
the post office	el correo	el kōrre'ō
the Protestant Church	la iglesia protestante ..	lä ēgle'syä prōtestän'te
... Square	la plaza	lä plä'sä
... Street	la calle	lä kä'lye
the station	la estación	lä estäsyōn'
the synagogue	la sinagoga	lä sēnägō'gä
a taxi stand	la parada/*Mex* el sitio/ de taxis	lä pärä'dä/el sē'tyō/de tä'ksēs

Is it far from here?
¿Está lejos?
estä' le'hōs

How far is it to the ...?
A qué distancia está ...?
ä ke dēstän'syä estä' ...

How many minutes on foot?
¿Cuántos minutos andando?
kōo·än'tōs mēnōo'tōs ändän'dō

A good distance. (Not far.)
Bastante. (No muy lejos.)
bästän'te (nō mōo'ē le'hōs)

Which direction is ...?
¿En qué dirección se encuentra ...?
en ke dēreksyōn' se enkōo·en'trä ...

What street is ... on?
¿En qué calle está ...?
en ke kä'lye estä' ...

There.	**Straight ahead.**	**To the right.**	**To the left.**
Allí.	Todo derecho/*Sp* seguido.	A la derecha.	A la izquierda.
älyē'	tō'dō dere'tshō/segē'dō	ä lä dere'tshä	ä lä ēskyer'dä

Bus, Taxi

Can I get there by bus?
¿Va el autobús/*Mex* el camión/a …?
vä el outōbōos'/el kämyōn'/ä …

Which bus goes to (the) …?
¿Qué autobús/*Mex* camión/va a …?
ke outōbōos'/kämyōn'/vä ä …

How many stops is it from here?
¿Cuántas paradas hay desde aquí?
kōō·än'täs pärä'däs ī dez'de äkē'

Do I have to change?
¿Tengo que cambiar de auto-
bús/*Mex* camión?
ten'gō ke kämbyär' de outōbōos'/kämyōn'

Where do I have to *get out (change)*?
¿Dónde tengo que *bajar (cambiar)*?
dōn'de ten'gō ke bähar' (kämbyär')

Would you please tell me when we get there?
¿Podría avisarme cuando lleguemos?
pōdrē'ä ävēsär'me kōō·än'dō lyege'mōs

A *one-way (transfer)* ticket to …
Un boleto/*Sp* billete/*de ida sólo (de correspondencia)* para …
ōon bōle'tō/bēlye'te/de ē'dä sō'lō (de kōrrespōnden'syä) pä'rä …

Where can I get a taxi?
¿Dónde puedo conseguir un taxi?
dōn'de pōō·e'dō kōnsegēr' ōon tä'ksē

Take me to …
Lléveme a …
lye'veme ä …

To the station, please.
A la estación, por favor.
ä lä estäsyōn', pōr fävōr'

How much is the fare to …?
Cuánto cuesta hasta …?
kōō·än'tō kōō·es'tä äs'tä …

Could you show us some of the sights?
¿Podría enseñarnos algunos monumentos importantes?
pōdrē'ä ensenyär'nōs älgōō'nōs mōnōō·men'tōs ēmpōrtän'tes

Please *wait (stop)* here for a minute.
Espere (Pare) aquí un momento, por favor.
espe're (pä're) äkē' ōon mōmen'tō, pōr fävōr'

Sightseeing and Excursions

Two tickets for the ... tomorrow, please.
Para mañana, dos plazas para ..., por favor.
pä'rä mänyä'nä, dōs plä'säs pä'rä ..., pōr fävōr'

Is lunch included?
¿Está incluido el almuerzo en el precio?
estä' ēnklōō·ē'dō el älmōō·er'sō en el pre'syō

When (Where) do we meet?
¿A que hora (Dónde) nos encontramos?
ä ke ō'rä (dōn'de) nōs enkōnträ'mōs

We'll be meeting ...
Nos encontramos ...
nōs enkōnträ'mōs ...

When do we get going?
¿A qué hora salimos?
ä ke ō'rä sälē'mōs

Will we be seeing the ... too?
¿Visitamos también ...?
vēsētä'mōs tämbyen' ...

Will we have some free time?
¿Disponemos de algún tiempo libre?
dēspōne'mōs de älgōōn' tyem'pō lē'bre

How much?
¿Cuánto?
kōō·än'tō

Will we be able to do some shopping?
¿Podemos ir de compras?
pōde'mōs ēr de kōm'präs

When do we get back?
¿Cuándo volveremos?
kōō·än'dō vōlvere'mōs

How long will we stay in ...?
¿Cuánto tiempo nos quedamos en ...?
kōō·än'tō tyem'pō nōs kedä'mōs en ...

Will we be going to ... too?
¿Iremos también a ...?
ēre'mōs tämbyen' ä ...

What's worth seeing in ...?
¿Qué cosas de interés turístico hay en ...?
ke kō'säs de ēnteres' tōōrēs'tēkō ī en ...

When does ... open (close)?
¿A qué hora *abren (cierran)* ...?
ä ke ō'rä äb'ren (sye'rrän) ...

How much does the admission (guided tour) cost?
¿Cuánto cuesta *la entrada (el guía)*?
kōō·än'tō kōō·es'tä lä enträ'dä (el gē'ä)

Is there an English speaking guide?
¿Hay un guía que hable inglés?
ī ōōn gē'ä ke äb'le ēngles'

I'd like to see the ...
Me gustaría ver ...
me gōōstärē'ä ver ...

Can we take a look at ... today?
¿Se puede visitar ... hoy?
se pōō·e'de vēsētär' ... oi

the castle	el castillo	el kästē'lyō
the cathedral	la catedral	lä kätedräl'
the church	la iglesia	lä ēgle'syä
the fortress	la fortaleza	lä fōrtäle'sä
the exhibition	la exposición	lä ekspōsēsyōn'
the gallery	la galería	lä gälerē'ä
the monument	el monumento	el mōnōōmen'tō
the museum	el museo	el mōōse'ō
the palace	el palacio	el pälä'syō
the zoo	el jardín zoológico	el härdēn' sō·ōlō'hēkō

When does the tour start?
¿A qué hora comienza la visita guiada?
ä ke ō'rä kōmyen'sä lä vēsē'tä gē·ä'dä

Can we take pictures?
¿Se puede sacar fotos?
se pōō·e'de säkär' fō'tōs

What is that *building (monument)*?
¿Qué *edificio (monumento)* es ése?
ke edēfē'syō (mōnōōmen'tō) es e'se

Who *painted this picture (sculpted this statue)*?
¿De quién es *este cuadro (esta estatua)*?
de kyen es es'te kōō·ä'drō (es'tä estä'tōō·ä)

What period does this ... date from?
¿De qué siglo es ...?
de ke sē'glō es ...

When was ... built?
¿Cuándo fue construido ...?
kōō·än'dō fōō·e' kōnstrōō·ē'dō ...

Who built ...?
¿Quién construyó ...?
kyen kōnstrōōyō' ...

Where can I find ...?
¿Dónde se encuentra ...?
dōn'de se enkōō·en'trä ...

Is this ...?
¿Es éste ...?
es es'te ...

*This is where ... *lived (was born, died)*.
Aquí *vivió* ... (*nació* ..., *murió* ...)
äkē' vēvyō' ... (näsyō' ..., mōōryō' ...)

Vocabulary

airport	aeropuerto *m*	ä·erōpōō·er'tō
alley	callejón *m*	kälye*h*ōn'
amusement park	parque *m* de atracciones	pär'ke de äträk-syō'nes
area	región *f*	re*h*yōn'
avenue	avenida *f*, paseo *m*	ävenē'dä, päse'ō
boat trip	excursión *f* en lancha	ekskōōrsyōn' en län'tshä
botanical gardens	jardín *m* botánico	*h*ärdēn' bōtä'nēkō
bridge	puente *m*	pōō·en'te
building	edificio *m*	edēfē'syō
bus	autobús *m*/*Mex* camión *m*	outōbōōs'/kämyōn'
capital	capital *f*	käpētäl'
castle	castillo *m*	kästē'lyō
cathedral	catedral *f*	kätedräl'
cave	cueva *f*	kōō·e'vä
cemetery	cementerio *m*	sementer'yō
church	iglesia *f*	ēgle'syä
churchyard	campo *m* santo	käm'pō sän'tō
city	ciudad *f*	syōōdäd'
city hall	alcaldía *f*/*Sp* ayuntamiento *m*	älkäldē'ä/äyōōntämyen'tō
consulate	consulado *m*	kōnsōōlä'dō
corner	esquina *f*	eskē'nä
countryside	campo *m*	käm'pō
courthouse	tribunal *m*, juzgado *m*	trēbōōnäl', *h*ōōzgä'dō
covered market	mercado *m* cubierto	merkä'dō kōōbyer'tō
dead-end street	callejón *m* sin salida	kälye*h*ōn' sēn sälē'dä
district of town	barrio *m*	bärr'yō
ditch	zanja *f*	sän'*h*ä
downtown	centro *m* ciudad, centro *m* urbano	sen'trō syōōdäd, sen'trō ōōrbä'nō
embassy	embajada *f*	embä*h*ä'dä
excavations	excavaciones *fpl*	ekskäväsyō'nes

excursion	excursión f	ekskōōrsyōn′
exhibition	exposición f	ekspōsēsyōn′
factory	fábrica f	fä′brēkä
farmhouse	granja f/Mex cortijo m	grän′hä/ kōrtē′hō
fire dept	bomberos mpl	bōmbe′rōs
first-aid	puesto m de socorros/ Mex "primeros auxi- lios"	pōō·es′tō de sō- kō′rrōs/prēme′rōs ouksē′lyōs
fountain	fuente f	fōō·en′te
gallery	galería f	gälerē′ä
garden	jardín m	härdēn′
gate	puerta f	pōō·er′tä
government office	oficina f pública	ōfēsē′nä pōō′blēkä
guide	guía m	gē′ä
harbor	puerto m	pōō·er′tō
high-rise	edificio m, torre f	edēfē′syō, tō′rre
hill	colina f, cerro m	kōlē′nä, se′rrō
hospital	hospital m	ōspētäl′
house	casa f	kä′sä
house number	número m (de la casa)	nōō′mero
landscape	paisaje m	pīsä′he
lane	camino m, sendero m	kämē′nō, sende′rō
library	biblioteca f	bēblē·ōte′kä
lost and found office	oficina f de objetos per- didos	ōfēsē′nä de ōb- he′tōs perdē′dōs
market	mercado m	merkä′dō
main street	calle f principal	kä′lye prēnsēpäl′
memorial	monumento m	mōnōōmen′tō
ministry	ministerio m	mēnēster′yō
moat	foso m	fō′sō
monument	monumento m	mōnōōmen′tō
mountain	montaña f	mōntä′nyä
mountain range	montañas fpl, sierra f, cordillera f	mōntä′nyäs, sye′- rrä, kōrdēlye′rä
museum	museo m	mōōse′ō
national park	parque m nacional	pär′ke näsyōnäl′
observatory	observatorio m	ōbservätōr′yō
old town	parte f antigua	pär′te äntē′gōō·ä
open market	mercado m	merkä′dō
palace	palacio m	pälä′syō

park	parque *m*	pär′ke
part of town	barrio *m*	bärr′yō
path	senda *f*	sen′dä
pavillion	pabellón *m*	päbelyōn′
pedestrian	peatón *m*	pe·ätōn′
– pedestrian crossing	paso *m* de peatones	pä′sō de pe·ätō′nes
police	policía *f*	pōlēsē′ä
police station	comisaría *f*/estación *f* de policía	kōmēsärē′ä/estä-syōn′ de pōlēsē′ä
policeman	policía *m*	pōlēsē′ä
port	puerto *m*	poo·er′tō
post office	correos *mpl*	kōrre·ōs
power station	central *f* eléctrica/*Mex* planta *f* eléctrica	senträl′ elek′trēkä/plän′tä elek′trēkä
public garden	jardín *m* público	*h*ärdēn′ poo′blēko
public rest room	baños *mpl*/*Sp* servicios *mpl*	bä′nyōs/servē′syōs
river	río *m*	rē′ō
road	camino *m*	kämē′nō
road sign	señal *f* de tráfico	senyäl′ de trä′fēkō
ruin	ruina *f*	roo·ē′nä
school	escuela *f*	eskoo·e′lä
sidewalk	acera *f*/*Mex* banqueta *f*	äse′rä/bängke′tä
shop	tienda *f*	tyen′dä
shopping mall	centro *m* comercial	sen′trō kōmersyäl′
side road	calle *f* lateral	kä′lye läteräl′
sightseeing	turismo *m*	toorēz′mō
square	plaza *f*	plä′sä
stadium	estadio *m*	estä′dyō
station	estación *f*	estäsyōn′
stop	parada *f*	pärä′dä
store	tienda *f*	tyen′dä
street	calle *f*	kä′lye
suburbs	afueras *fpl*	äfoo·e′räs
subway	métro *m*	me′trō
surroundings	alrededores *mpl*	älrededō′res
synagogue	sinagoga *f*	sēnägō′gä
taxi	taxi *m*	tä′ksē
taxi stand	parada *f*/*Mex* sitio *m*/de taxis	pärä′dä/sē′tyō/de tä′ksēs
temple	templo *m*	tem′plō

theater	teatro *m*	te·ä'trō
tomb	sepulcro *m*	sepōōl'krō
tower	torre *f*	tō'rre
town	ciudad *f*	syōōdäd'
traffic	tráfico *m*, circulación *f*	trä'fēkō, sērkōōläsyōn'
traffic light	semáforo *m*, disco *m*	semä'fōrō, dēs'kō
travel agency	agencia *f* de viajes	ä*h*en'syä de vyä'*h*es
university	universidad *f*	ōōnēversēdäd'
valley	valle *m*	vä'lye
village	pueblo *m*, aldea *f*	pōō·e'blō, älde·ä
wall *(city)*	muralla *f*	mōōrä'lyä
waterfall	cascada *f*, salto *m* de agua, caída *f* de agua	käskä'dä, säl'tō de ä'gōō·ä, kä·ē'dä de ä'gōō·ä
zebra crossing	paso *m* cebra	pä'sō se'brä
zoo	jardín *m* zoológico	*h*ärdēn' sō·ōlō'*h*ēkō

Religion, Churches

Where is the Catholic church?
¿Dónde está la iglesia católica?
dōn'de estä' lä ēgle'syä kätō'lēkä

What time *are services (is high mass)*?
¿A qué hora es *el oficio (la misa mayor)*?
ä ke ō'rä es el ōfē'syō (lä mē'sä mäyōr')

Is there *a wedding (christening)* today?
¿Se celebra hoy *una boda (un bautizo)*?
se sele'brä oi ōō'nä bō'dä (ōōn boutē'sō)

Who's preaching the sermon?
¿Quién predica?
kyen predē'kä

Are there church concerts?
¿Hay conciertos de música sacra?
ī kōnsyer'tōs de mōō'sēkä sä'krä

Have you been to church today?
¿Ha/Has *(fam)*/ido ya a la iglesia?
ä/äs/ē'dō yä ä lä ēgle'syä

Please call *a clergyman (priest)*!
¡Por favor, llame a *un clérigo (un cura)*!
pōr fävōr', lyä'me ä ōōn kle'rēgō (ōōn kōō'rä)

I am a	Soy	soi
Buddhist	budista *m*	bōōdēs'tä
Christian	cristiano *m*	krēstyä'nō
Jew	judío *m*	hōōdē'ō
Catholic	católico *m*	kätō'lēkō
Moslem	musulmán *m*	mōōsōōlmän'
Protestant	protestante *m*	prōtestän'te

I don't belong to any religious denomination.
No tengo confesión religiosa.
no ten'gō kōnfesyōn' relēhyō'sä

abbey	abadía *f*	äbädē'ä
altar	altar *m*	ältär'
arch	arco *m*	är'kō
baptism	bautismo *m*	boutēz'mō
Baroque	barroco	bärrō'kō
bell	campana *f*	kämpä'nä
candlestick	candelabro *m*	kändelä'brō
cathedral	catedral *f*	kätedräl'
Catholic	católico *m*	kätō'lēkō
cemetery	cementerio *m*	sementer'yō
chapel	capilla *f*	käpē'lyä
choir	coro *m*	kō'rō
Christ	Cristo	krēs'tō
christening	bautizo *m*	boutē'sō
Christian	cristiano *m*	krēstyä'nō
Christianity	cristianismo *m*	krēstyänēz'mō
church	iglesia *f*	ēgle'syä
church concert	concierto *m* de música sacra	kōnsyer'tō de mōō'sēkä sä'krä
churchyard	campo *m* santo	käm'pō sän'tō
circumcision	circuncisión *f*	sērkōōnsēsyōn'
clergyman	clérigo *m*	kle'rēgō
communion	comunión *f*	kōmōōnyōn'
confess	confesarse	kōnfesär'se
confession	confesión *f*	kōnfesyōn'
convent	convento *m*	kōnven'tō
creed	credo *m*	kre'dō
cross	cruz *f*	krōōs
crucifix	crucifijo *m*	krōōsēfē'hō
crypt	cripta *f*	krēp'tä

cupola	cúpula *f*	kōō'pōōlä
denomination	confesión *f* religiosa	kōnfesyōn' relēhyō'sä
dome	cúpula *f*, bóveda *f*	kōō'pōōlä, bō'vedä
font	pila *f* bautismal	pē'lä boutēzmäl'
fresco	fresco *m*	fres'kō
God	Dios	dyōs
Gospel	evangelio *m*	evän*h*e'lyō
Gothic	gótico	gō'tēkō
grave	sepultura *f*	sepōōltōō'rä
High Mass	misa *f* mayor	mē'sa mäyōr'
Islam	Islam	ēzläm'
Jewish	judío	*h*ōōdē'ō
Judaism	judaísmo *m*	*h*ōōdä·ēz'mō
mass	misa *f*	mē'sä
meditation	meditación *f*	medētäsyōn'
monastery	monasterio *m*	mōnäster'yō
mosaic	mosaico *m*	mōsī'kō
Moslem	musulmán *m*	mōōsōōlmän'
mosque	mezquita *f*	meskē'tä
nave	nave *f*	nä've
organ	órgano *m*	ōr'gänō
pastor	pastor *m*	pästōr'
pillar	columna *f*	kōlōōm'nä
portal	portal *m*	pōrtäl'
priest	cura *m*, padre *m*	kōō'rä, pä'dre
procession	procesión *f*	prōsesyōn'
Protestant	protestante *m*	prōtestän'te
pulpit	púlpito *m*	pōōl'pētō
rabbi	rabino *m*	räbē'nō
religion	religión *f*	relēhyōn'
religious	religioso	relēhyō'sō
Romanesque	románico	rōmä'nēkō
rosary	rosario *m*	rōsär'yō
sacristan	sacristán *m*	säkrēstän'
sacristy	sacristía *f*	säkrēstē'ä
sarcophagus	sarcófago *m*	särkō'fägō
sermon	sermón *m*, plática *f*	sermōn', plä'tēkä
service (*Protestant*)	oficio *m* religioso	ōfē'syō relēhyō'sō
sexton	sacristán *m*	säkrēstän'
Stations of the Cross	estaciones *fpl* de la vía Crucis	estäsyō'nes de lä vē'ä krōō'sēs

statue	estatua *f*	estä'tōō·ä
synagogue	sinagoga *f*	sēnägō'gä
tomb	tumba *f*	tōōm'bä
tower	torre *f*	tō'rre
vestibule	vestíbulo *m*	vestē'bōōlō

LET'S GO SHOPPING

General Words and Phrases

Where can I *get (buy)* ...?
¿Dónde se puede *conseguir (comprar)* ...?
dōn'de se pōō·e'de kōnsegēr' (kōmprär') ...

Is there a ... shop here?
¿Hay por aquí una tienda de ...?
ī pōr äkē' ōō'nä tyen'dä de ...

Please give me ...
Déme ..., por favor.
deme ..., pōr fävōr'

Have you got ...?
¿Tienen ...?
tye'nen ...

I'd (We'd) like ...
Quisiera (Quisiéramos) ...
kēsye'rä (kēsye'rämōs) ...

Please show me ...
Muéstreme/*Sp* enséñeme/..., por favor.
mōō·es'treme/ense'nyeme/..., pōr fävōr'

I need ...
Necesito ...
nesesē'tō ...

a bag	una bolsa de	ōō'nä bōl'sä de
a bottle	una botella de	ōō'nä bōte'lyä de
a box	una caja de	ōō'nä kä'hä de
a few	unos	ōō'nōs
a can	una lata de/*Mex* un bote de	ōō'nä lä'tä de/ōōm bo'te de
a pound	una libra de	ōō'nä lē'brä de
a *pack (packet)*	un paquete de	ōōm päke'te de
a pair	un par de	ōōm pär de
a piece	un trozo de	ōōn trō'sō de
a quart	*(approx)* un litro de	ōōn lē'trō de
a quarter pound	*(approx)* cien gramos de	syen grä'mōs de
a roll	un rollo de	ōōn rō'lyō de
a tube	un tubo de	ōōn tōō'bō de
two pounds	*(approx)* un kilo de	ōōn kē'lō de
a yard	*(approx)* un metro de	ōōn me'trō de

That's plenty.	**A little more.**	**Even more.**
Eso basta.	Algo más.	Todavía más.
e'sō bäs'tä	äl'gō mäs	tōdävē'ä mäs

Can you order it for me?
¿Puede encargarlo?
pōō·e'de enkärgär'lō

When will you get it in?
¿Cuándo lo tendrá?
kōō·än'dō lō tendrä'

Can I exchange it?
¿Puedo cambiarlo?
pōō·e'dō kämbyär'lō

I don't like *the shape (color)*.
No me gusta *la forma (el color)*.
nō me gōōs'tä lä fōr'mä (el kōlōr')

This is ...
Esto es ...
es'tō es ...

too big	demasiado grande	....	demäsyä'dō grän'de
too dark	demasiado oscuro	....	demäsyä'dō ōskōō'rō
too expensive	demasiado caro	....	demäsyä'dō kä'rō
too light (pale) ..	demasiado claro	......	demäsyä'dō klä'rō
too narrow	demasiado estrecho	...	demäsyä'dō estre'tshō
too small	demasiado pequeño	...	demäsyä'dō peke'nyō
too wide	demasiado ancho	.....	demäsyä'dō än'tshō
too much	demasiado	....	demäsyä'dō
not enough	muy poco	....	mōō'ē pō'kō

Have you got something *a little nicer (less expensive)*?
¿Tiene algo *mejor (no tan caro)*?
tye'ne äl'gō mehōr' (nō tän kä'rō)

I'll take it.
Me lo llevo.
me lō lye'vō

I like that.	**How much is that?**	**Thanks, that'll be all.**
Me gusta.	¿Cuánto vale?	Gracias, es todo.
me gōōs'tä	kōō·än'tō vä'le	grä'syäs, es tō'dō

Can you send my things to the ... Hotel please?
¿Podría mandarme las cosas al hotel ..., por favor?
pōdrē'ä mändär'me läs kō'säs äl ōtel' ... pōr fävōr

Do you take *credit cards (traveler's checks)*?
¿Aceptan *tarjetas de crédito (cheques de viaje)*?
äsep'tän tärhe'täs de kre'dētō (tshe'kes de vyä'he)

Stores

antique shop	tienda *f* de antigüedades	tyen'dä de äntēgōō·edä'des
art gallery	galería *f* de arte	gälerē'ä de är'te
bakery	panadería *f*	pänäderē'ä
barber shop	peluquería *f*	pelōōkerē'ä
beauty parlor	salón *m* de belleza	sälōn' de belye'sä
bookshop	librería *f*	lēbrerē'ä
butcher shop	carnicería *f*	kärnēserē'ä
candy store	confitería *f*	kōnfēterē'ä
china shop	artículos *mpl* de porcelana	ärtē'kōōlōs de pōrselä'nä
cosmetic salon	instituto *m* de belleza ..	ēnstētōō'tō de belye'sä
dairy	lechería *f*	letsherē'ä
department store	grandes almacenes *mpl*	grän'des älmäse'nes
dressmaker's shop ...	modista *f*	mōdēs'tä
drugstore *(cosmetics & sundries)*	droguería *f*	drōgerē'ä
drugstore (prescription pharmacy)	farmacia *f*	färmä'syä
dry cleaner's	tintorería *f*	tēntōrerē'ä
electrical appliance shop	(tienda *f* de) electrodomésticos *mpl*	(tyen'dä de) elektrōdōmes'tēkōs
fashion boutique	boutique *f*	bō·ōōtē'ke
fish market	pescadería *f*	peskäderē'ä
flower shop	florería *f*/*Sp* floristería *f*	flōrerē'ä/flōrēsterē'ä
fruit market	frutería *f*	frōōterē'ä
furrier	peletero *m*	pelete'rō
furniture store	tienda *f* de muebles ...	tyen'dä de mōō·e'bles
grocery store	tienda *f* de alimentación/*Mex* de abarrotes	tyen'dä de älēmentäsyōn'/de äbärrō'tes
hardware store	ferretería *f*	ferreterē'ä
hat shop	sombrería *f*	sōmbrerē'ä
jewelry store	joyería *f*	*h*ōyerē'ä
laundromat	lavandería *f* automática	lävänderē'ä outōmä'tēkä

laundry	lavandería *f*	lävänderē′ä
leather goods store	artículos *mpl* de piel, marroquinería *f*	ärtē′koolōs de pyel, märrōkēnerē′ä
lingerie shop	lencería *f*, corsetería *f*	lenserē′ä, kōrseterē′ä
liquor store	tienda *f* de bebidas alcohólicas/*Mex* licorerías	tyen′dä de bebē′däs älkō·ō′lēkäs/lēkōrerē′äs
music store	tienda *f* de música	tyen′dä de moo′sēkä
newsdealer	vendedor *m* de periódicos	vendedōr′ de perē·ō′dēkōs
optician	óptico *m*	ōp′tēkō
perfume shop	perfumería *f*	perfoomerē′ä
photo shop	tienda *f* de artículos fotográficos	tyen′dä de ärtē′koolōs fōtōgrä′fēkōs
photographer's studio	fotógrafo *m*	fōtō′gräfō
real estate agency	inmobiliaria *f*	ēnmōbēlyär′yä
record store	tienda *f* de discos/*Mex* discoteca *f*	tyen′dä de dēs′kōs/dēskōte′kä
second-hand bookshop	librería *f* de viejo/*Sp* de ocasión	lēbrerē′ä de vye′hō/de ōkäsyōn′
self-service	autoservicio *m*	outōservē′syō
shoemaker	zapatero *m*	säpäte′rō
shoe store	zapatería *f*	säpäterē′ä
souvenir shop	recuerdos *mpl*	rekoo·er′dōs
sporting goods store	tienda *f* de artículos de deporte	tyen′dä de ärtē′koolōs de depōr′te
stationery store	papelería *f*	päpelerē′ä
supermarket	supermercado *m*	soopermerkä′dō
tabacco store	tabaquería *f*/*Sp* estanco *m*	täbäkerē′ä/estäng′kō
tailor	sastre *m*	säs′tre
textile store	tienda *f* de tejidos	tyen′dä de tehē′dōs
toy store	juguetería *f*	hoogeterē′ä
travel agency	agencia *f* de viajes	ähen′syä de vyä′hes
vegetable market	verdulería *f*	verdoolerē′ä
watchmaker's shop	relojería *f*	relōherē′ä
wine shop	bodega *f*	bōde′gä

Flowers

bouquet	ramo *m* de flores	rä′mō de flō′res
carnation	clavel *m*	klävel′
flower pot	tiesto *m*, maceta *f* ...	tyes′tō, mäse′tä
flowers	flores *fpl*	flō′res
gladioli	gladiolos *mpl*	glädyō′lōs
lilacs	lilas *fpl*	lē′läs
orchids	orquídeas *fpl*	ōrkē′de·äs
roses	rosas *fpl*	rō′säs
tulips	tulipanes *mpl*	tōōlēpä′nes
vase	florero *m*	flōre′rō
violets	violetas *fpl*	vyōle′täs

Bookshop

autobiography	autobiografía *f*	outōbē·ōgräfē′ä
biography	biografía *f*	bē·ōgräfē′ä
book	libro *m*	lē′brō
brochure	folleto *m*	fōlye′tō
catalogue	catálogo *m*	kätä′lōgō
children's book	libro *m* para niños	lē′brō pä′rä nē′nyōs
city map	plano *m* de la ciudad ..	plä′nō de lä syōōdäd′
detective novel	novela *f* policíaca	nōve′lä pōlēsē′äkä
dictionary	diccionario *m*	dēksyōnär′yō
guide book	guía *f*	gē′ä
map	mapa *m*	mä′pä
novel	novela *f*	nōve′lä
paperback	libro *m* de bolsillo	lē′brō de bōlsē′lyō
phrase book	libro *m* de frases	lē′brō de frä′ses
record	disco *m*	dēs′kō
reference book	libro *m* de consulta	lē′brō de kōnsōōl′tä
road map	mapa *m* de carreteras .	mä′pä de kärrete′räs
story book	libro *m* de cuentos	lē′brō de kōō·en′tōs
street map	plano *m* de la ciudad ..	plä′nō de lä syōōdäd′
text book	manual *m*	mänōō·äl′
thriller	novela *f* de suspense, de	nōve′lä de sōōspen′se,
	misterio	de mēster′yō
translation	traducción *f*	trädōōksyōn′
volume	tomo *m*, volumen *m* ...	tō′mō, vōlōō′men

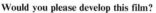

Photo Shop

Would you please develop this film?
¿Puede revelarme este rollo/*Sp* este carrete/por favor?
pōō·e'de revelär'me es'te rō'lyō/es'te kärre'te/pōr fävōr'

One print (enlargement) of each negative, please.
Una copia (una ampliación) de cada negativo, por favor.
ōō'nä kō'pyä (ōō'nä ämplē·äsyōn') de kä'dä negätē'vō, pōr fävōr'

– **three by four inches.**
– siete por diez centímetros.
– sye'te pōr dyes sentē'metrōs

– **three and a half by three and a half inches.**
– nueve por nueve centímetros.
– nōō·e've pōr nōō·e've sen- tē'metrōs

I'd like ...
Quisiera ...
kēsye'rä ...

– **a cartridge film.**
– un rollo/*Sp* un carrete.
– ōōn rō'lyō/ōōn kärre'te

– **a super eight color film.**
– una película súper de ocho milímetros, en color.
– ōō'nä pelē'kōōlä sōō'per de ō'tshō mēlē'metrōs, en kōlōr'

– **a sixteen millimeter color film.**
– una película de dieciséis milíme- tros, en color.
– ōō'nä pelē'kōōlä de dyesēse'ēs mēlē'metrōs en kōlōr'

– **a black and white eight millimeter film.**
– una película de ocho milímetros, en blanco y negro.
– ōō'nä pelē'kōōlä de ō'tshō mēlē'metrōs, en bläng'kō ē ne'grō

– **a thirty-five millimeter film.**
– una película de treinta y cinco milímetros.
– ōō'nä pelē'kōōlä de tre'ēntä e sēng'kō mēlē'metrōs

– **a film for color slides.**
– una película para transparencias/*Sp* diapositivas/en color.
– ōō'nä pelē'kōōlä pä'rä tränspären'syäs/dyäpōsētē'väs/en kōlōr'

– **a *twenty (thirty-six)* exposure film.**
– Un rollo/*Sp* un carrete/*de veinte (de treinta y seis)* fotografías.
– ōōn rō'lyō/ōōn kärre'te/de ve'ēnte (de tre'ēntä ē se'ēs) fōtōgräfē'äs

Would you please put the film in the camera for me?
Por favor, me puede poner el rollo/*Sp* el carrete?
pōr fävōr' me pōō·e'de pōner' el rō'lyō/el kärre'te

camera	máquina *f* fotográfica .	mä′kēnä fōtō-grä′fēkä
color film	película *f* en color	pelē′kōōlä en kōlōr′
daylight color film	película *f* en color para luz diurna	pelē′kōōlä en kōlōr′ pä′rä lōōs dyōōr′nä
develop	revelar, desarrollar	revelär′, desärrōlyär′
diaphragm	diafragma *m*	dyäfräg′mä
8-mm film	película *f* de ocho milímetros	pelē′kōōlä de ō′tshō mēlē′metrōs
enlargement	ampliación *f*	ämplē·äsyōn′
exposure	exposición *f*	ekspōsēsyōn′
exposure meter	fotómetro *m*	fōtō′metrō
film	1) rollo *m/Sp* carrete *m*	rō′lyō/kärre′te
	2) *for movies:* película *f*	pelē′kōōlä
film *(verb)*	filmar	fēlmär′
flash bulb	bombilla *f*, foco *m* de flash	bōmbē′lyä, fō′kō de fläsh
flash cube	cubo *m* de flash	kōō′bō de fläsh
lens	objetivo *m*	ōb*h*etē′vō
movie camera	tomavistas *m*, cámara *f*, filmadora *f*	tōmävēs′täs, kä′märä, fēlmädō′rä
negative	negativo *m*	negätē′vō
paper	papel *m*	päpel′
– glossy	brillante	brēlyän′te
– matte	mate	mä′te
photo	fotografía *f*	fōtōgräfē′ä
photograph *(verb)*	fotografiar	fōtōgräfē·är′
picture	foto *f*	fō′tō
print	copia *f*	kō′pyä
– color print	copia *f* en color	kō′pyä en kōlōr′
reversal film	película *f* reversible	pelē′kōōlä reversē′-ble
roll film	carrete *m*, rollo *m*	kärre′te, rō′lyō
shutter	obturador *m*	ōbtōōrädōr′
shutter (release)	disparador *m*	dēspärädōr′
slide	transparencia *f/Sp* diapositiva *f*	tränspären′syä/dyä-pōsētē′vä
take pictures	sacar fotos/*Mex* retratar	säkär′ fō′tōs/reträ-tär′
view finder	visor *m*	vēsōr′
yellow filter	filtro *m* amarillo	fēl′trō ämärē′lyō

Jeweler

amber	ámbar *m*	äm'bär
bracelet	pulsera *f*	poolse'rä
brooch	broche *m*, prendedor *m*	brō'tshe, prendedōr'
costume jewelry	bisutería *f*, fantasía *f*	bēsōōterē'ä, fäntäsē'ä
cufflinks	gemelos *mpl*/*Mex* man- cuernas *fpl*	*h*eme'lōs/män- koo·er'näs
diamond	diamante *m*	dyämän'te
earclips	zarcillos *mpl*, aretes *mpl*	särsē'lyōs, äre'tes
earrings	pendientes *mpl*	pendyen'tes
emerald	esmeralda *f*	ezmeräl'dä
gold	oro *m*	ō'rō
gold plated	dorado	dōrä'dō
jewelry	joyas *fpl*	*h*ō'yäs
necklace	collar *m*	kōlyär'
pearls	perlas *fpl*	per'läs
ring	sortija *f*, anillo *m*	sōrtē'*h*ä, änē'lyō
ruby	rubí *m*	rōōbē'
sapphire	zafiro *m*	säfē'rō
silver	plata *f*	plä'tä
silver plated	plateado	pläte·ä'dō
wedding ring	anillo *m* de boda	änē'lyō de bō'dä

Clothing

May I try it on?	**I take size …**	**This is …**
¿Me lo puedo probar?	Necesito la talla …	Esto es …
me lō pōō·e'dō prōbär'	nesesē'tō lä tä'lyä …	es'tō es …

too long	demasiado largo	demäsyä'dō lär'gō
too short	demasiado corto	demäsyä'dō kōr'tō
too tight	demasiado estrecho	demäsyä'dō estre'- tshō
too wide	demasiado ancho	demäsyä'dō än'tshō

Can it be altered?

¿Pueden arreglármelo (a mi medida)?
pōō·e'den ärreglär'melō (ä mē me- dē'dä)

… fits just fine (doesn't fit).

… me queda bien (no me queda).
… me ke'dä byen (nō me ke'dä)

apron	delantal *m*	deläntäl′
baby clothes	ropa *f* infantil	rō′pä enfäntēl′
bathing cap	gorro *m* de baño	gō′rrō de bä′nyō
bathing trunks	bañador *m* (*Sp*)	bänyädōr′
bathrobe	bata *f*/*Sp* albornoz *m*	bä′tä/älbōrnōs′
belt	cinturón *m*	sēntōōrōn′
bikini	bikini *m*	bēkē′nē
blouse	blusa *f*	blōō′sä
blue jeans	pantalón *m* vaquero, tejanos *mpl*, jeans *mpl*	päntälōn′ väke′rō, tehä′nōs, *h*ens
bra, brassiére	sostén *m*, sujetador *m*	sōsten′, sōō*h*etädōr′
cap	gorra *f*, gorro *m*	gō′rrä, gō′rrō
coat	sobretodo *m*/abrigo *m*	sōbretō′dō/äbrē′gō
corset	corpiño *m*	kōrpē′nyō
dress	vestido *m*	vestē′dō
dressing gown	bata *f*	bä′tä
fur coat	abrigo *m* de piel	äbrē′gō de pyel
fur jacket	chaquetón *m* de piel	tshäketōn′ de pyel
garter belt	portaligas *m*, liguero *m*	pōrtälē′gäs, lēge′rō
girdle	faja *f*	fä′*h*ä
gloves	guantes *mpl*	gōō-än′tes
handkerchief	pañuelo *m*	pänyōō-e′lō
hat	sombrero *m*	sōmbre′rō
– straw hat	sombrero *m* de paja	sombre′rō de pä′*h*ä
jacket *(lady's)*	chaqueta *f*	tshäke′tä
jacket *(man's)*	saco *m*/*Sp* americana *f*, chaqueta *f*	sä′kō/ämerēkä′nä, tshäke′tä
knee socks	medias *fpl* cortas	me′dyäs kōr′täs
leather coat	abrigo *m* de cuero	äbrē′gō de kōō-e′rō
leather jacket	chaquetón *m* de cuero	tshäketōn′ de kōō-e′rō
lingerie	ropa *f* interior	rō′pä ēnteryōr′
maternity clothes	ropa *f* pre-mamá	rō′pä pre-mämä′
night shirt	camisa *f* de dormir	kämē′sä de dōrmēr′
nightgown	camisón *m*	kämēsōn′
outfit	conjunto *m*	kōn*h*ōōn′tō
pajamas	pijama *m*	pē*h*ä′mä
panties	bragas *fpl*/*Mex* pantaletas *fpl*	brä′gäs/päntäle′täs

pants	pantalón *m*	päntälōn'
pants suit	traje *m* de pantalón	trä'*he* de päntälōn'
panty hose	panty *m/Mex* pantime-dias *fpl*	pän'tē/päntē-me'dyäs
parka	anorac *m*	änōräk'
petticoat	enaguas *fpl*	enä'gŏŏ-äs
raincoat	impermeable *m*	ēmperme·ä'ble
scarf	bufanda *f*	bŏŏfän'dä
shirt	camisa *f*	kämē'sä
– drip-dry	"no se plancha"	nō se plän'tshä
– short-sleeved	de manga corta	de män'gä kōr'tä
shorts	pantalón *m* corto	päntälōn' kōr'tō
skirt	falda *f*	fäl'dä
slacks	pantalones *mpl*	päntälō'nes
slip	combinación *f/Mex* medio fondo *m*	kōmbēnäsyōn'/me'dyō fōn'dō
socks	medias *fpl/Sp* calcetines *mpl*	me'dyäs/kälsetē'nes
sport shirt	camisa *f* deportiva	kämē'sä depōrtē'vä
sportswear	trajes *mpl* de deportes	trä'*hes* de depōr'tes
stockings	medias *fpl*	me'dyäs
stole	estola *f*	estō'lä
suède coat	abrigo *m* de ante	äbrē'gō de än'te
suède jacket	chaqueta *f* de ante	tshäke'tä de än'te
suit *(lady's)*	traje *m* de chaqueta, traje *m* sastre	trä'*he* de tshäke'tä, trä'*he* säs'tre
suit *(man's)*	traje *m*	trä'*he*
summer dress	vestido *m* de verano	vestē'dō de verä'nō
suspenders	tirantes *mpl*	tērän'tes
sweater	jersey *m*, suéter	*her*'sē, sŏŏ·e'ter
swimsuit	traje *m* de baño	trä'*he* de bä'nyō
tie	corbata *f*	kōrbä'tä
track suit	chandal *m/*sudadera *f*	tshändäl'/sŏŏdäde'rä
trench coat	gabardina *f*	gäbärdē'nä
two-piece	de dos piezas	de dōs pye'säs
underpants *(men's)*	calzoncillos *mpl*	kälsōnsē'lyōs
undershirt	camiseta *f*	kämēse'tä
underwear	ropa *f* interior	rō'pä ēnteryōr'
vest	chaleco *m*	tshäle'kō
windbreaker	cazadora *f*	käsädō'rä

Dry Goods

accessories	accesorios *mpl*	äksesōr'yōs
belt	cinturón *m*, correa *f*, cinto *m*	sēntōōrōn', kōrrē'ä, sēn'tō
buckle	hebilla *f*	ebē'lyä
button	botón *m*	bōtōn'
basting thread	hilo *m* para hilvanar	ē'lō pä'rä ēlvänär'
darning thread	hilo *m* para zurcir	ē'lō pä'rä sōōrsēr'
dry goods store	mercería *f*	merserē'ä
elastic	cinta *f* de goma, caucho *m*	sēn'tä de gō'mä, kou'tshō
garters	ligas *fpl*	lē'gäs
hooks and eyes	corchetes *mpl*, ganchos *mpl* de macho y hembra	kōrtshe'tes, gän'tshōs de mä'tshō ē em'brä
lining	forro *m*	fō'rrō
needle	aguja *f*	ägōō'hä
– sewing needle	aguja *f* de coser	ägōō'hä de kōser'
pin	alfiler *m*	älfēler'
ribbon	cinta *f*	sēn'tä
safety pin	imperdible *m/Mex* seguro *m*	ēmperdē'ble/ segōō'rō
scissors	tijeras *fpl*	tēhe'räs
silk thread	hilo *m* de seda	ē'lō de se'dä
snap	botón *m* de presión	bōtōn' de presyōn'
suspenders	tirantes *mpl*	tērän'tes
synthetic thread	hilo *m* sintético	ē'lō sēnte'tēkō
tape	cinta *f*	sēn'tä
tape measure	cinta *f* métrica	sēn'tä me'trēkä
thimble	dedal *m*	dedäl'
thread	hilo *m*	ē'lō
wool	lana *f*	lä'nä
zipper	cierre *m/Sp* cremallera *f*	sye'rre/kremälye're'rä

Fabrics

cloth	paño *m*, tela *f*	pä'nyō, te'lä
corduroy	pana *f*	pä'nä
cotton	algodón *m*	älgōdōn'

fabric	tela *f*	te′lä
– checked	a cuadros	ä kōō·ä′drōs
– printed	estampado	estämpä′dō
– solid color	de un solo color	de ōōn sō′lō kōlōr′
– striped	a rayas, rayado	ä rä′yäs, räyä′dō
flannel	franela *f*	fräne′lä
jersey	jersey *m*	*her*′sē
lace	encaje *m*	enkä′*he*
linen	lino *m*	lē′nō
material	tejido *m*, tela *f*	te*h*ē′dō, te′lä
nylon	nilón *m*	nēlōn′
silk	seda *f*	se′dä
– artificial	seda *f* artificial	se′dä ärtēfēsyäl′
synthetic fibre	fibra *f* sintética	fē′brä sēnte′tēkä
velvet	terciopelo *m*	tersyōpe′lō
wool	lana *f*	lä′nä
– pure wool	lana *f* pura	lä′nä pōō′rä
– pure virgen wool	pura lana *f* virgen	pōō′rä lä′nä vēr′hen
worsted	estambre *m*	estäm′bre

Cleaning, Alterations, Repairs

I'd like to have *this dress (suit)* cleaned.

Quiero que me limpien *este vestido (este traje)*.
kye′rō ke me lēm′pyen es′te vestē′dō (es′te trä′*he*)

I'd like to have these things laundered.

Quisiera mandar a lavar esta ropa.
kēsye′rä mändär′ ä lävär′ es′tä rō′pä

Would you please *press this (take out this stain)*?

¿Podría *plancharme esto (quitarme esta mancha)*?
pōdrē′ä pläntshär′me es′tō (kētär′me es′tä män′tshä)

Could you *darn this (sew on this button)*?

¿Puede *zurcirme esto (coserme este botón)*?
pōō·e′de sōōrsēr′me es′tō (kōser′me es′te bōtōn′)

Could you *lengthen (shorten)* this?

¿Podría *alargarme (acortarme)* esto?
pōdrē′ä älärgär′me (äkōrtär′me) es′tō

Optician

Can you fix these glasses?
¿Puede arreglarme estos lentes, anteojos/*Sp* estas gafas?
pōō·e′de ärreglär′me es′tōs len′tes, änte·ō′*h*ōs/es′täs gä′fäs

Can you replace these lenses?
¿Puede reponer los lentes?
pōō·e′de repōner′ lōs len′tes

I'm *near-sighted (far-sighted)*.
Soy *miope (présbita)*.
soi mē·ō′pe (pres′bētä)

binoculars	prismáticos *mpl*	prēsmä′tēkōs
compass	brújula *f*	brōō′*h*ōōlä
contact lenses	lentes *fpl* de contacto,	len′tes de kōn-
	lentillas *fpl*	täk′tō, lentē′lyäs
frame	montura *f*	mōntōō′rä
glasses	lentes *fpl*, anteojos *mpl*/	len′tes, änte·ō′*h*ōs/
	Sp gafas *fpl*	gä′fäs
sunglasses	lentes *fpl*, anteojos *mpl*/	len′tes, änte·ō′*h*ōs/
	Sp gafas *fpl*/de sol	gä′fäs/de sōl

Stationery

ball point pen	bolígrafo *m*/*Mex* pluma *f*	bōlē′gräfō/plōō′mä
crayons	lápices *mpl* de color	lä′pēses de kōlōr′
envelope	sobre *m*	sō′bre
eraser	goma *f*, borrador *m*	gō′mä, bōrrädōr′
fountain pen	pluma *f*	plōō′mä
glue	pegamento *m*	pegämen′tō
ink	tinta *f*	tēn′tä
pad	bloc *m*	blōk
– scratch pad	bloc *m* de notas	blōk de nō′täs
– sketch pad	bloc *m* de dibujos	blōk de dēbōō′*h*ōs
paper	papel *m*	päpel′
– typewriter paper	papel *m* para la máquina	päpel′ pä′rä lä
	de escribir	mä′kēnä de
		eskrēbēr′
– wrapping paper	papel *m* de envolver/*Sp* de	päpel′ de embōl-
	embalar	ver′/ de embälär′
– writing paper	papel *m* de carta	päpel′ de kär′tä
pencil	lápiz *m*	lä′pēs
photocopies	fotocopias *fpl*	fōtōkō′pyäs

Shoes

I take size ...	**I'd like a pair of ...**
Calzo el número ...	Quisiera un par de ...
käl′sō el nōō′merō ...	kēsye′rä ōōn pär de ...

beach sandals	sandalias *fpl* para la playa	sändä′lyäs pä′rä lä plä′yä
bedroom slippers ..	zapatillas *fpl*, pantuflas *fpl*	säpätē′lyäs, päntōōf′läs
boots	botas *fpl*	bō′täs
ladies' shoes	zapatos *mpl* de señora .	säpä′tōs de senyō′rä
loafers	zapatos *mpl* sin cordones, mocasín *m*	säpä′tōs sēn kōrdō′nes, mōkäsēn′
rubber boots	botas *fpl* de goma	bō′täs de gō′mä
sandals	sandalias *fpl*	sändä′lyäs
tennis shoes, gym shoes	zapatos *mpl* de tenis/*Sp* playeras *fpl*	säpä′tōs de te′nēs/ pläye′räs
walking shoes	botas *fpl* para caminar	bō′täs pä′rä kämēnär′

They're too *tight (wide)*.
Me están *estrechos (anchos)*.
me estän′ estre′tshōs (än′tshōs)

They pinch here.
Me aprietan aquí.
me äprē·e′tän äkē′

Could you fix these shoes for me?
¿Puede arreglarme estos zapatos?
pōō·e′de ärreglär′me es′tōs säpä′tōs

crepe sole	suela *f* de crepe	sōō·e′lä de kre′pe
heel	tacón *m*	täkōn′
– **flat**	bajo	bä′hō
– **high**	alto	äl′tō
in-sole	plantilla *f*	pläntē′lyä
leather	cuero *m*	kōō·e′rō
leather sole	suela *f* de cuero	sōō·e′lä de kōō·e′rō
rubber sole	suela *f* de goma	sōō·e′lä de gō′mä
shoe horn	calzador *m*	kälsädōr′
shoe laces	cordones *mpl*	kōrdō′nes
shoe polish	betún *m*	betōōn′
sole *(noun)*	suela *f*	sōō·e′lä
sole *(verb)*	poner suela	pōner′ sōō·e′lä
suède	ante *m*	än′te

Cigar Store

A pack of ... *cigarettes (tobacco)*, please.
Un paquete/*Mex* una cajetilla/de *cigarrillos*/*Mex cigarros*/*(tabaco)*, por favor.
ōōm päke'te/ōō'nä kä*h*etē'lyä/de sēgärrē'lyōs/sēgä'rrōs/(täbä'kō), pōr fävōr'

Do you have American cigarettes?
¿Tiene cigarrillos/*Mex* cigarros/norteamericanos?
tye'ne sēgärrē'lyōs/sēgä'rrōs/nōr'te·ämerēkä'nōs

A dozen cigars, please.
Doce puros, por favor.
dō'se pōo'rōs, pōr fävōr'

Would you please refill my lighter?
¿Puede llenarme el encendedor?
pōo·e'de lyenär'me el ensendedōr'

Could I please have a light?
¿Tiene fuego?
tye'ne fōo·e'gō

A box of matches, please.
Una caja de fósforos/*Sp* cerillas, *Mex* cerillos/por favor.
ōō'nä kä'*h*ä de fōs'fōrōs/serē'lyäs, serē'lyōs/pōr fävōr'

cigar	puro *m*	pōo'rō
cigarette	cigarrillo *m*/*Mex* cigarro *m*	sēgärrē'lyō/sēgä'rrō
– filtered	con filtro	kōn fēl'trō
– unfiltered	sin filtro	sēn fēl'trō
cigarillo	purito *m*	pōorē'tō
lighter	encendedor *m*	ensendedōr'
lighter fluid	gasolina *f* para el encendedor	gäsōlē'nä pä'rä el ensendedōr'
matches	fósforos *mpl*/*Sp* cerillas *fpl*, *Mex* cerillos *mpl*	fōs'fōrōs/serē'lyäs, serē'lyōs
pipe	pipa *f*	pē'pä
tobacco	tabaco *m*	täbä'kō

Toiletries

after shave	loción *f* para después del afeitado	lōsyōn' pä'rä despōo·es' del äfe·ētä'dō
bath salts	sales *fpl* de baño	sä'les de bä'nyō

bobby pins	horquillas *fpl*, clips *mpl*	ōrkē′lyäs, klĕps
body lotion	loción *f* corporal	lōsyōn′ kōrpōräl′
brush	cepillo *m*	sepē′lyō
comb	peine *m*	pe′ēne
compact	polvera *f*	pōlve′rä
cream	crema *f*	kre′mä
curler	rulero *m/Sp* rulo *m*	rōōle′rō/rōō′lō
deodorant	desodorante *m*	desōdōrän′te
dye	tinte *m*	tēn′te
eye liner	trazado *m* de párpado .	träsä′dō de pär′pädō
eye shadow	sombra *f* de ojos	sōm′brä de ō′hōs
eyebrow pencil	lápiz *m* de cejas	lä′pēs de se′häs
face cream	crema *f* para el cutis . .	kre′mä pä′rä el kōō′tēs
hair spray	spray *m*, laca *f*	spre′ē, lä′kä
hairbrush	cepillo *m* del pelo	sepē′lyō del pe′lō
hairpins	horquillas *fpl*, clips *mpl*	ōrkē′lyäs, klĕps
lipstick	lápiz *m* de labios/*Mex* colorete *m*	lä′pēs de lä′byōs/kōlōre′te
make up	maquillaje *m*	mäkēlyä′he
mascara	pestañina *f*/*Sp* rímel *m*	pestänyē′nä/rē′mel
mirror	espejo *m*	espe′hō
mouthwash	agua *f* dentífrica	ä′gōō·ä dentē′frēkä
nail file	lima *f* de uñas	lē′mä de ōō′nyäs
nail polish	esmalte *m*	ezmäl′te
nail polish remover	quitaesmalte *m*	kētä·ezmäl′te
nail scissors	tijeras *fpl* de uñas	tēhe′räs de ōō′nyäs
perfume	perfume *m*	perfōō′me
powder	polvos *mpl*	pōl′vōs
prophylactics	preservativos *mpl*	preservätē′vōs
razor (safety)	rasuradora *f*/*Sp* maquinilla *f* de afeitar	räsōōrädō′rä/mäkēnē′lyä de äfe·ētär′
– electric shaver . . .	máquina *f* de afeitar eléctrica	mä′kēnä de äfe·ētär′ elek′trēkä
– straight razor . . .	navaja *f*	nävä′hä
razor blades	hojas *fpl* de afeitar, cuchillas *fpl*	ō′häs de äfe·ētär′, kōōtshē′lyäs
sanitary napkins . . .	compresas *fpl*	kōmpre′säs
scissors	tijeras *fpl*	tēhe′räs
shampoo	champú *m*	tshämpōō′
shaving brush	brocha *f* de afeitar	brō′tshä de äfe·ētär′

shaving cream	crema *f* de afeitar	kre'mä de äfe·ētär'
shaving foam	espuma *f* de afeitar ...	espoo'mä de äfe·ētär'
shaving soap	jabón *m* de afeitar	häbōn' de äfe·ētär'
soap	jabón *m*	häbōn'
sponge	esponja *f*	espōn'hä
sun tan cream	crema *f* solar/*Mex* bronceadora *f*	kre'mä sōlär'/brōnse·ädō'rä
– sun tan lotion	loción *f* solar/*Mex* loción *f* para broncearse .	lōsyōn' sōlär'/lōsyōn' pä'rä brōnse·är'se
– sun tan oil	aceite *m* solar/*Mex* bronceador *m*	äse'ēte sōlär'/brōnse·ädōr'
talcum powder	talco *m*	täl'kō
tampon	tampón *m*	tämpōn'
tissues	pañuelos *mpl* de papel .	pänyoo·e'lōs de päpel'
toilet articles, toiletries	artículos *mpl* de tocador	ärtē'koolōs de tōkädōr'
toilet kit	neceser *m*	neseser'
toilet paper	papel *m* higiénico, papel *m* sanitario	päpel' ēhē·e'nēkō, päpel' sänētär'yō
toothbrush	cepillo *m* de dientes ...	sepē'lyō de dyen'tes
toothpaste	pasta *f* de dientes	päs'tä de dyen'tes
towel	toalla *f*	tō·ä'lyä
– bath towel	toalla *f* de baño	tō·ä'lyä de bä'nyō
tweezers	pinzas *fpl*	pēn'säs
wash cloth	manopla *f* de baño	mänō'plä de bä'nyō

Watchmaker

Can you fix this *watch (clock)*?
¿Puede arreglarme el *reloj*?
poo·e'de ärreglär'me el relō(h)'

How much will the repair cost?
¿Cuánto costará la reparación?
koo·än'tō kōstärä' lä repäräsyōn'

It's running *fast (slow)*.
Va *adelantado (atrasado)*.
vä ädeläntä'dō (äträsä'dō)

alarm clock	despertador *m*	despertädōr′
crystal	vidrio *m*/*Sp* cristal *m*	vē′drē·ō/krēstäl′
clock	reloj *m*	relō(h)′
face	esfera *f*	esfe′rä
hands	agujas *fpl*, manecillas *fpl*	agōō′häs, mäne-sē′lyäs
pocket watch	reloj *m* de bolsillo	relō(h)′ de bōlsē′lyō
spring	resorte *m*, muelle *m*	resōr′te, mōō·e′lye
stop watch	cronómetro *m*	krōnō′metrō
watch	reloj *m*	relō(h)′
watch band	pulsera *f* de reloj	pōōlse′rä de relō(h)′
wrist watch	reloj *m* de pulsera/*Mex* de pulso	relō(h)′ de pōōlse′rä/ de pōōl′sō

Sundries

ash tray	cenicero *m*	senēse′rō
bag	saco *m*, bolsa *f*	sä′kō, bōl′sä
ball	pelota *f*	pelō′tä
basket	cesta *f*, cesto *m*, canasta *f*	ses′tä, ses′tō, känäs′tä
battery	pila *f*, bateria *f*	pē′lä, bäterē′ä
beach bag	bolsa *f* para la playa	bōl′sä pä′rä lä plä′yä
bottle opener	destapador *m*/*Sp* abridor *m*	destäpädōr′/äbrēdōr′
briefcase	maletín *m*/*Sp* cartera *f*.	mäletēn′/kärte′rä
camp stove	brasero *m*	bräse′rō
can opener	abrelatas *m*	äbrelä′täs
candle	vela *f*	ve′lä
– beeswax	cera *f* de abejas	se′rä de äbe′häs
candlestick	candelero *m*	kändele′rō
candy	caramelos *mpl*	käräme′lōs
canned goods	conservas *fpl*, enlatados *mpl*	kōnser′väs, enlä-tä′dōs
cassette	cassette *m or f*	käse′te
ceramics	cerámica *f*	serä′mēkä
china	porcelana *f*	pōrselä′nä
computer	ordenador *m*	ōrdenädōr′
corkscrew	sacacorchos *m*, descorchador *m*	säkäkōr′tshōs, deskōrtshädōr′

detergent	detergente *m*	deter*h*en'te
doll	muñeca *f*	mōōnye'kä
figurine	figura *f*	fēgōō'rä
flashlight	linterna *f*/*Mex* foco *m*, luz *f*	lēnter'nä/fō'kō, lōōs
hammock	hamaca *f*	ämä'kä
handbag	bolso *m*, cartera *f*/*Mex* bolsa *f*	bōl'sō, kärte'rä/ bōl'sä
handicrafts	labores *mpl* de mano	läbō'res de mä'nō
kerchief	pañuelo *m* de cabeza	pänyōō·e'lō de käbe'sä
jackknife	navaja *f*	nävä'*h*ä
leash	cuerda *f*	kōō·er'dä
paper napkins	servilletas *fpl* de papel	servēlye'täs de päpel'
phonograph record	disco *m*	dēs'kō
picture	cuadro *m*	kōō·ä'drō
plastic bag	bolsa *f* de plástico	bōl'sä de pläs'tēkō
playing cards	cartas *fpl*, naipes *mpl*	kär'täs, nī'pes
pocket knife	navaja *f*	nävä'*h*ä
recording tape	cinta *f* magnetofónica	sēn'tä mägnetō-fō'nēkä
rucksack	mochila *f*	mōtshē'lä
Scotch tape	cinta *f* adhesiva/*Sp* cinta *f* celo	sēn'tä ädese'vä/ sēn'tä se'lō
sled	trineo *m*	trēne'ō
spot remover	quitamanchas *m*	kētämän'tshäs
string	cuerda *f*, cordel *m*	kōō·er'dä, kōrdel'
stuffed animal	animal *m* de trapo	änēmäl' de trä'pō
suitcase	maleta *f*	mäle'tä
tape recorder	magnetófono *m*/*Mex* grabadora *f*	mägnetō'fōnō/grä-bädō'rä
thermometer	termómetro *m*	termō'metrō
thermos bottle	termo *m*	ter'mō
toy	juguete *m*	*h*ōōge'te
umbrella	paraguas *m*	pärä'gōō·äs
vase	florero *m*	flōre'ō
video camera	cámara *f* de vídeo	kä'märä de vē'de·ō
video cassette	cassette *m or f* de vídeo	käse'te de vē'de·ō
wallet	monedero *m*	mōnede'rō
washing line	cuerda *f*, soga *f*, lazo *m*	kōō·er'dä, sō'gä, lä'sō
wood carvings	tallas *fpl* de madera	tä'lyäs de mäde'rä

Post Office

THE POST OFFICE

Where is the post office?
¿Dónde está el correo/*Sp* la oficina de correos?
dōn´de estä´ el kŏrre´ō/lä ōfēsē´nä de kŏrre´ōs

Where is there a mail box?
¿Dónde hay un buzón?
dōn´de ī ōōn bōōsōn´

How much is airmail for this postcard?
¿Cuánto cuesta esta postal por avión?
kōō·än´tō kōō·es´tä es´tä pōstäl´ pōr ävyōn´

– to Canada.
– para Canadá.
– pä´rä känädä´

– to the United States.
– para los Estados Unidos.
– pä´rä lōs estä´dōs ōōne´dōs

What's the postage for this letter?
¿Cuánto cuesta esta carta?
kōō·än´tō kōō·es´tä es´tä kär´tä

this air mail letter .	esta carta por avión ...	es´tä kär´tä pōr ävyōn´
this letter abroad ..	esta carta para el extranjero	es´tä kär´tä pä´rä el eksträn*he*´rō
this local letter	esta carta local	es´tä kär´tä lōkäl´
this local post card	esta postal local	es´tä pōstäl´ lōkäl´
this parcel	este paquete	es´te päke´te
this post card	esta (tarjeta) postal	es´tä (tär*he*´tä) pōstäl´
this printed matter .	estos impresos	es´tōs ēmpre´sōs
this registered letter	esta carta certificada, registrada	es´tä kär´tä sertēfē-kä´dä, re<u>h</u>ēsträ´dä
this small parcel ...	este paquete pequeño ..	es´te päke´te peke´nyō
this special delivery letter ...	esta carta exprés, urgente	es´tä kär´tä ekspres´, ōōr<u>h</u>en´te

Five two pesos stamps, please.
Cinco timbres *(Mex.)* de dos pesos, por favor.
sēng´kō tēm´bres de dōs pe´sōs, pōr fävōr´

Three twenty pesetas stamps, please.
Tres sellos *(Sp.)* de veinte pesetas, por favor.
tres se´lyōs de ve´ēnte pese´täs, pōr fävōr´

When sending letters or postcards to the US from Latin America or Spain be sure to specify por avión *(air mail), otherwise they might be sent by regular mail* (correo ordinario).

Do you have any special issues?
¿Tiene estampillas/*Sp* sellos, *Mex* timbres/especiales?
tye'ne estämpē'lyäs/se'lyōs, tēm'bres/espesyä'les

This set of stamps, please.
Esta serie, por favor.
es'tä ser'ye, pōr fävōr'

Two of each, please.
Dos de cada uno, por favor.
dōs de kä'dä ōo'nō, pōr fävōr'

Aerograms (thin, prestamped letter sheets) are handy for longer messages, and save the trouble of having to get paper, envelopes and stamps.

I'd like to send this letter by *registered mail (special delivery)*.
Quisiera enviar esta carta *registrada*/*Sp* certificada/(*exprés or urgente*).
kēsye'rä embyär' es'tä kär'tä rehēsträ'dä/sertēfēkä'dä/(ekspres', ōor-hen'te)

How long does it take for *a letter (package)* to get to …?
¿Cuánto tarda *una carta (un paquete)* para …?
kōo·än'tō tär'dä ōo'nä kär'tä (ōom päke'te) pä'rä …

Can I withdraw money from my postal savings account?
¿Puedo sacar dinero con mi libreta postal de ahorros?
pōo·e'dō säkär' dēne'rō kōn mē lēbre'tä pōstäl' de ä·ō'rrōs

Is there any mail here for me?
¿Hay correo para mí?
ī kōrre'ō pä'rä mē

My name is …
Mi nombre es …
mē nōm'bre es …

Where can I *mail (pick up)* a package?
¿Dónde puedo *enviar (recoger)* un paquete?
dōn'de pōo·e'dō embyär' (rekōher') ōom päke'te

*Sign here, please.
Firme aquí, por favor.
fēr'me äkē', pōr fävōr'

Do I need a customs declaration?
¿Hay que hacer una declaración de aduana?
ī ke äser' ōo'nä dekläräsyōn' de ädōo·ä'nä

This is my new address.
Aquí está mi dirección
(*or* están mis señas).
äkē' estä' mē dēreksyōn'
(estän' mēs se'nyäs)

I'd like to have my mail forwarded to …
Quisiera que me remitan mi correspondencia a …
kēsye'rä ke me remē'tän mē kōrrespōnden'syä ä …

Telegrams

A telegram form, please.
Un impreso de telegrama, por favor.
ōōn ēmpre'sō de telegrä'mä, pōr fävōr'

I'd like to send ...
Quisiera poner/*Mex* mandar/ ...
kēsye'rä pōner'/mändär'

a telegram	un telegrama	ōōn telegrä'mä
– with prepaid reply .	con respuesta pagada ..	kōn respōō·es'tä pagä'dä
an urgent telegram ..	un telegrama urgente ..	ōōn telegrä'mä ōōrhen'te

How much do ten words to ... cost?
¿Cuánto cuestan diez palabras para ...?
kōō·än'tō kōō·es'tän dyes pälä'bräs pä'rä ...

When will it arrive at ...?
¿Cuándo llegará a ...?
kōō·än'dō lyegärä' ä ...

Telephone

*It is wise to place long distance calls at the telephone office (*central de teléfonos; *in Mexico,* oficina de teléfonos*), as many hotels make sizeable surcharges for use of the phone.*

Where is the nearest phone?
¿Dónde está el teléfono más próximo?
dōn'de estä' el tele'fōnō mäs prō'ksēmō

May I use your phone?
¿Puedo utilizar su teléfono?
pōō·e'dō ōōtēlēsär' sōō tele'fōnō

Where can I make a phone call?
¿Dónde puedo telefonear?
dōn'de pōō·e'dō telefōne·är'

What's the area code for ...?
¿Cuál es el prefijo de ...?
kōō·äl' es el prefē'hō de ...

The phone book, please.
El directorio/*Sp* la guía (de teléfonos)/, por favor.
el dērektōr'yō/lä gē'ä (de tele'fōnōs)/pōr fävōr'

Can I direct dial to ...?
¿Puedo llamar directamente a ...?
pōō·e'dō lyämär' dērektämen'te ä ...

You can direct dial from both Spain and Mexico.
to US from Mexico: 95 & area code & tel. number
to US from Spain: 07-1 & area code & tel. number

A long distance call to ..., please.
Una llamada a larga distancia/*Sp* una conferencia/, por favor.
ōō'nä lyämä'dä ä lär'gä dēstän'syä/ ōō'nä kōmferen'syä/, pōr fävōr'

How long will that take?
¿Cuánto tiempo tardará?
kōō·än'to tyem'pō tärdärä'

Can I have some coins for the pay phone?
¿Tiene monedas (cambio) para el teléfono público?
tye'ne mōne'däs (käm'byō) pä'rä el tele'fōnō pōō'blēkō

How much does *a local call (call to ...)* cost?
¿Cuánto cuesta *una llamada urbana*/*Mex interna*/*(una llamada a ...)*?
kōō·än'tō kōō·es'tä ōōnä lyämä'dä ōōrbä'nä/ēnter'nä/(ōō'nä lyämä'dä ä ...)

What time does the night rate begin?
¿A partir de qué hora hay tarifa nocturna?
ä pärtēr' de ke ō'rä ī tärē'fä nōktōōr'nä

*What's your number?
¿Cuál es su número?
kōō·äl es sōō nōō'merō

*Your call is ready in booth four.
Su llamada/*Sp* su conferencia/es en la cabina cuatro.
sōō lyämä'dä/sōō kōmferen'syä/es en lä käbē'nä kōō·ä'trō

Wrong number!
¡Se ha equivocado de número!
se ä ekēvōkä'dō de nōō'merō

Please connect me with ...
Póngame con (comuníqueme con) ... por favor.
pōn'gäme kōn (kōmōōnē'keme kōn) ... pōr fävōr'

The line is *busy (out of order)*.
Está *ocupado (interrumpido)*.
estä' ōkōōpä'dō (ēnterrōōmpē'dō)

There's no answer at that number.
El número no contesta.
el nōō'merō nō kōntes'tä

Hello!
¡Díga(me)!/*Mex* ¡Bueno!
dē'gä(me)/bōō·e'nō

May I speak to *Mr. (Mrs., Miss)* ...?
¿Puedo hablar con *el señor (la señora, la señorita)* ...?
pōō·e'dō äblär' kōn el senyōr' (lä senyō'rä, lä senyōrē'tä) ...

Speaking!
¡Soy yo!
soi yō

This is ... speaking.
Aquí ...
äkē' ...

Who is this?
¿Quién habla?
kyen äb'lä

Please hold the line.
¡Por favor, no cuelgue!
pōr fävōr', nō kōō·el'ge

Would you please cancel that call.
Por favor, cancelen/*Sp* anulen/la llamada.
pōr fävōr', känse'len/änōō'len/lä lyämä'dä

Code Alphabet

A	Antonio	[äntō'nyō]	**M**	México	[me'*h*ēkō]
B	Bogotá	[bōgōtä']	**N**	Nicaragua	[nēkärä'gōo·ä]
C	Carmen	[kär'men]	**Ñ**	Ñoño	[nyō'nyō]
CH	Chocolate	[tshōkōlä'te]	**O**	Océano	[ōse'änō]
D	Dora	[dō'rä]	**P**	Paraguay	[pärägōo·ī']
E	Enrique	[enrē'ke]	**Q**	Querido	[kerē'dō]
F	Francisco	[fränsēs'kō]	**R**	Ramón	[rämōn']
G	Gibraltar	[*h*ēbrältär']	**S**	Sábado	[sä'bädō]
H	Historia	[ēstōr'yä]	**T**	Tomás	[tōmäs']
I	Inés	[ēnes']	**U**	Ulises	[ōolē'ses]
J	José	[*h*ōse']	**V**	Venezuela	[venesōo·e'lä]
K	Kilo	[kē'lō]	**W**	Washington	[ōo·äshēngtōn']
L	Lorenzo	[lōren'sō]	**X**	Xiquena	[*h*ēke'nä]
Ll	Llobregat	[lyōbregät']	**Y**	Yegua	[ye'gōo·ä]
			Z	Zaragoza	[särägō'sä]

address	dirección *f*/señas *fpl*	dēreksyōn'/se'nyäs
addressee	destinatario *m*	destēnätär'yō
air mail	correo *m* aéreo	kōrre'ō ä·er'e·ō
area code	prefijo *m*/*Mex* clave *f*	prefē'*h*ō/klä've
c.o.d.	envío *m* contra reembolso	embē'ō kōn'trä re·embōl'sō
counter	ventanilla *f*	ventänē'lyä
customs declaration	declaración *f* de aduana	dekläräsyōn' de ädōo·ä'nä
destination	destino *m*	destē'nō
dial *(noun)*	disco *m*	dēs'kō
dial *(verb)*	marcar	märkär'
direct dialing	llamada *f* directa	lyämä'dä dērek'tä
general delivery	lista *f* de correos	lēs'tä de kōrre'ōs
insured mail	correo *m* asegurado	kōrre'ō äsegōorä'dō
letter	carta *f*	kär'tä
local call	llamada *f* urbana/*Mex* interna	lyämä'dä ōorbä'nä/ēnter'nä
long distance call	conferencia *f*/*Mex* llamada *f* de larga distancia	kōmferen'syä/lyämä'dä de lär'gä dēstän'syä
mail box	buzón *m*	bōosōn'

operator	telefonista *m* & *f*/*Mex* operador *m* & *f*	telefōnēs'tä/ōperä- dōr'
package	paquete *m*	päke'te
parcel	paquete *m*	päke'te
post card	postal *f* or tarjeta *f* postal	pōstäl', tärhe'tä pōstäl'
postage	porte *m*, franqueo *m*	pōr'te, frängke'ō
postal clerk	empleado *m* de correos .	emple·ä'dō de kōrre'ōs
postal savings book	libreta *f* postal de aho- rros	lēbre'tä pōstäl' de ä·ō'rrōs
postman	cartero *m*	kärte'rō
printed matter .	impresos *mpl*	ēmpre'sōs
receipt	recibo *m*/*Sp* resguardo *m*	resē'bō/rezgo͞o·är'dō
register	certificar, registrar	sertēfēkär', rehēsträr'
registered letter	carta *f* certificada, registrada	kär'tä sertēfēkä'dä, rehēsträ'dä
registered parcel with declared value	paquete *m* registrado/*Sp* certificado/con declara- ción de valor	päke'te rehēsträ'dō/ sertēfēkä'dō/kōn dekläräsyōn' de välōr'
return postage .	porte *m* de vuelta	pōr'te de vo͞o·el'tä
sender	remitente *m*	remēten'te
small parcel	paquete *m* pequeño	päke'te peke'nyō
special delivery .	exprés, urgente, entrega *f* inmediata	ekspres', o͞orhen'te, entre'gä ēnmedyä'tä
special delivery letter	carta *f* exprés, carta *f* de entrega inmediata/*Sp* urgente	kär'tä ekspres', kär'tä de entre'gä ēnmedyä'tä/ o͞orhen'te
special issue stamp	estampilla *f*/*Sp* sello *m*, *Mex* timbre *m*/conmemo- rativo	estämpē'lyä/se'lyō, tēm'bre/kōnmemō- rätē'vō
stamp	estampilla *f*/*Sp* sello *m*, *Mex* timbre *m*	estämpē'lyä/se'lyō, tēm'bre
stamp (*verb*) ...	franquear	frängke·är'
stamp machine .	distribuidor *m* automá- tico de estampillas/*Sp* sellos, *Mex* timbres	dēstrēbo͞o·ēdōr' outō- mä'tēkō de estämpē'- lyäs/se'lyōs, tēm'bres
telegram	telegrama *m*	telegrä'mä
telephone	teléfono *m*	tele'fōnō
unstamped	sin franquear	sēn frängke·är'
value declaration	declaración *f* de valor ...	dekläräsyōn' de välōr'

BANK, CURRENCY EXCHANGE

Where can I change some money?
¿Dónde se puede cambiar dinero?
dōn'de se poō·e'de kämbyär' dēne'rō

Where is the bank?
¿Dónde está el banco?
dōn'de estä' el bäng'kō

I need a hundred dollars in ...
Quisiera cambiar cien dólares en ...
kēsye'rä kämbyär' syen dō'läres en ...

How much will I get for ...?
¿Cuánto me dan por ...?
koō·än'tō me dän pōr ...

What's the rate of exchange?
¿Cómo es el cambio?
kō'mō es el käm'byō

Can you change ... into *pesos (pesetas)* for me?
¿Puede cambiar ... en *pesos (pesetas)*?
poō·e'de kämbyär' ... en pe'sōs (pese'täs)

Could I have some change, please?
¿Tiene dinero suelto (cambio), por favor?
tye'ne dēne'rō soō·el'tō (käm'byō), pōr fävōr'

Can you change this?
¿Puede cambiar esto?
poō·e'de kämbyär' es'tō

I'd like to cash this *check (traveler's check)*.
Quisiera cobrar este *cheque (cheque de viaje)*.
kēsye'rä kōbrär' es'te tshe'ke (tshe'ke de vyä'he)

Has some money arrived for me?
¿Ha llegado dinero para mí?
ä lyegä'do dēne'rō pä'rä mē

amount	importe *m*	ēmpōr'te
bank	banco *m*	bäng'kō
bank account	cuenta *f* bancaria	koō·en'tä bäng-kär'yä
bank charges	derechos *mpl* del banco	dere'tshōs del bäng'kō
bank draft	cheque *m* del banco	tshe'ke del bäng'kō
bank note	billete *m* de banco	bēlye'te de bäng'kō
bank transfer	giro *m* bancario	hē'rō bängkär'yō
bill	billete *m*	bēlye'te
branch manager	gerente *m or* director *m* de la sucursal	heren'te (dērektōr') de lä soōkoōrsäl'

cash *(verb)*	cobrar	kōbrär′
change	cambio *m*	käm′byō
check	cheque *m*, talón *m*	tshe′ke, tälōn′
coin	moneda *f*	mōne′dä
credit	crédito *m*	kre′dētō
– **take out a loan**	tomar crédito	tōmär′ kre′dētō
credit card	tarjeta *f* de crédito	tär*h*e′tä de kre′dētō
currency	moneda *f*	mōne′dä
deposit	ingresar, consignar	ēngresär′, kōnsēgnär′
foreign currency	divisas *fpl*	dēvē′säs
form	formulario *m*	fōrmŌŌlär′yō
in cash	al contado	äl kōntä′dō
money	dinero *m*	dēne′rō
– **Canadian dollars**	dólares *mpl* canadienses	dō′läres känädyen′ses
– **English pounds**	libras *fpl* inglesas	lē′bräs ēngle′säs
– **American dollars**	dólares *mpl* americanos	dō′läres ämerēkä′nōs
money exchange	cambio *m* de moneda	käm′byō de mōne′dä
mortgage	hipoteca *f*	ēpōte′kä
on credit	al fiado, al crédito	äl fyä′dō, äl kre′dētō
pay out	pagar	pägär′
payment	pago *m*	pä′gō
rate of exchange	tipo *m* de cambio	tē′pō de käm′byō
receipt	recibo *m*	resē′bō
savings bank	caja *f* de ahorros	kä′*h*ä de ä·ō′rrōs
savings book	libreta *f* de ahorros	lēbre′tä de ä·ō′rrōs
security	fianza *f*	fyän′sä
share of stock	acción *f*	äksyōn′
signature	firma *f*	fēr′mä
stock	acciones *fpl*	äksyō′nes
telegraphic	telegráfico	telegrä′fēkō
teller's window	caja *f*	kä′*h*ä
transfer	giro *m*	*h*ē′rō
traveler's check	cheque *m* de viaje	tshe′ke de vyä′*h*e
withdraw	retirar	retērär′

POLICE STATION

STOP
POLICE

Reporting

I'd like to report …
Quisiera denunciar …
kēsye′rä denōōnsyär′ …

an accident	un accidente	ōōn äksēden′te
a blackmail attempt	una extorsión, un chantaje	ōō′nä ekstōrsyōn′, ōōn tshäntä′he
a hold-up	un atraco	ōōn äträ′kō
a kidnapping	un secuestro	ōōn sekōō·es′trō
a loss	una pérdida	ōō′nä per′dēdä
a murder	un asesinato	ōōn äsesēnä′tō
a theft	un robo	ōōn rō′bō

My … has been stolen.
Me han robado …
me än rōbä′dō …

I lost my …
He perdido mi …
e perdē′dō mē …

bag	el saco, la bolsa	el sä′kō, lä bōl′sä
billfold	la cartera	lä kärte′rä
bracelet	la pulsera	lä pōōlse′rä
briefcase	la cartera de documentos	lä kärte′rä de dōkōōmen′tōs
camera	la máquina fotográfica	lä mä′kēnä fōtōgrä′fēkä
car keys	las llaves del carro/*Sp* del coche	läs lyä′ves del kä′rrō/del kō′tshe
handbag	el bolso/*Mex* la bolsa	el bōl′sō/lä bōl′sä
jewelry	las joyas	läs hō′yäs
key	la llave	lä lyä′ve
money	el dinero	el dēne′rō
necklace	el collar	el kōlyär′
purse	el bolso/*Mex* la bolsa	el bōl′sō/lä bōl′sä
ring	el anillo, la sortija	el änē′lyō, lä sōrtē′hä
suitcase	la maleta	lä mäle′tä
umbrella	el paraguas	el pärä′gōō·äs
wallet	el monedero	el mōnede′rō
watch	el reloj	el relō(h)′
– wrist watch	el reloj de pulsera/*Mex* de pulso	el relō(h)′ de pōōlse′rä/de pōōl′sō

I have nothing to do with it *(this business)*.
Yo no tengo nada que ver con *eso (ese asunto)*.
yō nō ten'gō nä'dä ke ver kōn e'sō (e'se äsōōn'tō)

I'm innocent.
Yo soy inocente.
yō soi ēnōsen'te

I didn't do it.
Yo no lo he hecho.
yō nō lō e e'tshō

How long do I have to stay here?
¿Cuánto tiempo debo quedarme aquí?
kōō·än'tō tyem'pō de'bō kedär'me äkē'

This man is *bothering (following)* me.
Este hombre me está *molestando (persiguiendo)*.
es'te ōm'bre me estä' mōlestän'dō (persēgyen'dō)

arrest	detener	detener'
attorney	abogado *m*	äbōgä'dō
confiscate	confiscar	kōnfēskär'
court	tribunal *m*	trēbōōnäl'
crime	delito *m*	delē'tō
criminal	delincuente *m*	delēnkōō·en'te
custody	detención *f*	detensyōn'
– protective custody	custodia *f* preventiva	kōōstō'dyä preventē'vä
drugs	drogas *fpl*	drō'gäs
hold-up	atraco *m*	äträ'kō
judge	juez *m*	hōō·es'
lawyer	abogado *m*	äbōgä'dō
narcotics	narcóticas *fpl*	närkō'tēkäs
pickpocket	ratero *m*	räte'rō
police	policía *f*	pōlēsē'ä
police car	carro *m/Sp* coche *m*/de la policía	kä'rrō/kō'tshe/de lä pōlēsē'ä
police station	estación *f* de policía/*Sp* comisaría *f*	estäsyōn' de pōlēsē'ä/kōmēsärē'ä
prison	cárcel *f*	kär'sel
smuggling	contrabando *m*	kōnträbän'dō
thief	ladrón *m*	lädrōn'
verdict	sentencia *f*	senten'syä

BEAUTY SHOP, BARBER SHOP

Beauty Shop

May I make an appointment for Saturday?
¿Puede darme hora para el sábado?
pōō·e'de där'me ō'rä pä'rä el sä'bädō

Would you put me down for a permanent wave?
¿Puede hacerme la permanente?
pōō·e'de äser'me lä permänen'te

For tomorrow?
¿Para mañana?
pä'rä mänyä'nä

Will I have to wait?
¿Tengo que esperar?
ten'gō ke esperär'

Will it take long?
¿Tardará mucho tiempo?
tärdärä' mōō'tshō tyem'pō

Wash and set, please.
Lavar y enrular/*Sp* marcar/, por favor.
lävär' ē enrōōlär'/märkär'/, pōr fävōr'

I'd like a permanent (set), please.
Quisiera una permanente.
kēsye'rä ōō'nä permänen'te

Please set my hair for the evening.
Quisiera un peinado de noche.
kēsye'rä ōōm pe·ēnä'dō de nō'tshe

Please *dye (rinse)* my hair.
Por favor, podría *teñirme el pelo (dar reflejos al pelo)*.
pōr fävōr', pōdrē'ä tenyēr'me el pe'lō (där refle'hōs äl pe'lō)

Please cut my hair a little shorter.
Córteme el pelo un poco, por favor.
kōr'teme el pe'lō ōōm pō'kō, pōr fävōr'

Just trim it, please.
Sólo las puntas.
sō'lō läs pōōn'täs

Please cut it wet.
Corte en mojado, por favor.
kōr'te en mō*h*ä'dō, pōr fävōr'

Please pin it up in a bun.
Hágame el moño, por favor.
ä'gäme el mō'nyō, pōr fävōr'

Please tease it a little on the *top (sides)*.

Por favor, enredar/*Sp* cardar/sólo un poco *arriba (a los lados)*.
pōr fävōr', enredär'/kärdär'/sō'lō ōōm pō'kō ärrē'bä (ä lōs lä'dōs)

It's a little too hot under the drier.

Hace demasiado calor bajo el secador.
ä'se demäsyä'dō kälōr' bä'*h*ō el sekädōr'

No *setting lotion (hair spray)*, please.

No ponga *fijador (laca)*, por favor.
nō pōn'gä fē*h*ädōr' (lä'kä), pōr fävōr'

Could you give me a *manicure (pedicure)*?

¿Puede hacerme la *manicura (pedicura)*?
pōō·e'de äser'me lä mänēkōō'rä (pedēkōō'rä)

Please file my nails *round (to a point)*.

Hágame las uñas *redondas (en punta)*.
ä'gäme läs ōō'nyäs redōn'däs (em pōōn'tä)

Just polish them, please.	***With (without)* nail polish.**
Por favor, sólo pulir.	*Con (sin)* esmalte.
pōr fävōr', sō'lō pōōlēr'	kōn (sēn) ezmäl'te

Please *tweeze (shave)* my eyebrows.

Por favor, *maquilleme (depileme)* las cejas.
pōr fävōr', mäkē'lyeme (depē'leme) läs se'*h*äs

A *facial mask (face massage)*, please.

Por favor, *una mascarilla (un masaje facial)*.
pōr fävōr', ōō'nä mäskärē'lyä (ōon mäsä'*h*e fäsyäl')

Would you please put *this hairpiece (wig)* on for me?

Por favor, póngame *este postizo (esta peluca)*?
pōr fävōr', pōn'gäme es'te pōstē'sō (es'tä pelōō'kä)

Yes, thank you, that's just fine.	**Very nice!**
Sí, gracias, está bien así.	¡Muy bien!
sē, grä'syäs, estä' byen äse'	mōō'ē byen

Barber Shop

(Shave and) a haircut, please.
Cortar el pelo (y afeitar), por favor.
kōrtär' el pe'lō (ē äfe·ētär'), pōr fävōr'

Not too short, please.	**(Very) short, please.**
No demasiado corto, por favor.	(Muy) corto, por favor.
nō demäsyä'dō kōr'tō, pōr fävōr'	(moo'ē) kōr'tō, pōr fävōr'

– at the back.	– on top.	– in front.	– on the sides.
– por detras.	– arriba.	– por delante.	– a los lados.
– pōr deträs'	– ärrē'bä	– pōr delän'te	– ä lōs lä'dōs

A razor cut, please.	*With (without) part, please.*
Un corte a navaja, por favor.	*Con (sin) raya (carrera, línea),* por favor.
ōōn kōr'te ä nävä'hä, pōr fävōr'	kōn (sēn) rä'yä (kärre'rä, lē'ne·ä), pōr fävōr'

Part it on the *left (right)*, please.
Hágame la raya (carrera, línea) a la *izquierda (derecha).*
ä'gäme lä rä'yä (kärre'rä, lē'ne·ä) ä lä ēskyer'dä (dere'tshä)

A shampoo too, please.	**Scalp massage, please.**
Láveme también el pelo, por favor.	Un poco de masaje, por favor.
lä'veme tämbyen' el pe'lō, pōr fävōr'	ōōm pō'kō de mäsä'he, pōr fävōr'

Would you trim my *beard (moustache)*, please.
Arrégleme un poco *la barba (el bigote)*, por favor.
ärre'gleme ōōm pō'kō lä bär'bä (el bēgō'te), pōr fävōr'

Just a shave, please.	**Please don't shave against the grain.**
Sólo afeitar, por favor.	No me afeite a contrapelo, por favor.
sō'lō äfe·ētär', pōr fävōr'	no me äfe'ēte ä kōnträpe'lō, pōr fävōr'

Some hair tonic (a little brilliantine), please.
Loción (un poco de brillantina), por favor.
lōsyōn' (ōōm pō'kō de brēlyäntē'nä), pōr fävōr'

Please leave it dry.	**Yes, thank you, that's just great.**
No los moje, por favor.	Si, gracias, está bien asi.
nō lōs mō'he, pōr fävōr'	sē, grä'syäs, estä' byen äsē'

barber	peluquero *m*	pelōōke'rō
beard	barba *f*	bär'bä
beauty parlor . . .	salón *m* de belleza	sälōn' de belye'sä
brilliantine	brillantina *f*	brēlyäntē'nä
comb *(noun)*	peine *m*	pe'ēne
comb *(verb)*	peinar	pe·ēnär'
curls	rizos *mpl*	rē'sōs
cut	cortar	kōrtär'
dandruff	caspa *f*	käs'pä
dye	teñir	tenyēr'
hair	pelo *m*	pe'lō
– **dry hair**	seco	se'kō
– **greasy hair**	grasiento	gräsyen'tō
haircut	corte *m* de pelo	kōr'te de pe'lō
hair-do	peinado *m*	pe·ēnä'dō
hairdresser	peluquero *m*	pelōōke'rō
– **men's**	peluquero *m* de caba-	de käbälye'rōs
	lleros	
– **women's**	peluquero *m* de señoras .	de senyō'räs
hair drier	secador *m*	sekädōr'
hair loss	caída *f* del pelo	kä·ē'dä del pe'lō
hair style	peinado *m*	pe·ēnä'dō
hairpiece	postizo *m*	pōste'sō
lock of hair	mechón *m*	metshōn'
manicure	manicura *f*	mänēkōō'rä
moustache	bigote *m*	bēgō'te
part	raya *f*, carrera *f*, línea *f*	rä'yä, kärre·rä,
		lē'ne·ä
pedicure	pedicura *f*	pedēkōō'rä
permanent wave . . .	permanente *f*	permänen'te
scalp massage . . .	masaje *m* de la cabeza .	mäsä'he de lä käbe'sä
set	enrular/*Sp* marcar	enrōōlär'/märkär'
shave	afeitar	äfe·ētär'
sideburns	patillas *fpl*	pätē'lyäs
tease	cardar, crespar, enredar	kärdär', krespär',
		enredär'
tint	dar color, dar reflejos .	där kōlōr', där re-
		fle'hōs
toupé	postizo *m*	pōste'sō
wash	lavar	lävär'
wig	peluca *f*	pelōō'kä

HEALTH

Pharmacy

Where is the nearest pharmacy?
¿Dónde está la farmacia más cercana?
dōn'de estä' lä färmä'syä mäs serkä'nä

Which pharmacy has night duty?
¿Qué farmacia está de guardia *or* de turno?
ke färmä'syä est'ä de gōō·är'dyä, de tōōr'nō

I'd like this medicine, please.
Quisiera este medicamento, por favor.
kēsye'rä es'te medēkämen'tō, pōr fävōr'

Please give me something for …	**I'd like …**
Por favor, déme algo contra …	Quisiera …
pōr fävōr', de'me äl'gō kōn'trä …	kēsye'rä …

Do I need a prescription for this medicine?
¿Se necesita receta (fórmula) para este medicamento?
se nesesē'tä rese'tä (fōr'mōōlä) pä'rä es'te medēkämen'tō

Can you order this medicine for me?
¿Podría encargarme este medicamento?
pōdrē'ä enkärgär'me es'te medēkämen'tō

Where can I pick it up?	**Can I wait for it?**
¿Dónde puedo recogerlo?	¿Puedo esperar?
dōn'de pōō·e'dō rekōher'lō	pōō·e'dō esperär'

for external use	....	para uso externo ....
for internal use	....	para uso interno ....
before meals	....	antes de las comidas ....
after meals	....	después de las comidas ....
three times a day	....	tres veces al día ....
as prescribed	....	según prescripción médica ......
on an empty stomach	.....	en ayunas ....

Medication and Bandages

absorbent cotton	algodón *m* hidrófilo ...	älgōdōn' ēdrō'fēlō
adhesive bandage	tela *f* adhesiva	te'lä ädesē'vä
adhesive tape	esparadrapo *m*	espärädrä'pō
alcohol	alcohol *m*	älkō-ōl'
ampule	ampolla *f*	ämpō'lyä
antidote	antídoto *m*	äntē'dōtō
aspirin	aspirina *f*	äspērē'nä
bandage	vendaje *m*/*Mex* venda *f*	vendä'*he*/ven'dä
bicarbonate of soda ..	bicarbonato *m* sódico .	bēkärbōnä'tō sō'dēkō
boric acid ointment ..	agua *f* bórica	ä'gōō·ä bō'rēkä
burn ointment	pomada *f* para quemaduras	pōmä'dä pä'rä kemädōō'räs
camomile tea	manzanilla *f*	mänsänē'lyä
castor oil	aceite *m* de ricino	äse'ēte de rēsē'nō
charcoal pills	pastillas *fpl* de carbón .	pästē'lyäs de kärbōn'
contraceptive pills ...	píldoras *fpl* anticonceptivas	pēl'dōräs äntēkōnseptē'väs
corn plaster	parche *m* para callos ..	pär'tshe pä'rä kä'lyōs
cough medicine	calmante *m* de la tos ..	kälmän'te de lä tōs
cough syrup	jarabe *m* para tos	*h*ärä'be pä'rä tōs
dextrose	dextrosa *f*	dekstrō'sä
digestive tablets	pastillas *fpl* para el estómago	pästē'lyäs pä'rä el estō'mägō
digestive tonic	gotas *fpl* para el estómago	gō'täs pä'rä el estō'mägō
disinfectant	desinfectante *m*	desēnfektän'te
diuretic	diurético *m*	dyōōre'tēkō
drops	gotas *fpl*	gō'täs
ear drops	gotas *fpl* para los oídos	gō'täs pä'rä lōs ō·ēdōs
elastic bandage	venda *f* elástica	ven'dä eläs'tēkä
elastic stocking	media *f* elástica	me'dyä eläs'tēkä
emetic	emético *m*	eme'tēkō
enema	enema *f*	ene'mä
eye drops	gotas *fpl* para los ojos .	gō'täs pä'rä lōs ō'*h*ōs

eye ointment	pomada *f* para los ojos	pōmä′dä pä′rä lōs ō′hōs
fever cure	antipirético *m*, antitérmico *m*	äntēpēre′tēkō, än-tēter′mēkō
first-aid kit	botiquín *m*	bōtēkēn′
gargle	gárgaras *fpl*	gär′gäräs
gauze bandage	gasa *f*	gä′sä
glycerine	glicerina *f*	glēserē′nä
hydrogen peroxide	agua *f* oxigenada	ä′gōō·ä ōksēhenä′dä
injection	inyección *f*	ēnyeksyōn′
insect repellent	insecticida *m*	ēnsektēsē′dä
iodine	yodo *m*	yō′dō
laxative	laxante *m*	läksän′te
liniment	linimento *m*	lēnēmen′tō
medicine	medicina *f*	medēsē′nä
mouthwash	agua *f* para gargarismo	ä′gōō·ä pä′rä gär-gärēz′mō
ointment	pomada *f*	pōmä′dä
pain pills	analgésicos *mpl*	änälhe′sēkōs
peppermint	menta *f*	men′tä
pill	pastillas *fpl*, píldoras *fpl*	pästē′lyäs, pēl′dōräs
powder	talco *m*	täl′kō
prophylactics	preservativos *mpl*	preservätē′vōs
quinine	quinina *f*	kēnē′nä
remedy	remedio *m*	reme′dyō
salve	pomada *f*	pōmä′dä
sanitary napkins	compresas *fpl*	kōmpre′säs
sleeping pills	somníferos *mpl*	sōmnē′ferōs
suppository	supositorio *m*/*Mex a* calillo *m*	sōōpōsētōr′yō/kä-lē′lyō
tablet	comprimido *m*	kōmprēmē′dō
talcum powder	talco *m*	täl′kō
thermometer	termómetro *m*	termō′metrō
tincture of iodine	tintura *f* de yodo	tēntōō′rä de yō′dō
tonic	tónico *m*	tō′nēkō
tranquilizer	calmante *m*, sedante *m*	kälmän′te, sedän′te
valerian drops	gotas *fpl* de valeriana	gō′täs de väleryä′nä
vaseline	vaselina *f*	väselē′nä
vitamin pills	pastillas *fpl* de vitaminas	pästē′lyäs de vētämē′näs
wound salve	ungüento *m*	ōōngōō·en′tō

The doctor is in

Quick, call a doctor!
¡Pronto! Llame a un médico.
prōn'tō lyä'me ä ōōn me'dēkō

Is there a doctor in the house?
¿Hay un médico aquí?
ī ōōn me'dēkō äkē'

Please get a doctor!
¡Por favor, busque un médico!
pōr fävōr', bōōs'ke ōōn me'dēkō

Where is there a doctor?
¿Dónde hay un médico?
dōn'de ī ōōn me'dēkō

Can he come here?
¿Puede venir aquí?
pōō•e'de venēr' äkē'

Where is there a hospital?
¿Dónde hay un hospital?
dōn'de ī ōōn ōspētäl'

When does the doctor have office hours?
¿A qué hora tiene consulta?
ä ke ō'rä tye'ne kōnsōōl'tä

Would you please come to the ...
Por favor, venga a ...
pōr fävōr', ven'gä ä ...

I'm sick.
Estoy enfermo.
estoi' enfer'mō

My husband (my wife, our son, our daughter) is sick.
Mi esposo (mi esposa, nuestro hijo, nuestra hija)
está enfermo (-a).
mē espō'sō (mē espō'sä, nōō•es'trō ē'hō, nōō•es'-
trä ē'hä) estä' enfer'mō (-ä)

doctor	médico *m*	me'dēkō
dermatologist	dermatólogo *m*	dermätō'lōgō
ear, nose and throat specialist	otorrinolaringólogo *m* .	ōtōrrēnōlärēn-gō'lōgō
eye doctor	optometrista *m*	ōptōmetrēs'tä
general practitioner .	médico *m* general	me'dēkō heneräl'
gynecologist	ginecólogo *m*	hēnekō'lōgō
internist *m*	internista *m*	ēnternēs'tä
neurologist	neurólogo *m*	ne•ōōrō'lōgō
orthopedist	ortopedista *m*	ōrtōpedēs'tä
pediatrician	pediatra *m*	pedyä'trä

psychiatrist	psiquiatra *m*	sēkyä′trä
psychologist	psicólogo *m*	sēkō′lōgō
specialist	especialista *m*	espesyälēs′tä
surgeon	cirujano *m*	sērōō*h*ä′nō
urologist	urólogo *m*	ōōrō′lōgō
doctor's office	consultorio *m*	kōnsōōltōr′yō
office hours	horas *fpl* de consulta . .	ō′räs de kōnsōōl′tä
waiting room	sala *f* de espera	sä′lä de espe′rä

I haven't felt well the last few days.
Hace algunos días que no me encuentro bien.
ä′se älgōō′nōs dē′äs ke nō me enkōō·en′trō byen

My *head (throat, stomach)* hurts.
Me duele *la cabeza (la garganta, el estómago)*.
me dōō·e′le lä käbe′sä (lä gärgän′tä, el estō′mägō)

It hurts here.
Me duele aquí.
me dōō·e′le äkē′

I've got a *severe (sharp, dull)* pain here.
Tengo aquí dolores *fuertes (agudos, sordos)*.
ten′gō äkē′ dōlō′res fōō·er′tes (ägōō′dōs, sōr′dōs)

I've got a (high) fever. **I've caught a cold.**
Tengo (mucha) fiebre. Estoy resfriado./ *Sp* Estoy constipado.
ten′gō (mōō′tshä) fye′bre estoi′ resfrē·ä′dō/estoi′ kōnstēpä′dō

I can't handle *the heat (food)* here.
Me sienta mal *el calor (la comida)*.
me syen′tä mäl el kälōr′ (lä kōmē′dä)

I must have done something to my stomach. I ate . . .
Tengo una indigestión. Comí . . .
ten′gō ōō′nä ēndē*h*estyōn′ kōmē′ . . .

I threw up. **I feel sick.**
Vomité. Me siento mal.
vomēte′ me syen′tō mäl

I have *no appetite (diarrhea)*. **I'm constipated.**
No tengo apetito. (Tengo diarrea.) Tengo estreñimiento.
nō ten′gō äpetē′tō (ten′gō dyärre′ä) ten′gō estrenyēmyen′tō

My eyes hurt.
Me duelen los ojos.
me doo·e'len lōs ō'hōs

I have an earache.
Me duele el oído.
me doo·e'le el ō·ē'dō

I can't sleep.
No puedo dormir.
nō poo·e'dō dōrmēr'

I feel nauseated.
Me mareo.
me märe'ō

I've got chills.
Tengo escalofríos.
ten'gō eskälōfrē'ōs

I can't move ...
No puedo mover ...
nō poo·e'dō mōver' ...

I'm diabetic.
Soy diabético.
soi dyäbe'tēkō

I'm expecting a baby.
Estoy embarazada.
estoi' embäräsä'dä

I fell.
Me he caído.
me e kī'dō

I sprained my ankle.
Me he torcido el tobillo.
me e tōrsē'dō el tōbē'lyō

... is (are) swollen.
... *está(n)* hinchado*(s)*.
... estä(n)' ēntshä'dō(s)

Is it serious?
¿Es algo grave?
es äl'gō grä've

I'm feeling *a little (much)* better.
Ya me siento *algo (mucho)* mejor.
yä me syen'tō äl'gō (moo'tshō) mehōr'

Could you give me a prescription for ...?
¿Puede recetarme ...?
poo·e'de resetär'me ...

I'd like to be vaccinated against ...
Quiero vacunarme contra ...
kye'rō väkoonär'me kōn'trä ...

The doctor will tell you:

Take your clothes off, please.
Quítese la ropa, por favor.
kē'tese lä rō'pä, pōr fävōr'

Breathe deeply.
Respire profundamente.
respē're prōfoondämen'te

Does this hurt?
¿Le duele aquí?
le doo·e'le äkē'

Open your mouth.
Abra la boca.
ä'brä lä bō'kä

Let me see your tongue.
¡Saque la lengua!
sä′ke lä len′gōō·ä

Cough!
¡Tosa!
tō′sä

What have you been eating?
¿Qué ha comido usted?
ke ä kōmē′dō ōōste′

How long have you been ill?
¿Desde cuándo está enfermo?
dez′de kōō·än′dō estä′ enfer′mō

We'll have to do a *blood test (urinalysis)*.
Es necesario hacer un *análisis de sangre (de orina)*.
es nesesär′yō äser′ ōōn änä′lēsēs de säng′gre (de ōrē′nä)

You're going to need an operation.
Tiene que someterse a una operación.
tye′ne ke sōmeter′se ä ōō′nä ōperäsyōn′

I'll have to refer you to ...
Le remitiré a ...
le remētēre′ ä ...

You must stop *drinking (smoking)*.
Debe abstenerse de *beber (fumar)*.
de′be äbstener′se de beber′ (fōōmär′)

You'll have to stay *in bed (on a strict diet)*.
Debe *quedarse en cama (seguir una dieta rigurosa)*.
de′be kedär′se en kä′mä (segēr′ ōō′nä dye′tä rēgōōrō′sä)

Spend the next few days in bed.
Guarde cama algunos días.
gōō·är′de kä′mä älgōō′nōs dē′äs

Take *two tablets (ten drops)* three times a day.
Tome *dos comprimidos (diez gotas)* tres veces al día.
tō′me dōs kōmprēmē′dōs (dyes gō′täs) tres ve′ses äl dē′ä

It's nothing serious.
No es nada grave.
nō es nä′dä grä′ve

Come back and see me a week from now.
Vuelva a verme dentro de ocho días.
vōō·el′vä ä ver′me den′trō de ō′tshō dē′äs

Parts of the Body and their Functions

abdomen	abdomen *m*	äbdō′men
ankle	tobillo *m*	tōbē′lyō
appendix	apéndice *m*	äpen′dēse
arm	brazo *m*	brä′sō
armpit	sobaco *m*, axila *f*	sōbä′kō, äksē′lä
artery	arteria *f*	ärter′yä
back	espalda *f*	espäl′dä
bile	bilis *f*	bē′lēs
bladder	vejiga *f*	ve*h*ē′gä
blood	sangre *f*	säng′gre
blood pressure	presión *f* de la sangre, tensión *f*	presyōn′ de lä säng′gre, tensyōn′
body	cuerpo *m*	kōo·er′pō
bone	hueso *m*	ōō·e·sō
bowel movement	deposición *f*	depōsēsyōn′
brain	cerebro *m*	sere′brō
breast	pecho *m*, seno *m*	pe′tshō, se′nō
breathing	respiración *f*	respēräsyōn′
buttocks	nalgas *fpl*	näl′gäs
calf	pantorilla *f*	päntōrē′lyä
cheek	mejilla *f*	me*h*ē′lyä
chest	pecho *m*	pe′tshō
chin	barbilla *f*, mentón *m*	bärbē′lyä, mentōn′
circulation	circulación *f*	sērkōoläsyōn′
collarbone	clavícula *f*	klävē′kōolä
digestion	digestión *f*	dē*h*estyōn′
disc	disco *m* intervertebral	dēs′kō ēnterverte-bräl′
ear	oreja *f*	ōre′*h*ä
eardrum	tímpano *m*	tēm′pänō
elbow	codo *m*	kō′dō
eye	ojo *m*	ō′*h*ō
– eyeball	globo *m* del ojo	glō′bō del ō′*h*ō
– eyelid	párpado *m*	pär′pädō
face	cara *f*, rostro *m*	kä′rä, rōs′trō
finger	dedo *m*	de′dō
– thumb	pulgar *m*	pōolgär′
– index finger	dedo *m* índice	de′dō ēn′dēse
– middle finger	dedo *m* del corazón	de′dō del kōräsōn′

– **ring finger**	dedo *m* anular	de'dō änōōlär'
– **pinkie**	dedo *m* meñique	de'dō menyē'ke
foot	pie *m*	pye
forehead	frente *f*	fren'te
frontal sinus	seno *m* frontal	se'nō frōntäl'
gall bladder	vesícula *f*	väsē'kōōlä
genital organs	órganos *mpl* genitales	ōr'gänōs henētä'les
gland	glándula *f*	glän'dōōlä
hair	pelo *m*, cabello *m*	pe'lō, käbe'lyō
hand	mano *f*	mä'nō
head	cabeza *f*	käbe'sä
heart	corazón *m*	kōräsōn'
heel	talón *m*	tälōn'
hip	cadera *f*	käde'rä
intestine	intestino *m*	ēntestē'nō
– **large intestine**	intestino *m* grueso	ēntestē'nō grōō·e'sō
– **small intestine**	intestino *m* delgado	ēntestē'nō delgä'dō
jaw	maxilar *m*, mandíbula *f*	mäksēlär', mändē'bōōlä
– **upper jaw**	maxilar *m*, mandíbula *f* superior	-sōōperyōr'
– **lower jaw**	maxilar *m*, mandíbula *f* inferior	-ēnferyōr'
joint	articulación *f*	ärtēkōōläsyōn'
kidney	riñón *m*	rēnyōn'
knee	rodilla *f*	rōdē'lyä
kneecap	rótula *f*	rō'tōōlä
larynx	laringe *f*	lärēn'he
leg	pierna *f*	pyer'nä
– **thigh**	muslo *m*	mōōs'lō
limbs	miembros *mpl*	myemb'rōs
lip	labio *m*	lä'byō
liver	hígado *m*	ē'gädō
lung	pulmón *m*	pōōlmōn'
maxillary sinus	seno *m* maxilar	se'nō mäksēlär'
menstruation	menstruación *f*, período *m*	menstrōō·äsyōn', perē'ōdō

metabolism	metabolismo *m*	metäbōlēz'mō
mouth	boca *f*	bō'kä
mucous membrane	mucosa *f*	mōōkō'sä
muscle	músculo *m*	mōōs'kōōlō
nail	uña *f*	ōō'nyä
neck	cuello *m*	kōō·e'lyō
– nape of the neck	nuca *f*	nōō'kä
nerve	nervio *m*	ner'vyō
nerves	nervios *mpl*	ner'vyōs
nose	nariz *f*	närēs'
palate	paladar *m*	pälädär'
pancreas	páncreas *m*	pän'kre·äs
pelvis	pelvis *f*	pel'vēs
penis	pene *m*	pe'ne
pregnancy	embarazo *m*	embärä'sō
respiration	respiración *f*	respēräsyōn'
rib	costilla *f*	kōstē'lyä
shin	espinilla *f*	espēnē'lyä
shoulder	hombro *m*	ōm'brō
sinew	tendón *m*	tendōn'
skin	piel *f*, cutis *m*	pyel, kōō'tēs
skull	cráneo *m*	krä'ne·ō
sole	planta *f*	plän'tä
spinal cord	médula *f* espinal	me'dōōlä espēnäl'
spine	espina *f* dorsal	espē'nä dōrsäl'
spleen	bazo *m*	bä'sō
stomach	estómago *m*	estō'mägō
temple	sien *f*	syen
tendon	tendón *m*	tendōn'
thorax	tórax *m*	tōräks'
throat	garganta *f*	gärgän'tä
toe	dedo *m* del pie	de'dō del pye
tongue	lengua *f*	len'gōō·ä
tonsils	amígdalas *fpl*	ämēg'däläs
tooth	diente *m*	dyen'te
urine	orina *f*	ōrē'nä
uterus	útero *m*	ōō'terō
vagina	vagina *f*	vähē'nä
vein	vena *f*	ve'nä
wrist	muñeca *f*	mōōnye'kä

What's wrong?

abscess	absceso *m*	äbse′sō
AIDS	SIDA *m*	sē′dä
airsickness	mareo *m*	märe′ō
allergy	alergia *f*	äler′hyä
anemia	anemia *f*	äne′myä
appendicitis	apendicitis *f*	äpendēsē′tēs
arthritis	artritis *f*	ärtrē′tēs
asthma	asma *m*	äz′mä
attack	ataque *m*	ätä′ke
bite *(insect)*	mordedura *f*/*Mex* mordida *f*	mōrdedoo′rä/mōrdē′dä
bleeding	hemorragia *f*	emōrrä′hyä
blood poisoning	intoxicación *f* de la sangre	ēntōksēkäsyōn′ de lä säng′gre
blood pressure	presión *f* de la sangre, tensión *f*	presyōn′ de lä säng′gre, tensyōn′
– **high pressure**	tensión *f* alta	tensyōn′ äl′tä
– **low pressure**	tensión *f* baja	tensyōn′ bä′hä
breathing problems	dificultades *fpl* respiratorias	dēfēkooltä′des respērätōr′yäs
bronchitis	bronquitis *f*	brōngkē′tēs
bruise	contusión *f*	kōntoosyōn′
burn	quemadura *f*	kemädoo′rä
cardiac infarction	infarto *m* del miocardio	ēnfär′tō del mē·ō·kär′dyō
chicken pox	varicela *f*	värēse′lä
chills	escalofríos *mpl*	eskälōfrē′ōs
cholera	cólera *m*	kō′lerä
circulatory problems	trastornos *mpl* circulatorios	trästōr′nōs sērkoolätōr′yōs
cold	resfriado *m*	resfrē·ä′dō
colic	cólico *m*	kō′lēkō
concussion	conmoción *f* cerebral	kōnmōsyōn′ serebräl′
conjunctivitis	conjuntivitis *f*	kōnhoontēvē′tēs
constipation	estreñimiento *m*	estrenyēmyen′tō
cough	tos *f*	tōs
cramps	calambres *mpl*	käläm′bres
cut	herida *f*, corte *m*	erē′dä, kōr′te

diabetes	diabetes *f*	dyäbe′tes
diarrhea	diarrea *f*	dyärre′ä
diphtheria	difteria *f*	dēfte′ryä
disease	enfermedad *f*	enfermedäd′
– **contagious disease** .	enfermedad *f* contagiosa	enfermedäd′ kōntä*hy*ō′sä
dislocation	dislocación *f*	dēslōkäsyōn′
dizziness	mareo *m*, vértigo *m* ...	märe′ō, ver′tēgō
dysentery	disentería *f*	dēsenterē′ä
fainting	desmayo *m*	desmä′yō
fever	fiebre *f*/*Mex* calentura *f*	fye′bre/kälentoo′rä
flatulence	flatulencia *f*	flätoolen′syä
flu	gripe *f*	grē′pe
food poisoning	intoxicación *f* alimenticia	entōksēkäsyōn′ älementē′syä
fracture	fractura *f*/*Mex* *a* quebradura *f*	fräktoo′rä/kebrädoo′rä
gall stones	cálculos *mpl* biliares ...	käl′koolōs bēlyä′res
German measles	rubéola *f*	roobe′ōlä
hay fever	fiebre *f* del heno	fye′bre del e′nō
heart attack	ataque *m* cardíaco	ätä′ke kärdē′äkō
heart problems	problemas *mpl* cardíacas	prōble′mäs kärdē′äkäs
heartburn	ardor *m* del estómago .	ärdōr′ del estō′mägō
hemorrhage	hemorragia *f*	emōrrä′hyä
hemorrhoids	hemorroides *fpl*	emōrroi′des
hoarseness	ronquera *f*	rōnke′rä
hypertension	hipertensión *f*	epertensyōn′
indigestion	trastornos *mpl* digestivos	trästōr′nōs dē*hes*tē′vōs
inflammation	inflamación *f*	ēnflämäsyōn′
influenza	gripe *f*	grē′pe
injury	herida *f*, lesión *f*	erē′dä, lesyōn′
insomnia	insomnio *m*	ēnsōm′nyō
intestinal catarrh	enteritis *f*	enterē′tēs
jaundice	ictericia *f*	ēkterē′syä
kidney stones	cálculos *mpl* renales ...	käl′koolōs renä′les
liver problems	trastornos *mpl* del hígado	trästōr′nōs del ē′gädō

measles	sarampión *m*	särämpyōn′
middle ear inflammation	otitis *f* media	ōtē′tēs me′dyä
mumps	paperas *fpl*	päpe′räs
nausea	náuseas *fpl*	nou′se·äs
nephritis	nefritis *f*	nefrē′tēs
neuralgia	neuralgia *f*	ne·ōōräl*h*yä
nosebleed	hemorragia *f* nasal	emōrrä′*h*yä näsäl′
pain	dolor *m*	dōlōr′
paralysis	parálisis *f*	pärä′lēsēs
peptic ulcer	úlcera *f* gástrica	ōōl′serä gäs′trēkä
piles	almorranas *fpl*	älmōrrä′näs
pleurisy	pleuresía *f*	ple·ōōresē′ä
pneumonia	pulmonía *f*	pōōlmōnē′ä
poisoning	envenenamiento *m*, intoxicación *f*	envenenämyen′tō, ēntōksēkäsyōn′
pregnancy	embarazo *m*	embärä′sō
pulled tendon	distorsión *f* de un tendón	dēstōrsyōn′ de ōōn tendōn′
rash	erupción *f* cutánea/*Mex* salpullido *m*	erōōpsyōn′ kōōtä′ne·ä/sälpōōlye′dō
rheumatism	reumatismo *m*	re·ōōmätēz′mō
scarlet fever	escarlatina *f*	eskärlätē′nä
sciatica	ciática *f*	syä′tēkä
seasickness	mareo *m*	märe′ō
shock	shock *m* nervioso	shōk nervyō′sō
skin disease	enfermedad *f* de la piel	enfermedäd′ de lä pyel
skin lesion	lesión *f* de la piel	lesyōn′ de lä pyel
smallpox	viruela *f*	vērōō·e′lä
sore throat	dolor *m* de garganta	dōlōr′ de gärgän′tä
sprain	torcedura *f*, falseo *m*	tōrsedōō′rä, fälse′ō
sting	picadura *f*	pēkädōō′rä
stitch in the side	puntadas *fpl* en el costado	pōōntä′däs en el kōstä′dō
stomach pain	dolores *mpl* de estómago	dōlō′res de estō′mägō
stroke	apoplejía *f*	äpōple*h*ē′ä
sunburn	quemadura *f* del sol	kemädōō′rä del sōl
sunstroke	insolación *f*	ēnsōläsyōn′
suppuration	supuración *f*	sōōpōōräsyōn′
swelling	hinchazón *f*	ēntshäsōn′

tetanus	tétano *m*	te'tänō
tonsillitis	anginas *fpl*	än*h*ē'näs
tumor	tumor *m*	tōōmōr'
typhoid fever	tifoidea *f*	tēfoide'ä
ulcer	úlcera *f*	ōōl'serä
vomiting	náuseas *fpl*	nou'se·äs
wound	herida *f*	erē'dä

In the Hospital

anesthetic	anestesia *f*	äneste'syä
bed	cama *f* (de ruedas)	kä'mä (de rōō·e'däs)
bed pan	orinal *m*, bacín *m*	ōrēnäl', bäsēn'
blood count	hemograma *m*	emōgrä'mä
blood test	muestra *f* de sangre . . .	mōō·es'trä de säng'gre
blood transfusion . .	transfusión *f* de sangre	tränsfōōsyōn' de säng'gre
diagnosis	diagnóstico *m*	dyägnō'stēkō
discharge	dar de alta	där de äl'tä
doctor	médico *m*	me'dēkō
examination	1) *in lab:* análisis *m*	änä'lēsēs
	2) *of person:* reconoci- miento *m*	rekōnōsēmyen'tō
examine	examinar, reconocer . .	eksämēnär', rekōnōser'
head nurse	enfermera *f* jefe	enferme'rä *he*'fe
hospital	hospital *m*	ōspētäl'
infusion	infusión *f*	ēnfōōsyōn'
injection	inyección *f*	ēnyeksyōn'
intensive care unit	unidad *f* de cuidados in-tensivos	ōōnēdäd' de kōō·ē-dä'dōs ēntense'vōs
medical director . . .	médico-jefe *m*	me'dēkō-*he*'fe
night nurse	enfermera *f* de noche . .	enferme'rä de nō'tshe
nurse	enfermera *f*	enferme'rä
operate	operar	ōperär'
operation	operación *f*	ōperäsyōn'
patient	paciente *m* & *f*	päsyen'te
surgeon	cirujano *m*	sērōō*h*ä'nō

temperature	temperatura *f*	temperätoo′rä
temperature chart ...	curva *f* de temperatura	koor′vä de tempe-rätoo′rä
visiting hours	horas *fpl* de visita	ō′räs de vēsē′tä
ward	unidad *f*, sección *f*	oonēdäd′, seksyōn′
x-ray *(verb)*	hacer una radiografía .	äser′ oo′nä rädyō-gräfē′ä

Nurse, could you give me a *pain killer (sleeping pill)*?
¿Podría darme algo contra *el dolor (para dormir)*?
pōdrē′ä där′me äl′gō kōn′trä el dōlōr′ (pä′rä dōrmēr′)

When can I get out of bed?
¿Cuándo puedo levantarme?
koo·än′dō poo·e′dō leväntär′me

What's the diagnosis?
¿Cuál es el diagnóstico?
koo·äl′ es el dyägnōs′tēkō

At the Dentist's

Where is there a dentist here?
¿Dónde hay un dentista por aquí?
dōn′de ī oon dentēs′tä pōr äke′

I'd like to make an appointment.
Quisiera pedir hora (cita).
kēsye′rä pedēr ō′rä (sē′tä)

I've got a toothache.
Tengo dolor de muelas.
ten′gō dōlōr′ de moo·e′läs

This tooth hurts.
Me duele este diente.
me doo·e′le es′te dyen′te

– up here (an upper tooth).
– arriba.
– ärrē′bä

– down here (a lower tooth).
– abajo.
– äbä′hō

I've lost a filling.
Se ha caído una calza/*Sp* un empaste.
se ä kä·ē′dō oo′nä käl′sä/oon empäs′te

This tooth is loose.
Este diente se mueve.
es′te dyen′te se moo·e′ve

Does this tooth have to be pulled?
¿Es necesario sacar este diente?
es nesesär′yō säkär′ es′te dyen′te

... broke off.
... está roto.
... estä′ rō′tō

Can you do a temporary repair on this tooth?
¿Puede tratarme provisionalmente este diente?
poo·e′de trätär′me prōvēsyōnälmen′te es′te dyen′te

Can you fix these dentures?
¿Puede reparar esta dentadura postiza?
poo·e′de repärär′ es′tä dentädoo′rä pōstē′sä

*Please don't *eat anything (smoke)* for two hours.

¿Por favor, no *coma (fume)* hasta dentro de dos horas.

pōr fàvōr', nō kō'mä (fōo'me) äs'tä den'trō de dōs ō'räs

When do you want me to come back?

¿Cuándo tengo que volver?

kōo·än'dō ten'gō ke vōlver'

anesthesia	anestesia *f*	äneste'syä
braces	aparato *m* dental, frenillo *m*	äpärä'tō dentäl', frenē'lyō
bridge	puente *m* dental	pōo·en'te dentäl'
cavities	caries *fpl*	kär'yes
crown	corona *f*	kōrō'nä
dental clinic	clínica *f* dental	klē'nēkä dentäl'
dentist	dentista *m*	dentēs'tä
dentures	dentadura *f* postiza ...	dentädōo'rä pōstē'sä
extract	sacar, extraer	säkär', eksträ·er'
false tooth	diente *m* de espiga ...	dyen'te de espē'gä
fill	calza/*Sp* empastar ...	kälsär'/empästär'
filling	calza *f*/*Sp* empaste *m* ..	käl'sä/empäs'te
gums	encías *fpl*	ensē'äs
incisor	diente *m* incisivo	dyen'te ēnsēsē'vō
injection	inyección *f*	ēnyeksyōn'
jaw	mandíbula *f*	mändē'bōolä
molar	muela *f*	mōo·e'lä
nerve	nervio *m*	ner'vyō
oral surgeon	cirujano *m* oral	sērōohä'nō ōräl'
orthodontist	ortodoncista *m*	ōrtōdōnsēs'tä
plate	plancha *f*	plän'tshä
root	raíz *f* del diente	rä·ēs' del dyen'te
root canal work	tratamiento *m* de la raíz	trätämyen'tō de lä rä·ēs'
tartar	sarro *m* dental, tártaro *m*	sä'rrō dentäl', tär'tärō
temporary filling	empaste *m* provisional .	empäs'te prōvēsyōnäl'
tooth	diente *m*	dyen'te
toothache	dolor *m* de muelas	dōlōr' de mōo·e'läs
wisdom tooth	muela *f* del juicio	mōo·e'lä del hōo·ē'syō

Taking a Cure

bath	baño *m*	bä'nyō
bath attendant	bañero *m*	bänye'rō
convalescent home	casa *f* de reposo	kä'sä de repō'sō
cure	cura *f*, tratamiento *m*	kōō'rä, trätä-myen'tō
cure tax	impuesto *m* de turismo	ēmpōō·es'tō de tōōrēz'mō
diet	régimen *m*, dieta *f*	re'*h*ēmen, dye'tä
gymnastics	gimnasia *f*	*h*ēmnä'syä
health resort	estación *f* climática	estäsyōn' klēmä'tē-kä
hot spring	fuente *f* termal	fōō·en'te termäl'
inhale	inhalar	ēnälär'
massage *(noun)*	masaje *m*	mäsä'*h*e
massage *(verb)*	dar masaje	där mäsä'*h*e
masseur	masajista *m*	mäsä*h*ēs'tä
masseuse	masajista *f*	mäsä*h*ēs'tä
medicinal spring	aguas *fpl* medicinales	ä'gōō·äs medēsēnä'les
mineral bath	baño *m* de aguas minerales	bä'nyō de ä'gōō·äs mēnerä'les
mineral spring	aguas *fpl* minerales	ä'gōō·äs mēnerä'les
minerals	minerales *mpl*	mēnerä'les
mud	lodo *m*	lō'dō
mud bath	baño *m* de lodo	bä'nyō de lō'dō
mud pack	envoltura *f*	envōltōō'rä
radiation therapy	radioterapia *f*	rädyōterä'pyä
rest cure	cura *f* de reposo	kōō'rä de repō'sō
sanatorium	sanatorio *m*	sänätōr'yō
sauna	sauna *f*	sou'nä
sea water	agua *f* de mar	ä'gōō·ä de mär
short wave	onda *f* corta	ōn'dä kōr'tä
spa	balneario *m*	bälne·är'yō
steam bath	baño *m* de vapor, baño *m* turco	bä'nyō de väpōr', bä'nyō tōōr'kō
sunlamp	lámpara *f* solar ultravioleta	läm'pärä sōlär' ōōlträvyōle'tä
ultrasonics	ultrasonido *m*	ōōlträsōnē'dō

CONCERT, THEATER, MOVIES

▐ Box Office

What's on tonight?
¿Qué dan esta noche?
ke dän es'tä nō'tshe

When does *the performance (the concert)* start?
¿A qué hora empieza *la función (el concierto)*?
ä ke ō'rä empye'sä lä fōōnsyōn' (el kōnsyer'tō)

Where can we get tickets?
¿Dónde se venden (se despachan) los boletos/*Sp* las entradas?
dōn'de se ven'den (se despä'tshän) lōs bōle'tōs/läs enträ'däs

Are there any discounts for …?
¿Hay una reducción del precio para …?
ī ōō'nä redōōksyōn' del pre'syō pä'rä …

Are there still tickets available for *this (tomorrow)* evening?
¿Quedan boletos/*Sp* entradas/para *esta noche (mañana)*?
ke'dän bōle'tōs/enträ'däs/pä'rä es'tä nō'tshe (mänyä'nä)

One ticket in the *third (tenth)* row, please.
Un asiento en la *tercera (décima)* fila, por favor.
ōōn äsyen'tō en lä terse'rä (de'sēmä) fē'lä, pōr fä'vōr'

Two seats in the third row, orchestra, please.
Dos asientos en el patio (la luneta), tercera fila, por favor.
dōs äsyen'tōs en el pä'tyō (lä lōōne'tä), terse'rä fē'lä, pōr fävōr'

– in the middle.	**– on the side.**
– en el centro.	– lateral(es).
– en el sen'trō	– läteräl'(es)

▐ Concert, Theater

accompaniment	acompañamiento *m* ...	äkōmpänyä-myen'tō
act	acto *m*	äk'tō
actor	actor *m*	äktōr'
actress	actriz *f*	äktrēs'

advance ticket sales	venta *f* anticipada	ven'tä äntēsēpä'dä
alto	alto *m*	äl'tō
applause	aplausos *mpl*	äplou'sōs
aria	aria *f*	är'yä
ballet	ballet *m*	bäle'
balcony	paraíso *m*/*Mex* chilla *f*	pärä-ē'sō/tshē'lyä
band	conjunto *m*, banda *f*	kōn*h*ōon'tō, bän'dä
baritone	barítono *m*	bärē'tōnō
bass	bajo *m*	bä'*h*ō
box office	taquilla *f*	täkē'lyä
box seats	palcos *mpl*	päl'kōs
chamber music	música *f* de cámara	mōō'sēkä de kä'märä
check room	guardarropa *m*	gōō-ärdärrō'pä
chorus	coro *m*	kō'rō
coat check	ficha *f* del guardarropa	fē'tshä del gōō-ärdärrō'pä
comedy	comedia *f*	kōme'dyä
composer	compositor *m*	kōmpōsētōr'
concert	concierto *m*	kōnsyer'tō
concert hall	sala *f* de conciertos	sä'lä de kōnsyer'tōs
conductor	director *m* de orquesta	dērektōr' de ōrkes'tä
contralto	contralto *m*	kōnträl'tō
costumes	trajes *mpl*	trä'*h*es
costume designer	figurinista *m*	fēgōōrēnēs'tä
curtain	telón *m*	telōn'
curtain time	comienzo *m*	kōmyen'sō
dancer	bailarín *m*	bīlärēn'
director	director *m*	dērektōr'
drama	drama *m*	drä'mä
dress circle	anfiteatro *m*	änfēte·ä'trō
duet	dúo *m*	dōō'ō
final curtain	fin *m*	fēn
grand piano	piano *m* de cola	pē·ä'nō de kō'lä
intermission	descanso *m*, intermedio *m*, entreacto *m*	deskän'sō, ēnterme'dyō, entre·äk'tō
libretto	libreto *m*	lēbre'tō
lobby	foyer *m*	fōyer' (fōye')
music	música *f*	mōō'sēkä
musical	musical *m*	mōōsēkäl'

note	nota *f*	nō′tä
opera	ópera *f*	ō′perä
opera glasses	gemelos *mpl* (de teatro)	*heme*′lōs (de te·ä′trō)
operetta	opereta *f*	ōpere′tä
orchestra	orquesta *f*	ōrkes′tä
orchestra seats	patio *m* (de butacas), platea *f*/luneta *f*	pä′tyō (de bo͞otä′-käs), pläte′ä/lo͞one′tä
overture	obertura *f*	ōberto͞o′rä
part/role	papel *m*	päpel′
– leading role	papel *m* principal	päpel′ prēnsēpäl′
performance	representación *f*	representäsyōn′
pianist	pianista *m*	pē·änēs′tä
piano recital	recital *m* (de piano)	resētäl′ (de pē·ä′nō)
piece of music	composición *f*	kōmpōsēsyōn′
play	pieza *f* de teatro	pye′sä de te·ä′trō
producer	productor *m*	prōdo͞oktōr′
production	puesta *f* en escena	po͞o·es′tä en ese′nä
program	programa *m*	prōgrä′mä
scenery/settings	decoración *f*	dekōräsyōn′
set designer	escenógrafo *m*	esenō′gräfō
singer	cantante *m*	käntän′te
singing	canto *m*	kän′tō
soloist	solista *m & f*	sōlēs′tä
song	canción *f*	känsyōn′
– folk song	canción *f* popular	känsyōn′ pōpo͞olär′
song recital	recital *m* (de canto)	resētäl′ (de kän′tō)
soprano	soprano *m*	sōprä′nō
stage	escena *f*, escenario *m*	ese′nä, esenär′yō
stage director	director *m* de escena	dērektōr′ de ese′nä
symphony concert	concierto *m* sinfónico	kōnsyer′tō sēnfō′nēkō
tenor	tenor *m*	tenōr′
theater	teatro *m*	te·ä′trō
theater schedule	programa *m*	prōgrä′mä
ticket	boleto *m/Sp* entrada *f*.	bōle′tō/enträ′dä
ticket sales	despacho *m* de localidades	despä′tshō de lōkälēdä′des
tragedy	tragedia *f*	trä*h*e′dyä
violin recital	recital *m* (de violín)	resētäl′ (de vē·ōlēn′)
work	obra *f*	ō′brä

Movies

What's on tonight at the movies?
¿Qué película ponen *or* dan hoy?
ke pelē'kōōlä pō'nen (dän) oi

What time does *the box office open (the film start)*?
¿Cuándo empieza *la venta de boletos/Sp entradas (la película)*?
kōō·än'dō empye'sä lä ven'tä de bōle'tōs/enträ'däs (lä pelē'kōōlä)

How long is the picture?
¿Cuánto dura la sesión?
kōō·än'tō dōō'rä lä sesyōn'

audience	espectadores *mpl*	espektädō'res
auditorium	sala *f*	sä'lä
cartoon	dibujos *mpl* animados/ *Am a* monitos *mpl*	dēbōō'hōs änēmä'dōs/mōnē'tōs
cinema	cine *m*	sē'ne
color film	película *f* en color	pelē'kōōlä en kōlōr'
documentary	documental *m*	dōkōōmentäl'
drive-in movie	cine *m* al aire libre	sē'ne äl ī're lē'bre
dubbed	doblado	dōblä'dō
dubbing	doblaje *m*	dōblä'he
educational film	documental *m*	dōkōōmentäl'
feature film	largometraje *m*	lärgōmeträ'he
film	película *f*, film(e) *m*	pelē'kōōlä, fēlm(e)
film actor	actor *m* de cine	äktōr' de sē'ne
film festival	festival *m* cinematográfico	festēväl' sēnemätōgrä'fēkō
film screening	sesión *f* de cine	sesyōn' de sē'ne
motion picture theater	cine *m*	sē'ne
movie	película *f*	pelē'kōōlä
movies	cine *m*	sē'ne
preview	avance *m*	ävän'se
screen	pantalla *f*	päntä'lyä
screenplay	guión *m*	gē·ōn'
short subject	cortometraje *m*	kōrtōmeträ'he
subtitled	subtitulado	sōōbtētōōlä'dō
thriller	película *f* escalofriante	pelē'kōōlä eskälōfrē·än'te
usher	acomodador *m*	äkōmōdädōr'

PASTIMES

Fun and Games

Where is there …?
¿Dónde hay …
dōn'de ī …

a bar	un bar	ōōn bär
a discothèque	una discoteca	ōō'nä dēskōte'kä
an ice skating rink .	una pista de hielo	ōō'nä pēs'tä de ye'lō
a miniature golf course	un minigolf	ōōn mēnēgōlf'
a night club	un club nocturno	ōōn klōōb nōktōōr'nō
a pool hall	una sala de billar	ōō'nä sä'lä de bēlyär'
a riding stable	una cuadra	ōō'nä kōō·ä'drä
a sailing school	una escuela de vela	ōō'nä eskōō·e'lä de ve'lä
a tennis court	una pista *or* cancha de tenis	ōō'nä pēs'tä (kän'tshä) de te'nēs

I'd like to …
Quisiera …
kēsye'rä …

play badminton	jugar al badminton/*Sp* al volante	hōō'gär äl bädmēn- tōn'/äl vōlän'te
play miniature golf	jugar al minigolf	hōō'gär äl mēnēgōlf'
play ping pong	jugar al ping pong	hōōgär' äl pēnpōn'
watch the fashion show	mirar el desfile de mo- das	mē'rär el desfē'le de mō'däs

Do you have television?
¿Tienen televisión?
tye'nen televēsyōn'

Can I listen to the radio here?
¿Puedo escuchar el radio/*Sp* la radio?
pōō·e'dō eskōōtshär' el rä'dyō/lä rä'dyō

What station is that?
¿Qué emisora es ésta?
ke emēsō'rä es es'tä

What's on today?
¿Qué programa hay hoy?
ke prōgrä'mä ī oi

Do you play *chess (ping pong)*?
¿Juega/juegas *(fam)*/ al ajedrez *(ping pong)*?
hōō·e'gä/hōō·e'gäs/äl ähedres' (pēnpōn')

amusement	pasatiempo *m*	päsätyem′pō
bowling alley	bolera *f*	bōle′rä
card game	juego *m* de cartas	hōō•e′gō de kär′täs
– cut	cortar	kōrtär′
– deal	dar	där
– shuffle	barajar	bärä*h*är′
– ace	as *m*	äs
– jack	valet *m*	välet′
– queen	dama *f*	dä′mä
– king	rey *m*	re′ē
– clubs	tréboles *mpl*	tre′bōles
– diamonds	diamantes *mpl*	dyämän′tes
– hearts	corazones *mpl*	kōräsō′nes
– spades	picos *mpl*	pē′kōs
– joker	comodín *m*	kōmōdēn′
– trick	baza *f*	bä′sä
– trump	triunfo *m*	trē-ōōn′fō
cheekers	damas *fpl*	dä′mäs
chess	ajedrez *m*	ä*h*edres′
chessboard	tablero *m*	täble′rō
chessman	pieza *f*	pye′sä
– square	casilla *f*	käsē′lyä
– bishop	alfil *m*	älfēl′
– castle	torre *f*	tō′rre
– king	rey *m*	re′ē
– knight	caballo *m*	käbä′lyō
– pawn, rook	peón *m*	pe-ōn′
– queen	reina *f*	re′ēnä
chip	ficha *f*	fē′tshä
circus	circo *m*	sēr′kō
club	club *m*	klōōb
country fair	fiesta *f* popular	fyes′tä pōpōōlär′
crossword puzzle	crucigrama *m*	krōōsēgrä′mä
dice	dados *mpl*	dä′dōs
– shoot dice	jugar a los dados	hōōgär′ ä lōs dä′dōs
gambling casino	casino *m*	käsē′nō
gambling	juego *m*	hōō•e′gō
– banker	banquero *m*	bängke′rō
– bet	apostar	äpōstär′
– draw	mover, jugar	mōver′, hōōgär′
– move	jugada *f*	hōōgä′dä

– **piece**	peón *m*, pieza *f*	pe·ōn′, pye′sä
– **play**	jugar	hōōgär′
– **stake**	puesta *f*	pōō·es′tä
magazine	revista *f*	revēs′tä
– **fashion magazine** . .	revista *f* de modas . . .	revēs′tä de mō′däs
– **glossy**	revista *f* ilustrada	revēs′tä ēlōōsträ′dä
newspaper	periódico *m*	peryō′dēkō
party games	juegos *mpl* de sociedad	hōō·e′gōs de sōsye-dä′d
pastime	pasatiempo *m*	päsätyem′pō
ping pong	ping pong *m*	pēnpōn′
radio	radio *m*, *Sp f*	ra′dyō
– **FM**	frecuencia *f* modulada .	frekōō·en′syä mōdōōlä′dä
– **long wave**	onda *f* larga	ōn′dä lär′gä
– **medium wave**	onda *f* media	ōn′dä me′dyä
– **short wave**	onda *f* corta	ōn′dä kōr′tä
– **radio play**	radioteatro *m*	rä′dyōte·ä′trō
record	disco *m*	dēs′kō
record player	tocadiscos *m*	tōkädēs′kōs
table tennis	ping pong *m*	pēnpōn′
tape recorder	magnetófono *m*	mägnetō′fōnō
television	televisión *f*	televēsyōn′
– **announcer**	presentador *m*	presentädōr′
– **breakdown**	interferencia *f*	ēnterferen′syä
– **news**	noticias *fpl*	notē′syäs
– **program**	programa *m*	prōgrä′mä
– **program schedule** . .	programas *mpl* de la semana	prōgrä′mäs de lä semä′nä
– **turn off**	apagar	äpägär′
– **turn on**	poner	pōner′
– **television play**	telefilm *m*	telefēlm′

Getting acquainted

Hope you don't mind if I talk to you.
Perdone que me dirija a usted. (*Fam:* Quisiera hablar contigo si no te importa.)

perdō′ne ke me dērē′hä ä ōōste′ (kēsye′rä äblär′ kōntē′gō sē nō te ēmpōr′tä)

Mind if I join you?
¿Puedo sentarme a su/tu *(fam)*/lado?
pōō·e'dō sentär'me ä sōō/tōō/lä'dō

May I treat you to a *drink (coffee, tea)*?
¿Lo/*Sp* le/te *(fam)*/invito a tomar *algo (un café, un té)*?
lō/le/te/ēmbē'tō ä tōmär' äl'gō (ōōn käfe', ōōn te)

Are you doing anything this evening?
¿Tiene/tienes *(fam)*/un compromiso para esta noche?
tye'ne/tye'nes/ōōn kōmprōmē'sō pä'rä es'tä nō'tshe

Shall we dance?
¿Bailamos?
bīlä'mōs

Is there *a discothèque (a dance hall)* nearby?
¿Hay por aquí *una discoteca (una sala de baile)*?
ī pōr äkē' ōō'nä dēskōte'kä (ōō'nä sä'lä de bī'le)

May I have the next dance?
¿Me reserva/reservas *(fam)*/el próximo baile?
me reser'vä/reser'väs/el prō'ksēmō bī'le

We can chat undisturbed here.
Aquí podemos hablar sin que nadie nos moleste.
äkē' pōde'mōs äblär' sēn ke nä'dye nōs mōles'te

May I invite you to a party?
¿Puedo invitarlo/*Sp* le/te *(fam)*/a una fiesta?
pōō·e'dō ēmbētär'lō/le/te/ä ōō'nä fyes'tä

I'll be expecting you at ...
Lo/*Sp* le/te *(fam)*/esperaré a las ...
lō/le/te/esperäre' ä läs ...

You look good in that dress.
Ese vestido le/te *(fam)*/queda muy bien.
e'se vestē'dō le/te/ke'dä mōō'ē byen

When can you come visit me?
¿Cuándo me va/vas *(fam)*/a visitar?
kōō·än'dō me vä/väs/ä vēsētär'

When can we meet again?
¿Cuándo podemos vernos otra vez?
kōō·än'dō pōde'mōs ver'nōs ōt'rä ves

May I give you a lift home?
¿Puedo llevarlo/*Sp* le/te *(fam)*/a casa?
pōō·e'dō lyevär'lō/le/te/ä kä'sä

Where do you live?
¿Dónde vive/vives *(fam)*?
dōn'de vē've/vē'ves

Won't you come in for a minute?
¿Quiere/quieres *(fam)*/pasar un
momentito?
kye're/kye'res/pä'sär ōōn mōmentē'tō

May I walk part of the way with you?
¿Puedo acompañarlo/*Sp* le/te *(fam)*/un trecho?
pōō·e'dō äkōmpänyär'lō/le/te/ōōn tre'tshō

Thanks very much for a nice evening.
Gracias por una tarde muy a̱gradable.
grä'syäs pōr ōō'nä tär'de mōō'ē ägrädä'ble

accompany	acompañar	äkōmpänyär'
chat	charlar/*Mex a* platicar	tshärlär'/plätēkär'
dance *(noun)*	baile *m*	bī'le
dance *(verb)*	bailar	bīlär'
dance hall	sala *f* (salón *m*) de baile	sä'lä (sälōn') de bī'le
discothèque	discoteca *f*	dēskōte'kä
enjoy oneself	divertirse	dēvertēr'se
expect somebody	esperar a	esperär' ä
flirt	flirteo *m*	flērte'ō
invite	invitar	ēmbētär'
kiss *(noun)*	beso *m*	be'sō
kiss *(verb)*	besar	besär'
live	vivir	vēvēr'
love *(noun)*	amor *m*	ämōr'
love *(verb)*	amar	ämär'
make love	hacer el amor	äser' el ämōr'
meet	encontrarse	enkōnträr'se
meet again	volver a verse	vōlver' ä ver'se
party	fiesta *f*	fyes'tä
take a walk	pasear, dar una vuelta	päse·är', där ōō'nä vōō·el'tä
visit	visitar	vēsētär'

On the Beach

Where can we go swimming here?
¿Dónde podemos bañarnos?
dōn'de pōde'mōs bänyär'nōs

Can we go swimming here?
¿Podemos bañarnos aquí?
pōde'mōs bänyär'nōs äkē'

Two tickets (with cabaña), please.
Dos boletos/*Sp* entradas/(con caseta).
dōs bōle'tōs/enträ'däs/(kōn käse'tä)

Can we swim nude here?
¿Podemos bañarnos desnudos aquí?
pōde'mōs bänyär'nōs desnoo'dōs
äkē'

How far out can we swim?
¿Hasta dónde se puede nadar?
äs'tä dōn'de se poo·e'de nädär'

How *deep (warm)* is the water?
¿Qué *profundidad (temperatura)* tiene el agua?
ke prōfoondēdäd' (temperätoo'rä) tye'ne el ä'goo·ä

Is it dangerous for children?
¿Es peligroso para los niños?
es pelēgrō'sō pä'rä lōs nē'nyōs

No swimming!
¡Prohibido bañarse!
prō·ēbē'dō bänyär'se

Is there an undertow here?
¿Hay aquí corrientes?
ī äkē' kōrryen'tes

Where is the lifeguard?
¿Dónde está el vigilante?
dōn'de estä' el vēhēlän'te

A deck chair (umbrella), please.
Por favor, *una hamaca or silla extensible (una sombrilla).*
pōr fävōr', oo'nä ämä'kä, sē'lyä ekstensē'ble (oo'nä sōmbrē'lyä)

How much does ... cost?
¿Cuánto cuesta ...?
koo·än'tō koo·es'tä ...

I'd like to rent *a cabaña (boat).*
Quisiera alquilar/*Mex* rentar/*una caseta (un bote).*
kēsye'rä älkēlär'/rentär'/oo'nä käse'tä (oom bō'te)

Where *is (are)* ...?
¿Dónde *está (están)* ...?
dōn'de estä' (estän') ...

I'd like to go water skiing.
Quisiera practicar el esquí acuático.
kēsye'rä präktēkär' el eskē' akoo·ä'tēkō

Where can I go fishing?
¿Dónde se puede pescar?
dōn'de se poo·e'de peskär'

Would you be good enough to keep an eye on my gear.
Hágame/házme *(fam)*/el favor de cuidar/*Sp* vigilar/mis cosas.
ä'gäme/äz'me/el fävōr' de koo·ēdär'/vēhēlär'/mēs kō'säs

air mattress	colchón *m* de aire	kōltshōn' de ī're
air temperature ...	temperatura *f* del aire .	temperätoo'rä del ī're
bathing cap	gorro *m* de baño	gō'rrō de bä'nyō
bathing suit	traje *m* de baño	trä'*h*e de bä'nyō
– **trunks**	bañador *m* (*Sp*)	bänyädōr'
bathrobe	bata *f*/*Sp* albornoz *m* ..	bä'tä/älbōrnōs'
bay	bahía *f*	bä-ē'ä
boat	barca *f*, lancha *f*	bär'kä, län'tshä
– **dinghy**	bote *m*	bō'te
– **motorboat**	lancha *f* motora, voladora *f*, *Mex* motonauta *f*	län'tshä mōtō'rä, vōlädō'rä, mōtōnou'tä
– **pedal boat**	patín *m*	pätēn'
– **sailboat**	barco *m* de vela	bär'kō de ve'lä
cabaña	caseta *f*	käse'tä
dive	bucear	boose-är'
diving board	trampolín *m*	trämpōlēn'
dune	duna *f*	doo'nä
jellyfish	medusa *f*/*Mex* malagua *f*	medoo'sä/mälä'goo-ä
locker room	vestuario *m*	vestoo-är'yō
non-swimmer	no-nadador *m*	nō-nädädōr'
saline content	salinidad *f*	sälēnēdäd'
sandy beach	playa *f* de arena	plä'yä de äre'nä
scuba diving	bucear	boose-är'
scuba equipment ..	escafandra *f*, equipo *m* de bucear	eskäfän'drä, ekē'pō de boose-är'
shells	conchas *fpl*	kōn'tshäs
shower	ducha *f*, regadera *f*	doo'tshä, regäde'rä
swim	nadar, bañarse	nädär', bänyär'se
swimmer	nadador *m*	nädädōr'
take a sunbath	tomar el sol	tōmär' el sōl
water	agua *f*	ä'goo-ä
water temperature	temperatura *f* del agua	temperätoo'rä del ä'goo-ä
wave	ola *f*	ō'lä

Sports

What sport events do they have here?

¿Qué pruebas deportivas se organizan aquí?

ke proo-e'bäs depōrtē'väs se ōrgänē'sän äkē'

Where's *the stadium (soccer field)*?
¿Dónde está el estadio (el campo de fútbol)?
dōn'de estä' el estä'dyō (el käm'pō de fōot'bōl)

... is playing today against ...	**What sports do you like to play?**
Hoy juega ... contra ...	¿Qué deportes practica/practicas
oi hōō·e'gä ... kōn'trä ...	(fam)/?
	ke depōr'tes präktē'kä/präktē'käs/

I'd love to see *the game (race, fight)*.
Tengo ganas de ver el partido (la carrera, la pelea).
ten'gō gä'näs de ver el pärtē'dō (lä kärre'rä, lä pele'ä)

When (Where) is the soccer game?
¿Cuándo (Dónde) se juega el partido de fútbol?
kōō·än'dō (dōn'de) se hōō·e'gä el pärtē'dō de fōot'bōl

Can you get us tickets for it?	**Goal!**
¿Podría/podrías (fam)/facilitarnos boletos/Sp entradas?	¡Gol!
pōdrē'ä/pōdrē'äs/fäsēlētär'nōs bōle'tōs/enträ'däs	gōl

What's the score?	**The score is three to two for ...**
¿Cómo está el partido?	Está tres a dos a favor de ...
kō'mō estä' el pärtē'dō	estä' tres ä dōs ä fàvōr' de ...

Is there an *outdoor (indoor)* swimming pool here?
¿Hay aquí una piscina/Mex alberca/(cubierta)?
ī äkē' ōō'nä pēsē'nä/älber'kä/(kōōbyer'tä)

I'm ...	**I play ...**	**I'm fond of ...**
Soy ...	Juego ...	Soy aficionado a ...
sōi ...	hōō·e'gō ...	sōi äfēsyōnä'dō ä ...

athlete	atleta m & f	ätle'tä
auto racing	motorismo m	mōtōrēz'mō
– race	carrera f	kärre'rä
– race car driver	corredor m	kōrredōr'
– racing car	carro m/Sp coche m/de	kä'rrō/kō'tshe/de
	carreras	kärre'räs
basketball	baloncesto m	bälōnses'tō
bicycling	ciclismo m	sēklēz'mō
– bicycle	bicicleta f	bēsēkle'tä
– bicycle race	carrera f ciclista	kärre'rä sēklēs'tä
– bicycle rider	ciclista m	sēklēs'tä
– ride a bike	ir en bicicleta	ēr en bēsēkle'tä
bowling	bolos mpl	bō'lōs
– bowling alley	bolera f	bōle'rä

boxing	boxeo *m*	bōkse'ō
– box	boxear	bōkse·är'
– boxer	boxeador *m*	bōkse·ädōr'
bullfight	corrida *f* (de toros)	kōrrē'dä de tō'rōs
– bull	toro *m*	tō'rō
– bullfighter	torero *m*, matador *m*	tōre'rō, mätädōr'
– bullring	plaza *f* de toros	plä'sä de tō'rōs
competition	competición *f*, concurso *m*	kōmpetēsyōn', kōnkōōr'sō
– championship	campeonato *m*	kämpe·ōnä'tō
– defeat	derrota *f*	derrō'tä
– draw	empate *m*	empä'te
– free style	carrera *f* libre	kärre'rä lē'bre
– game	juego *m*	hōō·e'gō
– goal	gol *m*	gōl
– half time	medio tiempo *m*	me'dyō tyem'pō
– match	partido *m*	pärtē'dō
– play	jugar	hōōgär'
– point	punto *m*	pōōn'tō
– practice	entrenarse	entrenär'se
– result	resultado *m*	resōōltä'dō
– start	salida *f*	sälē'dä
– victory	victoria *f*	vēktō'ryä
– win	ganar	gänär'
fencing	esgrima *f*	esgrē'mä
figure skating	patinaje *m* artístico	pätēnä'he ärtēstē'kō
– skate	patinar	pätēnär'
– skates	patines *mpl*	pätē'nes
– skater	patinador *m*	pätēnädōr'
fishing	pesca *f*	pes'kä
– fishing rod	caña *f*	kä'nyä
– go fishing	pescar (con caña)	peskär' (kōn kä'nyä)
– fishing license	licencia *f* de pescar	lēsen'syä de peskär'
golf	golf *m*	gōlf
gymnastics	gimnasia *f*	hēmnä'syä
– gymnast	gimnasta *m* & *f*	hēmnäs'tä
– gymnastics with apparatus	gimnasia *f* con aparatos	hēmnä'syä kōn äpärä'tōs
– horizontal bar	barra *f* fija	bä'rrä fē'hä
– parallel bars	paralelas *fpl*	päräle'läs
– rings	anillas *fpl*	änē'lyäs

handball	balonmano *m*	bälōnmä′nō
hockey	hockey *m*	*hō′kē*
marksmanship	tiro *m*	tē′rō
– clay pigeon shooting	tiro *m* al plato	tē′rō äl plä′tō
– rifle range	campo *m* de tiro	käm′pō de tē′rō
– shoot	tirar	tērär′
– target	blanco	bläng′kō
mountain climbing	montañismo *m*, alpinismo *m*	mōntänyēz′mō, älpēnēz′mō
– mountain climber	montañero *m*, alpinista *m*	mōntänye′rō, älpēnēs′tä
ninepins	bolos *mpl*	bō′lōs
player	jugador *m*	*hōō*gädōr′
referee	árbitro *m*	är′bētrō
riding	equitación *f*	ekētäsyōn′
– horse	caballo *m*	käbä′lyō
– horse race	carrera *f* de caballos	kärre′rä de käbä′lyōs
– jumping	salto *m*	säl′tō
– ride	montar a caballo	mōn′tär ä käbä′lyō
– rider	jinete *m*	*hē*ne′te
rowing	remo *m*	re′mō
– scull	barca *f* de remos	bär′kä de re′mōs
– oarsman	remero *m*	reme′rō
– coxswain	timonel *m*	tēmonel′
sailing	deporte *m* de vela	depōr′te de ve′lä
– sail *(noun)*	vela *f*	ve′lä
– sail *(verb)*	navegar a la vela	nävegär′ ä lä ve′lä
– sailboat	barco *m* de vela	bär′kō de ve′lä
skiing	esquí *m*	eskē′
– ski *(noun)*	esquí *m*	eskē′
– ski *(verb)*	esquiar	eskē·är′
– ski binding	fijación *f*	fē*h*äsyōn′
– ski jump	trampolín *m* de saltos	trämpōlēn′ de säl′tōs
– ski lift	telesquí *m*	teleskē′
soccer	fútbol *m*	fōōt′bōl
– ball	balón *m*	bälōn′
– corner	saque *m* de esquina	sä′ke de eskē′nä
– forward	delantero *m*	delänte′rō
– free kick	golpe *m* franco	gōl′pe fräng′kō
– fullback	defensa *m*	defen′sä

– kick a goal	meter un gol	meter' o͞on gōl
– goal	gol *m*	gōl
– goalie	portero *m*	pōrte'rō
– off-side	fuera de juego	fo͞o·e'rä de ho͞o·e'gō
– penalty kick	penalty *m*	penäl'tē
– play soccer	jugar al fútbol	ho͞ogär' äl fo͞ot'bōl
– player	jugador *m*	ho͞ogädōr'
– throw-in	saque *m* de línea	sä'ke de lē'ne·ä
sports	deportes *m*	depōr'tes
– athletic club	club *m* deportivo	klo͞ob depōrtē'vō
– sports fan	aficionado *m*	äfēsyōnä'dō
swimming	natación *f*	nätäsyōn'
– dive	salto *m*	säl'tō
– diving board	trampolín *m*	trämpōlēn'
– swimmer	nadador *m*	nädädōr'
team	equipo *m*	ekē'pō
tennis	tenis *m*	te'nēs
– singles/doubles	individual/dobles *mpl*	ēndēvēdo͞o·äl/dō'bles
– play tennis	jugar al tenis	ho͞ogär' äl te'nēs
– tennis ball	pelota *f* de tenis	pelō'tä de te'nēs
– tennis court	pista *f*, cancha *f* de tenis	pēs'tä, kän'tshä de te'nēs
– tennis racket	raqueta *f* de tenis	räke'tä de te'nēs
– ping pong	ping pong *m*	pēnpōn'
tobogganing	ir en trineo	ēr en trēne'ō
– toboggan	trineo *m*	trēne'ō
track and field	atletismo *m* en pista	ätletēz'mō en pēs'tä
umpire	árbitro *m*	är'bētrō
volleyball	vol(e)ibol *m*/*Sp* balón-volea *m*	vōlēbōl'/bälōn'-vōle'ä
wrestling	lucha *f*	lo͞o'tshä
– wrestle	luchar	lo͞otshär'
– wrestler	luchador *m*	lo͞otshädōr'

The most popular sport in Spain and Latin America is fútbol
*(soccer), which draws enormous crowds every week. American
football is virtually unknown.*

Signs

APPENDIX

A LA DERECHA ..	to the right	ä lä dere'tshä
A LA IZQUIERDA .	to the left	ä lä ēskyer'dä
¡ATENCION!	Caution!	ätensyōn'
CABALLEROS	Men	käbälye'rōs
CERRAR LA PUERTA	Close the door	serrär' lä pōō·er'tä
¡CUIDADO! ¡PERRO!	Beware of the dog ...	kōō·ēdä'dō, pe'rrō
¡DESPACIO!	Slow!	despä'syō
¡EMPUJAR!	Push!	empōōhär'
ENTRADA LIBRE .	free entrance	enträ'dä lē'bre
ESTACIONAMIENTO/*Sp* APARCAMIENTO	Parking	estäsyōnämyen'tō/ äpärkämyen'tō
FUMADORES	Smokers	fōōmädō'res
LLEGADA	Arrival	lyegä'dä
¡OBRAS!/*Mex* ¡HOMBRES TRABAJANDO!..	Construction	ō'bräs/ ōm'bres träbähän'dō
PARADA	Stop	pärä'dä
¡PELIGRO!	Danger!	pelē'grō
PRIVADO	private	prēvä'dō
PROHIBIDO BAÑARSE	No Swimming	prō·ēbē'dō banyär'se
PROHIBIDO EL PASO	Road Closed	prō·ēbē'dō el pä'sō
PROHIBIDO FIJAR AFICHES/ *Sp* CARTELES ...	Post no bills	prō·ēbē'dō fēhär' äfē'tshes/kärte'les
PROHIBIDA LA ENTRADA ...	No Entry	prō·ēbē'dä lä enträ'dä
SALIDA	Exit	sälē'dä
SE ALQUILA/ *Mex* SE RENTA ..	For Rent	se älkē'lä/se ren'tä
SEÑORAS	Ladies	senyō'räs
SE PROHIBE FUMAR	No Smoking	se prō·ē'be fōōmär'
SE VENDE	For Sale	se ven'de
¡JALE!/*Sp* ¡TIRAR!	Pull	hä'le/tērär'

Abbreviations

a/c	al cuidado de .... [äl kōō·ēdä'dō de]	**care of**
apdo	apartado (de correos) .... [äpärtä'dō (de kōrre'ōs)]	**Post Office Box**
avda	avenida [ävenē'dä]	**avenue**
C/	calle [kä'lye]	**street**
Cía	Companía [kōmpänyē'ä]	**company**
D. Dª ...	Don, Doña [dōn, dō'nyä].....	**terms of respect, forms of address**
dcha	derecha [dere'tshä]	**right**
D. F. ...	Distrito Federal .... [dēstrē'tō federäl']	**Mexico City (Federal District)**
EE. UU.	Estados Unidos .... [estä'dōs ōōnē'dōs]	**United States**
gral.	general [heneräl']	**general**
izq., izda.	izquierda [ēskyer'dä]	**left**
Kg.	kilogramo [kēlōgrä'mō]	**kilogram**
Km. ...	kilómetro [kēlō'metrō]	**kilometer**
m. ...	metro [me'trō]	**meter**
M.N. ...	Moneda Nacional .... [mōne'dä näsyōnäl']	**Mexican peso ("national currency")**
Nº	número [nōō'merō]	**number**
pág.	página [pä'hēnä]	**page**
Ptas. ...	pesetas [pese'täs]	**Spanish pesetas**
P.V.P. ..	precio de venta al público ..... [pre'syō de ven'tä äl pōō'blēkō]	**sale price to the public (Spain)**
RENFE .	Red Nacional de los Ferrocarri- les Españoles .... [red näsyōnäl' de lōs ferrōkä- rrē'les espänyō'les]	**Spanish national railroad**
S. A. ...	Sociedad Anónima .... [sōsyedäd' änō'nēmä]	**Corporation, Incorporated**
Sr.	Señor [senyōr']	**Mr.**
Sra.	Señora [senyō'rä]	**Mrs.**
Srta. ...	Señorita [senyōrē'tä]	**Miss**
tel., teléf.	teléfono [tele'fōnō]	**telephone**
Ud.	usted [ōōste']	**you**
Vd.	usted [ōōste']	**you**

Weights and Measures

1 millimeter	un milímetro	ōon mēlē′metrō
1 centimeter	un centímetro	ōon sentē′metrō
1 decimeter	un decímetro	ōon desē′metrō
1 meter	un metro	ōon me′trō
1 kilometer	un kilómetro	ōon kēlō′metrō
1 inch	una pulgada	ōo′nä pōolgä′dä
1 foot	un pie	ōom pye
1 yard	una yarda	ōo′nä yär′dä
1 (statute) mile	una milla	ōo′nä mē′lyä
1 nautical mile	una milla marítima or náutica	ōo′nä mē′lyä märē′tēmä, nou′tēkä
1 square foot	un pie cuadrado	ōom pye kōo·ädrä′dō
1 square yard	una yarda cuadrada	ōo′nä yär′dä kōo·ädrä′dä
1 square meter	un metro cuadrado	ōon me′trō kōo·ädrä′dō
1 square mile	una milla cuadrada	ōo′nä mē′lyä kōo·ädrä′dä
1 cubic foot	un pie cúbico	ōom pye kōo′bēkō
1 liter	un litro	ōon lē′trō
1 pint	una pinta	ōo′nä pēn′tä
1 quart	un cuarto de galón	ōon kōo·är′tō de gälōn′
1 gallon	un galón	ōon gälōn′
1 ounce	una onza	ōo′nä ōn′sä
1 pound	una libra	ōo′nä lē′brä
1 hundredweight	*approx.* un quintal	ōon kēntäl′
1 ton	una tonelada	ōo′nä tōnelä′dä
a piece (of ...)	una parte, un trozo de	ōo′nä pär′te, ōon trō′sō de
a pair (of ...)	un par de	ōom pär de
a dozen	una docena	ōo′nä dōsē′nä
a pack(et) of	un paquete de	ōom päke′te de

Colors

beige	beige	be'ēhe
black	negro	ne'grō
blonde	rubio	rōō'byō
blue	azul	äsōōl'
– **light blue**	azul claro	äsōōl' klä'rō
– **navy blue**	azul marino	äsōōl' märē'nō
– **turquoise**	azul turquesa	äsōōl' tōōrke'sä
brown	marrón/*Mex* café	märrōn'/käfe'
– **chestnut brown**	castaño	kästä'nyō
brunette	moreno	mōre'nō
color	color	kōlōr'
– **colored**	de colores	de kōlō'res
– **colorful**	de muchos colores	de mōō'tshōs kōlō'res
– **solid-color**	de un solo color	de ōōn sō'lō kōlōr'
gold	dorado	dōrä'dō
gray	gris	grēs
– **ash gray**	gris ceniza	grēs senē'sä
– **dark gray**	gris oscuro	grēs ōskōō'rō
– **pale gray**	gris claro	grēs klä'rō
green	verde	ver'de
– **dark green**	verde oscuro	ver'de ōskōō'rō
– **light green**	verde claro	ver'de klä'rō
lavender/mauve	lila, malva	lē'lä, mäl'vä
orange	naranja	närän'hä
pink	rosa	rō'sä
purple	morado	mōrä'dō
red	rojo, colorado	rō*h*ō, kōlōrä'dō
– **bright red**	rojo vivo	rō'*h*ō vē'vō
– **dark red**	rojo oscuro	rō*h*ō ōskōō'rō
silver	plateado	pläte·ä'dō
violet	violeta	vyōle'tä
white	blanco	bläng'kō
yellow	amarillo	ämärē'lyō

IMPORTANT GRAMMAR RULES

I. Stress and Accent

1. A word consisting of more than two syllables and ending in **n, s,** or a vowel is stressed on the second last syllable; e.g. *tomo* [tō'mō] I take, *naciones* [näsyō'nes] nations, *joven* [hō'ven] young.

2. A word consisting of more than two syllables and ending in another consonant or in y is stressed on the last syllable; e.g. *papel* [päpel'] paper, *Madrid* [mädrēd'], *estoy* [estōi'] I am.

3. Exceptions to the above rules are indicated by accent marks over the syllable to be stressed; e.g. *está* [estä'] he, she, it is, *nación* [näsyōn'] nation, *jóvenes pl.* [hō'venes] young people, *fácil* [fä'sēl] easy.

4. **i** (and **y** at the end of a word) and **u** next to another vowel are the unstressed (weak) vowels in diphthongs: *auto* [ou'tō] car, *bien* [byen] well, *buey* [bōo·ei'] ox. When i or u are stressed, an accent mark is placed over them.

5. Words of one syllable do not need accent marks, but some are accented in order to distinguish them from words which sound the same but have a different meaning; e.g. *se* [se] -self, *sé* [se] I know.

6. All question words have an accent, e.g. *¿dónde?* where?, *¿quién?* who?.

II. Orthography

Different Spellings for the Same Sound

k = **c:** *saco* [sä'kō] I take out.
         qu before e, i: *saque usted* [sä'ke ōōsted'] take out (polite command form)

g = **g:** *pagar* [pägär'] to pay
         gu before e, i: *paguemos* [päge'mōs] let's pay

x = **j:** me *dirijo* [me dērē'hō] I turn towards
         g before e, i: *dirigirse* [dērēhēr'se] to turn towards

ĭ, j = **i:** *perdió* [perdyō'] he (she) lost
         y between vowels: *creyó* [kreyō'] he (she) believed

In Spain:

θ = **z:** la *voz* [lä vōθ] the voice
         c before e, i: las *voces* [läs vō'θes] the voices

III. The Article

1. Spanish nouns are either masculine or feminine.

2. The Definite Article:

masculine (*m*): **el** [el], plural (*pl.*) **los** [lōs]; feminine (*f*): **la** [lä], plural **las** [läs]. – *el año* [el ä′nyō] the year, *los años* [lōs ä′nyōs] the years; *el libro* [el lē′brō] the book, *los libros* [lōs lē′brōs] the books; *la casa* [lä kä′sä] the house, *las casas* [läs kä′säs] the houses; *la voz* [lä vōs] the voice, *las voces* [läs vō′ses] the voices.

3. The neuter article **lo** [lō] precedes adjectives when they are used as nouns, numbers and possessive pronouns; e.g. *lo bueno* [lō boo‧e′nō] the good thing, *lo primero* [lō prēme′rō] the first thing, *lo mío* [lō mē‧ō] mine.

4. The Indefinite Article:

un *m* [oon] a, an, **unos** *pl* [oo′nōs] some, a few **una** *f* [oo′nä] a, an, **unas** *pl* [oo′näs] some, a few; e.g.

un año [oon ä′nyō] a year, *unos años* [oo′nōs ä′nyōs] some years; *una voz* [oonä vōs] a voice, *unas voces* [oo′näs vō′ses] some voices.

5. Before a feminine noun beginning with a stressed a or ha, el is used instead of la and un instead of una; e.g. *el agua* (*f*) [el ä′goo‧ä] the water, *un hacha f* [oon ä′tshä] an axe; *pl. las, unas.*

IV. The Noun

Plural

1. Nouns and adjectives ending in a vowel form their plurals by adding -s; those ending in a consonant or -y add -es; e.g. *el próximo año* [el prōg′sēmō ä′nyō] next year, *pl. los próximos años*; *un país fértil* [oom päēs′ fer′tēl] a fertile country, *pl. los países fértiles*; *la ley* [lä lei] the law, *pl. las leyes* [läs le′yes].

2. The addition of -es changes the accentuation: *la región* [lä rehyōn] the region, *pl. las regiones* [läs rehyō′nes].

V. The Prepositions de and a

1. The preposition **de** [de] is used to indicate possession; in conjunction with the masculine singular definite article (el) it forms the contracted form **del** [del]. When used with the masculine singular el, the preposition **a** forms **al** [äl]; e.g. *la casa* [lä kä′sä] the house, *de la casa, a la casa*; *el mes* [el mes] the month, *del mes, al mes*; *pl. los meses* [lōs me′ses] the months, *de los meses, a los meses*.

2. As in English, subject and object are distinguished by their place in the sentence (preceding or following the verb). When the direct object is a

person or one of the indefinites (alguien, nadie, alguno(s), ninguno(s)) it is preceded by **a**; e.g. *pierdo el tren* [pyer'dō el tren] I miss the train; but: *llamo al camarero* [lyä'mō äl kämäre'rō] I call the waiter.

3. When a number or an indefinite article precedes a direct object referring to a person, the **a** is dropped: *busco una secretaria* [bōōs'kō ōō'nä sekretä'ryä] I'm looking for a secretary.

VI. Adjectives and Adverbs

1. Adjectives agree in number and gender with the noun or pronoun they describe.

2. The plural of adjectives is formed in the same way as the plural of nouns.

3. Adjectives ending in **-o** form the feminine by changing the **-o** to **-a**; e.g. *alto* [äl'tō] high, tall, *f alta*; *pl. altos, altas*.

4. All other adjectives have the same form in the masculine and feminine; e.g. *un año feliz* [ōōn ä'nyō felēs'] a happy year; *una hora feliz* [ōō'nä ō'rä felēs'] a happy hour.

5. Adjectives referring to nationality, whatever their ending, can always have a feminine form with **a**; e.g. *español m* [espänyōl'] Spanish, *f española*; as a noun *el español* the Spaniard (*m*), *la española* the Spaniard (*f*).

6. Certain adjectives drop the -o when they precede a masculine singular noun, thus *bueno* [bōōe'·nō] good becomes **buen** [bōō·en'], *malo* [mä'lō] bad becomes **mal** [mäl].

7. The adjective usually follows the noun; demonstrative and indefinite adjectives as well as cardinal numbers precede the noun. Other adjectives may also precede the noun for emotional effect.

8. The adverb is formed by adding **-mente** to the feminine singular form of the adjective: e.g. *lento* [len'tō] slow – *lentamente* [lentämen'te] slowly.

9. Irregular Adverbs: **bien** [byen] well, **mal** [mäl] badly.

10. **"Very"** = muy [mōō·ē] before adjectives and adverbs; **"very much"** = mucho [mōō'tshō] after the verb.

VII. Comparison

1. The comparison of adjectives is formed by placing **más** [mäs] before the adjective; the superlative is obtained by placing the definite article before the comparative; e.g. *más alto* [mäs äl'tō] higher, *el más alto* the highest.

2. Irregular Comparisons: **mejor** [mehōr'] better, **peor** [pe·ōr'] worse; **mayor** [mäyōr] bigger, older, **menor** [menōr'] smaller, younger.

3. **"Than"** after the comparative = que [ke], before numbers de [de], and when the Spanish sentence has two verbs de lo que [de lō ke]; e.g. *España es más grande que Portugal* [Espä'nyä es mäs grän'de ke Pōrtōōgäl'] Spain is bigger than Portugal; *más de tres veces* [mäs de tres ve'ses] more than three times; *España es mas grande de lo que yo pensaba* [Espä'nyä es mäs grän'de de lō ke yō pensä'bä] Spain is bigger than I thought.

VIII. Pronouns

Personal Pronouns

A. Personal Pronouns used in the Accusative and Dative with the Verb

1. Singular (*sg.*)   Plural (*pl.*)

me	[me]	me, to me	*nos*	[nōs]	us, to us
te	[te]	you, to you	*os*	[ōs]	you, to you (*m*)
lo	[lō]	him, it	*los*	[lōs]	them, you (*m*)
la	[lä]	her, it, you	*las*	[läs]	them, you (*f*)
le	le]	him, you, to him, to her, to you	*les*	[les]	them, you, to them, to you
se	[se]	yourself, himself, herself, itself, yourselves, themselves			

2. Position: The unstressed personal pronouns precede the verb; e.g. *lo sé* [lō se] I know it. However, they are attached to the end of the direct affirmative command, the infinitive and the gerund; e.g. *sigame usted* [sē'gäme ōosted'] follow me (but: *no me siga usted* [nō me sē'gä ōosted'] don't follow me).

3. **se** can be used instead of the passive and to express the impersonal form (the English "one"); e.g. *cigarrillos se venden en estancos* [sēgärrē'lyōs se ven'den en estän'kōs] cigarettes are sold in tobacco stores; *aquí se come bien* [äkē' se kō'me byen] one can eat well here.

4. When both the direct and indirect object pronouns are in the third person singular in one sentence, the indirect precedes the direct and is written **se** [se] instead of "le" or "les"; le(s) + lo(s), la(s) = se lo(s), la(s).

B. Stressed Personal Pronouns

1. Subject Pronouns:

Singular	Plural
yo [yō] I	*nosotros f -as* [nōsō'trōs, -äs] we
tú [tōō] you (familiar)	*vosotros f -as* [vōsō'trōs, -äs] you (familiar)

él [el] he   *ellos f -as* [e'lyōs, -äs] they
ella [e'lyä] she   *Ustedes* [ōōste'des] you (*pl.*) (polite)
Usted [ōōsted'] you (polite)

The subject pronoun is usually omitted; it is used when necessary for clarification or emphasis.

2. Pronouns as objects of a preposition; e.g. *a mí* [ä mē] to me, me; *de ti* [de tē] from you, of you; *para él* [pä'rä el] for him; *con ella* [kōn e'lyä] with her; *por ello* [pōr e'lyō] because of that.

3. Irregular: *conmigo* [kōnmē'gō] with me, *contigo* [cōntē'gō] with you, *consigo* [kōnsē'gō] with him, her, it(self) and yourself (polite form).

4. **usted (Ud.)** [ōōsted'] you (sing. polite), *ustedes* (Uds.) [ōōste'des] you (*pl.* polite); also see Remarks.

5. The object pronouns before the verb are often supplemented by the prepositional pronoun when ambiguity exists (that is, in the polite form of "you"); e.g. **le** *buscaba* **a usted** [le bōōskä'bä ä ōōsted'] I looked for you; *le buscaba* can stand alone when the meaning is clear from the context.

Possessive Pronouns

1. Preceding the noun:

mi [mē] my   *nuestro, f -a* [nōō·es'trō] our
tu [tōō] your   *vuestro, f -a* [vōō·es'trō] your
su [sōō] his, her, your, their

2. Nominative function:

el mío [el mē·ō], *la mía* [lä mē·ä] mine
el tuyo [el tōō'yō], *la tuya* [lä tōō'yä] your
el suyo [el sōōy'ō], *la suya* [lä sōō'yä] his, hers, theirs
el nuestro [el nōō·es'trō], *la nuestra* [lä nōō·es'trä] ours
el vuestro [el vōō·es'trō], *la vuestra* [lä vōō·es'trä] your

3. Plurals are formed in the same way as the plural of nouns.

4. *Estas casas son mías* [es'täs kä'säs sōn mē'äs] these houses are mine. – *un amigo suyo* [ōōn ämē'gō sōō'yō] a friend of his, hers, theirs; *un amigo de usted* [ōōn ämē'gō de ōōsted'] a friend of yours.

5. *su amigo de usted* [sōō ämē'gō de ōōsted'] your friend.

Demonstrative Pronouns

1. Preceding the noun: *este m* [es'te], *esta f* [es'tä], *pl. estos, estas* this, these (near speaker).

esa f [e'sä], *ese m* [e'se], *pl. esos, esas* that, those (near listener); *aquel m* [äkel'], *aquella f* [äke'lyä], *pl. aquellos, -as* that, those (over there).

2. When used as the subject or object of a verb or when standing alone, the demonstrative pronouns have an accent placed on the stressed vowel: e.g. *éstos son míos* [es'tōs sōn mē·'ōs] these are mine.

3. Demonstratives are used with prepositions in the same way as nouns.

Question Words

1. *¿quién? pl. ¿quiénes?* [kyen, kye'nes] who?
   ¿qué? [ke] what? which? (before noun)
   ¿cuál? pl. ¿cuáles? [kōō·äl, kōō·ä'les] which? (before *de* "of" and the verb *ser* "to be").
   ¿cuánto, -a, -os, -as? [kōō·än'tō, -ä, -os, -äs] how much?, how many?

2. Interrogatives are used with prepositions in the same way as nouns, e.g. *¿de quién* [de kyen] whose?, *¿a quién?* [ä kyen] to whom?, *¿de qué?* [de ke] what about?

Relative Pronouns

que [ke]: most frequent relative pronoun, meaning who, that, which; sometimes with the definite article: *el (la, los, las) que*

el (la) cual, los (las) cuales [el (lä) kōō·äl, lōs (läs) kōō·ä'les]: used mostly after prepositions with more than two syllables to mean, who, which, or whom.

quien(es) [kyen'(es)]: whom, refers only to persons, especially following prepositions of one syllable.

cuyo(s), cuya(s) [kōō'yō(s), kōō'yä(s)]: always in adjective meaning "whose", agrees in number and gender with the noun it modifies.

lo que [lō ke], *lo cual* [lō kōō·äl], what, which; *todo lo que* [tō'dō lō ke] everything that.

Definite Pronouns

= the definite article; e.g. *el que* [el ke], he who.

IX. The Verb

Conjugation of regular verbs

Endings are attached to the stem of the verb except in the future and conditional tenses, when they are added to the infinitive.

Verbs are divided into three conjugations with the endings **-ar, -er** and **-ir.**

Infinitive

First Conjugation: *tomar* [tōmär'] to take (stem: *tom-*)
Second Conjugation: *vender* [vender'] to sell (stem: *vend-*)
Third Conjugation: *vivir* [vēvēr'] to live (stem: *viv-*)
Gerund: *tomando* taking, *vendiendo* selling, *viviendo* living. y instead of i is written between two vowels, e.g. *creer* [kre·er] to believe: *Ger. creyendo* [kreyen'dō] believing.
Participle: *tomado* taken, *vendido* sold, *vivido* lived
With an accent: *creer* to believe: *creído* [kre·ē'dō] believed.

Endings

	1st sing.	3rd sing.		2nd pl.	
		2nd sing.		1st pl.		3rd pl.

Present Indicative
I take, etc.

		1st sing.	2nd sing.	3rd sing.	1st pl.	2nd pl.	3rd pl.
stem	tom-	o	as	a	amos	áis	an
	vend-	o	es	e	emos	éis	en
	viv-	o	es	e	imos	ís	en

Present Subjunctive
(that) I (may) take

		1st sing.	2nd sing.	3rd sing.	1st pl.	2nd pl.	3rd pl.
stem	tom-	e	es	e	emos	éis	en
	vend- }	a	as	a	amos	áis	an
	viv- }						

Imperfect
I used to take,
I was taking, etc.

		1st sing.	2nd sing.	3rd sing.	1st pl.	2nd pl.	3rd pl.
stem	tom-	aba	abas	aba	ábamos	abais	aban
	vend- }	ía	ías	ía	íamos	íais	ían
	viv- }						

Preterite
I took, etc.

stem $\left\{\begin{array}{l}\text{tom-}\\ \text{vend-}\\ \text{viv-}\end{array}\right\}$	é í	aste iste	ó ió	amos imos	asteis isteis	aron ieron

1. Imperfect Subjunctive (-ra)
(that) I might take, etc.

stem $\left\{\begin{array}{l}\text{tom-}\\ \text{vend-}\\ \text{viv-}\end{array}\right\}$	ara iera	aras ieras	ara iera	áramos iéramos	arais ierais	aran ieran

2. Imperfect Subjunctive (-se)

stem $\left\{\begin{array}{l}\text{tom-}\\ \text{vend-}\\ \text{viv-}\end{array}\right\}$	ase iese	ases ieses	ase iese	ásemos iésemos	aseis ieseis	asen iesen

Imperative
take, etc.

stem $\left\{\begin{array}{l}\text{tom-}\\ \text{vend-}\\ \text{viv-}\end{array}\right\}$	a e e		ad ed id

Future
I will take, etc.

Infin-itive $\left\{\begin{array}{l}\text{tomar}\\ \text{vender}\\ \text{vivir}\end{array}\right\}$	é	ás	á	emos	éis	án

Conditional
I would take, etc.

Infin-itive $\left\{\begin{array}{l}\text{tomar}\\ \text{vender}\\ \text{vivir}\end{array}\right\}$	ía	ías	ía	íamos	íais	ían

Remarks

1. The familiar forms of address are tú [tōo] you *sing.* and vosotros [vōsō′trōs] you *pl.* (only in Spain). The polite forms of address are usted [ōōsted′] you *sing.* and ustedes [ōōste′des] you *pl.*

2. The active compound tenses are formed with the auxiliary verb **haber** + the participle. The participle does not change.

Examples:

1. Present Perfect: *he tomado* [e tōmä′dō] I have taken, *hemos estado* [e′mōs estä′dō] we have been.

2. Pluperfect: *habían vendido* [äbē·'än vendē'do] they had sold, *habíamos venido* [äbē'ämōs venē'dō] we had come.

3. The passive is often expressed by an impersonal reflexive construction (se) in the third person singular. It is also expressed, as in English, by the auxiliary verb to be (ser) + past participle + by (por); e.g. *fué vendido por mí* [fōō·e' vendē'dō pōr mē] it was sold by me.

4. The imperfect is used to describe a past progressive action (what was happening or what used to happen) or a physical or emotional state in an incomplete past time. The preterite records an event or a series of events as a single completed occurrence in the past. The present perfect refers to an event in the past which extends into the present.

5. The affirmative command form of *tú* is the same as the third person of the present indicative, except for *tener, poner, venir, salir, hacer, ser, decir* and *ir*, whose forms are *ten, pon, ven, sal, haz, sé, di, ve*. The affirmative imperative of vosotros is formed by changing the final -r of the infinitive to -d. All other persons form the imperative by taking the corresponding form of the present subjunctive (with the negative commands being preceded by *no*); e.g. *toma* [tō'mä] (2nd pers. sing.) take – but: *no tomes* [nō tō'mes] (2nd pers. sing.) don't take; *tome usted* [tō'me ōōsted'] (3rd pers. sing.) take, *tomen ustedes* [tō'men ōōste'des] (3rd pers. pl.) take; *tomemos* [tōme'mos] let us take; also *vamos a tomar*.

6. The subjunctive expresses: 1. doubt on the part of the speaker: *no creo que venga* [nō kre'·ō ke ven'gä] I don't think he'll come. – 2. desire and the expression of will: *deseaba que viniese* or *viniera* [deseä'bä ke vēnye'se or vēnye'rä] I wanted him to come; commands (see paragraph 5). – 3. possibility: *es posible que venga* [es pōsē'ble ke ven'gä] he might come. – 4. expressions of emotion: *siento que estés enfermo* [syen'tō ke estes' emfer'mō] I'm sorry you're sick.

7. Progressive Action: Progressive action in the present is expressed by the verb estar ("to be") and the present participle of the verb, which is formed by adding -ando to the stem of the -ar verbs and -iendo to the stem of the -er and -ir verbs: *estoy fumando* [estoi' fōōmän'dō] I am smoking – *seguir* [segēr'], *continuar* [kōntēnōō·är'] + Gerund = to keep on doing something: *sigo* (or *continúo*) *fumando* I keep on smoking.

ENGLISH – SPANISH DICTIONARY

The translations are followed by phonetic transcriptions and page references, so that this dictionary serves as an index as well.

A

abbey abadía f [äbädē'ä] 124
abdomen abdomen m [äbdō'men] 166
above sobre [sō'bre] 25
abscess absceso m [äbse'sō] 169
absorbent cotton algodón m hidrófilo [älgōdōn' ēdrō'fēlō] 160
accelerator acelerador m [äselerädōr'] 51
access road acceso m [äkse'sō] 42
accessories accesorios m/pl. [äksesōr'yōs] 136
accident accidente m [äksēden'te] 153
accommodations alojamiento m [älōhämyen'tō] 81
accompany acompañar [äkōmpänyär'] 184
ace as m [äs] 181
act acto m [äk'tō] 176
actor actor m [äktōr'] 176
actress actriz f [äktrēs'] 176
adapter plug enchufe m intermedio [entshōō'fe ēnterme'dyō] 90
address dirección f [dēreksyōn'] 48
addressee destinatario m [destēnätär'yō] 149
admission entrada f [enträ'dä] 118
advance reservation reserva f de plaza [reser'vä de plä'sä] 90
advance ticket sales venta f anticipada [ve'ntä äntēsēpä'dä] 176
after después [despōō·es'] 159
after shave loción f para después del afeitado [lōsyōn' pä'rä despōō·es' del äfe·ētä'dō] 140
afternoon tarde f [tär'de] 31; **good ~**

buenas tardes [bōō·e'näs tär'des] 12; **in the ~** por la tarde [pōr lä tär'de] 31; **this ~** esta tarde [es'tä tär'de] 31
again otra vez [ō'trä ves] 184
against contra [kōn'trä] 164
age edad f [edäd'] 35; **under ~** menor de edad [menō'r de edäd'] 35
ago: a month ~ hace un mes [ä'se ōōn mes] 32
air aire m [ī're] 26; **~ filter** filtro m de aire [fēl'trō de ī're] 51; **~ pump** bomba f de aire [bōm'bä de ī're] 57; **~ sickness** mareo m [märe'ō] 70; **~ temperature** temperatura f del aire [temperätōō'rä del ī're] 185; **~ mattress** colchón m de aire [kōltshōn' de ī're] 185; **~ jet** tobera f de aire fresco [tōbe'rä de ī're fres'kō] 70; **~ conditioning** aire m acondicionado [ī're äkōndēsyōnä'dō] 75; **~ mail** por avión [pōr ävyōn'] 145; correo m aéreo [kōrre'ō ä·e'reō] 149
aircraft avión m [ävyōn'] 70
airline compañía f aérea [kōmpänyē'ä ä·e'reä] 70
airport aeropuerto m [ä·erōpōō·er'tō] 68; **~ service charge** tasa f del aeropuerto [tä'sä del ä·erōpōō·er'tō] 68
alcohol alcohol m [älkō·ōl] 101
all todo [tō'dō] 80
allergy alergia f [äler'hyä] 169
alley callejón m [kälyehōn'] 120
almond almendra f [älmen'drä] 111
alone solo [sō'lō] 14
already ya [yä] 70
altar altar m [ältär'] 124

alto alto [äl'tō] 176

a.m.: nine ~ las nueve de la mañana [läs nōō·e've de lä mänyä'nä] 30

amber ámbar m [äm'bär] 133

ambulance ambulancia f [ämbōōlän'syä] 49

American americano, [ämerēkä'nō] 152; **~ dollars** dólares m/pl americanos [dō'läres ämerēkä'nōs] 152; **~ plan** pensión f completa [pensyōn' kömple'tä] 90; **~ studies** estudios m/pl. americanos [estōō'dyōs ämerēkä'nōs] 39

amount importe m [ēmpōr'te] 151

ampule ampolla f [ämpō'lyä] 160

amusement pasatiempo m [päsätyem'pō] 181; **~ park** parque m de atracciones [pär'ke de äträksyō'nes] 120

anchor ancla f [ang'klä] 75

anchovies anchoas f/pl [äntshō'äs] 104

anemia anemia f [äne'myä] 169

anesthesia anestesia f [äneste'syä] 174

anesthetic anestesia f [äneste'syä] 172

ankle tobillo m [tōbē'lyō] 166

announcer presentador m [presentädōr'] 182

annually todos los años [tōdōs lōs ä'nyōs] 32

another otro [ōt'rō] 83

antidote antídoto m [äntē'dōtō] 160

anyone alguien [äl'gyen] 85

anything algo [äl'gō] 80

apartment apartamento m [äpärtämen'tō] 81; **~ building** casa f de pisos [kä'sä de pē'sōs] 90

apologize pedir perdón [pedēr' perdōn'] 22

appendicitis apendicitis f [äpendēsē'tēs] 169

appendix apéndice m [äpen'dēse] 166

appetite apetito m [äpetē'tō] 163

applause aplausos m/pl [äplou'sōs] 177

apple manzana f [mänsä'nä] 111

appointment hora f, cita f [ō'rä, sē'tä] 173

apprentice aprendiz m [äprendēs'] 36

approach (plane) vuelo m de aproximación [vōō·e'lō de äprōksēmäsyōn'] 70

apricot damasco m, albaricoque m (Sp), chabacano m (Mex) [dämäs'kō, älbärēkō'ke, tshäbäkä'nō] 111

April abril m [äbrēl'] 33

apron delantal m [deläntäl'] 134

arch arco m [är'kō] 124

archaeology arqueología f [ärke·ōlōhē'ä] 39

architecture arquitectura f [ärkētektōō'rä] 39

area región f [rehyōn'] 120; **~ code** prefijo m, (Mex) clave f [prefē'hōō, klä've] 149

aria aria f [ä'ryä] 177

arm brazo m [brä'sō] 166

armchair butaca f, sillón m [bōōtä'kä, sē'lyōn] 90

armpit sobaco m, axila f [sōbä'kō, äksē'lä] 166

arrest detener [detener'] 154

arrival llegada f [lyegä'dä] 67

art arte m [är'te] 39; **~ gallery** galería f de arte [gälerē'ä de är'te] 128; **~ history** historia f de arte [ēstōr'ya de är'te] 39

artery arteria f [ärter'ya] 166

arthritis artritis f [ärtrē'tēs] 169

artichoke alcachofa f [älkätschō'fä] 109

articles objetos m/pl [ōbhe'tōs] 80

artist artista m + f [ärtēs'tä] 36

ash tray cenicero m [senēse'rō] 87

ashore: to go ~ desembarcar [desembärkär'] 72

asparagus espárragos m/pl [espä'rrägōs] 110

aspirin aspirina f [äspērē'nä] 160

asthma asma m [äz'mä] 169

athlete atleta *m* + *f* [ätle'tä] 187

athletic club club *m* deportivo [klōōb depōrtĕ'vō] 189

atmospheric pressure presión *f* atmosférica [presyōn' ätmōsfe'rēkä] 26

attack ataque *m* [ätä'ke] 169

attorney abogado *m* [äbōgä'dō] 154

audience espectadores *m/pl* [espektädō'res] 179

auditorium sala *f* [sä'lä] 179

August agosto *m* [ägōs'tō] 33

aunt tía *f* [tē'ä] 35

auto racing motorismo [*m* mōtōrēz'-mō] 187

autobiography autobiografía *f* [outōbē-ōgräfē'ä] 130

automatic transmission dispositivo *m* automático [dĕspōsētĕ'vō ōŭtōmä'-tēkō] 51

automobile club automóvil club *m* [outōmō'vĕl klōōb] 42

avenue avenida *f*, paseo *m* [ävenē'dä, päse'ō] 120

avocado aguacate *m* [ägōō·äkä'te] 109

axle eje *m* [e'he] 51

B

back *(noun)* espalda *f* [espäl'dä] 166; ~ **seat** asiento *m* trasero [äsyen'tō träse'rō] 55; ~ **wheel** rueda *f* trasera [rōō·e'dä träse'rä] 47

backache dolores *m/pl* de la espalda [dōlō'res de lä espäl'dä] 169

backfire petardeo *m* [petärde'ō] 51

backwards de espaldas [de espäl'däs] 66

bacon tocino *m* [tōsē'nō] 100

badminton badminton *m*, volante *m* *(Sp)* [bädmēntōn', vōlän'te] 180

bag bolsa *f* [bōl'sä] 126; **beach** ~ bolsa *f* para la playa [bōl'sä pä'rä lä plä'yä] 143; **plastic** ~ bolsa *f* de plástico [bōl'sä de pläs'tēkō] 144; **traveling** ~

bolso *m*, bolsa *f* de viaje [bōl'sō, bōl'-sä de vyä'he] 63

baggage equipaje *m* [ekēpä'he] 63; ~ **check** resguardo *m*, (Sp) talón *m* [rezgōō·är'dō, tälōn'] 84; ~ **check area** consigna *f*, (Mex) "guarda equipaje" [kōnsēg'nä, gōō·är'dä ekēpä'-he] 63; ~ **claim area** entrega *f* de equipaje, (Mex) andenes *m/pl* de equipaje [entre'gä de ekēpä'he, än-de'nes de ekēpä'he] 63

baked asado, horneado [äsä'dō, ōrne·ä'dō] 102

baker panadero *m* [pänäde'rō] 36

bakery panadería *f* [pänäderē'ä] 128

balance beam barra *f* de equilibrio [bä'rra de ekēlē'brē·ō] 188

balcony balcón *m* [bälkōn] 82; ~ *(theater)* paraíso, (Mex) chilla [pärä·ē'sō, tshē'lyä] 177

ball pelota *f* [pelō'tä] 143; ~ **bearings** cojinete *m* de bolas, (Mex) baleros *m/pl* [kōhēne'te de bō'läs, bäle'rōs] 51; ~ **point pen** bolígrafo *m*, (Mex) pluma *f* [bōlē'gräfō, plōō'mä] 138

ballet ballet *m* [bäle'] 177

banana plátano *m* [plä'tänō] 112

band conjunto *m*, banda *f* [kōnhōōn'-tō, bän'dä] 177

bandage vendaje *m*, (Mex) venda *f* [vendä'he, ven'dä] 160

bank *(money)* banco *m* [bäng'kō] 151; ~ **savings** ~ caja *f* de ahorros [kä'hä de ä·ō'rrōs] 152; ~ **account** cuenta *f* bancaria [kōō·en'tä bängkär'yä] 151; ~ **charges** derechos *m/pl* del banco [dere'tshōs del bäng'ko] 151; ~ **note** billete *m* de banco [bēlye'te de bäng'kō] 151; ~ **transfer** giro *m* bancario [hē'ro bängkär'yō] 151

bank *(river)* orilla *f* [ōrē'lyä] 75

banker banquero *m* [bängke'rō] 181

baptism bautismo *m* [boutēz'mō] 124

bar bar *m* [bär] 74

barber shop peluquería f [peloōokerēˈä] 74

barge barcaza f, (Mex) chalana f [bärkäˈsä, tshäläˈnä] 75

baritone barítono m [bärēˈtōnō] 177

barometer barómetro m [bärōˈmetrō] 25

Baroque barroco m [bärrōˈkō] 124

barrier barrera f [bärreˈrä] 67

basement sótano m [sōˈtänō] 90

bass bajo m [bäˈhō] 177

bath baño m [bäˈnyō] 82; ~ **attendant** bañero m [bänyeˈrō] 175; ~ **salts** sales f/pl de baño [säˈles de bäˈnyō] 140; **mineral** ~ baño m de aguas minerales [bäˈnyō de äˈgoō·äs mēnerä-ˈles] 175; **steam** ~ baño m de vapor, baño m turco [bäˈnyō de väpōr, bäˈ-nyō toōrˈkō] 175; **take a** ~ bañarse [bänyärˈse] 97

bathing cap gorro m de baño [gōˈrro de bäˈnyō] 186

bathing suit traje m de baño [träˈhe de bäˈnyō] 186

bathing trunks bañador m (Sp) [bänyä-dōrˈ] 186

bathrobe bata f (Sp) albornoz m [bäˈtä, älbōrnōsˈ] 134

bathroom cuarto m de baño [koō·ärˈtō de bäˈnyō] 90

battery (car) batería f, acumulador m (Mex) [bäterēˈä, äkoōmoōlädōrˈ] 51

bay bahía f [bä·ēˈä] 75

beach playa f [pläˈyä] 81; **private** ~ playa f privada [pläˈyä prēväˈdä] 93; **sandy** ~ playa f de arena [pläˈyä de äreˈnä] 186

beans frijoles m/pl, judías f/pl (Sp) [frē-hōˈles, hoōdēˈäs] 110; **green** ~ ejotes m/pl. (Mex), judías verdes f/pl (Sp) [ehōˈtes, hoōdēˈäs verˈdes] 110

beard barba f [bärˈbä] 157

beauty contest concurso m de belleza [kōnkoōrˈsō de belyeˈsä] 181

beauty parlor salón m de belleza [sälōnˈ de belyeˈsä] 158

bed cama f [käˈmä] 90; ~ **and two meals** media pensión f [meˈdyä pen-syōnˈ] 90; ~ **linen** ropa f de cama [rōˈpä de käˈmä] 90; ~ **rug** alfombrilla f, pie m de cama [älfōmbrēˈlyä, pye de käˈmä] 90; ~ **side table** mesita f de noche [mesēˈtä de nōˈtshe] 90; ~ **spread** colcha f, cubrecama m, sobrecama m [kōlˈtshä, koōbrekäˈmä, sōbrekäˈmä] 90; **day** ~ sofá-cama m [sōfäˈ-käˈmä] 91

bedroom dormitorio m, alcoba f, recámara f (Mex) [dōrmētōrˈyō, älkōˈbä, rekäˈmärä] 93

beer cerveza f [serveˈsä] 113; **bottled** ~ cerveza f de botella [serveˈsä de bō-teˈlyä] 113; **dark** ~ cerveza f negra [serveˈsä neˈgrä] 113; **draft** ~ cerveza f de barril [serveˈsä de bärrēlˈ] 113; **light** ~ cerveza f clara, rubia (Sp) [serveˈsä kläˈrä, roōˈbyä] 113

beeswax cera f de abejas [seˈrä de äbeˈhäs] 143

beets remolachas f/pl [remōläˈtshäs] 110

beige beige [be·ēˈhe] 194

bell campana f [kämpäˈnä] 124

belt cinturón m [sēntoōrōnˈ] 134

bet apostar [äpōstärˈ] 181

bicycle bicicleta f [bēsēkleˈtä] 41; ~ **race** carrera f ciclista [kärreˈrä sēklēsˈ-tä] 187; ~ **rider** ciclista m [sēklēsˈtä] 187; **ride a** ~ ir en bicicleta [ēr en bēsēkleˈtä] 187

bicycling ciclismo m [sēklēzˈmō] 187

big grande [gränˈde] 127

bike lane pista f de bicicletas [pēsˈtä de bēsēkleˈtäs] 42

bikini bikini m [bēkēˈnē] 134

bile bilis f [bēˈlēs] 166

bill (money) billete m [bēlyeˈte] 151

bill cuenta f [koō·enˈtä] 89

billfold cartera f [kärte'rä] 153

binoculars prismáticos m/pl [présmä'-tēkōs] 138

biography biografía f [bē-ōgräfē'ä] 130

biology biología f [bē-ōlōhē'ä] 39

birthday cumpleaños m [kōōmple-·ä'nyōs] 22; **Happy** ~ ¡Feliz cumpleaños! [felēs' kōōmple·ä'nyōs] 23

bishop (chess) alfil m [älfēl'] 181

black negro [ne'grō] 194

blackmail attempt extorsión f, chantaje m [ekstōrsyōn', tshäntä'he] 153

bladder vejiga f [vehē'gä] 166

blanket cobija f, frazada f, manta f (Sp) [kōbē'hä, fräsä'dä, män'tä] 87

bleeding hemorragia f [emōrrä'hyä] 169

blinker intermitente m [ēntermēten'te] 51

blizzard ventisca f [ventēs'kä] 26

blonde rubio [rōō'byō] 194

blood sangre f [säng'gre] 166; ~ **count** hemograma m [emōgrä'mä] 172; ~ **poisoning** intoxicación f de la sangre [ēntōksēkäsyōn' de lä säng'gre] 169; ~ **pressure** presión f de la sangre, tensión f [presyōn' de lä säng'gre, tensyōn'] 169; ~ **test** muestra f de sangre [mōō·es'trä de säng'gre] 172; ~ **transfusion** transfusión f de sangre [tränsfōōsyōn' de säng'gre] 172

blouse blusa f [blōō'sä] 134

blown (fuse) fundido [fōōndē'dō] 55

blow-out pinchazo m, reventón m [pēntshä'sō, reventōn'] 47

blue azul [äsōōl'] 194; **dark** ~ azul marino [äsōōl' märē'nō] 194; **light** ~ azul claro [äsōōl' klä'rō] 194; ~ **jeans** pantalón m vaquero, tejanos m/pl, jeans m/pl [päntälōn' väke'rō, tehä'nōs, hēns] 134

boar (wild) jabalí m [häbälē'] 108

board (to) ir a bordo [ēr ä bōr'dō] 75;

on ~ a bordo [ä bōr'dō] 75

boarding house casa f de huéspedes [kä'sa de ōō·es'pedes] 81

boarding school internado m [ēnter-nä'dō] 38

boat barco m, lancha f [bär'kō, län'-tshä] 75; **pedal** ~ patín m [pätēn'] 186; ~ **trip** excursión f en lancha [ekskōōrsyōn' en län'tshä] 120

body cuerpo m [kōō·er'pō] 166

body (car) carrocería f [kärrōserē'ä] 51; ~ **and fender damage** daños m/pl en la carrocería [dä'nyōs en lä kä-rrōserē'ä] 49

boiled cocido [kōse'dō] 102

bolt tornillo m [tōrnē'lyō] 51; ~ **nut** tuerca f [tōō·er'kä] 51

bone hueso m [ōō·e'sō] 166

book libro m [lē'brō] 130; ~ **shop** librería f [lēbrerē'ä] 128; **children's** ~ libro m para niños [lē'brō pä'rä nē'-nyōs] 130; **guide** ~ guía f [gē'ä] 130; **phrase** ~ libro m de frases [lē'brō de frä'ses] 130; **reference** ~ libro m de consulta [lē'brō de kōnsōōl'tä] 130; **story** ~ libro m de cuentos [lē'brō de kōō·en'tōs] 130; **text** ~ manual m [mänōō·äl'] 130

bookkeeper tenedor m de libros [tene-dōr' de lē'brōs] 36

bookseller librero m [lēbre'rō] 36

booth cabina f [käbē'nä] 148

boots botas f/pl [bō'täs] 139

border frontera f [frōnte'rä] 78; ~ **crossing** paso m de la frontera [pä'so de lä frōnte'rä] 80

botanical gardens jardín m botánico [härdēn' bōtä'nēkō] 120

bottle botella f, frasco m (Mex) [bōte'-lya, fräs'kō] 199

bouquet ramo m de flores [rä'mō de flō'res] 147

bow (ship) proa f [prō'ä] 75

bowel movement deposición f [depōsēsyōn¹] 166

bowl tazón m [täsōn¹] 99

bowling bolos m/pl [bō¹lōs] 187; ~ **alley** bolera f [bōle¹rä] 187

box (verb) boxear [bōkse·är¹] 187

box (noun) caja f [kä¹hä] 126; ~ **lunch** bolsa f de merienda [bōl¹sä de meryen¹dä] 86; ~ **office** taquilla f [täkē¹lyä] 177

boxer boxeador m [bōkse·ädōr¹] 187

boxing boxeo m [bōkse·ō] 187

boy niño m, muchacho m [nē¹nyō, mōōtshä¹tshō] 35

bra sostén m, sujetador m [sōsten¹, sōōhetädōr¹] 134

bracelet pulsera f [pōōlse¹rä] 133

braces aparato m dental, frenillo m [äpärä¹tō dentäl¹, frenē¹lyō] 174

brain cerebro m [sere¹brō] 166

brake drum tambor m de freno [tämbōr¹ de fre¹nō] 51

brake fluid líquido m de frenos [lē¹kēdō de fre¹nōs] 51

brake lights luces f/pl de freno [lōō¹ses de fre¹nō] 51

brake pedal pedal m de freno [pedäl¹ de fre¹no] 51

brakes frenos m/pl [fre¹nōs] 51

branch manager gerente m or director m de la sucursal [heren¹te, dērektōr¹ de lä sōōkōōrsäl] 151

brandy coñac m [kōnyäk¹] 113

bread pan m [pän] 111; **whole wheat** ~ pan m de trigo integral [pän de trē¹gō ēntegräl¹] 100; ~ **basket** cestilla f, canasta f del pan [sestē¹lyä, känäs¹ tä del pän] 99

breakdown falla mecánica f, avería f [fä¹lyä mekä¹nēkä, äverē¹ä] 48

breakfast desayuno m [desäyōō¹nō] 90; **to have** ~ desayunar [desäyōōnär¹] 90; ~ **room** sala f de desayuno [sä¹lä desäyōō¹nō] 90

breast pecho m, seno m [pe¹tshō,

se¹nō] 166

breathing respiración f [respēräsyōn¹] 166; ~ **problems** dificultades f/pl respiratorias [dēfēkōōltä¹des respērätō¹ryäs] 169

breeze brisa f [brē¹sä] 75

bricklayer albañil m [älbänyēl¹] 36

bridge puente m [pōō·en¹te] 42

bridge (on ship) puente m de mando [pōō·en¹te de män¹do] 75

briefcase maletín m, cartera f (Sp) [mäletēn¹, kärte¹rä] 143

brilliantine brillantina f [brēlyäntē¹nä] 158

broccoli brécol m, brócoli m [bre¹kōl, brō¹kōlē] 110

brochure folleto m [fōlye¹tō] 130

broken roto [rō¹tō] 23

bronchitis bronquitis f [brōngkē¹tēs] 169

brooch broche m, prendedor m [brō¹tshe, prendedōr¹] 133

broth caldo m [käl¹dō] 105; **chicken** ~ caldo m de gallina [käl¹dō de gälyē¹nä] 105

brother hermano m [ermä¹nō] 35; ~ **-inlaw** cuñado m [kōōnyä¹dō] 35

brown marrón, café (Mex) [märrōn¹, käfe¹] 194; **chestnut** ~ castaño [kästä¹nyō] 194

bruise contusión f [kōntōōsyōn¹] 169

brush cepillo m [sepē¹lyō] 141; **clothes** ~ cepillo m de ropa [sepē¹lyō de rō¹pä] 141

Brussel sprouts coles f/pl de Bruselas [kō¹les de brōōse¹läs] 110

bucket cubo m, balde m [kōō¹bō, bäl¹de] 90

buckle hebilla f [ebē¹lyä] 136

building edificio m [edēfē¹syō] 119

bulb bombilla f [bōmbē¹lyä] 51; **light** ~ bombillo m, bombilla f (Sp), foco m (Mex) [bōmbē¹lyō, bōmbē¹lyä, fō¹kō] 92

bumper parachoques m, defensa f [pä-rätshō'kes, defen'sä] 51

bungalows bungalows m/pl, bungalos m/pl, cabañas f/pl. (Mex) [bōōngä'lōs, bōōngä'lōs, käbä'nyäs] 81

buoy boya m [bō'yä] 75

burn (noun) quemadura f [kemädōō'rä] 169

burned out (bulb) fundida(-o) [fōōndē'dä(-ō)] 88

bus autobús m, camión m (Mex) [outōbōōs', kämyōn'] 59; ~ **terminal** estación f de autobuses [estäsyōn' de outōbōō'ses] 59

bus stop parada f de autobuses, de camiones (Mex) [pärä'dä de outōbōō'ses, de kämyō'nes] 116

business administration economía f de empresas [ekōnōmē'ä de empre'säs] 39

business school escuela f de comercio [eskōō·e'lä de kōmer'syō] 39

busy ocupado [ōkōōpä'dō] 148

butcher carnicero m [kärnēse'rō] 36

butter mantequilla f [mäntekē'lyä] 102

buttocks nalgas f/pl [näl'gäs] 166

button botón m [bōtōn'] 136

buy comprar [kōmprär'] 126

C

cabaña caseta f [käse'tä] 185

cabbage repollo m [repō'lyō] 110

cabin (on ship) camarote m, cabina f (Mex) [kämärō'te, käbē'nä] 75; **double** ~ camarote m, cabina f (Mex) doble [kämärō'te, käbē'nä dō'ble] 73; **inside** ~ camarote m, cabina f (Mex) interior [kämärō'te, käbē'nä ēnteryōr'] 73; **outside** ~ camarote m, cabina f (Mex) exterior [kämärō'te, käbē'nä eksteryōr'] 73; **single** ~ camarote m, cabina f (Mex) individual [kämärō'te, käbē'nä ēndēvē-

dōō·äl'] 73

cabinetmaker ebanista m [ebänēs'tä] 36

cable cable m [kä'ble] 52

cake tarta f, torta f [tär'tä, tōr'tä] 113

calf (of leg) pantorilla f [päntōrē'lyä] 166

call (noun) llamada f [lyämä'dä] 148; **make a phone** ~ telefonear [telefōne·är'] 147; **collect** ~ cobro m revertido, por cobrar (Mex) [kō'brō revertē'dō, pōr cōbrär'] 149; **long distance** ~ conferencia f, llamada f de larga distancia (Mex) [kōmferen'syä, lyämä'dä de lär'gä destän'syä] 149

call (at port) hacer escala [äser' eskä'lä] 75

camera máquina f fotográfica [mä'kēnä fōtōgrä'fēkä] 132; **movie** ~ tomavistas m, cámara f, filmadora f [tōmävēs'täs, kä'märä, fēlmädō'rä] 132

camomile tea manzanilla f [mänsänē'lyä] 160

camp (out) acampar [äkämpär'] 95; ~ **bed** cama f de campaña [kä'mä de kämpä'nyä] 96; ~ **site** camping m campamento m (Mex) [kämpēn', kämpämen'tō] 96; ~ **stove** brasero m [bräse'ro] 143

camper vehicle cámper m [käm'per] 40

camping camping m, campismo m (Mex) [kämpēn', kämpēz'mō] 96; ~ **ID** tarjeta f de camping [tärhe'tä de kämpēn'] 96; ~ **trailer** caravana f, trayler m (Mex) [kärävä'nä, trīler] 40

camshaft árbol m de levas [är'bōl de le'väs] 51

can opener abrelatas m [äbrelä'täs] 143

canal canal m [känäl'] 75

cancel anular [änōōlär'] 69

cancer cáncer m [kän'ser] 169

candle vela f [ve'lä] 143

candlestick candelero m [kändele'rō] 143

candy caramelos *m/pl* [käräme'lōs] 143

canned goods conservas *f/pl*, enlatados *m/pl* [kōnser'väs, enlätä'dōs] 143

cap gorra *f*, gorro *m* [gō'rrä, gō'rrō] 134

capers alcaparras *f/pl* [älkäpä'rräs] 102

capital capital *f* [käpētäl'] 120

capon capón *m* [käpōn'] 107

captain capitán *m* [käpētän'] 75; **~'s table** mesa *f* del capitán [me'sä del käpētän'] 75

car automóvil *m* [outōmō'vēl] 40; **~ (railroad)** coche *m*, vagón *m* [kō'-tshe, vägōn'] 67; **~ door** puerta *f* del carro, del coche *(Sp)* [pōō·er'tä del kä'rrō, del kō'tshe] 52; **~ ferry** transbordador *m* [tränsbōrdädōr'] 72; **~ keys** llaves *f/pl* del carro, del coche [lyä'ves del kä'rrō, del kō'tshe] 52; **~ repair service** taller *m* mecánico [tälyer' mekä'nēkō] 45; **to go by ~** ir en carro, coche *(Sp)* [ēr en kä'rrō, kō'-tshe] 42

carafe garrafa *f* [gärrä'fä] 99

caraway semillas *f/pl* de Alcaravea [semē'lyäs de älkäräve'ä] 103

carburetor carburador *m* [kärbōōrädōr'] 52; **~ jet** esprea *f* [espre'ä] 52

card *(post)* tarjeta *f* postal [tärhe'tä pōstäl'] 145; **~ game** juego *m* de cartas [hōō·e'gō de kär'täs] 181; **greeting ~ telegram** telegrama *m* de felicitación [telegrä'mä de felēsētäsyōn'] 147

cardiac infarction infarto *m* del miocardio [ēnfär'tō del mē·ōkär'dyō] 169

careful! ¡atención! [ätensyōn'] 49

carp carpa *f* [kär'pä] 106

carpenter carpintero *m* [kärpēnte'rō] 36

carpet moqueta *f*, tapete *m (Mex)* [mōke'tä, täpe'te] 90

carrots zanahorias *f/pl* [sänä·ō'ryäs] 110

cartoon dibujos *m/pl* animados, monitos *m/pl* [dēbōō'hōs änēmä'dōs, mōnē'tōs] 179

cash *(verb)* cobrar [kōbrär'] 151

cassette cassette *m or f* [käse'te] 143

castle castillo *m* [kästē'lyō] 119

castor oil aceite *m* de ricino [äse'ēte de rēsē'nō] 160

catalogue catálogo *m* [kätä'lōgō] 130

category categoría *f* [kätegōrē'ä] 90

cathedral catedral *f* [kätedräl'] 119

cauliflower coliflor *f* [kōlēflōr'] 110

cave cueva *f* [kōō·e'vä] 120

cavities caries *f/pl* [kär'yes] 174

ceiling techo *m* [te'tshō] 90

celery apio *m* [ä'pyō] 109

cellar sótano *m* [sō'tänō] 90

cemetery cementerio *m* [semente'ryō] 120

centimeter centímetro *m* [sentē'metrō] 193

ceramics cerámica *f* [serä'mēkä] 143

cereal cereales *m/pl* [cere·ä'les] 100

certainly desde luego [dez'de lōō·e'gō] 21

chains cadenas *f/pl* [käde'näs] 52

chair silla *f* [sē'lyä] 91; **deck ~** silla *f* de cubierta, hamaca *f*, tumbona *f* [sē'-lyä de kōōbyer'tä, ämä'kä, tōōmbō'-nä] 91

chamber music música *f* de cámara [mōō'sēkä de kä'marä] 177

championship competición *f*, concurso *m* [kōmpetēsyōn', kōnkōōr'sō] 188

change *(noun)* cambio *m* [käm'byō] 152

change *(verb)* cambiar [kämbyär'] 85

chapel capilla *f* [käpē'lyä] 124

charcoal pills pastillas *f/pl* de carbón [pästē'lyäs de kärbōn'] 160

charter plane avión *m* charter [ävyōn' tshär'ter] 70

chassis chasís *m*, *chasis* *m* (Sp) [tshäsēs¹, tshä¹sēs] 52

chauffeur chófer *m* [tshō¹fer] 41

check *(noun)* cuenta *f* [kōō·en¹tä] 115; ~ **room** guardarropa *m* [gōō·ärdä-rrō¹pä] 177;

check *(verb)* revisar [revēsär¹] 50; ~ **in** inscribirse [ēnskrēbēr¹se] 91

checked a cuadros [ä kōō·ä¹drōs] 137

checkers damas *f/pl* [dä¹mäs] 181

check-in inscripción *f* [ēnskrēpsyōn¹] 91

cheek mejilla *f* [mehē¹lyä] 166

cheers! ¡salud! [sälōōd¹]101

cheese queso *m* [ke¹sō] 110; **goat** ~ queso *m* de cabra [ke¹sō de kä¹brä] 110; **grated** ~ queso *m* rallado [ke¹sō rälyä¹dō] 111; **smoked** ~ queso *m* ahumado [ke¹sō ä·ōōmä¹dō] 110; **Swiss** ~ queso *m* suizo [ke¹sō sōō·ē¹sō] 111; **white** ~ queso *m* blanco [ke¹sō bläng¹kō] 110

chef jefe *m* de cocina [he¹fe de kōsē¹-nä] 36

chemistry química *f* [kē¹mēkä] 39

cherry cereza *f* [sere¹sä] 111

chess ajedrez *m* [ähedres¹] 180

chessman pieza *f* [pye¹sä] 181

chest pecho *m* [pe¹tshō] 166

chicken pollo *m* [pō¹lyō] 107; ~ **pox** varicela *f* [värēse¹lä] 169

children niños *m/pl* [nē¹nyōs] 185

chills escalofríos *m/pl* [eskälōfrē¹ōs] 169

chimney chimenea *f* [tshēmene¹ä] 91

chin barbilla *f*, mentón *m* [bärbē¹lyä, mentōn¹] 166

china porcelana *f* [pōrselä¹nä] 143

chip ficha *f* [fē¹tshä] 181

chisel cincel *m* [sēnsel¹] 57

chives cebollino *m* [sebōlyē¹nō] 103

chocolate chocolate *m* [tshōkōlä¹te] 100

choir coro *m* [kō¹rō] 124

cholera cólera *m* [kō¹lerä] 169

chop *(noun)* chuleta *f* [tshōōle¹tä] 108

chorus coro *m* [kō¹rō] 177

christening bautizo *m* [boutē¹sō] 124

church iglesia *f* [ēgle¹syä] 124; **Catholic** ~ iglesia *f* católica [ēgle¹syä kätō¹lēkä] 123; **Protestant** ~ iglesia *f* protestante [ēgle¹syä prōtestän¹te] 116; ~ **concert** concierto *m* de música sacra [kōnsyer¹tō de mōō¹sēkä sä¹krä] 124

churchyard campo *m* santo [käm¹pō sän¹tō] 124

cider sidra *f* [sē¹drä] 114

cigar puro *m* [pōō¹rō] 140

cigarette cigarrillo *m*, cigarro *m* (Mex) [sēgärrē¹lyo, sēgä¹rrō] 140; **filtered** ~ con filtro [kōn fēl¹trō] 140; **unfiltered** ~ sin filtro [sēn fēl¹trō] 140

cigarillo purito *m* [pōōrē¹tō] 140

cinema cine *m* [sē¹ne] 179

cinnamon canela *f* [käne¹lä] 103

circulation circulación *f* [sērkōōläs-yōn¹] 166

circulatory problems trastornos *m/pl* circulatorios [trästōr¹nōs sērkōōlä-tō¹ryōs] 169

circus circo *m* [sēr¹kō] 181

city ciudad *f* [syōōdäd¹] 120; ~ **hall** alcaldía *f*, ayuntamiento *m* (Sp) [älkäl-dē¹ä, ayōōntämyen¹tō] 120

civil servant funcionario *m* [fōōnsyō-nä¹ryō] 36

claim *(luggage)* recoger [rekōher¹] 63; ~ **check** talón *m*, recibo *m*, resguardo *m* [tälōn¹, resē¹bō, rezgōō·är¹dō] 63

clam almeja *f* [älme¹hä] 106

class clase *f* [klä¹se] 73; **first** ~ primera clase [prēme¹rä klä¹se] 73; **tourist** ~ clase *f* turista [klä¹se tōōrēs¹tä] 73

clay pigeon shooting tiro *m* al plato [tē¹rō äl plä¹tō] 181

clear *(sky)* despejado [despehä¹dō] 26

clergyman clérigo *m* [kle¹rēgō] 36

climate clima *m* [klē'mä] 26

clock reloj *m* [relōh'] 142; **alarm ~** despertador *m* [despertädōr'] 143

close cerrar [serär'] 65

closet armario *m* [ärmär'yō] 91

cloth paño *m* [pä'nyō] 57

clothes hanger percha *f*, gancho *m* [per'tshä, gän'tshō] 87

cloud nube *f* [nōō'be] 26; **~ cover** nuboso, nublado [nōōbō'sō, nōōblä'-dō] 26

cloudburst chaparrón *m* [tshäpärrōn'] 26

cloves clavos *m/pl* de especia [klä'vōs de espe'syä] 103

club club *m* [klōōb] 181

clubs *(cards)* tréboles *m/pl* [tre'bōles] 181

clutch cloche *m*, embrague *m (Sp)* [klō'tshe, embrä'ge] 52; **~ pedal** pedal *m* del embrague [pedäl' del embrä'ge] 52

coast costa *f* [kōs'tä] 75

coastal road camino *m* de la costa [kämē'nō de lä kōs'tä] 43

coat sobretodo *m*, abrigo *m* [sōbretō'-dō, äbrē'gō] 134; **~ check** ficha *f* del guardarropa [fē'tshä del gōō·ärdärrō'pä] 177

coconut coco *m* [kō'kō] 111

cod bacalao *m* [bäkälä'·ō] 106

c.o.d. envío *m* contra reembolso [envē'ō kōn'trä re·embōl'sō] 149

coffee café *m* [käfe'] 100; **black ~** *(espresso)* café *m* solo, expreso *m (Mex)* [käfe' sō'lō, espre'sō] 100; **decaffeinated ~** descafeinado [deskäfe·ēnä'dō] 100; **~ and milk** café *m* con leche [käfe' kōn le'tshe] 100

cognac coñac *m* [kōnyäk'] 113

coins monedas *f/pl*, cambio *m* [mōne'-däs, käm'byō] 148

cold *(noun)* resfriado *m* [resfrē·ä'dō] 169

cold *(adj.)* frío [frē'ō] 25; **~ cuts** fiambres *m/pl*, carnes *f/pl* frías *(Mex)* [fyäm'bres, kär'nes frē'äs] 100

colic cólico *m* [kō'lēkō] 169

collarbone clavícula *f* [klävē'kōōlä] 166

collect call cobro *m* revertido, por cobrar *(Mex)* [kō'brō revertē'dō, pōr kōbrär'] 149

collision choque *m* [tshō'ke] 49

cologne agua *m* de colonia [ä'gōō·ä de kōlō'nyä] 141

color color *m* [kōlōr'] 127

colored de colores [de kōlō'res] 194

colorful de muchos colores [de mōō'-tshōs kōlō'res] 194

comb *(noun)* peine *m* [pe'ēne] 141

comb *(verb)* peinar [pe·ēnär'] 158

come venir [venēr'] 15; **~ in!** ¡adelante! ¡pase! [ädelän'te, pä'se] 16

comedy comedia *f* [kome'dyä] 177

communion comunión *f* [kōmōōnyōn'] 124

compact polvera *f* [pōlve'rä] 141

compartment departamento *m*, compartim(i)ento *m* [depärtämen'tō, kōmpärtēm(y)en'tō] 67

compass brújula *f* [brōō'hōōlä] 138

competition competición *f*, concurso *m* [kōmpetēsyōn', kōnkōōr'sō] 188

complaint reclamación *f*, reclamo *m* [reklämäsyōn', reklä'mō] 91; **register a ~** hacer una reclamación, un reclamo [äser' ōō'nä reklämäsyōn', ōōn reklä'mō] 23

composer compositor *m* [kōmpōsē-tōr'] 177

compression compresión *f* [kōmpre-syōn'] 52

concert concierto *m* [kōnsyer'tō] 177; **~ hall** sala *f* de conciertos [sä'lä de kōnsyer'tōs] 177

concierge conserje *m* [kōnser'he] 91

concussion conmoción *f* cerebral [kōnmōsyōn' serebräl'] 169

condenser condensador *m* [kŏndensä-dŏr¹] 52

condolences pésame *m* [pe¹säme] 23

conductor conductor *m* [kŏndōōktŏr¹] 67; ~ *(orchestra)* director *m* de orquesta [dērektŏr¹ de ŏrkes¹tä] 177

confectioner pastelero *m* [pästele¹rō] 36

confess confesarse [kŏnfesär¹se] 124

confession confesión *f* [kŏnfesyŏn¹] 124

confiscate confiscar [kŏnfēskär¹] 154

congratulations! ¡felicitaciones! [felē-sētäsyŏ¹nes] 22

conjunctivitis conjuntivitis *f* [kŏnhōōn-tēvē¹tēs] 169

connecting rod biela *f* [bye¹lä] 52; ~ **bearing** conjinete *m* de biela, metales *m/pl* de bielas [kŏhēne¹te de bye¹lä, metä¹les de bye¹läs] 52

connection conección *f*, correspondencia *f* [kŏnegsyŏn¹, kŏrrespŏnden¹syä] 67

constipation estreñimiento *m* [estrenyēmyen¹tō] 169

consulate consulado *m* [kŏnsōōlä¹dō] 120

contact contacto *m* [kŏntäk¹tō] 52; ~ **lenses** lentes *f/pl* de contacto, lentillas *f/pl* [len¹tes de kŏntäk¹tō, lentē¹lyäs] 138

contraceptive pills píldoras *f/pl* anticonceptivas [pēl¹dōräs äntēkŏnseptē¹väs] 160

convalescent home casa *f* de reposo [kä¹sä de repō¹sō] 175

convent convento *m* [kŏnven¹tō] 124

cook *(verb)* cocinar [kōsēnär¹] 96

cook *(noun)* cocinero *m* [kōsēne¹rō] 36

cookies galletas *f/pl*, pastas *f/pl (Sp)* [gälye¹täs, päs¹täs] 112

cooking utensils batería *f* de cocina [bäterē¹ä de kōsē¹nä] 96

coolant agua *f* para el radiador [a¹-gōō·ä pä¹rä el rädyädōr¹] 45

cordial cordial [kŏrdyäl¹] 12

cordially yours con un saludo cordial [kŏn ōōn sälōō¹dō kŏrdyäl¹] 13

corduroy pana *f* [pä¹nä] 136

corkscrew sacacorchos *m*, descorchador *m* [säkäkŏr¹tshōs, deskŏrtshä-dŏr¹] 143

corn maíz *m* [mēs] 110; ~ **plaster** parche *m* para callos [pär¹tshe pä¹rä kä¹lyōs] 160

corner esquina *f* [eskē¹nä] 120; ~ *(sports)* saque *m* de esquina [sä¹ke de eskē¹nä] 189

corridor pasillo *m*, corredor *m* [päsē¹-lyō, kŏrrēdŏr¹] 91

corset corpiño *m* [kŏrpē¹nyō] 134

cosmetic salon instituto *m* de belleza [ēnstētōō¹tō de belye¹sä] 128

costumes trajes *m/pl* [trä¹hes] 177; ~ **designer** figurinista *m* [fēgōōrēnēs¹-tä] 177

cotton algodón *m* [älgōdōn¹] 136

couchette car coche *m* literas, camas *f/pl (Mex)* [kŏ¹tshe lēte¹räs, kä¹mäs] 64

cough tos *f* [tŏs] 169; ~ **medicine** calmante *m* de la tos [kälmän¹te de lä tōs] 160; ~ **syrup** jarabe *m* para tos [härä¹be pä¹rä tŏs] 160

counter ventanilla *f* [ventänē¹lyä] 149

country fair fiesta *f* popular [fyes¹tä pōpōōlär¹] 181

country road camino *m* vecinal [kä-mē¹nō vesēnäl¹] 43

countryside campo *m* [käm¹pō] 120

course rumbo *m* [rōōm¹bō] 75; **of** ~ por supuesto [pŏr sōōpōō·es¹tō] 21

court tribunal *m* [trēbōōnäl¹] 154

courthouse tribunal *m*, juzgado *m* [trēbōōnäl¹, hōōzgä¹dō] 120

cousin *(female)* prima *f* [prē¹mä] 35

cousin *(male)* primo *m* [prē¹mō] 35

covered market mercado *m* cubierto [merkä¹dō kōōbyer¹tō] 120

coxswain timonel *m* [tēmōnel'] 189

crab cangrejo *m* [kängre'hō] 107

cramps calambres *m/pl* [käläm'bres] 169

crankshaft cigüeñal *m* [sēgōō-enyäl'] 52

crayons lápices *m/pl* de color [lä'pēses de kōlōr'] 138

cream crema *f* [kre'mä] 141; **whipped ~** crema *f* batida; nata *f (Sp)* [kre'mä bätē'dä, nä'tä] 112, 113

credit crédito *m* [kre'dētō] 152; **~ card** tarjeta *f* de crédito [tärhe'tä de kre'dētō] 152

creed credo *m* [kre'dō] 124

crew tripulación *f* [trēpōōläsyōn'] 75

crib cuna *f* [kōō'nä] 83

crime delito *m* [delē'tō] 154

criminal delincuente *m* [delēnkōō-en'te] 154

croissant croissant *m* [krō-äsänt'] 100

cross cruz *f* [krōōs] 124; **~ road** travesía *f* [trävesē'ä] 43

crossing travesía *f* [trävesē'ä] 75

crown corona *f* [kōrō'nä] 124

crucifix crucifijo *m* [krōōsēfē'hō] 124

cruise crucero *m* [crōōse'rō] 75

crystal vidrio *m*, cristal *m (Sp)* [vē'drē-ō, krēstäl'] 143

cubic cúbico [kōō'bēkō] 193

cufflinks gemelos *m/pl*, mancuernas *f/pl (Mex)* [heme'lōs, mänkōō-er'näs] 133

cup taza *f* [tä'sä] 99

cure cura *f*, tratamiento *m* [kōō'rä, trätämyen'tō] 175; **~ tax** impuesto *m* de turismo [ēmpōō-es'tō de tōōrēz'mō] 175; **rest ~** cura *f* de reposo [kōō'rä de repō'sō] 175

curler rulero *m*, rulo *m (Sp)* [rōōle'rō, rōō'lō]141

curls rizos *m/pl* [rē'sōs] 158

currency moneda *f* [mōne'dä] 152; **foreign ~** divisas *f/pl* [dēvē'säs] 152

current corriente *f* [kōrryen'te] 90; **alternating ~** corriente *f* alterna [kōrryen'te älter'nä] 90

curtain cortina *f* [kōrtē'nä] 91

curtain *(theater)* telón *m* [telōn'] 177; **~ time** comienzo *m* [kōmyen'sō]177; **final ~** fin *m* [fēn] 177

curve curva *f* [kōōr'vä] 42

custody detención *f* [detensyōn'] 154; **protective ~** custodia *f* preventiva [kōōstō'dyä preventē'vä] 154

customs aduana *f* [ädōō-ä'nä] 80; **~ control** control *m* aduanero [kōntrōl' adōō-ä'ne'rō] 80; **~ declaration** declaración *f* de aduana [dekläräsyōn' de ädōō-ä'nä] 80; **~ office** edificio *m* de aduanas [edēfē'syō de ädōō-änäs] 80; **~ officer** aduanero *m* [ädōō-äne'rō] 80

cut *(noun)* herida *f*, corte *m* [erē'dä, kōr'te] 169

cut *(verb)* cortar [kōrtär'] 181

cutlery cubiertos *m/pl* [kōōbyer'tōs] 99

cylinder cilindro *m* [sēlēn'drō] 52; **~ head** culata *f*, cabeza *f (Mex)* del cilindro [kōōlä'tä, käbe'sä del sēlēn'drō] 52; **~ head gasket** junta *f* de la culeta, empaque *m* de cabeza *(Mex)* [hōōn'tä de lä kōōlä'tä, empä'ke de käbe'sä] 52

Canadian dollars dólares *m/pl* canadienses [dō'läres känädyen'ses] 152

Catholic católico *m* [kätō'lēkō] 124

Christ cristo [krēs'tō] 124

Christian cristiano *m* [krēstyä'nō] 124

Christianity cristianismo *m* [krēstyänēz'mō] 124

Christmas Navidad *f* [nävēdäd'] 33; **Merry ~** ¡Feliz Navidad! [felēs' nävēdäd'] 23

D

daily todos los días [tōdōs lōs dē'äs] 31

dairy lechería f [letsherē'ä] 128

damage *(noun)* daños m/pl [dä'nyōs] 49

dance *(verb)* bailar [bīlär'] 184

dance *(noun)* baile m [bī'le] 183; **~ hall** sala f de baile [sä'lä de bī'le] 183

dancer bailarín m [bīlärēn'] 177

dandruff caspa f [käs'pä] 158

danger! ¡peligro! [pelē'grō] 191

dangerous peligroso [pelēgrō'sō] 185

dark oscuro [ōskō'rō] 127

darn zurcir [sōōrsēr'] 137

darning thread hilo m para zurcir [ē'lō pä'rä sōōrsēr'] 137

date of birth fecha f de nacimiento [fe'tshä de näsēmyen'tō] 79

daughter hija f [ē'hä] 35

dawn madrugada f [mädrōōgä'dä] 26

day día m [dē'ä] 31; **New Year's ~** Año Nuevo [ä'nyō nōō·e'vō] 33; **~ room** sala f de estar [sä'lä de estär'] 96

dead end street callejón m sin salida [kälyehōn' sēn sälē'dä] 120

deal *(cards)* dar [där] 181

dealership garage taller m concesionario [tälyer' kōnsesyōnä'ryō] 49

decanter jarra f [hä'rrä] 99

December diciembre m [dēsyem'bre] 33

decimeter decímetro m [desē'metrō] 193

deck *(ship)* cubierta f [kōōbyer'tä] 76; **boat ~** cubierta f de botes [kōōbyer'tä de bō'tes] 76; **fore ~** cubierta f de proa [kōōbyer'tä de prō'ä] 76; **main ~** cubierta f principal [kōōbyer'tä prēnsēpäl'] 76; **poop ~** cubierta f de popa [kōōbyer'tä de pō'pä] 76; **promenade ~** cubierta f de paseo [kōōbyer'tä de päse'ō] 76; **steerage ~** entrepuente m [entrepōō·en'te] 76;

sun ~ cubierta f del sol [kōōbyer'tä del sōl] 76; **upper ~** cubierta f superior [kōōbyer'tä sōōperyōr'] 76; **~ chair** silla f de cubierta, tumbona f, hamaca f [sē'lyä de kōōbyer'tä, tōōmbō'nä, ämä'ka] 76

declare declarar [deklärär'] 80

defeat derrota f [derrō'tä] 188

delicious! ¡muy rico! [mōō·ē rē'kō] 101

delivery truck furgoneta f, camioneta f [fōōrgōne'tä, kämyōne'tä] 40

denomination *(religious)* confesión f religiosa [kōnfesyōn' relēhyō'sä] 125

dental clinic clínica f dental [klē'nēkä dentäl'] 174

dentist dentista m [dentēs'tä] 174

dentistry odontología f [ōdōntōlōhē'ä] 39

dentures dentadura f/pl postiza [dentädōō'rä pōstē'sä] 174

deodorant desodorante m [desōdōrän'te] 141

depart salir [sälēr'] 67

departure salida f [sälē'dä] 67

deposit *(noun)* pago m a cuenta [pä'gō ä kōō·en'ta] 91

deposit *(verb)* ingresar, consignar [ēngresär', kōnsēgnär'] 152

dermatologist dermatólogo m [dermätō'lōgō] 162

destination destino m [destē'nō] 149

detergent detergente m [deterhen'te] 144

detour desviación f, desvío m [desvē·äsyōn', desvē'ō] 42

develop desarrollar, revelar [desärrōlyär', revelär'] 132

dew rocío m [rōsē'ō] 26

diabetes diabetes f [dyäbe'tes] 170

diabetic diabético [dyäbe'tēkō] 164

diagnosis diagnóstico m [dyägnō'stēkō] 172

dial *(noun)* disco m [dēs'kō] 149

dial *(verb)* marcar [mär'kär'] 149

diamond diamante *m* [dyämän'te] 153

diamonds diamantes *m/pl* [dyämän'-tes] 181

diaphragm diafragma *m* [dyäfräg'mä] 132

diarrhea diarrea *f* [dyärre'ä] 170

dice dados *m/pl* [dä'dōs] 181; **shoot ~** jugar a los dados [hōōgär' ä lōs dä'-dōs] 181

dictionary diccionario *m* [dēksyōnä'-ryō] 130

diesel gasóleo *m*, diesel *m (Mex)* [gä-sō'le·ō, dyesel] 45; **~ motor** motor *m* diesel [mōtōr' dyesel'] 54; **~ nozzle** tobera *f* [tōbe'rä] 52

diet dieta *f* [dye'tä] 165

differential diferencial *m* [dēferensyäl'] 52

digestion digestión *f* [dēhestyōn'] 166

digestive tablets pastillas *f/pl* para el estómago [pästē'lyäs pä'rä el estō'mägō] 160

digestive tonic gotas *f/pl* para el estómago [gō'täs pä'rä el estō'mägō] 160

dill eneldo *m* [enel'dō] 103

dinghy bote *m* [bō'te] 186

dining car coche-restaurante *m* [kō'-tshe-restourän'te] 61

dining room comedor *m* [kōmedōr'] 74

dip stick varilla *f* del nivel de aceite [vä-rē'lyä del nēvel' de äse'ēte] 52

diphtheria difteria *f* [dēfte'ryä] 170

dipped headlights luz *f* de cruce [lōōs de krōō'se] 53

direct directo [dērek'tō] 68; **~ dial** llamar directamente [lyämär' dērektämen'te] 147

direction dirección *f* [dēreksyōn'] 59; **~ sign** indicador *m* de camino [ēn-dēkädōr de kämē'nō] 42

director director *m* [dērektōr'] 177

disc disco *m* intervertebral [dēs'kō ēn-tervertebräl'] 166; **~ brake** freno *m* de disco [fre'nō de dēs'kō] 51

discharge dar de alta [där de äl'tä] 172

discothèque discoteca *f* [dēskōte'kä] 180

discount reducción *f* del precio [re-dōōksyōn' del pre'syō] 176

disease enfermedad *f* [enfermedäd'] 170; **contagious ~** enfermedad *f* contagiosa [enfermedäd' kōntähyō'-sä] 170

disembark desembarcar [desembär-kär'] 76

dish plato *m* [plä'tō] 101

dishes vajilla *f* [vähē'lyä] 96

disinfectant desinfectante *m* [desēn-fektän'te] 160

dislocation dislocación *f* [dēslōkä-syōn'] 170

distilled water agua *f* destilada [a'-gōō·ä destēlä'dä] 45

distributor distribuidor *m* [dēstrē-bōō·ēdōr'] 52

district of town barrio *m* [bä'rryō] 120

ditch zanja *f* [sän'hä] 120

diuretic diurético *m* [dyōōre'tēkō] 160

dive bucear [bōōse·är'] 186

diving board trampolín *m* [trämpōlēn'] 186

divorced divorciado (-a) [dēvōrsyä'dō (-ä)] 79

dizziness mareo *m*, vértigo *m* [märe'ō, ver'tēgō] 170

dock *(noun)* muelle *m*, embarcadero *m* [mōō·e'lye, embärkäde'rō] 76

dock *(verb)* atracar [äträkär'] 76

doctor médico *m* + *f* [me'dēkō] 36; **~'s office** consultorio *m* [kōnsōōltō'ryō] 163

documentary documental *m* [dōkōō-mentäl'] 179

dog perro *m* [pe'rrō] 191; **beware of the ~** ¡cuidado! ¡perro! [kōō·ēdä'dō, pe'rrō] 191

doll muñeca *f* [mōōnye'kä] 144

dome cúpula *f*, bóveda *f* [kōō'pōōlä,

bōˈvedä] 125

door puerta f [pōō·erˈtä] 91; ~ **handle**
picaporte m [pĕkäpōrˈte] 91; ~ **lock**
cerradura f, chapa f [serrädōōˈrä,
tshäˈpä] 52

dormitory dormitorio m [dōrmĕtōrˈyō]
96

doubles dobles m/pl [dōˈbles] 189

downtown centro m ciudad, centro m
urbano [senˈtrō syōōdädˈ, senˈtrō
ōōrbäˈnō] 120

dozen docena f [dōseˈnä] 193

draft corriente f [kōrryenˈte] 26

drain desagüe m [desäˈgōō·e] 88

drama drama m [dräˈmä] 177

draw (cards) mover, jugar [mōverˈ,
hōōgärˈ] 181

draw (noun) empate m [empäˈte] 188

drawer cajón m, gaveta f [kähōnˈ, gä-
veˈtä] 91

dress vestido m [vesteˈdō] 134

dressing gown bata f [bäˈtä] 134

dressmaker costurera f [kōstōōreˈrä]
36

drier secador m [sekädōrˈ] 156

drill taladro m [tälädˈrōˈ] 57

drink (noun) refresco m [refresˈkō]
114; ~**ing water** agua f potable [äˈ-
gōō·ä pōtäˈble] 96

drip-dry "no se plancha" [nō se plänˈ-
tshä] 135

drive shaft árbol m del cardán [ärˈbōl
del kärdänˈ] 52

drive-in movie cine m al aire libre [sēˈ-
ne äl īˈre lēˈbre] 179

driver conductor m, chófer m [kōn-
dōōktōrˈ, tshōˈfer] 36

driver's license carnet m de conducir,
licencia f de manejar (Mex) [kärnetˈ
de kōndōōsērˈ, lēsenˈsyä de mäne-
härˈ] 42

driver's seat asiento m del conductor
[äsyenˈtō del kōndōōktōrˈ] 55

driveway calzada f [kälsäˈdä] 42

driving instructor profesor m de auto-
escuela [prōfesōrˈ de outō-es-
kōō·eˈlä] 36

drops gotas f/pl [gōˈtäs] 160; **ear** ~ gotas f/pl para los oídos [gōˈtäs päˈrä
lōs ō·ēˈdōs] 160; **eye** ~ gotas f/pl para los ojos [gōˈtäs päˈrä lōs ōˈhōs]
160

drugs drogas f/pl [drōˈgäs] 154

dry secar [seˈkär] 92; ~ **cleaner's** tinto-
rería f [tĕntōrerēˈä] 128; ~ **goods
store** mercería f [merserēˈä] 136

dubbed doblado [dōblä'dō] 179

dubbing doblaje m [dōbläˈhe] 179

duck pato m [päˈtō] 107

duet dúo m [dōōˈō] 177

dune duna f [dōōˈnä] 186

during the morning durante la mañana
[dōōränˈte lä mänyäˈnä] 31

dusk crepúsculo m [krepōōsˈkōōlō] 26

duty derechos m/pl de aduana [dereˈ-
tshōs de ädōō·äˈnä] 80; **pay** ~ pagar
derechos de aduana [pägärˈ dereˈ-
tshōs de ädōō·äˈnä] 80; **export** ~ derechos m/pl de salida [dereˈtshōs de
säleˈdä] 80; **import** ~ derechos m/pl
de entrada [dereˈtshōs de enträˈdä]
80

dye tinte m [tĕnˈte] 141

dynamo dínamo m + f (Sp f) [dēˈnämō]
52

dysentery disentería f [dēsenterēˈä]
170

E

ear oreja f [ōreˈhä] 166; ~ **clips** zarci-
llos m/pl, aretes m/pl [särsēˈlyōs,
äreˈtes] 133

eardrum tímpano m [tĕmˈpänō] 166

earlier antes [änˈtes] 32

early temprano [tempräˈnō] 31

earrings pendientes m/pl [pendyenˈ-
tes] 133

Easter Pascua f [päsˈkōō·ä] 33

economics ciencias f/pl económicas [syen'syäs ekōnō'mēkäs] 39

economy class clase f turista [klä'se tōōrēs'tä] 69

education *(subject)* pedagogía f [pedägōhē'ä] 39

eel anguila f [ängē'lä] 106

egg huevo m, blanquillo m *(Mex)* [ōō·e'vō, blängkē'lyō] 100; **soft-boiled ~** huevo m pasado por agua, tibio *(Mex)* [ōō·e'vō päsä'dō pōr ä'gōō·ä, tē'byō] 100; **bacon and eggs** huevos m/pl con tocino [ōō·e'vōs kōn tōsē'nō] 100; **fried eggs** huevos m/pl fritos, estrellados *(Mex)* [ōō·e'vōs frē'tōs, estrelyä'dōs] 100; **ham and eggs** huevos m/pl con jamón [ōō·e'vōs kōn hämōn'] 100; **scrambled eggs** huevos m/pl revueltos [ōō·e'vōs revōō·el'tōs] 100

egg cup huevera f [ōō·eve'rä] 99

eight ocho [ō'tshō] 28

eighty ochenta [ōtshen'tä] 28

elastic cinta f de goma, caucho m [sēn'tä de gō'mä, kou'tshō] 136; **~ bandage** venda f elástica [ven'dä eläs'tēkä] 160; **~ stocking** media f elástica [me'dyä eläs'tēkä] 160

elbow codo m [kō'dō] 166

electric shaver máquina f de afeitar eléctrica [mä'kēnä de äfe·etär elek'trēkä] 141

electrical connections enchufes m/pl, soquetes m/pl, dados m/pl *(Mex)* [entshōō'fes, sōke'tes, dä'dōs] 95

electrician electricista m [elektrēsēs'tä] 36

elevator ascensor m, elevador m *(Mex)* [äsensōr', elevädōr'] 91

embassy embajada f [embähä'dä] 120

emerald esmeralda f [ezmeräl'dä] 133

emergency brake *(train)* alarma f 66

emergency chute rampa f de emergencia [räm'pä de emer*hen*'syä] 70

emergency exit salida f de emergencia [sälē'dä de emer*hen*'syä] 70

emergency landing aterrizaje m forzoso [äterrēsä'*h*e fōrsō'sō] 70

emergency ward sala f de emergencias [sä'lä de emer*hen*'syäs] 49

emetic emético m [eme'tēkō] 160

endive escarola f [eskärō'lä] 110

enema enema f [ene'mä] 160

engine motor m [mōtōr'] 70

engineer *(scientific)* ingeniero m [ēn*henye*'rō] 36; **~** *(railroad)* maquinista m [mäkēnēs'tä] 36

English inglés m [ēngles'] 24

enjoy oneself divertirse [dēvertēr'se] 184

enlargement ampliación f [ämplē·äsyōn'] 131

enough suficiente [sōōfēsyen'te] 46; **not ~** muy poco [mōō'·ē pō'kō] 127

entrance entrada f [enträ'dä] 67

entry entrada f [enträ'dä] 79; **~ visa** visa f, visado m *(Sp)* de entrada [vē'sä, vēsä'dō de enträ'dä] 79

envelope sobre m [sō'bre] 138

eraser goma f, borrador m [gō'mä, bōrrädōr'] 138

essentials: the ~ lo más necesario [lō mäs nesesä'ryō] 50

eve: New Year's Eve Año Viejo [ä'nyō vye'*h*ō] 33

evening noche f [nō'tshe] 183; **Good ~!** ¡Buenas noches! [bōō·e'näs nō'tshes] 12; **in the ~** por la tarde or noche [pōr lä tär'de, nō'tshe] 31; **this ~** esta tarde [es'tä tär'de] 31

every cada, todos los [kä'dä, tōdōs lōs] 31; **~ day** todos los días [tōdōs lōs dē'äs] 31

everything todo [tō'dō] 83

exact exacto [eksäk'tō (-ä)] 30

examination *(lab)* análisis m [änä'lēsēs] 172; **~** *(of person)* reconocimiento m [rekōnōsēmyen'tō] 172

examine examinar, reconocer [eksä-mēnär', rekōnōser'] 172

excavations excavaciones f/pl [ekskä-väsyō'nes] 12

excess baggage exceso m de equipaje [ekse'sō de ekēpä'he] 68

exchange *(verb)* cambiar [kämbyär'] 127; **money ~** *(noun)* cambio m de moneda [käm'byō de mōne'dä] 152; **rate of ~** cambio m [käm'byō] 151

excursion excursión f [ekskōōrsyōn'] 76; **~ program** programa m de la excursión f [prōgrä'mä de lä ekskōōr-syōn] 76; **land ~s** excursiones a tierra [ekskōōrsyō'nes ä tye'rrä] 72

excuse me! *(apology)* ¡discúlpeme!, ¡discúlpame! [dēskōōl'peme, dēskōōl'päme] 22

excuse me? *(when passing)* ¿permiso? [permē'sō] 20

exhaust escape m [eskä'pe] 52

exhibition exposición f [ekspōsēsyōn'] 121

exit salida f [sälē'dä] 42; **~ visa** visa f, visado m (Sp) de salida [vē'sä, vēsä'-dō de sälē'dä] 79

expensive caro [kä'rō] 127

exposure exposición f [ekspōsēsyōn'] 132; **~ meter** fotómetro m, exposímetro m [fōtō'metrō, ekspōse'metrō] 132

express train expreso m [ekspre'sō] 60

extend prorogar [prōrōgär'] 79

extension cord cordón m, cable m de empalme, cable m de extensión (Mex) [kōrdōn', kä'ble de empäl'me, kä'ble de ekstensyōn'] 91

external externo [ekster'nō] 159

extra week semana f suplementaria [semä'nä sōōplementär'yä] 91

extract sacar, extraer [säkär', ekstră-er'] 174

eye ojo m [ō'hō] 166; **~ doctor** optometrista m + f [ōptōmetrēs'tä] 162;

~ liner trazado m de párpado [träsä'dō de pär'pädō] 141; **~ shadow** sombra f de ojos [sōm'brä de ō'hōs] 141

eyeball globo m del ojo [glō'bō del ō'hō] 166

eyebrow ceja f [se'hä] 156; **~ pencil** lápiz m de cejas [lä'pēs de se'häs] 141

eyelid párpado m [pär'pädō] 166

F

fabric tela f [te'lä] 137

face cara f, rostro m [kä'rä, rōs'trō] 166; **~** *(of clock)* esfera f [esfe'rä] 143; **~ mask** mascarilla f [mäskärē'-lyä] 156; **~ massage** masaje m facial [mäsä'he fäsyäl] 156

factory fábrica f [fä'brēkä] 121

falling rocks desprendimiento m de piedras, zona f de derrumbes (Mex) [desprendēmyen'tō de pye'dräs, sō'nä de derrōōm'bes] 42

false tooth diente m de espiga [dyen'te de espē'gä] 174

family familia f [fämē'lyä] 35

fan ventilador m [ventēlädōr'] 53; **~ belt** correa f de ventilador, banda f de ventilador [kōrre'ä de ventēlädōr', bän'dä de ventēlädōr'] 53

far lejos [le'hōs] 59; **as ~ as** hasta [äs'-tä] 40; **how far?** ¿ a qué distancia? [ä ke dēstän'syä] 40

fare precio m del boleto, billete (Sp) [pre'syō del bōle'tō, bēlye'te] 62; **pay the excess ~** pagar la diferencia [pägär' lä dēferen'syä] 66; **~ discount** tarifa f reducida [tärē'fä re-dōōsē'dä] 67

farewell dinner comida f de despedida [kōmē'dä de despedē'dä] 76

farmer agricultor m [ägrēkōōltōr'] 36

farmhouse granja f, cortijo m (Mex)

[grän'hä, körtē'hō] 121

far-sighted présbita [pres'bētä] 138

fashion boutique boutique f [bō·ōōtē'-ke] 128

fashion show desfile m de modas [desfē'le de mō'däs] 180

fast rápido [rä'pēdō] 42; **~ (clock)** adelantado [ädeläntä'dō] 31; **~ train** tren m rápido [tren rä'pēdō] 60

fat (noun) grasa f [grä'sä] 102

father padre m, papá m (Mex) [pä'dre, päpä'] 35; **~ -in-law** suegro m [sōō·e'grō] 35

fatty grasiento [gräsyen'tō] 115

faucet grifo m [grē'fō] 88

February febrero m [febre'rō] 33

fee tarifa f [tärē'fä] 97; **rental ~** tarifa f de alquiler [tärē'fä de älkēler'] 97

fencing esgrima f [esgrē'mä] 188

fender guardabarros m [gōō·ärdäbä'rrōs] 53

ferry transbordador m, ferry m [tränsbōrdädōr', fe'rrē] 72; **train ~** transbordador m de trenes [tränsbōrdädōr' de tre'nes] 76

fever fiebre f, calentura f (Mex) [fye'bre, kälentōō'rä] 170; **~ cure** antipirético m, antitérmico m [äntēpēre'tēkō, äntēter'mēkō] 161

fiancé prometido m, novio m [prōmetē'dō, nō'vyō] 14

fiancée prometida f, novia f [prōmetē'dä, nō'vyä] 14

fibre fibra f [fē'brä] 137; **synthetic ~** fibra f sintética [fē'brä sēnte'tēkä] 137

fight (noun) pelea f [pele'ä] 187

fig higo m [ē'gō] 111

figure skating patinaje m artístico [pätēnä'he ärtēstē'kō] 188

figurine figura f [fēgōō'rä] 144

file (noun) lima f [lē'mä] 57

fill (tooth) calzar, empastar (Sp) [käl-sär', empästär'] 174; **~ in** (re)llenar

[(re)lyenär'] 78; **~ it up** lleno [lye'nō] 45

fillet filete m [fēle'te] 108

filling calza f, empaste m (Sp) [käl'sä, empäs'te] 174; **temporary ~** empaste m provisional [empäs'te prōvēsyōnäl'] 174

film (noun) rollo m, carrete m (Sp) [rō'lyō, kärre'te] 132; **~ (movie)** película f [pelē'kōōlä] 132; **~ (verb)** filmar [fēlmär'] 132; **~ actor** actor m de cine [äktōr' de sē'ne] 179; **~ festival** festival m cinematográfico [festēväl' sēnemätōgrä'fēkō] 179; **~ screening** sesión f de cine [sesyōn' de sē'ne] 179; **cartridge ~** rollo m, carrete m (Sp) [rō'lyō, kärre'te] 131; **color ~** película f en color [pelē'kōōlä en kōlōr'] 132; **daylight color ~** película f en color para luz diurna [pelē'kōōlä en kōlōr' pä'rä lōōs dyōōr'nä] 132; **educational ~** documental m [dōkōōmentäl'] 179; **feature ~** largometraje m [lärgōmeträ'he] 179; **reversal ~** película f reversible [pelē'kōōlä reversē'ble] 132; **roll ~** carrete m, rollo m [kärre'te, rō'lyō] 132; **sixteen millimeter color ~** película f de dieciséis milímetros, en color [pelē'kōōlä de dyesēse'ēs mēlē'metrōs, en kōlōr'] 131; **thirty-five millimeter ~** película f de treinta y cinco milímetros [pelē'kōōlä de tre'ēntä ē sēng'kō mēlē'metrōs] 131; **thirty-six exposure ~** rollo m, carrete m (Sp) de treinta y seis fotografías [rō'lyō, kärre'te de tre'ēntä ē se'ēs fōtōgräfē'äs] 131; **twenty exposure ~** rollo m, carrete m (Sp) de veinte fotografías [rō'lyō, kärre'te de ve'ēnte fōtōgräfē'äs] 131

filter filtro m [fēl'trō] 132

fine muy bien [mōō'ē byen] 12

finger dedo m [de'dō] 167; **index ~** dedo m índice [de'dō ēn'dēse] 167;

middle ~ dedo *m* del corazón [de'dō del kōräsōn'] 167; **ring** ~ dedo *m* anular [de'dō änōōlär'] 167

fire department bomberos *m/pl* [bōmbe'rōs] 49

fire extinguisher extintor *m*, extinguidor *m* [ekstēngtōr', ekstēngōō·ēdōr'] 53

fireplace chimenea *f* [tshēmene'ä] 91

first (1st) primero [prēme'rō] 29

first class primera clase [prēme'rä klä'se] 62

first-aid puesto *m* de socorros, "primeros auxilios" *(Mex)* [pōō·es'tō de sōkō'rrōs, prēme'rōs ouksē'lyōs] 121; ~ **kit** botiquín *m* [bōtēkēn'] 161; ~ **station** puesto *m* de socorro, "primeros auxilios" *(Mex)* [pōō·es'tō de sōkō'rrō, prēme'rōs ouksē'lyōs] 49

fish *(noun)* pescado *m* [peskä'dō] 107

fish *(verb)* pescar [peskär'] 185

fish market pescadería *f* [peskäderē'ä] 128

fisherman pescador *m* [peskädōr'] 36

fishing pesca *f* [pes'kä] 188; ~ **license** licencia *f* de pescar [lēsen'syä de peskär'] 188; ~ **rod** caña *f* [kä'nyä] 188; ~ **trawler** barco *m* pesquero [bär'kō peske'rō] 75

fit ataque *m* [ätä'ke] 170

five cinco [sēng'kō] 28

fix arreglar [arreglär'] 50

flannel franela *f* [fräne'lä] 137

flash bulb bombilla *f*, foco *m* de flash [bōmbē'lyä, fō'kō de fläsh] 132

flash cube cubo *m* de flash [kōō'bō de fläsh] 132

flashing signal avisador *m* luminoso [ävēsadōr' lōōmēnō'sō] 53

flashlight linterna *f*, foco *m (Mex)*, luz *f* [lēnter'nä, fō'kō, lōōs] 144

flat *(shoes)* bajo [bä'hō] 139

flatulence flatulencia *f* [flätōōlen'syä] 170

flight vuelo *m* [vōō·e'lō] 68; ~ **attendant** azafata *f*, aeromoza *f*, cabinera *f* [äsäfä'tä, ä·erōmō'sä, käbēne'rä] 71

flint piedra *f* [pye'drä] 140

flirt flirteo *m* [flērte'ō] 184

float *(car)* flotador *m* [flōtädōr'] 53

floor piso *m* [pē'sō] 91; **second** ~ segundo piso [segōōn'dō pē'sō] 82

flower pot tiesto *m*, maceta *f* [tyes'tō, mäse'tä] 130

flowers flores *f/pl* [flō'res] 130

flu gripe *f* [grē'pe] 170

fly *(verb)* volar [vōlär'] 71

flying time duración *f* de vuelo [dōōräsyōn' de vōō·e'lō] 71

FM frequencia *f* modulada [frekōō·en'syä mōdōōlä'dä] 182

fog niebla *f* [nye'blä] 27

fond of aficionado a [äfēsyōnä'dō ä] 187

font pila *f* bautismal [pē'lä boutēzmäl'] 125

food comida *f* [kōmē'dä] 163; **diet** ~ platos *m/pl* de régimen [plä'tōs de re'hēmen] 98; **vegetarian** ~ platos *m/pl* vegetarianos [plä'tōs vehetäryä'nōs] 98; ~ **poisoning** intoxicación *f* alimenticia [ēntōksēkäsyōn' älēmentē'syä] 170

foot pie *m* [pye] 167; **on** ~ andando [ändän'dō] 116; ~ **brake** freno *m* de pedal [fre'nō de pedäl'] 51

footpath senda *f* [sen'dä] 42

for sale se vende [se ven'de] 191

forehead frente *f* [fren'te] 167

forest ranger guarda *m* forestal [gōō·är'dä fōrestäl'] 36

fork tenedor *m* [tenedōr'] 99

form *(noun)* formulario *m* [fōrmōōlä'ryō] 78

fortress fortaleza *f* [fōrtäle'sä] 119

forward *(sports)* delantero *m* [delänte'rō] 189

fountain fuente *f* [fōō·en'te] 121

four cuatro [kōō·ä'trō] 28

fracture fractura f, quebradura f (Mex) [fräktōō'rä, kebrädōō'rä] 170

frame (eyeglass) montura f [mōntōō'rä] 138

free libre [lē'bre] 44; ~ **kick** golpe m franco [gōl'pe fräng'kō] 189; ~ **style** carrera f libre [kärre'rä lē'bre] 188; ~ **wheel** (hub) rueda f libre [rōō·e'dä lē'bre] 138

freighter carguero m [kärge'rō] 77

French francés [fränses'] 24

fresco fresco m [fres'kō] 125

fresh fresco [fres'kō] 102

Friday viernes m [vyer'nes] 33; **Good** ~ viernes m santo [vyer'nes sän'tō] 33

fried frito [frē'tō] 102

friend (male) amigo m [ämē'gō] 14

friend (female) amiga f [ämē'gä] 14

front (of train) puertas f/pl delanteras [pōō·er'täs delänte'räs] 66; **up** ~ en la cabeza [en lä käbe'sä] 65; ~ **desk** recepción f [resepsyōn'] 91; ~ **door** puerta f de entrada [pōō·er'tä de enträ'dä] 91; ~ **seat** asiento m delantero [äsyen'tō delänte'rō] 55; ~ **passenger seat** asiento m delantero del pasajero [äsyen'tō delänte'rō del päsähe'rō] 55; ~ **wheel** rueda f delantera [rōō·e'dä delänte'rä] 47

frontal sinus seno m frontal [se'nō frōntäl'] 167

frost helada f [elä'dä] 27

frostbite congelación f [kōnheläsyōn'] 170

fruit fruta f [frōō'tä] 112; ~ **cocktail** coctel m de frutas, macedonia f de frutas (Sp) [kōktel' de frōō'täs, mäsedō'nyä de frōō'täs] 112; ~ **market** frutería f [frōōterē'ä] 128

fuel gasolina f [gäsōlē'nä] 53; ~ **injector** bomba f de inyección [bōm'bä de ēnyeksyōn'] 53; ~ **lines** conducto m de gasolina [kōndōōk'tō de gäsōlē'-

nä] 53; ~ **pump** bomba f de gasolina [bōm'bä de gäsōlē'nä] 53

full beam luz f de carretera [lōōs de kärrete'rä] 53

full coverage insurance seguro m [segōō'rō] 41

full-fare precio m normal [pre'syō nōrmäl'] 59

fullback defensa m [defen'sä] 189

funnel embudo m [embōō'dō] 57

fur coat abrigo m de piel [äbrē'gō de pyel] 134

fur jacket chaquetón m de piel [tshäketōn' de pyel] 134

furrier peletero m [pelete'rō] 128

fuse fusible m [fōōsē'ble] 53

G

gall bladder vesícula f [vesē'kōōlä] 167

gall stones cálculos m/pl biliares [käl'kōōlōs bēlyär'yes] 170

gallery galería f [gälerē'ä] 119

gallon galón m [gälōn'] 193

gambling casino casino m [käsē'nō] 181

game juego m [hōō·e'gō] 181

gangway plancha f [plän'tshä] 76

garage garaje m [gärä'he] 44; ~ (workshop) taller m mecánico [tälyer' mekä'nēkō] 50

garden jardín m [härdēn'] 121

gardener jardinero m [härdēne'rō] 36

gargle gárgaras f/pl [gär'gäräs] 161

garlic ajo m [ä'hō] 103

garter belt portaligas m, liguero m [pōrtälē'gäs, lēge'rō] 134

garters ligas f/pl [lē'gäs] 136

gas gasolina f [gäsōlē'nä] 53; ~ **bottles** botellas f/pl, cilindros m/pl de gas [bōte'lyäs, sēlēn'drōs de gäs] 95; ~ **station** gasolinera f, estación f de servicio [gäsōlēne'rä, estäsyōn' de servē'syō] 45

gasket junta f, empaque m [hōōn'tä, empä'ke] 53

gasoline gasolina f [gäsōlē'nä] 45; ~ **can** bidón m de gasolina [bēdōn' de gäsōlē'nä] 45

gate puerta f [pōō·er'tä] 121

gauze bandage gasa f [gä'sä] 161

gear (car) marcha f, engrane m (Mex) [mär'tshä, engrä'ne] 53; ~ **lever** palanca f de cambios [pälän'kä de käm'byōs] 53; ~ **oil** aceite m lubricante [äse'ēte lōōbrēkän'te] 46; **put in** ~ meter la marcha [meter' lä mär'tshä] 53

gear box caja f de cambios [kä'hä de käm'byōs] 53

general delivery lista f de correos [lēs'tä de kōrre'ōs] 149

general practitioner médico m general [me'dēkō heneräl'] 162

genital organs órganos m/pl genitales [ōr'gänōs henētä'les] 167

gentlemen señores m/pl, caballeros m/pl [senyō'res, käbälye'rōs] 13

geology geología f [he·ōlōhē'ä] 39

German alemán [älemän'] 24

German measles rubéola f [rōōbe'ōlä] 170

get conseguir [kōnsegēr'] 20; **get in** (vehicle) subir (a) [sōōbēr' (ä)] 67; **get off, out of** (véhicle) bajar (de) [bähär' (de)] 67, 117

gin ginebra f [hēne'brä] 113

ginger jengibre m [henhē'bre] 103

girdle faja f [fä'hä] 134

girl niña f, muchacha f [nē'nyä, mōōtshä'tshä] 35

gladioli gladiolos m/pl [glädyō'lōs] 130

gland glándula f [glän'dōōlä] 167

glass vaso m [vä'sō] 99; **water** ~ vaso m para agua [vä'sō pä'rä ä'gōō·ä] 99; **wine** ~ vaso m para vino [vä'sō pä'rä vē'nō] 99

glasses lentes f/pl, anteojos m/pl, gafas f/pl (Sp) [len'tes, änte·ō'hōs, gä'fäs] 138

glazier vidriero m [vēdrē·e'rō] 37

glossy (adj.) brillante [brēlyän'te] 132

glossy (noun) revista f ilustrada [revēs'tä ēlōōsträ'dä] 182

gloves guantes m/pl [gōō·än'tes] 134

glue pegamento m [pegämen'tō] 138

glycerine glicerina f [glēserē'nä] 161

goal gol m [gōl] 187; **kick a** ~ meter un gol [meter' ōōn gōl] 190

goalie portero m [pōrte'rō] 190

God Dios [dyōs] 125

gold oro m [ō'rō] 133; ~ **plated** dorado [dōrä'dō] 133

golf golf m [gōlf] 188

good-bye! ¡adiós! [ädyōs'] 17; **say** ~ despedirse [despedēr'se] 17

goods mercancías f/pl [merkänsē'äs] 70

goose ganso m [gän'sō] 107

gospel evangelio m [evänhe'lyō] 125

gothic gótico [gō'tēkō] 125

government office oficina f pública [ōfēsē'nä pōō'blēkä] 121

grain (noun) contrapelo m [kōnträpe'lō] 157

grand piano piano m de cola [pē·ä'nō de kō'lä] 177

grandchild nieto m [nye'tō] 35

granddaughter nieta f [nye'tä] 35

grandfather abuelo m [äbōō·e'lō] 35

grandmother abuela f [äbōō·e'lä] 35

grandparents abuelos m/pl [äbōō·e'lōs] 35

grandson nieto m [nye'tō] 35

grape uva f [ōō'vä] 112

grapefruit pomelo m [pōme'lō] 112; ~ **juice** jugo m, zumo m (Sp) de pomelo, de toronja (Mex) [hōō'gō, sōō'mō de pōme'lō, de tōrōn'hä] 100

grateful agradecido [ägrädesē'dō] 21

grave (noun) sepultura f [sepōōltōō'rä] 125

gray gris [grēs] 194; **ash ~** gris ceniza [grēs senē'sä] 194; **dark ~** gris oscuro [grēs ōskōō'rō] 194; **pale ~** gris claro [grēs klä'rō] 194

grease grasa f [grä'sä] 53

greasy grasiento [gräsyen'tō] 158

green verde [ver'de] 194; **dark ~** verde oscuro [ver'de ōskōō'rō] 194; **light ~** verde claro [ver'de klä'rō] 194

grill room parrilla f [pärrē'lyä] 91

grilled asado a la parrilla [äsä'dō ä lä pärrē'lyä] 102

grocery store tienda f de comestibles, de abarrotes (Mex) [tyen'dä de kōmestē'bles, de äbärrō'tes] 95

group fare ticket boleto m colectivo [bōle'tō kōlektē'vō] 62

guarded vigilado [vēhēlä'dō] 44

guest house casa f de huéspedes [kä'sä de ōō·e·s'pedes] 91

guide guía m [gē'ä] 121

gums encías f/pl [ensē'äs] 174

gym shoes zapatos m/pl de tenis, playeras [säpä'tōs de te'nēs, plä·ye'räs] 139

gymnast gimnasta m + f [hēmnäs'tä] 188

gymnastics gimnasia f [hēmnä'syä] 188; **~ with apparatus** gimnasia f con aparatos [hēmnä'syä kōn äpärä'tōs] 188

gynecologist ginecólogo m [hēnekō'lōgō] 162

H

hair pelo m [pe'lō] 155; **~ spray** laca f [lä'kä] 156; **~ tonic** loción f [lōsyōn'] 157; **~ drier** secador m [sekädōr'] 158; **~ loss** caída f del pelo [kä·ē'dä del pe'lō] 158; **~ style** peinado m [pe·ēnä'dō] 158

hairbrush cepillo m del pelo [sepē'lyō del pe'lō] 141

haircut corte m [kōr'te] 157

hair-do peinado m [pe·ēnä'dō] 158

hairdresser peluquero m [pelōōke'rō] 158

hairpiece postizo m [pōstē'sō] 158

hairpins horquillas f/pl, clips m/pl [ōrkē'lyäs, klēps] 141

half fare boleto m de media tarifa [bōle'tō de me'dya tärē'fä] 62

half past six las seis y media [läs se'ēs ē me'dyä] 30

half time medio tiempo m [me'dyō tyem'pō] 188

hall hall m, vestíbulo m [äl, vestē'bōōlō] 92

ham jamón m [hämōn'] 108

hammer martillo m [märtē'lyō] 57

hammock hamaca f [ämä'kä] 144

hand mano f [mä'nō] 167; **~s** (on clock) agujas f/pl, manecillas f/pl [ägōō'häs, mänesē'lyäs] 30; **~ brake** freno m de mano [fre'nō de mä'nō] 51; **~ luggage** bultos m/pl de mano [bōōl'tōs de mä'nō] 63

handbag bolso m, bolsa f (Mex) [bōl'sō, bōl'sä] 153

handball balonmano m [bälōnmä'nō] 189

handicrafts labores m/pl de mano [läbō'res de mä'nō] 144

handkerchief pañuelo m [pänyōō·e'lō] 134

handle manecilla f, manija f [mänesē'lyä, mänē'hä] 53

harbor puerto m [pōō·er'tō] 76; **~ police** policía f del puerto [pōlēsē'ä del pōō·er'tō] 76

hare liebre f [lye'bre] 108

hat sombrero m [sōmbre'rō] 134; **straw ~** sombrero m de paja [sōmbre'rō de pä'hä] 134

hay fever fiebre f del heno [fye'bre del e'nō] 170

hazelnut avellana f [ävelyä'nä] 111

head cabeza f [käbe'sä] 167; ~ **clerk** jefe m de recepción [he'fe de resep-syōn'] 91; ~ **nurse** enfermera f jefe [enferme'rä he'fe] 172

headlight faro m, focos m/pl (Mex) [fä'rō, fō'kōs] 53

head-on collision choque m de frente [tshō'ke de fren'te] 49

health resort estación f climática [estä-syōn' klēmä'tēkä] 175

heart corazón m [kōräsōn'] 167; ~ **attack** ataque m cardíaco [ätä'ke kär-dē'äkō] 170; ~ **problems** problemas m/pl cardíacas [prōble'mäs kärdē'ä-käs] 170

heartburn ardor m del estómago [är-dōr' del estō'mägō] 170

hearts (cards) corazones m/pl [kōrä-sō'nes] 181

heat calor m [kälōr'] 27

heating system calefacción f [kälefäk-syōn'] 53; **central** ~ calefacción f central [kälefäksyōn' senträl'] 90

heel (shoe) tacón m [täkōn'] 139

heel (foot) talón m [tälōn'] 167

helicopter helicóptero m [elēkōp'terō] 71

helm timón m [tēmōn'] 76

helmsman timonel m [tēmōnel'] 76

help ayuda f [äyōō'dä] 21

hemmorrhage hemorragia f [emōrrä'-hyä] 170

hemorrhoids hemorroides f/pl [emō-rrō-ē'des] 170

herbs hierbas f/pl [yer'bäs] 103

here aquí [äkē'] 14

herring arenque m [ären'ke] 106

high alto [äl'tō] 139; ~ **mass** misa f mayor [mē'sä mäyōr'] 123; ~ **pressure** (system) anticiclón m [äntēsē-klōn'] 27; ~ **school** instituto m de bachillerato [ēnstētōō'tō de bätshē-lyerä'tō] 39; ~ **test** (gas) gasolina f extra [gäsōlē'nä eks'trä] 45

high-rise (building) edificio m, torre f [edēfē'syō, tō'rre] 121

highway autopista f [outōpēs'tä] 42; ~ **patrol** policía f de tráfico [pōlēsē'ä de trä'fēkō] 42

hill colina f, cerro m [kōlē'nä, se'rrō] 121

hip cadera f [käde'rä] 167

history historia f [ēstōr'yä] 39

hitch-hike hacer auto-stop, viajar por aventón (Mex) [äser' ou'tō-stōp', vē-ähär' pōr äventōn'] 43

hoarseness ronquera f [rōnke'rä] 170

hockey hockey m [hō'kē] 189

hold-up atraco m [äträ'kō] 153

home casa f [kä'sä] 15; at ~ en casa [en kä'sä] 15

honey miel f [myel] 100

hood capó m, capota f [käpō', käpō'tä] 53

horizontal bar barra f fija [bä'rrä fē'hä] 188

horn bocina f, claxon m, pito m [bōsē'-nä, klä'ksōn, pē'tō] 53

horse caballo m [käbä'lyō] 189; ~ **cart** carro m, carreta f (Mex) [kä'rrō, kä-rre'tä] 41; ~ **race** carrera f de caba-llos [kärre'rä de käbä'lyōs] 189

horseradish rábano m picante [rä'bä-nō pēkän'te] 103

hospital hospital m [ōspētäl'] 49

hostal father encargado m del al-bergue [enkärgä'dō del älber'ge] 96; **hostal mother** encargada f del al-bergue [enkärgä'dä del älber'ge] 96; **hostel parents** encargados m/pl del albergue [enkärgä'dōs del älber'ge] 96

hot caliente [kälyen'te] 94; ~ (spicy) pi-cante [pēkän'te] 102; ~ **chocolate** chocolate m [tshōkōlä'te] 100; ~ **spring** fuente f termal [fōō-en'te ter-mäl'] 175

hotel hotel m [ōtel'] 92; **beach** ~ hotel

m de playa [ōtelʲ de plāʲyä] 92; ~ **restaurant** restaurante *m* del hotel [re-
stourānʲte del ōtelʲ] 92

hour hora *f* [ōʲrä] 31; **every** ~ cada hora [käʲdä ōʲrä] 31; **quarter** ~ cuarto
de hora [kōō·ärʲtō de ōʲrä] 87; **half** ~
media hora [meʲdyä ōʲrä] 87

house casa *f* [käʲsä] 92; ~ **key** llave *f*
de la casa [lyäʲve de lä käʲsä] 92; ~
number número *m* (de la casa)
[nōōʲmerō de lä käʲsä] 121

how como [kōʲmō] 12; ~ **are you?** ¿cómo está usted? [kōʲmō estäʲ ōōsteʲ]
12; ~ **far** a qué distancia [ä ke dē-
stänʲsyä] 72

hub cubo *m* [kōōʲbō] 53; ~ **cap** tapa-
cubos *m*, copa *f* [täpäkōōʲbōs, kōʲ-
pä] 53

hundred cien, ciento [syen, syenʲtō] 28

hundredweight *(approx.)* un quintal
[ōōn kēntälʲ] 193

hunting caza *f* [käʲsä] 188; ~ **license**
licencia *f* de caza [lēsenʲsyä de käʲ-
sä] 188

hurt herido [erēʲdō] 49

husband esposo *m*, marido *m* [espōʲ-
sō, märēʲdō] 13

hydrogen peroxide agua *f* oxigenada
[äʲgōō·ä ōksēhenäʲdä] 161

hypertension hipertensión *f* [ēperten-
syōnʲ] 170

I

ice hielo *m* [yeʲlō] 27; ~ **cream** helado
m [eläʲdō] 112; **chocolate** ~ **cream**
helado *m* de chocolate [eläʲdō de
tshōkōläʲte] 112; **strawberry** ~
cream helado *m* de fresa [eläʲdō de
freʲsä] 112; **vanilla** ~ **cream** helado
m de vainilla [eläʲdō de vēnēʲlyä] 112;
~ **skating rink** pista *f* de hielo [pēsʲtä
de yeʲlō] 180

icy road carretera *f* helada [kärreteʲrä
eläʲdä] 27

identity card documento *m*, carnet *m*
de identidad [dōkōōmenʲtō, kärnetʲ
de ēdentēdädʲ] 79

ignition encendido *m* [ensendēʲdō] 54;
~ **cable** cable *m* del encendido [käʲ-
ble del ensendēʲdō] 54; ~ **key** llave *f*
de contacto [lyäʲve de kōntäkʲtō] 54;
~ **lock** interruptor *m* (del encendido) [ēnterrōōptōrʲ (del ensendēʲdō)]
54

illness enfermedad *f* [enfermedädʲ]
170

inch pulgada *f* [pōōlgäʲdä] 193

incisor diente *m* incisivo [dyenʲte ēnsē-
sēʲvō] 174

included incluido [ēnklōō·ēʲdō] 83

indigestion trastornos *m/pl* digestivos
[trästōrʲnōs dēhestēʲvōs] 170

inflammation inflamación *f* [ēnflämä-
syōnʲ] 170

influenza gripe *f* [grēʲpe] 170

information información *f* [ēnfōrmä-
syōnʲ] 67

infusion infusión *f* [ēnfōōsyōnʲ] 172

inhale inhalar [ēnälärʲ] 175

injection inyección *f* [ēnyeksyōnʲ] 174

injured *(noun)* heridos *m/pl* [erēʲdōs]
48

injury herida *f* [erēʲdä] 49

ink tinta *f* [tēnʲtä] 138

inn posada *f*, hostal *m* [pōsäʲdä, ōstälʲ]
81

inner tube cámara *f*, tubo *(Mex)* de aire
[käʲmärä, tōōʲbō de īʲre] 46

innocent inocente [ēnōsenʲte] 154

inquiry informe *m* [ēnfōrʲme] 92

insect repellent insecticida *m* [ēnsek-
tēsēʲdä] 161

inside dentro [denʲtrō] 47

in-sole plantilla *f* [pläntēʲlyä] 139

insomnia insomnio *m* [ēnsōmʲnyō] 170

inspection light lámpara *f* piloto *or* de
prueba [lämʲpärä pēlōʲtō, de prōō·eʲ-
bä] 57

insulation aislamiento *m* [īzlämyen'tō] 54

insurance seguro *m* [segōō'rō] 49; **~ certificate** tarjeta *f* de seguro [tärhe'- tä de segōō'rō] 79

insure asegurar [asegōōrär'] 63

insured mail correo *m* asegurado [kō- rre'ō äsegōōrä'dō] 149

intensive care unit unidad *f* de cuida- dos intensivos [ōōnēdäd' de kōō·ē- dä'dōs ēntensē'vōs] 172

intermission descanso *m*, intermedio *m*, entreacto *m* [deskän'sō, ēnter- me'dyō, entre·äk'tō] 177

internal interno [ēnter'nō] 159

internist internista *m + f* [ēnternēs'tä] 162

interpreter intérprete *m + f* [ēnter' pre- te] 36

interrupt interrumpir [ēnterrōōmpēr'] 62

interrupter ruptor *m* [rōōptōr'] 54

intersection cruce *m*, crucero *m* (Mex) [krōō'se, krōōse'rō] 42

intestinal catarrh enteritis *f* [enterē'tēs] 170

intestine intestino *m* [ēntestē'nō] 167

invitation invitación *f* [ēmbētäsyōn'] 16

invite invitar [ēmbētär'] 183

iodine yodo *m* [yō'dō] 161

iron planchar [pläntshär'] 92

Islam Islam *m* [ēzläm'] 125

island isla *f* [ēz'lä] 76

J

jack (cards) valet *m* [välet'] 181

jack (tool) gato *m* [gä'tō] 57

jacket (lady's) chaqueta *f* [tshäke'tä] 134

jacket (man's) saco *m*, americana *f* (Sp), chaqueta *f* [sä'kō, ämerēkä'nä, tshäke'tä] 134

jackknife navaja *f* [nävä'hä] 144

jam mermelada *f* [mermelä'dä] 100

January enero *m* [ene'rō] 33

jaundice ictericia *f* [ēkterē'syä] 170

jaw maxilar *m*, mandíbula *f* [mäksēlär', mändē'bōōlä] 167; **upper ~** maxilar *m*, mandíbula *f* superior [mäksēlär', mändē'bōōlä sōōperyōr'] 167; **lower ~** maxilar *m*, mandíbula *f* inferior [mäksēlär', mändē'bōōlä ēnferyōr'] 167

jersey jersey *m* [her'sē] 137

jet plane jet *m*, avión *m* a reacción (Sp) [het, ävyōn' ä re·äksyōn'] 71

jetty malecón *m*, muelle *m* [mälekōn', mōō·e'lye] 76

Jew judío *m* [hōōdē'ō] 124

jewelry joyas *f/pl* [hō'yäs] 133; **costu- me ~** bisutería *f*, fantasía *f* [bēsōōte- rē'ä, fäntäsē'ä] 133

Jewish judío [hōōdē'ō] 125

joint articulación *f* [ärtēkōōläsyōn'] 167

joker (cards) comodín *m* [kōmōdēn'] 181

journalism periodismo *m* [peryōdēz'- mō] 39

journalist periodista *m + f* [peryōdēs'- tä] 37

journey viaje *m* [vyä'he] 43

Judaism judaísmo *m* [hōōdä·ēz'mō] 125

judge juez *m + f* [hōō· es'] 37

judo yudo *m*, judo *m* (Sp) [yōō'dō, hōō'dō] 188

juice jugo *m*, zumo *m* (Sp) [hōō'gō, sōō'mō] 100; **fruit ~** jugo *m*, zumo *m* (Sp) [hōō'gō, sōō'mō] 100; **grape- fruit ~** jugo *m*, zumo *m* (Sp) de po- melo, de toronja (Mex) [hōō'gō, sōō'mō de pōme'lō, de tōrōn'hä] 100; **orange ~** jugo *m*, zumo *m* (Sp) de naranja [hōō'gō, sōō'mō de nä- rän'hä] 100

juicy jugoso [hōōgō'sō] 102

July julio *m* [hŌŌ'lyō] 33
jumping salto *m* [säl'tō] 189
June junio *m* [hŌŌ'nyō] 33

K

kerchief pañuelo *m* de cabeza [pänyŌŌ·e'lō de käbe'sä] 144
ketchup salsa *f* de tomate [säl'sä de tōmä'te] 103
key llave *f* [lyä've] 85
kidnapping secuestro *m* [sekŌŌ·es'trō] 153
kidney riñón *m* [rēnyōn']; 167; ~ **stones** cálculos *m/pl* renales [käl'kŌŌlōs renä'les] 170
kilometer kilómetro *m* [kēlō'metrō] 193
king rey *m* [re'ē] 181
kiss *(noun)* beso *m* [be'sō] 184
kiss *(verb)* besar [besär'] 184
kitchen cocina *f* [kōsē'nä] 92
kitchenette rincón-cocina *m*, cocineta *f* [rēnkōn'-kōsē'nä, kōsēne'tä] 103
knee rodilla *f* [rōdē'lyä] 167; ~ **socks** medias *f/pl* cortas [me'dyäs kōr'täs] 134
kneecap rótula *f* [rō'tŌŌlä] 167
knife cuchillo *m* [kŌŌtshē'lyō] 99; **pocket** ~ navaja *f* [nävä'hä] 144
knight *(chess)* caballo *m* [käbä'lyō] 181
knot nudo *m* [nŌŌ'dō] 76

L

ladies señoras *f/pl*, damas *f/pl* [senyō'räs, dä'mäs] 13; ~ **shoes** zapatos *m/pl* de señora [säpä'tōs de senyō'rä] 139
lake lago *m* [lä'gō] 76
lamb cordero *m* [kōrde'rō] 108; **baby** ~ cordero *m* lechal [kōrde'rō letshäl'] 108
lamp lámpara *f* [läm'pärä] 92; **reading** ~ lámpara *f* para leer [läm'pärä pä'rä le·er'] 93

land *(noun)* tierra *f* [tye'rrä] 76
land *(verb)* tomar tierra [tōmar' tye'rrä] 76
land *(planes)* aterrizar [äterrēsär'] 71
landing aterrizaje *m* [äterrēsä'he] 71
landing gear tren *m* de aterrizaje [tren de äterrēsä'he] 71
landing stage embarcadero *m* [embärkäde'rō] 76
landscape paisaje *m* [pīsä'he] 121
lane *(highway)* carril *m* [kärrēl'] 42
lane camino *m*, sendero *m* [kämē'nō, sende'rō] 121; **get in** ~ *(merge)* tomar fila [tōmär' fē'lä] 43
larynx laringe *f* [lärēn'he] 167
last último [ŌŌl'tēmō] 59; ~ **stop** terminal *m* + *f* [termēnäl'] 59; ~ **year** año *m* pasado [ä'nyō päsä'dō] 32
late tarde [tär'de] 17; ~ *(trains, planes)* retraso *m* [reträ'sō] 61
later más tarde [mäs tär'de] 15
launch *(noun)* lancha *f* [län'tshä] 75
laundromat lavandería *f* automática [lävänderē'ä outōmä'tēkä] 128
laundry lavandería *f* [lävänderē'ä] 92
lavender lila *f* [lē'lä] 194
law *(subject)* derecho *m* [dere'tshō] 39
lawyer abogado *m* + *f* [äbōgä'dō] 37
laxative laxante *m* [läksän'te] 161
lean magro, macizo *(Mex)* [mägrō, mäsē'sō] 102
leash cuerda *f* [kŌŌ·er'dä] 144
leather cuero *m* [kŌŌ·e'rō] 139; ~ **coat** abrigo *m* de cuero [äbrē'gō de kŌŌ·e'rō] 134; ~ **jacket** chaquetón *m* de cuero [tshäketōn' de kŌŌ·e'rō] 134
leave dejar [dehär'] 44
left izquierda [ēskyer'dä] 40
leg pierna *f* [pyer'nä] 167
lemon limón *m*, lima *f* *(Mex)* [lēmōn', lē'mä] 103

lemonade limonada *f* [lēmōnäʻdä] 114

lend prestar [prestärʻ] 48

lengthen alargar [älärgärʻ] 137

lens *(camera)* objetivo *m* [obhetēʻvō] 132

lenses lentes *m/pl* [lenʻtes] 138

letter carta *f* [kärʻtä] 34; **local** ~ carta *f* local [kärʻtä lōkälʻ] 145; **registered** ~ carta *f* certificada, registrada [kärʻtä sertēfēkäʻdä, rehēsträʻdä] 145; **special delivery** ~ carta *f* exprés, urgente [kärʻtä ekspresʻ, ōōrhenʻte 145; ~ **abroad** carta *f* para el extranjero [kärʻtä päʻrä el ekstränheʻrō] 145

librarian bibliotecario *m* [bēblē-ōtekärʻyō] 37

library biblioteca *f* [bēblē-ōteʻkä] 121

libretto libreto *m* [lēbreʻtō] 177

license plate matrícula *f*, placa *f* [mätrēʻkōōlä, pläʻkä] 54

life belt salvavidas *m* [sälvävēʻdäs] 76

life jacket chaleco *m* salvavidas [tshäleʻkō sälvävēʻdäs] 71

lifeboat bote *m* salvavidas [bōʻte sälvävēʻdäs] 75

lifeguard vigilante *m* [vēhēlänʻte] 185

light *(adj.)* claro [kläʻrō] 127

light luz *f* [lōōs] 88

lighter encendedor *m*, mechero *m* [ensendedōrʻ, metsheʻrō] 140; ~ **fluid** gasolina *f* para el encendedor [gäsōlēʻnä päʻrä el ensendedōrʻ] 140

lighthouse faro *m* [fäʻrō] 76

lighting system alumbrado *m*, luces *f/pl* [älōōmbräʻdō, lōōʻses] 54

lightning relámpago *m* [relämʻpägō] 27

lights luces *f/pl* [lōōʻses] 92

lilacs lilas *f/pl* [lēʻläs] 190

limbs miembros *m/pl* [myemʻbrōs] 167

linen lino *m* [lēʻnō] 137

lingerie ropa *f* interior [rōʻpä enteryōrʻ] 134

liniment linimento *m* [lēnēmenʻtō] 161

lining forro *m* [fōʻrrō] 136

lip labio *m* [läʻbyō] 167

lipstick lápiz *m* de labios, colorete *m* *(Mex)* [läʻpēs de läʻbyōs, kōlōreʻte] 141

liter litro *m* [lēʻtrō] 193

liver hígado *m* [ēʻgädō] 108; ~ **problems** trastornos *m/pl* del hígado [trästōrʻnōs del ēʻgädō] 170

living room salón *m*, sala *f* de estar [sälōnʻ, säʻlä de estärʻ] 93

loafers zapatos *m/pl* sin cordones, mocasín *m* [säpäʻtōs sēn kōrdōʻnes, mōkäsēnʻ] 139

loan prestar [prestärʻ] 57

lobby foyer *m* [fōyerʻ (fōyeʻ)] 177

lobster bogavante *m* [bōgävänʻte] 106; **spiny** ~ langosta *f* [läng-gōsʻtä] 106

local call llamada *f* urbana, interna *(Mex)* [lyämäʻdä ōōrbäʻnä, ēnterʻnä] 149

lock cerrar con llave [serrärʻ kōn lyäʻve] 92; ~ **up** encerrar [enserrärʻ] 92

locker room vestuario *m* [vestōō-ärʻyō] 186

locksmith cerrajero *m* [serräheʻrō] 37

locomotive locomotora *f* [lōkōmōtōʻrä] 67

long largo [lärʻgō] 133; **how** ~ cuánto tiempo [kōō-änʻtō tyemʻpō] 18; ~ **distance express** expreso *m* de largo recorrido [ekspreʻsō de lärʻgō rekōrrēʻdō] 60; ~ **wave** onda *f* larga [ōnʻdä lärʻgä] 182

loss pérdida *f* [perʻdēdä] 153

lounge salón *m* [sälōnʻ] 74

love *(noun)* amor *m* [ämōrʻ] 184

love *(verb)* amar [ämärʻ] 184

low pressure *(system)* de baja presión [de bäʻhä presyōnʻ] 27

lubricant lubricante *m* [lōōbrēkänʻte] 54

lubrication lubricación *f* [lōōbrēkäsyōnʻ] 46

luck suerte *f* [sōō-erʻte] 23; **good** ~

mucha suerte [mōō'tshä sōō·er'te] 23

luggage equipaje m [ekēpä'he] 59; ~ **car** furgón m [fōōrgōn'] 64; ~ **locker** consigna f automática [kōnsēg'nä outōmä'tēkä] 63; ~ **rack** rejilla f [rehē'lyä] 67

lunch almuerzo m, comida f [älmōō·er'sō, kōmē'dä] 92

lung pulmón m [pōōlmōn'] 167

M

mackerel caballa f [käbä'lyä] 106

magazine revista f [revēs'tä] 182; **fashion** ~ revista f de modas [revēs'tä de mō'däs] 182

maid camarera f, recamarera f [kämäre'rä, rekämäre'rä] 92

maiden name nombre m de soltera [nōm'bre de sōlte'rä] 79

mail correo [kōrre'ō] 89; ~ **box** buzón m [bōōsōn'] 145

mailman cartero m [kärte'rō] 149

main road carretera f principal [kärrete'rä prēnsēpäl'] 43

main station estación f central [estäsyōn' senträl'] 60

main street calle f principal [kä'lye prēnsēpäl'] 121

manager director m, gerente m [dērektōr', heren'te] 23

manicure manicura f [mänēkōō'rä] 156

manufacturer's spare parts piezas f/pl de repuesto originales [pye'säs de repōō·es'tō ōrēhēnä'les] 50

map mapa m [mä'pä] 130; **city** ~ plano m de la ciudad [plä'nō de lä syōōdäd'] 130; **road** ~ mapa m de carreteras [mä'pä de kärrete'räs] 130; **street** ~ plano m de la ciudad [plä'nō de lä syōōdäd'] 130

March marzo m [mär'sō] 33

margarine margarina f [märgärē'nä] 103

marital status estado m civil [estä'dō sēvēl'] 79

marksmanship tiro m [tē'rō] 189

marriage boda f [bō'dä] 22

married casado [käsä'dō (-ä)] 79

mascara pestañina f, rímel m (Sp) [pestänyē'nä, rē'mel] 141

mass misa f [mē'sä] 125

massage (noun) masaje m [mäsä'he] 175; **massage** (verb) dar masaje [där mäsä'he] 175

masseur masajista m [mäsähēs'tä] 175

masseuse masajista f [mäsähēs'tä] 175

mast mástil m [mäs'tēl] 76

match (sports) partido m [pärtē'dō] 188

matches fósforos m/pl, cerillas f/pl (Sp), cerillos m/pl (Mex) [fōs'fōrōs, serē'lyäs, serē'lyōs] 140

material tejido m, tela f [tehē'dō, te'lä] 137

mathematics matemáticas f/pl [mätemä'tēkäs] 39

matte mate [mä'te] 132

mattress colchón m [kōltshōn'] 90

mauve malva [mäl'vä] 194

maxillary sinus seno m maxilar [se'nō mäksēlär'] 167

maximum speed velocidad f máxima [velōsēdäd' mä'ksēmä] 42

May mayo m [mä'yō] 33

maybe quizá(s) [kēsä(s)'] 21

mayonnaise mayonesa f [mäyōne'sä] 103

meals comidas f/pl [kōmē'däs] 86

meanwhile mientras tanto [myen'träs tän'tō] 32

measles sarampión m [särämpyōn'] 171

meat carne f [kär'ne] 108; **ground** ~ carne f molida, picada (Sp) [kär'ne mōlē'dä, pēkä'dä] 108

mechanic mecánico m [mekä'nēkō] 48

mechanical engineering construcción f mecánica [kōnstrōōksyōn' mekä'nēkä] 39

medical director médico-jefe m [me'dēkō-he'fe] 172

medicinal spring aguas f/pl medicinales [ä'gōō-äs medēsēnä'les] 175

medicine medicamento m [medēkämen'tō] 159

medicine (discipline) medicina f [medēsē'nä] 39

meditation meditación f [medētäsyōn'] 125

medium (done) medio cocido, medio asado (Sp) [me'dyō kō sē'dō, me'dyō äsä'dō] 102

meet encontrarse [enkōnträr'se] 184; **glad to ~ you** encantado [enkäntä'dō] 14

melon melón m [melōn'] 112; **water ~** sandía f [sändē'ä] 112

membership card tarjeta f, carnet m de miembro (Sp) [tärhe'tä, kärnet' de myem'brō] 96

memorial monumento m [mōnōōmen'-tō] 121

men's room caballeros [käbälye'rōs] 92

menstruation menstruación f, período m [menstrōō·äsyōn', perē'ōdō] 167

menu carta f [kär'tä] 98

metabolism metabolismo m [metäbōlēz'mō] 168

metalworker metalúrgico m [metäl-ōōr'hēkō] 37

meter metro m [me'trō] 193

middle centro m [sen'trō] 65; **~ ear inflammation** otitis f media [ōtē'tēs me'dyä] 171

midnight medianoche f [medyänō'-tshe] 31

midwife comadrona f, partera f [kōmädrō'nä, pärte'rä] 37

mile milla f [mē'lyä] 193; **nautical ~**

milla f marítima or náutica [mē'lyä märē'tēma, nou'tēkä] 193

mileage indicator cuentakilometros m [kōō·entäkēlō'metrōs] 54

milk leche f [le'tshe 100; **condensed ~** leche f evaporada [le'tshe eväpōrä'-dä] 100

millimeter milímetro m [mēlē'metrō] 193

mine mío [mē'ō] 80

miner minero m [mēne'rō] 37

minerals minerales m/p. [mēnerä'les] 175

miniature golf minigolf m [mēnēgōlf] 180; **~ course** minigolf m [mēnēgōlf] 180

ministry ministerio m [mēnēster'yō] 121

minute minuto m [mēnōō'tō] 86; **just a ~** un momento [ōōn mōmen'tō] 16

mirror espejo m [espe'hō] 92

miss señorita f [senyōrē'tä] 13

mist neblina f [neblē'nä] 27

molar muela f [mōō·e'lä] 174

mole malecón m, muelle m [mälekōn', mōō·e'lye] 76

moment momento m [mōmen'tō] 87; **at the ~** de momento [de mōmen'tō] 32

monastery monasterio m [mōnäste'-ryō] 125

Monday lunes m [lōō'nes] 33

money dinero m [dēne'rō] 151; **~ exchange** oficina f de cambio [ōfē-sē'nä de käm'byō] 60

month mes m [mes] 32

monument monumento m [mōnōō-men'tō] 119

moon luna f [lōō'nä] 27

moped ciclomotor m [sēklōmōtōr'] 41

morning mañana f [mänyä'nä] 31; **good ~** buenos días [bōō·e'nōs dē'äs] 12; **in the ~** por la mañana [pōr lä mänyä'nä] 31; **this ~** esta mañana [es'tä mänyä'nä] 31

mortgage hipoteca f [ēpôte'kä] 152

mosaic mosaico m [mōsī'kō] 125

Moslem musulmán m [mōōsōōlmän'] 125

mosque mezquita f [meskē'tä] 125

motel motel m [mōtel'] 81

mother madre f, mamá f (Mex) [mä'dre, mämä'] 35

mother-in-law suegra f [sōō·e'grä] 35

motor motor m [mōtōr'] 54; **~ scooter** escúter m [eskōō'ter] 41; **~ oil** aceite m para el motor [äse'ēte pä'rä el mōtōr'] 46

motorail service autotrén m [outōtren'] 60

motorboat lancha f motora, voladora f, motonauta f (Mex) [län'tshä mōtō'rä, vōlädō'rä, mōtōnou'tä] 75

motorcycle motocicleta f, moto f [mōtōsēkle'tä, mō'tō] 41

mountain montaña f [mōntä'nyä] 122; **~ range** montañas f/pl, sierra f, cordillera f [mōntä'nyäs, sye'rä, kōrdēlye'rä] 122; **~ climber** montañero m, alpinista m + f [mōntänye'rō, älpēnēs'tä] 189; **~ climbing** montañismo m, alpinismo [mōntänyēz'mō, älpēnēz'mō] 189

moustache bigote m [bēgō'te] 157

mouth boca f [bō'kä] 168

mouthwash agua m dentífrica [ä'gōō·ä dentē'frēkä] 141

move (verb) mover [mōver'] 164

move (e.g. apt.) mudarse [mōōdär'se] 92; **~ in** instalarse [ēnstälär'se] 92; **~ out** abandonar [äbändōnär'] 92

move (e.g. game) jugada f [hōōgä'dä] 181

movie película f [pelē'kōōlä] 179

movies cine m [sē'ne] 179

Mr. señor [senyōr'] 13

Mrs. señora [senyō'rä] 13

mucous membrane mucosa f [mōōkō'sä] 168

mud lodo m [lō'dō] 175; **~ bath** baño m de lodo [bä'nyō de lō'dō] 175; **~ pack** envoltura f [envōltōō'rä] 175

mumps paperas f/pl [päpe'räs] 171

murder asesinato m [äsesēnä'tō] 153

muscle músculo m [mōōs'kōōlō] 168

museum museo m [mōōse'ō] 116

mushrooms champiñones m/pl [tshämpēnyō'nes] 110

music música f [mōō'sēkä] 177; **piece of ~** composición f [kōmpōsēsyōn'] 178

musical musical m [mōōsēkäl'] 177

musician músico m + f [mōō'sēkō] 37

musicology música f [mōō'sēkä] 39

mussels mejillones m/pl [mehēlyō'nes] 107

mustard mostaza f [mōstä'sä] 103

mutton carnero m [kärne'rō] 108

my mi [mē] 80

N

nail (finger) uña f [ōō'nyä] 168

nail (tool) clavo m [klä'vō] 57; **~ file** lima f de uñas [lēmä de ōō'nyäs] 141; **~ polish** esmalte m [ezmäl'te] 141; **~ polish remover** quitaesmalte m [kētä·ezmäl'te] 141; **~ scissors** tijeras f/pl de uñas [tēhe'räs de ōō'nyäs] 141

name nombre m [nōm'bre] 79; **first ~** nombre m de pila [nōm'bre de pē'lä] 79; **middle ~** nombre m segundo [nōm'bre segōōn'dō] 79; **last ~** apellido m [äpelyē'dō] 79; **what's your ~** como se llama [kō'mō se lyä'mä] 19

napkin servilleta f [servēlye'tä] 99

narcotics narcóticas f/pl [närkō'tēkäs] 154

narrow estrecho [estre'tshō] 127

national park parque m nacional [pär'ke näsyōnäl'] 122

nationality nacionalidad f [näsyōnälē-

däd'] 79; ~ **plate** placa f de nacionalidad [plä'kä de näsyönälēdäd'] 79

nausea náuseas f/pl [nou'se·äs] 171

nave nave f [nä've] 125

near cerca [ser'kä] 44; ~ **here** cerca de
aquí [ser'kä de äkē'] 44

nearest cercano [serkä'nō] 50

near-sighted miope [mē·ō'pe] 138

neck cuello m [kōō·e'lyō] 168; **nape of
the** ~ nuca f [nōō'kä] 168

necklace collar m [kōlyär'] 133

needle aguja f [ägōō'hä] 136; **sewing**
~ aguja f de coser [ägōō'hä de kōse-
r'] 136

negative negativo m [negätē'vō] 131

nephew sobrino m [sōbrē'nō] 35

nephritis nefritis f [nefrē'tēs] 171

nerve nervio m [ner'vyō] 174

nerves nervios m/pl [ner'vyōs] 168

neuralgia neuralgia f [ne·ōōräl'hyä]
171

neurologist neurólogo m [ne·ōōrō'lō-
gō] 162

neutral *(car)* punto m muerto [pōōn'tō
mōō·er'tō] 53

never nunca [nōōng'kä] 21

new nuevo [nōō·e'vō] 50

news noticias f/pl [notē'syäs] 182

newsdealer vendedor m de periódicos
[vendedor' de perē·ō'dēkōs] 129

newspaper periódico m [peryō'dēkō]
181

next próximo [prō'hēmō] 183

nice agradable [ägrädä'ble] 184

niece sobrina f [sōbrē'nä] 35

night noche f [nō'tshe] 83; **all** ~ toda la
noche [tō'dä lä nō'tshe] 44; **at** ~ por
la noche [pōr lä nō'tshe] 31; **good** ~
buenas noches [bōōe'näs nō'tshes]
17; ~ **club** club m nocturno [klōōb
nōktōōr'nō] 180; ~ **duty** guardia f or
turno m [gōō·är'dyä, tōōr'nō] 159; ~
rate tarifa f nocturna [tärē'fä
nōktōōr'nä] 148; ~ **shirt** camisa f de

dormir [kämē'sä de dōrmēr'] 134

nightgown camisón m [kämēsōn'] 134

night's lodging alojamiento m para
una noche [älōhämyen'tō pä'rä ōō'-
nä nō'tshe] 92

nine nueve [nōō·e've] 28

ninepins bolos m/pl [bō'lōs] 189

no no [nō] 21

nobody nadie [nä'dye] 49

non-swimmer no-nadador [nō-nädä-
dōr'] 186

noodles fideos m/pl [fēde'ōs] 105

noon mediodía m [medyōdē'ä] 31; **at** ~
a mediodía [ä medyōdē'ä] 31; **this** ~
hoy al mediodía [oi äl medyōdē'ä] 32

nose nariz f [närēs'] 168

nosebleed hemorragia f nasal [emō-
rrä'hyä näsäl'] 171

notary notario m [nōtär'yō] 37

note nota f [nō'tä] 177

nothing nada [nä'dä] 21

novel novela f [nōve'lä] 130

November noviembre m [nōvyem'bre]
33

now ahora [ä·ō'rä] 32; ~ **and then** a
veces [ä veses] 32

nude desnudo [desnōō'dō] 185

number número m [nōō'merō] 79

nurse enfermera f [enferme'rä] 172;
male ~ enfermero m [enferme'rō]
37; **night** ~ enfermera f de noche
[enferme'rä de nō'tshe] 172

nursery cuarto m de niños [kōō·är'tō
de nē'nyōs] 93

nutmeg nuez f moscada [nōō·es' mōs-
kä'dä] 103

nut nuez f [nōō·es'] 111

nylon nilón m [nēlōn'] 137

O

oarsman remero m [reme'rō] 189

observatory observatorio m [ōbservä-
tōr'yō] 121

occupation profesión f [prŏfĕsyŏn'] 79

occupied ocupado [ŏkōōpä'dō] 66

ocean océano m [ōse'änō] 77

October octubre m [ŏktōō'bre] 33

offer ofrecer [ōfreser'] 16

office oficina f [ōfēsē'nä] 121; **lost and found** ~ oficina f de objetos perdidos [ōfēsē'nä de ōbhe'tōs perdē'dōs] 121; ~ **hours** horas f/pl de consulta [ō'räs de kōnsōōl'tä] 163

officer oficial m [ōfēsyäl' 74; **deck** ~ oficial m de guardia [ōfēsyäl' de gōō·är'dyä] 74; **first** ~ segundo comandante m [segōōn'dō kōmändän'te] 76

off-side fuera de juego [fōō·e'rä de hōō·e'gō] 190

oil aceite m [äse'ēte] 45; **please check the** ~ revise el nivel de aceite [revē'se el nēvel' de äse'ēte] 46; ~ **can** aceitera f [äse·ēte'rä] 46; ~ **change** cambio m de aceite [käm'byō de äse'ēte] 46; ~ **filter** filtro m de aceite [fēl'trō de äse'ēte] 54; ~ **level** nivel m de aceite [nēvel' de äse'ēte] 46; ~ **pump** bomba f de aceite [bōm'bä de äse'ēte] 54

ointment pomada f [pōmä'dä] 161; **boric acid** ~ agua f bórica [ä'gōō·ä bō'rēkä] 160; **burn** ~ pomada f para quemaduras [pōmä'dä pä'rä kemädōō'räs] 160

eye ~ pomada f para los ojos [pōmä'dä pä'rä lōs ō'hōs] 160

olives aceitunas f/pl [äse'ētōō'näs] 104

one un, uno [ōōn, ōō'nō] 28

one way ticket boleto m de ida [bōle'tō de ē'dä] 62

onion cebolla f [sebō'lyä] 103

open abierto [äbyer'tō] 44

open (verb) abrir [äbrēr'] 65

open market mercado m [merkä'dō] 121

opera ópera f [ō'perä] 177; ~ **glasses**

gemelos m/pl (de teatro) [jeme'lōs (de te·ä'trō)] 178

operate operar [ōperär'] 172

operating room quirófano m [kērō'-fänō] 172

operation operación f [ōperäsyōn'] 172

operator telefonista m + f, operador m + f (Mex) [telefōnēs'tä, ōperädōr'] 150

operetta opereta f [ōpere'tä] 177

optician óptico m [ōp'tēkō] 129

oral surgeon cirujano m oral [sērōō-hä'nō ōräl'] 174

orange naranja f [närän'hä] 112; ~ **juice** jugo m, zumo m (Sp), de naranja [hōō'gō, sōō'mō de närän'hä] 100

orange (color) naranja [närän'hä] 194

orangeade naranjada f [näränhä'dä] 114

orchestra orquesta f [ōrkes'tä] 178; ~ **seats** patio m (de butacas), platea f, luneta f [pä'tyō (de bōōtä'käs), plä-te'ä, lōōne'tä] 178

orchids orquídeas f/pl [ōrkē'de·äs] 130

organ órgano m [ōr'gänō] 125

orthodontist ortodontista m + f [ōrtō-dōntēs'tä] 174

orthopedist ortopedista m + f [ōrtōpe-dēs'tä] 162

ounce onza f [ōn'sä] 193

overture obertura f [ōbertōō'rä] 178

oysters ostras f/pl, ostiones f/pl (Mex) [ōs'träs, ōstyō'nes] 104

P

pack (packet) paquete m [päke'te] 126

pad bloc m [blōk] 138; **scratch** ~ bloc m de notas [blōk de nō'täs] 138; **sketch** ~ bloc m de dibujos [blōk de dēbōō'hōs] 138

pail balde m, cubo m (Sp), cubeta f (Mex) [bäl'de, kōō'bō, kōōbe'tä] 92

pain dolor m [dōlōr'] 171; ~ **killer** algo

contra el dolor [äl'gō kōn'trä el dō-lōr'] 173; ~ **pills** analgésicos *m/pl* [änälhe'sēkōs] 161

paint *(noun)* pintura *f*, barniz *m (Sp)* [pēntōō'rä, bärnēs'] 54

painter pintor *m* [pēntōr'] 37

pair par *m* [pär] 126

pajamas pijama *m* [pēhä'mä] 134

palace palacio *m* [pälä'syō] 119

palate paladar *m* [pälädär'] 168

pancreas páncreas *m* [pän'kre·äs] 168

panties bragas *f/pl*, pantaletas *f/pl (Mex)* [brä'gäs', päntäle'täs] 134

pants pantalón *m* [päntälōn'] 135; ~ **suit** traje *m* de pantalón [trä'he de päntälōn'] 135

paper papel *m* [päpel'] 132

paperback libro *m* de bolsillo [lē'brō de bōlsē'lyō] 130

paper napkins servilletas *f/pl* de papel [servēlye'täs de päpel'] 144

papers documentación *f* [dōkōōmen-täsyōn'] 78

paprika pimentón *m* [pēmentōn'] 103

parallel bars paralelas *f/pl* [päräle'läs] 188

paralysis parálisis *f* [pärä'lēsēs] 171

parcel paquete *m* [päke'te] 145

pardon perdón [perdōn'] 22

parents padres *m/pl* [pä'dres] 35

park *(verb)* estacionar, aparcar *(Sp)* [estäsyōnär, äpärkär'] 43

park *(noun)* parque *m* [pär'ke] 121

parka anorac *m* [änōräk] 135

parking estacionamiento *m* [estäsyō-nämyen'tō] 42; **no** ~ estacionamiento *m* prohibido [estäsyōnämyen'tō prō·ēbē'dō] 42; ~ **disc** disco *m* de estacionamiento [dēs'kō de estäsyō-nämyen'tō] 42; ~ **lights** luz *f* de población [lōōs de pōbläsyōn'] 53; ~ **lot** aparcamiento *m*, estacionamiento *m* [äpärkämyen'tō, estäsyōnä-myen'tō] 42; ~ **meter** parquímetro *m*

[pärkē'metrō] 42

parsley perejil *m* [perehēl'] 103

part *(in hair)* raya *f*, carrera *f*, línea *f* [rä'yä, kärre'rä, lē'ne·ä] 157

part *(in theater)* papel *m* [päpel'] 178

part of town barrio *m* [bärr'yō] 121

partridge perdiz *f* [perdēs'] 107

party fiesta *f* [fyes'tä] 183; ~ **games** juegos *m/pl* de sociedad [hōō·e' gōs de sōsyedäd'] 182

pass *(on road)* adelantar [ädeläntär'] 42

pass *(mountain)* puerto *m* (de monta-ña) [pōō·er'tō (de mōntä'nyä)] 42

passenger pasajero *m* [päsähe'rō] 77

passport pasaporte *m* [päsäpōr'te] 79; ~ **control** control *m* de pasaportes [kōntrōl' de päsäpōr'tes] 79

pastime pasatiempo *m* [päsätyem'pō] 182

pastor pastor *m* [pästōr'] 125

pastry chef pastelero *m* [pästele'rō] 37

path camino *m* [kämē'nō] 42

patient paciente *m* + *f* [päsyen'te] 172

patio patio *m* [pä'tyō] 92

pavillion pabellón *m* [päbelyōn'] 122

pawn *(chess)* peón *m* [pe·ōn'] 181

pay pagar [pägär'] 80

payment pago *m* [pä'gō] 152

peas chícharos *m/pl (Mex)*, guisantes *m/pl (Sp)* [tshē'tshärōs, gēsän'tes] 110

peach durazno *m*, melocotón *m (Sp)* [dōōräz'nō, melōkōtōn'] 111, 112

peanuts cacahuates *m/pl (Mex)*, caca-huetes *m/pl (Sp)* [käkä·ōō·ä'tes, kä-kä·ōō·e'tes] 110

pear pera *f* [pe'rä] 112

pearls perlas *f/pl* [per'läs] 133

pedal pedal *m* [pedäl'] 54

pedestrian peatón *m* [pe·ätōn'] 122; ~ **crossing** paso *m* de peatones [pä'sō de pe·ätō'nes] 122

pediatrician pediatra *m* + *f* [pedyä'trä] 162

pedicure pedicura *f* [pedēkōō'rä] 156

pelvis pelvis *f* [pel'vēs] 168

pen *(fountain)* pluma *f* [plōō'mä] 138

penalty kick penalty *m* [penäl'tē] 190

pencil lápiz *m* [lä'pēs] 138

penis pene *m* [pe'ne] 168

pension pensión *f* [pensyōn'] 81

people personas *f/pl* [persō'näs] 41

pepper *(spice)* pimienta *f* (negra) [pē-myen'tä (ne'grä)] 103; ~ **mill** molinillo *m* de pimienta [mōlēnē'lyō de pē-myen'tä] 99; ~ **shaker** pimentero *m* [pēmente'rō] 99

peppermint menta *f* [men'tä] 161

peptic ulcer úlcera *f* gástrica [ōōl'serä gäs'trēkä] 171

perch perca *f* [per'kä] 107

performance *(at the theater)* función *f* [fōōnsyōn'] 176

performance *(of a work)* representación *f* [representäsyōn'] 178

perfume perfume *m* [perfōō'me] 141

perhaps quizá(s) [kēsä(s)'] 21

permanent wave permanente *f* [permänen'te] 155

personal personal [persōnäl'] 80

petticoat enaguas *f/pl* [enä'gōō·äs] 135

pharmacist farmacéutico *m* [färmäse'·ōōtēkō] 37

pharmacy farmacia *f* [färmä'syä] 159

pheasant faisán *m* [fīsän'] 107

phone *(verb)* telefonear [telefone·är'] 78

phone *(noun)* teléfono *m* [tele'fōnō] 147; ~ **book** directorio *m*, guía *f* (de teléfonos) *(Sp)* [dērektōr'yō, gē'ä (de tele'fōnōs)] 147; ~ **booth** cabina *f* [käbē'nä] 148; ~ **call** *(make a)* telefonear [telefone·är'] 85; **pay** ~ teléfono *m* público [tele'fōnō pōō'blēkō] 148

photo fotografía *f* [fōtōgräfē'ä] 132

photocopies fotocopias *f/pl* [fōtōkō'-pyäs] 138

photograph *(verb)* fotografiar [fōtōgrä-fē·är'] 132

photographer fotógrafo *m* [fōtō'gräfō] 74

photographer's studio fotógrafo *m* [fō-tō'gräfō] 129

physics física *f* [fē'sēkä] 39

pianist pianista *m* + *f* [pē·änēs'tä] 178

piano recital recital *m* (de piano) [resē-täl' (de pē·ä'nō)] 178

pick up recoger [rekōher'] 41

pickles pepinillos *m/pl* [pepēnē'lyōs] 103

pickled escabechado [eskäbetshä'dō] 102

picture cuadro *m* [kōō·ä'drō] 144

piece parte *f*, trozo *m* [pär'te, trō'sō] 193

pier embarcadero *m* [embärkäde'rō] 77

pike lucio *m* [lōō'syō] 107

piles almorranas *f/pl* [älmōrrä'näs] 171

pills pastillas *f/pl*, píldoras *f/pl* [pästē'-lyäs, pēl'dōräs] 161

pillar columna *f* [kōlōōm'nä] 125

pillow almohada *f* [älmō·ä'dä] 87

pillowcase funda *f* [fōōn'dä] 90

pilot piloto *m* [pēlō'tō] 71

pin alfiler *m* [älfēler'] 136; **bobby** ~ horquillas *f/pl*, clips *m/pl* [ōrkē'lyäs, klēps] 140

pincers tenazas *f/pl* [tenä'säs] 57

pineapple piña *f* [pē'nyä] 112

ping pong ping pong *m* [pēnpōn'] 182

pink rosa [rō'sä] 194

pinkie dedo *m* meñique [de'dō menyē'-ke] 167

pint pinta *f* [pēn'tä] 193

pipe tubo *m* [tōō'bō] 54

pipe *(to smoke)* pipa *f* [pē'pä] 140; ~ **cleaner** escobilla *f* [eskōbē'lyä] 140

piston émbolo *m*, pistón *m* [em'bōlō, pēstōn'] 54; ~ **ring** segmento *m* de émbolo (de pistón) [segmen'tō de em'bōlō (de pēstōn')] 54

pitcher jarra *f* [hä'rrä] 99; **cream ~** jarra *f* para leche [hä'rrä pä'rä le'tshe] 99

pity lástima *f*, pena *f* [läs'tēmä, pe'nä] 22

place of birth lugar *m* de nacimiento [lōōgär' de näsēmyen'tō] 79

place of residence lugar *m* de residencia [lōōgär' de resēden'syä] 79

plane avión *m* [ävyōn'] 68

plate *(dentistry)* plancha *f* [plän'tshä] 174

plate *(table service)* plato *m* [plä'tō] 99; **bread ~** platillo *m* [plätē'lyō] 99; **soup ~** plato *m* sopero [plä'tō sōpe'rō] 99

platform andén *m* [ändēn'] 67

play *(verb)* jugar [hōōgär'] 182

play *(noun)* pieza *f* de teatro [pye'sä de te·ä'trō] 178

player jugador *m* [hōōgädōr'] 189

playground parque *m* infantil [pär'ke ēnfäntēl'] 96

playing cards cartas *f/pl*, naipes *m/pl* [kär'täs, nī'pes] 144

please por favor [pōr fävōr'] 20

pleasure gusto *m* [gōōs'tō] 21

pleurisy pleuresía *f* [ple·ōōresē'ä] 171

pliers alicates *m/pl*, pinzas *f/pl* [älēkä'tes, pēn'säs] 57

plug clavija *f* de enchufe [klävē'hä de entshōō'fe] 92

plum ciruela *f* [sērōō·e'lä] 111

plumber plomero *m*, fontanero *m (Sp)* [plōme'rō, fōntäne'rō] 37

pneumonia pulmonía *f* [pōōlmōnē'ä] 171

point punto *m* [pōōn'tō] 188

poisoning envenenamiento *m*, intoxicación *f* [envenenämyen'tō, ēntōksēkäsyōn'] 171

police policía *f* [pōlēsē'ä] 154; **~ car** carro *m*, coche *m (Sp)* de la policía [kä'rrō, kō'tshe de lä pōlēsē'ä] 154;

~ station estación *f* de policía, comisaría *f (Sp)* [estäsyōn' de pōlēsē'ä, kōmēsärē'ä] 154

policeman policía *m* [pōlēsē'ä] 122

polish pulir [pōōlēr'] 156

political science ciencias *f/pl* políticas [syen'syäs pōlē'tēkäs] 39

pool hall sala *f* de billar [sä'lä de bē'lyär] 180

pork cerdo *m*, puerco *m* [ser'dō, pōō·er'kō] 108

port *(land)* puerto *m* [pōō·er'tō] 77

port *(side)* babor *m* [bäbōr'] 77; **~ fees** tasa *f* portuaria [tä'sä pōrtōō·är'yä] 77

portal portal *m* [pōrtäl'] 125

porter mozo *m* [mō'sō] 64

portion ración *f* [räsyōn'] 98

possible posible [pōsē'ble] 22

post office correos *m/pl* [kōrre'ōs] 122

postage porte *m*, franqueo *m* [pōr'te, fränke'ō] 150

postal clerk empleado *m* de correos [emple·ä'dō de kōrre'ōs] 150

postal savings book libreta *f* postal de ahorros [lēbre'tä pōstäl' de ä·ō'rrōs] 150

postcard postal *f* [pōstäl'] 85

postman cartero *m* [kärte'rō] 150

pot olla *f* [ō'lyä] 99; **coffee ~** cafetera *f* [käfete'rä] 99; **tea ~** tetera *f* [tete'rä] 99

potatoes papas *f/pl*, patatas *f/pl* [pä'päs, pätä'täs] 110

pound libra *f* [lē'brä] 193

powder polvos *m/pl* [pōl'vōs] 141; **~ puff** borla *f* de polvos [bōr'lä de pōl'vōs] 141

power brake servofreno *m* [servōfre'nō] 54

power station central *f* eléctrica, planta *f* eléctrica *(Mex)* [senträl' elek'trēkä, plän'tä elek'trēkä] 122

power steering servodirección *f* [servōdĕreksyōn'] 54

practice *(train)* entrenarse [entrenär'-se] 188

precipitation precipitaciones *f/pl* [presēpētäsyō'nes] 27

pregnancy embarazo *m* [embärä'sō] 168

prescription receta *f,* fórmula *f* [rese'tä, fōr'mōōlä] 159

present regalo *m* [regä'lō] 80

press *(verb)* planchar [pläntshär'] 137

preview avance *m* [ävän'se] 179

previously antes [än'tes] 32

price precio *m* [pre'syō] 92

priest cura *m* [kōō'rä] 123

print *(film)* copia *f* [kō'pyä] 131

printed estampado [estämpä'dō] 137

printed matter impresos *m/pl* [ēmpre'-sōs] 145

prison cárcel *f* [kär'sel] 154

probably probablemente [prōbäblemen'te] 21

procession procesión *f* [prōsesyōn'] 125

producer productor *m* [prōdōōktōr'] 178

production puesta *f* en escena [pōō·es'tä en ese'nä] 178

program programa *m* [prōgrä'mä] 178; ~ **schedule** programas *m/pl* de la semana [prōgrä'mäs de lä semä'nä] 182

prophylactics preservativos *m/pl* [preservätē'vōs] 161

Protestant protestante [prōtestän'te] 125

psychiatrist psiquiatra *m + f* [sēkyä'-trä] 163

psychologist psicólogo *m* [sēkō'lōgō] 163

psychology psicología *f* [sēkōlōhē'ä] 39

public garden jardín *m* público [härdēn' pōō'blēkō] 122

public rest room baños *m/pl,* servicios *m/pl (Sp)* [bä'nyōs, servē'syōs] 122

pulpit púlpito *m* [pōōl'pētō] 125

pumpkin calabaza *f* [käläbä'sä] 110

puncture pinchazo *m* [pēntshä'sō] 47

pupil alumno *m* [älōōm'nō] 37

purple morado [mōrä'dō] 194

purse bolso *m,* bolsa *f (Mex)* [bōl'sō, bōl'sä] 153

purser contador *m* [kōntädōr'] 74

Q

quay muelle *m* [mōō·e'lye] 77

quails codornices *f/pl* [kōdōrnē'ses] 107

quart *(approx.)* litro *m* [lē'trō] 126

quarter cuarto [kōō·är'tō] 30

quarter *(year)* trimestre *m* [trēmes'tre] 32

queen *(chess)* dama *f* [dä'mä] 181

quickly en seguida [en segē'dä] 48

quinine quinina *f* [kēnē'nä] 161

R

rabbi rabino *m* [räbē'nō] 125

rabbit conejo *m* [kōne'hō] 108

race carrera *f* [kärre'rä] 187; ~ **car driver** corredor *m* [kōrredōr'] 187

racing car carro *m,* coche *m (Sp)* de carreras [kä'rrō, kō'tshe de kärre'-räs] 187

radiation therapy radioterapia *f* [rädyō-terä'pyä] 175

radiator radiador *m* [rädyädōr'] 93

radio radio *m, (Sp) f* [rä'dyō] 182; ~ **play** radioteatro *m* [rä'dyōte·ä'trō] 182; ~ **room** cabina *f* de radio [käbē'nä de rä'dyō] 74

rag trapo *m* [trä'pō] 57

railroad ferrocarril *m* [ferrōkärrēl'] 67; ~ **crossing** paso *m* a nivel, cruce *m* de F.C. *(Mex)* [pä'sō ä nēvel', krōō'se de e'fe se] 42; ~ **man** ferroviario *m* [ferrōvyär'yō] 37; ~ **station** estación f [estäsyōn'] 72

rain *(noun)* lluvia f [lyoō'vyä] 88

rain *(verb)* llover [lyōver'] 25

raincoat impermeable m [ēmperme·ä'-ble] 135

raisins pasas f/pl [pä'säs] 103

ranch station wagon camioneta f, combi f *(Mex)* [kämyōne'tä, kōm'bē] 40

rare casi crudo, a la inglesa *(Sp)* [kä'sē krōō'dō, ä lä ēngle'sä] 102

rash erupción f cutánea, salpullido m *(Mex)* [erōōpsyōn' kōōtä'ne·ä, sälpōōlyē'dō] 171

raw crudo [krōō'dō] 102

razor *(safety)* rasuradora f, maquinilla f de afeitar *(Sp)* [räsōōrädō'rä, mäkē-nē'lyä de äfe·ētär'] 141; ~ **blades** hojas f/pl de afeitar, cuchillas f/pl [ō'häs de äfe·ētär', kōōtshē'lyäs] 141; ~ **cut** corte m a navaja [kōr'te ä nävä'hä] 157; **straight** ~ navaja f [nävä'hä] 141

reading room sala f de lectura [sä'lä de lektōō'rä] 74

ready listo [lēs'tō] 50

real estate agency inmobiliaria f [ēnmōbēlyär'yä] 129

rear trasero [träse'rō] 54; **at the** ~ en la cola [en lä kō'lä] 65; ~ **lights** luz f trasera [lōōs träse'rä] 53; ~ **motor** motor m trasero [mōtōr' träse'rō] 54; ~ **view mirror** espejo m retrovisor [espe'hō retrōvēsōr'] 55; ~ **-end collision** accidente m en cadena [äksē-den'te en käde'nä] 49

receipt recibo m, resguardo m *(Sp)* [resē'bō, rezgōō·är'dō] 150

recently recientemente [resyentemen'-te] 32

reception desk recepción f [resep-syōn'] 92

recommend recomendar [rekōmen-

där'] 81

record disco m [dēs'kō] 130; ~ **player** tocadiscos m/pl [tōkädēs'kōs] 182; **phonograph** ~ disco m [dēs'kō] 144

recording tape cinta f magnetofónica [sēn'tä mägnetōfō'nēkä] 144

recreation room salón m de recreo [salón' de rekre'ō] 96

red rojo, colorado [rō'hō, kōlōrä'dō] 194; **bright** ~ rojo vivo [rō'hō vē'vō] 194; **dark** ~ rojo oscuro [rō'hō ōs-kōō'rō] 194; ~ **cabbage** berza f, lombarda f [ber'sä, lōmbär'dä] 110

reduced fare ticket boleto m a precio reducido [bōle'tō a pre'syō redōōsē'-dō] 62

reduced rates rebaja f, descuento m [rebä'hä, deskōō·en'tō] 83

referee árbitro m [är'bētrō] 189

refrain from smoking no fumen [nō fōō'men] 70

refrigerator frigorífico m, refrigerador m *(Mex)* [frēgōrē'fēkō, refrēherädōr'] 93

register *(in hotel)* inscribir [ēnskrēbēr'] 84

register *(letter)* certificar, registrar [sertēfēkär', rehēsträr'] 150

registered letter carta f certificada, registrada [kär'tä sertēfēkä'dä, rehēs-trä'dä] 150

registration *(car)* papeles m/pl del carro, del coche *(Sp)* [päpe'les del kä'-rrō, del kō'tshe] 43

registration inscripción f [ēnskrēp-syōn'] 93

regret pesar m [pesär'] 22

regular *(gas)* normal f [nōrmäl'] 45

religion religión f [relēhyōn'] 125

religious religioso [relēhyō'sō] 125

remedy remedio m [reme'dyō] 161

renew renovar [renōvär'] 79

rent *(noun)* alquiler m, arriendo m [äl-kēler', ärryen'dō] 93

rent *(verb)* alquilar, rentar [älkēlär', rentär'] 93

repair *(verb)* arreglar [ärreglär'] 46

repair *(noun)* reparación f [repäräsyōn'] 55; **~ shop** taller m mecánico [tälyer' mekä'nēkō] 48

replace reponer [repōner'] 138

reply respuesta f [respōō·es'tä] 147

report *(to police)* denunciar [denōōnsyär'] 153

reservation reserva f [reser'vä] 71

reserve reservar [reservär'] 62; **~ fuel can** tarro m de reserva, bidón m de reserva [tä'rrō de reser'vä, bēdōn' de reser'vä] 55; **~ wheel** rueda f de repuesto [rōō·e'dä de repōō·es'tō] 47

respiration respiración f [respēräsyōn'] 168

rest room baños m/pl, servicios m/pl *(Sp)* [bä'nyōs, servē'syōs] 93

restaurant restaurante m [restourän'te] 60

result resultado m [resōōltä'dō] 188

retailer comerciante m [kōmersyän'te] 37

retiree pensionista m + f [pensyōnēs'tä] 37

retread recauchutar [rekoutshōōtär'] 46

return flight vuelo m de regreso [vōō·e'lō de regre'sō] 71

return postage porte m de vuelta [pōr'te de vōō·el'tä] 150

reverse *(gear)* marcha f atrás [mär'tshä äträs'] 53

rheumatism reumatismo m [re·ōōmätēz'mō] 171

rib costilla f [kōstē'lyä] 168

ribbon cinta f [sēn'tä] 136

rice arroz m [ärōs'] 105

ride *(on train)* viajar [vyähär'] 66

ride *(horse)* montar a caballo [mōntär' ä käbä'lyō] 189

rider jinete m [hēne'te] 189

riding equitación f [ekētäsyōn'] 189; **~ stable** cuadra f [kōō·ä'drä] 180

rifle range campo m de tiro [käm'pō de tē'rō] 188

right! ¡eso es! [e'sō es] 21

right derecha dere'tshä 40; **~ of way** preferencia f de paso [preferens'yä de pä'sō] 43; **~ away** en seguida [en segē'dä] 98

ring sortija f, anillo m [sōrtē'hä, änē'lyō] 133; **wedding ~** anillo m de boda [änē'lyō de bō'dä] 133

rinse *(hair)* dar reflejos *(al pelo)* [där refle'hōs äl pe'lō] 155

river río m [rē'ō] 70

road camino m [kämē'nō] 122; **~ sign** señal f de circulación [senyäl' de sērkōōläsyōn'] 43; **~ under construction** obras f, hombres trabajando *(Mex)* [ō'bräs, ōm'bres träbähän'dō] 43

roast beef rosbif m [rōsbēf'] 108

roasted horneado, asado *(Sp)* [ōrne·ä'dō, äsä'dō] 108

rod *(fishing)* caña f [kä'nyä] 188

role *(theater)* papel m [päpel'] 178; **leading ~** papel m principal [päpel' prēnsēpäl'] 178

roll *(bread)* panecillo m, bolillo m *(Mex)* [pänesē'lyō, bōlē'lyō] 100

roll rollo m [rō'lyō] 126

Romance languages filología f románica [fēlōlōhē'ä rōmä'nēkä] 39

Romanesque románico [rōmä'nēkō] 125

roof *(car)* capota f [käpō'tä] 55

rook peón m [pe·ōn'] 181

room cuarto m [kōō·är'tō] 93; **~ referral** oficina f de alojamiento [ōfēsē'nä de älōhämyen'tō] 60; **double ~** habitación f, cuarto m *(Mex)* doble [äbētäsyōn', kōō·är'tō dō'ble] 82; **single ~** habitación f, cuarto m *(Mex)* individual, sencillo *(Mex)* [äbētäsyōn', kōo·är'tō ēndēvēdōo·äl', sensē'lyō] 82; **quiet** ~ habitación f, cuarto m *(Mex)* tranquilo [äbētäsyōn', kōo·är'-tō trängkē'lō (-ä)] 82

root *(tooth)* raíz f del diente [rä·ēs' del dyen'te] 174; ~ **canal work** tratamiento m de la raíz [trätämyen'tō de lä rä·ēs'] 174

rope cuerda f, cabo m [kōo·er'dä, kä'bō] 77

rosemary romero m [rōme'rō] 103

roses rosas f/pl [rō'säs] 130

rough seas marejada f [märehä'dä] 77

round redondo [redōn'dō] 156

round-trip ticket boleto m, billete m *(Sp)* de ida y vuelta [bōle'tō, bēlye'te de ē'dä ē vōo·el'tä] 69

route ruta f [rōo'tä] 43

route *(plane)* trayecto m [träyek'tō] 71

row fila f [fē'lä] 176

rowing remo m [re'mō] 189

rubber boots botas f/pl de goma [bō'täs de gō'mä] 139

ruby rubí m [rōobē'] 133

rucksack mochila f [mōtshē'lä] 144

rudder timón m [tēmōn'] 77

ruin ruina f [rōo·ē'nä] 122

S

sacristan sacristán m [säkrēstän'] 125

sacristy sacristía f [säkrēstē'ä] 125

safety pin imperdible m, seguro m *(Mex)* [ēmperdē'ble, segōo'rō] 136

sail *(noun)* vela f [ve'lä] 189

sail *(verb)* navegar a la vela [nävegär' ä lä ve'lä] 189

sailboat barco m de vela [bär'kō de ve'lä] 189

sailing deporte m de vela [depōr'te de ve'lä] 189; ~ **school** escuela f de vela [eskōo·e'lä de ve'lä] 180

sailor marinero m [märēne'rō] 77

salad ensalada f [ensälä'dä] 104

salesperson dependiente m [dependyen'te] 37

saline content salinidad f [sälēnēdäd'] 186

salmon salmón m [sälmōn'] 107

salt sal f [säl] 103; ~ **shaker** salero m [säle'rō] 99

salted salado [sälä'dō] 102

salty salado [sälä'dō] 115

salve pomada f [pōmä'dä] 161

sanatorium sanatorio m [sänätōr'yō] 175

sandals sandalias f/pl [sändä'lyäs] 139; **beach** ~ sandalias f/pl para la playa [sändä'lyäs pä'rä lä plä'yä] 139

sandpaper papel m de lija [päpel' de lē'hä] 57

sanitary napkins compresas f/pl [kōmpre'säs] 161

sapphire zafiro m [säfē'rō] 133

sardines sardinas f/pl [särdē'näs] 104

Saturday sábado m [sä'bädō] 33

sauce salsa f [säl'sä] 103

saucer platillo m [plätē'lyō] 99

sauna sauna f [sou'nä] 175

sausage salchicha f [sältshē'tshä] 100

savings book caja f de ahorros [kä'hä de ä·ō'rrōs] 152

scarf bufanda f [bōofän'dä] 135

scarlet fever escarlatina f [eskärlätē'nä] 171

scenery/settings decoración f [dekōräsyōn'] 178

scheduled flight avión m de línea [ävyōn' de lē'ne·ä] 71

scholar erudito m [erōodē'tō] 37

school escuela f [eskōo·e'lä] 38

sciatica ciática f [syä'tēkä] 171

scientist científico m [syentē'fēkō] 37

scissors tijeras f/pl [tēhe'räs] 136

Scotch tape cinta f adhesiva, cinta f celo *(Sp)* [sēn'tä ädesē'vä, sēn'tä se'lō] 144

screen pantalla f [päntä'lyä] 179

screenplay guíon *m* [gē'ōn] 179

screw tornillo *m* [törnē'lyō] 57

screwdriver destornillador *m*, desarmador *m (Mex)* [destörnēlyädör', desärmädör'] 57

scuba diving bucear [bōōse·är'] 186

scuba equipment escafandra *f*, equipo *m* de bucear [eskäfän'drä, ekē'pō de bōōse·är'] 186

scull barca *f* de remos [bär'kä de re'mōs] 189

sculptor escultor *m* [eskōōltör'] 37

sea mar *m* [mär] 77

seasickness mareo *m* [märe'ō] 171

season temporada *f* [tempōrä'dä] 93

seasoned condimentado [köndēmentä'dō] 102

seasoning *(spice)* especias *f/pl* [espe'syäs] 103

seat asiento *m* [äsyen'tō] 62; **~ belt** cinturón *m* de seguridad [sēntōōrōn' de segōōrēdäd'] 55; **~ reservation** reserva *f* de asiento [reser'vä de asyen'tō] 62

second segundo *m* [segōōn'dō] 32

second class segunda clase *f* [segōōn'dä klä'se] 62

secretary secretaria *f* [sekretär'yä] 37

security fianza *f* [fyän'sä] 152

see ver [ver] 18; **~ you soon** hasta luego [äs'tä lōō·e'gō] 17; **~ you tomorrow** hasta mañana [äs'tä mänyä'nä] 17

self-service autoservicio *m* [outōservē'syō] 129

send mandar [mändär'] 147

send *(luggage)* facturar [fäktōōrär'] 63

sender remitente *m* [remēten'te] 150

separate separado [sepärä'dō] 115

September se(p)tiembre *m* [se(p)tyem'bre] 33

serious grave [grä've] 164

sermon sermón *m*, plática *f* [sermōn', plä'tēkä] 125

service *(church)* oficio *m* [ōfē'syō] 123

service servicio *m* [servē'syō] 83; **~ station** gasolinera *f* [gäsōlēne'rä] 48

serving dish fuente *f* [fōō·en'te] 99

set *(hair)* enrular, marcar *(Sp)* [enrōōlär', märkär'] 158

set designer escenógrafo *m* [esenō'gräfō] 178

setting lotion fijador *m* [fēhädōr'] 156

seven siete [sye'te] 28

sew coser [kōser'] 137

shampoo champú *m* [tshämpōō'] 141

shape forma *f* [fōr'mä] 127

share of stock acción *f* [äksyōn'] 152

sharp *(pain)* agudo [ägōō'dō] 163; **eleven ~** las once en punto [läs ōn'se em pōōn'tō] 30

shave afeitar [äfe·ētär'] 158

shaving brush brocha *f* de afeitar [brō'tshä de äfe·ētär'] 141

shaving cream crema *f* de afeitar [kre'mä de äfe·ētär'] 142

shaving foam espuma *f* de afeitar [espōō'mä de äfe·ētär'] 142

shaving soap jabón *m* de afeitar [häbōn' de äfe·ētär'] 142

sheets sábanas *f/pl* [sä'bänäs] 90

shellfish mariscos *m/pl* [märēs'kōs] 107

shells conchas *f/pl* [kōn'tshäs] 186

sherry jerez *m* [heres'] 113

shin espinilla *f* [espēnē'lyä] 168

ship barco *m*, buque *m* [bär'kō, bōō'-ke] 77; **passenger ~** barco *m* de pasajeros [bär'kō de päsähe'rōs] 77

shipboard party fiesta *f* de a bordo [fyes'tä de ä bōr'dō] 77

shipping agency agencia *f* marítima [ähen'syä märē'tēmä] 77

shipping company compañía *f* naviera [kömpänyē'ä nävye'rä] 77

ship's doctor médico *m* de a bordo [me'dēkō de ä bōr'dō] 77

shirt camisa *f* [kämē'sä] 135

shock shock *m* nervioso [shŏk nervyŏ'-sō] 171; ~ **absorber** amortiguador *m* [ämŏrtēgōō·ädŏr'] 55

shoe zapato *m* [säpä'tō] 139; ~ **horn** calzador *m* [kälsädŏ'r] 139; ~ **laces** cordones *m/pl* [kŏrdō'nes] 139

shoemaker zapatero *m* [säpäte'rō] 37

shoot tirar [tērär'] 189

shop tienda *f* [tyen'dä] 122; **antique ~** tienda *f* de antigüedades [tyen'dä de äntēgōō·edä'des] 128; **barber ~** peluquería *f* [pelōōkerē'ä] 128; **butcher ~** carnicería *f* [kärnēserē'ä] 128; **china ~** artículos *m/pl* de porcelana [ärtē'kōōlōs de pŏrselä'nä] 128; **dressmaker's ~** modista *f* [mōdēs'tä] 128; **electrical appliance ~** (tienda *f* de) electrodomésticos [(tyen'dä de) elektrōdōmes'tēkōs] 128; **flower ~** florería *f*, floristería *f*, (Sp) [flŏrerē'ä, flŏrēsterē'ä] 128; **hat ~** sombrería *f* [sŏmbrerē'ä] 128; **lingerie ~** lencería *f*, corsetería *f* [lenserē'ä, kŏrseterē'ä] 129; **photo ~** tienda *f* de artículos fotográficos [tyen'dä de ärtē'kōōlōs fōtōgrä'fēkō's 129; **shoe ~** zapatería *f* [säpäterē'ä] 129; **souvenir ~** recuerdos *m/pl* [rekōō·er'dōs] 129; **tailor ~** sastre *m* [säs'tre] 129; **textile ~** tienda *f* de tejidos [tyen'dä de tehē'dōs] 129; **watchmaker's ~** relojería *f* [relōherē'ä] 129; **wine ~** bodega *f* [bōde'gä] 129

shopping *(go)* ir de compras [ēr de kŏm'präs] 118; ~ **mall** centro *m* comercial [sen'trō kōmersyäl'] 122

shore *(on)* en tierra [en tye'rrä] 77

short corto [kŏr'tō] 133; ~ **circuit** cortocircuito [kŏrtōserkōō·ē'tō] 55; ~ **-sleeved** de manga corta [de män'gä kŏr'tä] 135; ~ **subject** cortometraje *m* [kŏrtōmeträ'he] 179; ~ **wave** onda *f* corta [ōn'dä kŏr'tä] 175

shorten acortar [äkŏrtär'] 137

shorts pantalón *m* corto [päntälōn' kŏr'tō] 135

shoulder hombro *m* [ōm'brō] 168

shower ducha *f*, regadera *f (Mex)* [dōō'tshä, regäde'rä] 82

shower *(weather)* chubasco *m*, aguacero *m* [tshōōbäs'kō, ägōō·äse'rō] 27

shrimp gambas *f/pl*, camarones *m/pl (Mex)* [gäm'bäs, kämärō'nes] 104

shuffle barajar [bärähär'] 181

shutter obturador *m* [ōbtōōrädŏr'] 132; ~ **release** disparador *m* [dēspärädŏr'] 132; **automatic ~** disparador *m* automático [dēspärädŏr' outōmä'tēkō] 132

sick enfermo [enfer'mō] 162; **I feel ~** me siento mal [me syen'tō mäl] 70; ~ **bay** hospital *m* [ōspētäl'] 74

side *(on the)* lateral(es) [läteräl'(es)] 176; ~ **road** calle *f* lateral [kä'lye läteräl'] 122; ~ **wind** viento *m* de costado [vyen'tō de kŏstä'dō] 43

sideburns patillas *f/pl* [pätē'lyäs] 158

sidewalk acera *f*, banqueta *f (Mex)* [äse'rä, bängke'tä] 122

sightseeing turismo *m* [tōōrēz'mō] 122

sign up inscribir [ēnskrēbēr'] 85

signature firma *f* [fēr'mä] 84

silk seda *f* [se'dä] 137; **artificial ~** seda *f* artificial [se'dä ärtēfēsyäl'] 137; ~ **thread** hilo *m* de seda [ē'lō de se'dä] 136

silver *(adj.)* plateado [pläte·ä'dō] 194

silver *(noun)* plata *f* [plä'tä] 133; ~ **plated** plateado [pläte·ä'dō] 133

silverware vajilla *f* de plata [vähē'lyä de plä'tä] 99

since desde [des'de] 32

sinew tendón *m* [tendōn'] 168

singer cantante *m* [käntän'te] 178

singing canto *m* [kän'tō] 178

single soltero [sōlte'rō (-ä)] 79

singles *(tennis)* individual [ēndēve·

dōō·äl'] 190

sink lavabo *m*, lavatorio *m* [lävä'bō, lävätōr'yō] 93

sir señor *m* [senyōr'] 13

sister hermana *f* [ermä'nä] 35; ~ **-in-law** cuñada *f* [kōōnyä'dä] 35

six seis [se'ēs] 28

size talla *f* [tä'lyä] 133

skate patinar [pätēnär'] 188

skater patinador *m* [pätēnädōr'] 188

skates patines *m/pl* [pätēn'es] 188

ski *(verb)* esquiar [eskē·är'] 189

ski *(noun)* esquí *m* [eskē'] 189; ~ **binding** fijación *f* [fēhäsyōn'] 189; ~ **jump** trampolín *m* de saltos [trämpō-lēn' de säl'tōs] 189; ~ **lift** telesquí *m* [teleskē'] 189

skiing esquí *m* [eskē'] 189

skin piel *f*, cutis *m* [pyel, kōō'tēs] 168; ~ **disease** enfermedad *f* de la piel [enfermedäd' de lä pyel] 171; ~ **lesion** lesión *f* de la piel [lesyōn' de lä pyel] 171

skirt falda *f* [fäl'dä] 135

skull cráneo *m* [krä'ne·ō] 168

sky cielo *m* [sye'lō] 26

slack flojo [flō'hō] 51

slacks pantalones *m/pl* [päntälō'nes] 135

Slavic languages eslavística *f* [es-läväs'tēkä] 39

sled trineo *m* [trēne'ō] 144

sleep dormir [dōrmēr'] 164

sleeper/sleeping car coche-cama *m*, camarín *m*, alcoba *f (Mex)* [kō'tshe-kä'mä, kämärēn', älkō'bä] 60; ~ **reservation** boleto *m*, billete *m (Sp)* de coche-cama, de alcoba, de camarín *(Mex)* [bōle'tō, bēlye'te de kō'tshe-kä'mä, de älkō'bä, de kämärēn'] 62

sleeping bag saco *m*, bolsa *f (Mex)* de dormir [sä'kō, bōl'sä de dōrmēr'] 96

sleeping pills somníferos *m/pl* [sōm-nē'ferōs] 161

slide transparencia *f*, diapositiva *f (Sp)* [tränspären'syä, dyäpōsētē'vä] 132; ~ **frame** marquito *m* [märke'tō] 132

sliding sun roof techo *m* corredizo [te'tshō korredē'sō] 55

slippers zapatillas *f/pl*, pantuflas *f/pl* [säpätē'lyäs, päntōōf'läs] 139

slippery resbaladizo, resbaloso [resbä-lädē'sō, resbälō'sō] 25; ~ **road** piso *m* resbaloso, resbaladizo [pē'sō res-bälō'sō, resbälädē'sō] 43

slow despacio [despä'syō] 42

slow *(clock)* retrasado [reträsä'dō] 31

small pequeño [peke'nyō] 127

smallpox viruela *f* [vērōō·e'lä] 171

smoked ahumado [ä·ōōmä'dō] 102

smoking *(sign)* fumadores [fōōmädō'-res] 66; **no** ~ *(sign)* no fumadores [nō fōōmädō'res] 66

smuggling contrabando *m* [kōnträ-bän'dō] 154

snails cangrejos *m/pl* [kängre'hōs] 104

snow *(verb)* nevar [nevär'] 25

snow *(noun)* nieve *f* [nye've] 27; ~ **chains** cadenas *f/pl* antideslizantes [käde'näs äntēdezlēsän'tes] 52; ~ **flurries** copos *m/pl* de nieve [kō'pōs de nye've] 27

soap jabón *m* [häbōn'] 87; **cake of** ~ pastilla *f* de jabón [pästē'lya de hä-bōn'] 87

soccer fútbol *m* [fōōt'bōl] 189; ~ **game** partido *m* de fútbol [pärtē'dō de fōōt'bōl] 187; **play** ~ jugar al fútbol [hōōgär' äl fōōt'bōl] 189

sociology sociología *f* [sōsyōlōhē'ä] 39

socket enchufe *m*, soquet *m (Mex)* [entshōō'fe, sōket'] 88; ~ **wrench** llave *f* de dado [lyä've de dä'dō] 57

socks medias *f/pl*, calcetines *m/pl (Sp)* [me'dyäs, kälsetē'nes] 135

soda *(bicarbonate of)* bicarbonato *m* sódico [bēkärbōnä'tō sō'dēkō] 160

soft blando [blän'dō] 102; ~ **drink** refresco *m* [refres'kō] 114

solder soldar [sōldär'] 55

sole *(verb)* poner suela [pōner' sōo·e'lä] 139

sole *(noun)* suela *f* [sōo·e'lä] 139; **leather ~** suela *f* de cuero [sōo·e'lä de kōo·e'rō] 139; **rubber ~** suela *f* de goma [sōo·e'lä de gō'mä] 139

sole *(fish)* lenguado *m* [leng·gōo·ä'dō] 107

solid color de un solo color [de ōon sō'lō kōlōr'] 137

soloist solista *m* + *f* [sōlēs'tä] 178

somebody alguien [al'gyen] 41

sometimes a veces [ä ve'ses] 32

son hijo *m* [ē'hō] 35

song canción *f* [känsyōn'] 178; **folk ~** canción *f* popular [känsyōn' pōpōo·lär'] 178; **~ recital** recital *m* (de canto) [resētäl' (de kän'tō)] 178

soon pronto [prōn'tō] 32

soprano soprano *m* [sōprä'nō] 178

sore throat dolor *m* de garganta [dōlōr' de gärgän'tä] 171

sorry (I'm) lo siento [lō syen'tō] 22

soup sopa *f* [sō'pä] 105; **fish ~** sopa *f* de pescado [sō'pä de peskä'dō] 105; **garlic ~** sopa *f* de ajo [sō'pä de ä'hō] 105; **lentil ~** sopa *f* de lentejas [sō'pä de lente'häs] 105; **noodle ~** sopa *f* de fideos [sō'pä de fēde'ōs] 105; **to-mato ~** sopa *f* de tomate [sō'pä de tōmä'te] 105; **vegetable ~** sopa *f* de verduras [sō'pä de verdōo'räs] 105

sour agrio [ä'grē·ō] 115

souvenir recuerdo *m* [rekōo·er'dō] 80

spa balneario *m* [bälne·är'yō] 175

space sitio *m* [sē'tyō] 44

spades *(cards)* picos *m/pl* [pē'kōs] 181

spare parts piezas *f/pl* de repuesto [pye'säs de repōo·es'tō] 50

spare wheel rueda *f* de recambio, de repuesto [rōo·e'dä de rekäm'byō, de repōo·e'stō] 50

spark chispa *f* [tshēs'pä] 55; **~ plug** bujía *f* [bōohē'ä] 55

speak hablar [äblär'] 15

speaking! *(on telephone)* ¡soy yo! [soi yō] 148

special especial [espesyäl'] 46; **~ delivery** exprés, urgente, entrega *f* inmediata [ekspres', ōōrhen'te, entre'gä ēnmedyä'tä] 150; **~ delivery letter** carta *f* exprés, carta *f* de entrega inmediata, urgente *(Sp)* [kär'tä ekspres', kär'tä de entre'gä ēnmedyä'tä, ōōrhen'te] 150; **~ issue stamp** estampilla *f*, sello *m (Sp)*, timbre *m (Mex)* conmemorativo [estämpē'lyä, se'lyō, tēm'bre kōnmemōrätē'vō] 150

specialist especialista *m* [espesyälēs'tä] 163; **ear, nose and throat ~** otorrinolaringólogo *m* + *f* [ōtōrrēnōlärēngō'lōgō] 162

speed velocidad *f* [velōsēdäd'] 43; **~ limit** límite *m* de velocidad [lē'mēte de velōsēdäd'] 43

speedometer taquímetro *m* [täkē'metrō] 55

spell deletrear [deletre·är'] 24

spinach espinacas *f/pl* [espēnä'käs] 110

spinal cord médula *f* espinal [me'dōolä espēnäl'] 168

spine espina *f* dorsal [espē'nä dōrsäl'] 168

spleen bazo *m* [bä'sō] 168

sponge esponja *f* [espōn'hä] 142

spoon cuchara *f* [kōotshä'ra] 99; **soup ~** cuchara *f* sopera [kōotshä'ra sōpe'rä] 99; **tea ~** cucharita *f* [kōotshärē'tä] 99

sport shirt camisa *f* deportiva [kämē'sä depōrtē'vä] 135

sports deportes *m/pl* [depōr'tes] 187; **~ event** pruebas *f/pl* deportivas [prōo·e'bäs depōrtē'väs] 186; **~ fan**

aficionado *m* [äfēsyōnä'dō] 190

sportswear trajes *m/pl* de deportes [trä'hes de depōr'tes] 135

spot remover quitamanchas *m* [kētämän'tshäs] 144

sprain *(noun)* torcedura *f*, falseo *m* [tōrsedōō'rä, fälse'ō] 171

spring ballesta *f* [bälyes'tä] 55

spring *(season)* primavera *f* [prēmäve'-rä] 33

square *(adj.)* cuadrado [kōō·ädrä'dō] 193

square *(noun)* plaza *f* [plä'sä] 122

square *(chess)* casilla *f* [käsē'lyä] 181

stadium estadio *m* [estä'dyō] 122

stage escena *f*, escenario *m* [ese'nä, esenär'yō] 178; ~ **director** director *m* de escena [dērektōr' de ese'nä] 178

stain mancha *f* [män'tshä] 137

staircase escalera *f* [eskäle'rä] 93

stairwell hueco *m* de escalera [ōō·e'kō de eskäle'rä] 93

stake puesta *f* [pōō·es'tä] 182

stamp *(verb)* franquear [fränke·är'] 150

stamp *(noun)* estampilla *f*, sello *m* (Sp), timbre *m* (Mex) [estämpē'lyä, se'lyō, tēm'bre] 150; ~ **machine** distribuidor *m* automático de estampillas, sellos (Sp), timbres (Mex) [dēstrēbōō·ēdōr' outōmä'tēkō de estämpē'-lyäs, se'lyōs, tēm'bres] 150

standard *(oil)* normal [nōrmäl'] 46

star estrella *f* [estre'lyä] 27

starboard estribor *m* [estrēbōr'] 77

start *(of race)* salida *f* [sälē'dä] 188

starter arranque *m*, marcha *f* (Mex) [ärrän'ke, mär'tshä] 55

station *(train)* estación *f* [estäsyōn'] 67

station *(TV etc.)* emisora *f* [emēsō'rä] 180; ~ **master** jefe *m* de estación [he'fe de estäsyōn'] 67; ~ **wagon** camioneta *f*, combi *m* (Mex) [kämyōne'-tä, kōm'bē] 40

Stations of the Cross estaciones *f/pl* de la vía Crucis [estäsyō'nes de lä vē'ä krōō'sēs] 125

statue estatua *f* [estä'tōō·ä] 119

steak bistec *m* [bēstek'] 108

steamed cocido al vapor [kōsē'dō äl väpōr'] 102

steamer vapor *m* [väpōr'] 77

steep downgrade bajada *f* (peligrosa) [bähä'dä (pelēgrō'sä)] 43

steep upgrade cuesta *f*, subida *f* [kōō·es'tä, sōōbē'dä] 43

steering dirección *f* [dēreksyōn'] 56; ~ **wheel** volante *m* [vōlän'te] 56

stern popa *f* [pō'pä] 77

stew potaje *m* [potä'he] 105

steward camarero *m* [kämäre'rō] 74; **chief** ~ jefe *m* de camareros [he'fe de kämäre'rōs] 74

stewed estofado, guisado [estōfä'dō, gēsä'dō] 102

still aún [ä·ōōn'] 31

stitch in the side puntadas *f/pl* en el costado [pōōntä'däs en el kōstä'dō] 171

stock acciones *f/pl* [äksyō'nes] 152

stockings medias *f/pl* [me'dyäs] 135

stole estola *f* [estō'lä] 135

stomach estómago *m* [estō'mägō] 168; ~ **pain** dolores *m/pl* de estómago [dōlō'res de estō'mägō] 171

stop parada *f* [pärä'dä] 59

stop *(verb)* parar [pärär'] 43

stopover escala *f* [eskä'lä] 71

stopped up tapado, atascado [täpä'dō, ätäskä'dō] 88

stopping (no) prohibido detenerse [prō·ēbē'dō detener'se] 42

store tienda *f* [tyen'dä] 128; **candy** ~ confitería *f* [kōnfēterē'ä] 128; **department** ~ grandes almacenes *m/pl* [grän'des älmäse'nes] 128; **drug** ~ *(sundries)* droguería *f* [drōgerē'ä] 128; **drug** ~ *(pharmacy)* farmacia *f* [färmä'syä] 128; **furniture** ~ tienda *f* de muebles [tyen'dä de mōō·e'bles] 128; **grocery** ~ tienda f de alimentación, de abarrotes *(Mex)* [tyen'dä de älēmentäsyōn', de äbärrō'tes] 128; **hardware** ~ ferretería f [ferreterē'ä] 128, **jewelry** ~ joyería f [hōyerē'ä] 128; **leather goods** ~ artículos m/pl de piel, marroquinería f [ärtē'kōōlōs de pyel, marrōkēnerē'ä] 129; **liquor** ~ tienda f de bebidas alcohólicas, licorerías *(Mex)* [tyen'dä de bebē'däs älkō·ō'lēkäs, lēkōrerē'äs] 129; **music** ~ tienda f de música [tyen'dä de mōō'sēkä] 129; **record** ~ tienda f de discos, discoteca f *(Mex)* [tyen'dä de dēs'kōs, dēskōte'kä] 129; **shoe** ~ zapatería f [säpäterē'ä] 129; **sporting goods** ~ tienda f de artículos de deporte [tyen'dä de ärtē'kōōlōs de depōr'te] 129; **stationery** ~ papelería f [päpelerē'ä] 129; **toy** ~ juguetería f [hōōgeterē'ä] 129

storekeeper tendero m [tende'rō] 37

storm tormenta f [tōrmen'tä] 27

stove estufa f, cocina f *(Sp)* [estōō'fä, kōsē'nä] 93

straight ahead todo derecho [tō'dō dere'tshō] 40

strait estrecho m [estre'tshō] 77

strawberry fresa f [fre'sä] 111

street calle f [kä'lye] 192

strict riguroso [rēgōōrō'sō] 165

string cordel m, cuerda f [kōrdel', kōō·er'dä] 57

stroke apoplejía f [äpōplehē'ä] 171

student estudiante m + f [estōōdyän'te] 37

stuffed relleno m [relye'nō] 102; ~ **animal** animal m de trapo [änēmäl' de trä'pō] 144

subject asignatura f [äsēgnätōō'rä] 39

subtitled subtitulado [sōōbtētōōlä'dō] 179

suburbs afueras f/pl [äfōō·e'räs] 122

suburban train tren m de cercanías, tren m local *(Mex)* [tren de serkänē'äs, tren lōkäl'] 60

subway métro m [me'trō] 122

success éxito m [e'ksētō] 23

suède ante m [än'te] 139; ~ **coat** abrigo m de ante [äbrē'gō de än'te] 135; ~ **jacket** chaqueta f de ante [tshäke'tä de än'te] 135

sugar azúcar m [äsōō'kär] 100; ~ **bowl** azucarera f, azucarero m *(Sp)* [äsōōkäre'rä, äsōōkäre'rō] 99

suit traje m de chaqueta, traje m sastre [trä'he de tshäke'tä, trä'he säs'tre] 135

suit *(man's)* traje m [trä'he] 135

suitcase maleta f [mäle'tä] 63

summer verano m [verä'nō] 33; ~ **dress** vestido m de verano [vestē'dō de verä'nō] 135

sun sol m [sōl] 27; ~ **tan cream** crema f solar, bronceadora f [kre'mä sōlär', brōnse·ädō'rä] 142; ~ **tan lotion** loción f solar, loción f para broncearse [lōsyōn' sōlär', lōsyōn' pä'rä brōnse·ō'hōs] 142; ~ **tan oil** aceite m solar, bronceador m *(Mex)* [äse'ētē sōlär', brōnse·ädōr'] 142

sun roof techo m corredizo [te'tshō kōrredē'sō] 55

sunbath: take a ~ tomar el sol [tōmär' el sōl] 186

sunburn quemadura f del sol [kemädōō'rä del sōl] 171

Sunday domingo m [dōmēn'gō] 33

sunglasses lentes f/pl, anteojos m/pl, gafas f/pl *(Sp)* de sol [len'tes, änte·ō'hōs, gä'fäs de sōl] 138

sunlamp lámpara f solar ultravioleta [lämp'ärä sōlär' ōōlträvyōle'tä] 175

sunrise salida f del sol [sälē'dä del sōl] 27

sunset puesta f del sol [pōō·es'tä del sōl] 27

sunstroke insolación f [ēnsōläsyōn'] 171

supermarket supermercado m [sōō-permerkä'dō] 129

supplement suplemento m [sōōplemen'tō] 66

suppository supositorio m, calillo m (Mex) [sōōpōsētōr'yō, kälē'lyō] 161

suppuration supuración f [sōōpōōräsyōn'] 171

surcharge suplemento m [sōōplemen'tō] 83; seasonal ~ suplemento m por temporada [sōōplemen'tō pōr tempōrä'dä] 83

surgeon cirujano m [sērōōhä'nō] 163

surroundings alrededores m/pl [älrededō'res] 122

suspenders tirantes m/pl [tērän'tes] 135

sweater jersey m, suéter m [her'sē, sōō·e'ter] 135

swelling hinchazón f [ēntshäsōn'] 171

swim nadar, bañarse [nädär', bänyär'se] 186

swimmer nadador m [nädädōr'] 186

swimming (go ~) ir a nadar, ir a bañarse [ēr ä nädär', ēr ä bänyär'se] 96

swimming (noun) natación f [nätäsyōn'] 190; no ~ ¡prohibido bañarse! [prō·ebē'dō bänyär'se] 185; ~ pool piscina f [pēsē'nä] 74

swimsuit traje m de baño [trä'he de bä'nyō] 135

switch interruptor m [ēnterrōōptōr'] 56

swollen hinchado [ēntshä'dō] 164

symphony concert concierto m sinfónico [kōnsyer'tō sēnfō'nēkō] 178

synagogue sinagoga f [sēnägō'gä] 122

synthetic thread hilo m sintético [ē'lō sēnte'tēkō] 136

system time table (trains) guía f de ferrocarriles [gē'ä de ferrōkärrē'les] 67

system time table (planes) horario m de vuelos [ōrär'yō de vōō·e'lōs] 71

T

table mesa f [me'sä] 93; ~ tennis ping pong m [pēn pōn'] 182

tablecloth mantel m [mäntel'] 93

tablet comprimido m [kōmprēmē'dō] 161

tailor sastre m [säs'tre] 37

take off despegue m, descolaje m [despe'ge, deskōlä'he] 71

talcum powder talco m [täl'kō] 161

tampon tampón m [tämpōn'] 142

tangerine mandarina f [mändärē'nä] 111

tape cinta f [sēn'tä] 136; ~ measure cinta f métrica [sēn'tä me'trēkä] 136; ~ recorder magnetófono m [mägnetō'fōnō] 182

target blanco [bläng'kō] 189

tartar sarro m dental, tártaro m [sä'rrō dentäl', tär'tärō] 174

taxi taxi m [tä'ksē] 89; ~ stand parada f, sitio m (Mex) de taxis [pärä'dä, sē'tyō de tä'ksēs] 116

tea té m [te] 100; camomile ~ té m de manzanilla [te de mänsänē'lyä] 100; mint ~ té m de menta, de hierba buena (Mex) [te de men'tä, de yer'bä bōō·e'nä] 100

teacher profesor m, maestro m [prōfesōr', mä·es'trō] 37

tease (hair) enredar, cardar (Sp) [enredär', kärdär'] 156

technical técnico [tek'nēkō] 39; ~ college escuela f superior técnica [eskōō·e'lä sōōperyōr tek'nēkä] 39

technician técnico m [tek'nēkō] 38

telegram telegrama m [telegrä'mä] 147; ~ form impreso m de telegrama [ēmpre'sō de telegrä'mä] 147

telegraphic telegráfico [telegrä'fēkō] 152

telephone teléfono m [tele'fōnō] 150

television televisión f [televēsyōn']

182; ~ **play** telefilm *m* [telefēlm] 182

tell decir [desēr'] 20

teller's window caja *f* [kä'hä] 152

temperature temperatura *f* [temperätōō'rä] 27; **what's the ~?** ¿a cuántos estamos? [ä kōō·än'tōs estä'mōs] 25; ~ **chart** curva *f* de temperatura [kōōr'vä de temperätōō'rä] 173

temple *(of head)* sien *f* [syen] 168

temple templo *m* [tem'plō] 122

temporarily por el momento [pōr el mōmen'tō] 32

temporary provisionalmente [prōvēsyōnälmen'te] 173

ten diez [dyes] 28

tender tierno [tyer'nō] 102

tendon tendón *m* [tendōn'] 168; **pulled ~** distorsión *f* de un tendón [dēstōrsyōn' de ōōn tendōn'] 171

tennis tenis *m* [te'nēs] 190; **play ~** jugar al tenis [hōōgär' äl te'nēs] 190; ~ **ball** pelota *f* de tenis [pelō'tä de te'nēs] 190; ~ **court** pista *f*, cancha *f* de tenis [pēs'tä, kän'tshä de te'nēs] 190

tenor tenor *m* [tenōr'] 178

tent carpa *f*, tienda *f (Sp)*, casita *f (Mex)* de campaña [kär'pä, tyen'dä, käsē'tä de kämpä'nyä] 97

terrace terraza *f* [terrä'sä] 93

terrific ¡estupendo! [estōōpen'dō] 21

tetanus tétano *m* [te'tänō] 172

thank you gracias [grä'syäs] 21

thanks a lot ¡muchas gracias! [mōō'tshäs grä'syäs] 21

thaw deshielo *m* [desye'lō] 27

theatre teatro *m* [te·ä'trō] 178; ~ **schedule** programa *m* [prōgrä'mä] 178

theft robo *f* [rō'bō] 153

there allá [älyä'] 40

thermometer termómetro *m* [termō'metrō] 144

thermos bottle termo *m* [ter'mō] 144

thermostat termostato *m*, toma *f* de agua *(Mex)* [termōstä'tō, tō'mä de ä'gōō·ä] 56

thief ladrón *m* [lädrōn'] 154

thigh muslo *m* [mōōs'lō] 167

thimble dedal *m* [dedäl'] 136

third tercero [terse'rō] 29

thorax tórax *m* [tō'räks] 168

thread hilo *m* ē'lō 136; **screw ~** rosca *f* [rōs'kä] 56

three tres [tres] 28

thriller novela *f* de suspense, de misterio [nōve'lä de sōōspen'se, de mēster'yō] 130

throat garganta *f* [gärgän'tä] 168

throw-in saque *m* de línea [sä'ke de lē'ne·ä] 190

thumb pulgar *m* [pōōlgär'] 167

thunder trueno *m* [trōō·e'nō] 27

thunderstorm tempestad *f* [tempestä'] 27

Thursday jueves *m* [hōō·e'ves] 33

ticket boleto *m*, billete *m (Sp)* [bōle'tō, bēlye'te] 59

ticket *(plane)* billete *m*, pasaje *m* [bēlye'te, päsä'he] 71; **one-way ~** boleto *m*, billete *m*, pasaje *m* de ida solo [bōle'tō, bēlye'te, päsä'he de e'dä sō'lō] 117; ~ **sales** despacho *m* de localidades [despä'tshō de lōkälēdä'des] 178; **transfer ~** boleto *m*, billete *m*, pasaje *m* de correspondencia [bōle'tō, bēlye'te, päsä'he de kōrrespōnden'syä] 117; ~ **window** despacho *m* de billetes, taquilla *f* [despä'tshō de bēlye'tes, täkē'lyä] 60

tie corbata *f* [kōrbä'tä] 133

tight *(brakes)* tenso [ten'sō] 51

tight *(shoes)* estrecho [estre'tshō] 139

tighten apretar [äpretär'] 55

time hora *f* [ō'rä] 30; **at what ~?** a qué hora [ä ke ō'rä] 15; **what ~ is it?** ¿qué hora es? [ke ō'rä es] 30; **have a**

good ~ diviértase, diviertete *(fam)* [dēvyer'täse, dēvyer'tete] 20; **from ~ to ~** de vez en cuando [de ves en kōō·än'dō] 32; **any ~** de un momento a otro [de ōōn mōmen'tō ä ō'trō] 32; **in ~** a la hora, a tiempo [ä lä ō'rä, ä tyem'pō] 32; **~ table** horario *m* [ōrär'yō] 60

tincture of iodine tintura *f* de yodo [tēntōō'rä de yō'dō] 161

tint dar color, dar reflejos [där kōlōr', där refle'*h*ōs] 158

tire neumático *m*, llanta *f (Mex)* [ne·ōōmä'tēkō, lyän'tä] 47; **~ change** cambio *m* de neumático, de llanta *(Mex)* [käm'byō de ne·ōōmä'tēkō, de lyän'tä] 47; **~ pressure** presión *f* de los neumáticos, de las llantas *(Mex)* [presyōn' de lōs ne·ōōmä'tēkōs, de läs lyän'täs] 47

tires neumáticos *m/pl*, llantas *f/pl (Mex)* [ne·ōōmä'tēkōs, lyän'täs] 47

tissues pañuelos *m/pl* de papel [pänyōō·e'lōs de päpel'] 142

toast pan *m* tostado [pän töstä'dō] 100

tobacco tabaco *m* [täbä'kō] 140

tobaggan trineo *m* [trēne'ō] 190

tobagganing ir en trineo [ēr en trēne'ō] 190

today hoy [oi] 68

toe dedo *m* del pie [de'dō del pye] 168

together junto [*h*ōōn'tō] 115

toilet wáter *m*, lavabo *m*, excusado *m (Mex)* [ōō·ä'ter, lävä'bō, ekskōōsä'dō] 82; **~ articles** artículos *m/pl* de tocador [ärtē'kōōlōs de tōkädōr'] 142; **~ kit** neceser *m* [neseser'] 142; **~ paper** papel *m* higiénico, papel *m* sanitario [päpel' ē*h*ē·e'nēkō, päpel' sänētär'yō] 142

tomato tomate *m (Sp)* jitomate *m (Mex)* [tōmä'te, *h*ētōmä'te] 110

tomb sepulcro *m* [sepōōl'krō] 123

tomorrow mañana [mänyä'nä] 31; **the**

day after ~ pasado mañana [päsä'dō mänyä'nä] 31

ton tonelada *f* [tōnelä'dä] 193

tongue lengua *f* [len'gōō·ä] 168

tonic tónico *m* [tō'nēkō] 161; **~ water** tónica *f* [tō'nēkä] 114

tonight esta noche [es'tä nō'tshe] 31

tonsilitis anginas *f/pl* [än*h*ē'näs] 172

tonsils amígdalas *f/pl* [ämēg'däläs] 168

too también [tämbyen'] 47

too *(degree)* demasiado [demäsyä'dō] 31

tool box *(kit)* caja *f* de herramientas *f/pl* [kä'*h*ä de errämyen'täs] 57

tools herramientas *f/pl* [errämyen'täs] 57

tooth diente *m* [dyen'te] 168; **~ brush** cepillo *m* de dientes [sepē'lyō de dyen'tes] 142; **~ paste** pasta *f* de dientes [päs'tä de dyen'tes] 142; **wisdom ~** muela *f* del juicio [mōō·e'lä del *h*ōō·ē'syō] 174

toothache dolor *m* de muelas [dōlōr' de mōō·e'läs] 174

toothpick palillo *m* [pälē'lyō] 99

top *(car)* capota *f* [käpō'tä] 56

tough duro [dōō'rō] 102

toupé postizo *m* [pōstē'sō] 158

tour visita *f* [vēsē'tä] 119; **guided ~** visita *f* guiada [vēsē'tä gē·ä'dä] 119; **~ guide** guía *m* [gē'ä] 94

tour guide's office dirección *f* del crucero [dēreksyōn' del krōōse'rō] 74

tow remolcar [remōlkär'] 48; **~ line** cable *m* de remolque [kä'ble de remōl'ke] 49; **~ truck** grúa *f*, coche *m* grúa *(Sp)* [grōō'ä, kō'tshe grōō'ä] 49

towel toalla *f* [tō·ä'lyä] 142; **bath ~** toalla *f* de baño [tō·ä'lyä de bä'nyō] 142

tower torre *f* [tō'rre] 123

towing service servicio *m* de remolque [servē'syō de remōl'ke] 49

town ciudad *f* [syōōdäd'] 123

toy juguete *m* [*h*ōōge'te] 144

track vía f [vē'ä] 67; ~ **and field** atletismo m en pista [ätletēz'mō en pēs'tä] 190; ~ **suit** chándal m, sudadera f [tshän'däl, sōōdäde'rä] 135

traffic tráfico m, circulación f [trä'fēkō, sērkōōläsyōn'] 123; ~ **light** semáforo m, disco m [semä'fōrō, dēs'kō] 123; ~ **regulations** reglamentos m/pl de la circulación [reglämen'tōs de lä sērkōōläsyōn'] 43

tragedy tragedia f [trähe'dyä] 178

trailer remolque m [remōl'ke] 41; **camping** ~ caravana f, trayler m (Mex) [kärävä'nä, trīler] 40

train tren m [tren] 60; **suburban** ~ tren m de cercanías, tren local (Mex) [tren de serkänē'äs, tren lōkäl'] 60

trainee aprendiz m [äprendēs'] 38

tranquilizer calmante m, sedante m [kälmän'te, sedän'te] 161

transfer (bus) correspondencia f [kōrrespōnden'syä] 59

transfer (money) giro m [hē'rō] 152

translate traducir [trädōōsēr'] 24

translation traducción f [trädōōksyōn'] 130

translator traductor m [trädōōktōr'] 38

transmission transmisión f [tränsmēsyōn'] 56

travel agency agencia f de viajes [ähen'syä de vyä'hes] 82

traveler's cheque cheque m de viaje [tshe'ke de vyä'he] 127

tray charola f, bandeja f (Sp) [tshärō'lä, bände'hä] 99

trick (cards) baza f [bä'sä] 181

trip viaje m [vyä'he] 61; **have a good** ~ buen viaje [bōō-em' byä'he] 17

tripe callos m/pl [kä'lyōs] 108

tripod trípode m [trē'pōde] 132

trout trucha f [trōō'tshä] 107

truck camión m [kämyōn'] 40; ~ **driver** chófer m, camionero m [tshō'fer, kämyōne'rō] 38

trump triunfo m [trē-ōōn'fō] 181

trunk portamaletas m, maletero m, cajuela f (Mex) [pōrtämäle'täs, mälete'rō, kähōō-e'lä] 56

tube tubo m [tōō'bō] 126

tubeless (tire) neumático m, llanta f (Mex) sin cámara [ne-ōōmä'tēkō, lyän'tä sēn kä'märä] 47

Tuesday martes m [mär'tes] 33

tug remolcador m [remōlkädōr'] 77

tulips tulipanes m/pl [tōōlēpä'nes] 130

tumor tumor m [tōōmōr'] 172

tuna atún m [ätōōn'] 106

turbot rodaballo m [rōdäbä'lyō] 107

turkey guajolote m (Mex), pavo m (Sp) [gōō-ähōlō'te, pä'vō] 107

turn (the car) dar la vuelta, virar [där lä vōō-el'tä, vērär] 43

turn (into a road) entrar en [enträr' en] 43

turn off (a road) doblar, torcer (Sp) [dōblär', tōrser'] 43

turn off apagar [äpägär'] 182

turn on poner [pōner'] 182

turnip nabo m [nä'bō] 110

tweezers pinzas f/pl [pēn'säs] 142

two dos [dōs] 28

two-piece de dos piezas [de dōs pye'säs] 135

two-stroke motor motor m de dos tiempos [mōtōr' de dōs tyem'pōs] 54

typewriter máquina f de escribir [mä'kēnä de eskrēbēr'] 138; ~ **paper** papel m para la máquina de escribir [päpel' pä'rä lä mä'kēnä de eskrēbēr'] 138

typhoid fever tifoidea f [tēfō-ēde'ä] 172

U

ulcer úlcera f [ōōl'serä] 172

ultrasonics ultrasonido m [ōōlträsōnē'dō] 175

umbrella paraguas m [pärä'gōō-äs]

144; **garden** ~ sombrilla *f*, parasol *m* [sŏmbrē'lyä, päräsōl'] 91

umpire árbitro *m* [är'bētrō] 190

uncle tío *m* [tē'ō] 35

underpants *(men's)* calzoncillos *m/pl* [kälsōnsē'lyōs] 135

undershirt camiseta *f* [kämēse'tä] 135

undertow corrientes *f/pl* [kōrryen'tes] 185

underwear ropa *f* interior [rō'pä ēnteryōr'] 135

university universidad *f* [ōōnēversēdäd'] 39

unlock abrir con llave [äbrēr' kōn lyä've] 92

unstamped sin franquear [sēn frängke·är'] 150

until hasta [äs'tä] 32

urgent urgente [ōōrhen'te] 147

urine orina *f* [ōrē'nä] 168

urinalysis análisis *m* de orina [änä'lēsēs de ōrē'nä] 165

urologist urólogo *m* [ōōrō'lōgō] 163

use uso *m* [ōō'sō] 80

usher acomodador *m* [äkōmōdädōr'] 179

uterus útero *m* [ōō'terō] 168

V

vacant libre [lē'bre] 65

vacation vacaciones *f/pl* [väkäsyō'nes] 78

vaccinate vacunar [väkōōnar'] 164

vaccination vacunación *f* [väkōōnäsyōn'] 78; ~ **certificate** certificado *m* de vacunación [sertēfēkä'dō de väkōōnäsyōn'] 78

vagina vagina *f* [vähē'nä] 169

valerian drops gotas *f/pl* de valeriana [gō'täs de väleryä'nä] 161

valid válido [vä'lēdō] 62

valley valle *m* [vä'lye] 123

valuables objetos *m/pl* de valor [ōbhe'-

tōs de välōr'] 84

value declaration declaración *f* de valor [dekläräsyōn' de välōr'] 150

valve válvula *f* [väl'vōōlä] 56

vanilla vainilla *f* [vīnē'lyä] 103

vase florero *m* [flōre'rō] 130

vaseline vaselina *f* [väselē'nä] 161

veal ternera *f*, ternero *m (Mex)* [terne'rä, terne'rō] 108

vegetable market verdulería *f* [verdōōlerē'ä] 129

vehicle vehículo *m* [ve·ē'kōōlō] 41

vein vena *f* [ve'nä] 168

velvet terciopelo *m* [tersyōpe'lō] 137

venereal disease enfermedad *f* venérea [enfermedäd' vene're·ä] 172

ventilation ventilación *f* [ventēläsyōn'] 94

verdict sentencia *f* [senten'syä] 154

very muy [mōō'ē] 21

vest chaleco *m* [tshäle'kō] 135

veterinarian veterinario *m* [veterēnär'yō] 38

veterinary medicine veterinaria *f* [veterēnär'yä] 38

victory victoria *f* [vēktōr'yä] 188

video cassette cassette *m* + *f* de vídeo [käse'te de vē'de'ō] 144

view finder visor *m* [vēsōr'] 132

village pueblo *m*, aldea *f* [pōō·e'blō, älde'ä] 123

vinegar vinagre *m* [vēnä'gre] 103

vintage wine vino *m* añejo [vē'nō änye'hō] 113

violet *(adj.)* violeta [vyōle'tä] 194

violets violetas *f/pl* [vyōle'täs] 130

violin recital recital *m* de violín [resētäl' de vē·ōlēn'] 178

visa visa *f*, visado *m (Sp)* [vē'sä, vēsä'dō] 78

visit visitar [vēsētär'] 183

visiting hours horas *f/pl* de visita [ō'räs de vēsē'tä] 173

vitamin pills pastillas *f/pl* de vitaminas

[pästē'lyäs de vētämē'näs] 161

vocational school escuela *f* de formación profesional [eskōō·e'lä de fōr-mäsyōn' prōfesyōnäl] 39

vodka vodka *f* [vōd'kä] 114

volleyball vol(e)ibol *m*, balónvolea *m* *(Sp)* [vōlēbōl', bälōnvōle'ä] 190

voltage voltaje *m* [vōltä'he] 86

volume *(of series)* tomo *m*, volumen *m* [tō'mō, vōlōō'men] 130

vomiting náuseas *f/pl* [nou'se·äs] 172

voyage *(sea)* viaje *m* (por mar) [vyä'he (pōr mär)] 77

W

wait esperar [esperär'] 87

waiter camarero *m*, mesero *m (Mex)* [kämäre'rō, mese'rō] 98

waiting room sala *f* de espera [sä'lä de espe'rä] 60

waitress camarera *f*, mesera *f (Mex)* [kämäre'rä, mese'rä] 38

walk *(take a ~)* pasear, dar una vuelta [päse·är', där ōō'nä vōō·el'tä] 184

walking shoes botas *f/pl* para caminar [bō'täs pä'rä kämēnär'] 139

wall *(city)* muralla *f* [mōōrä'lyä] 123

wall pared *f*, tabique *m* [päred', täbē'-ke] 94

wallet monedero *m* [mōnede'rō] 144

ward unidad *f*, sección *f* [ōōnēdäd', seksyōn'] 173

warning triangle triángulo *m* de peligro [trē·än'gōōlō de pelē'grō] 56

warship buque *m* de guerra [bōō'ke de ge'rrä] 77

wash lavar [lävär'] 155; **~ and set** lavar y enrular [lävär' ē enrōōlär'] 155; **~ cloth** manopla *f* de baño [mänō'plä de bä'nyō] 142; **~ rooms** lavabos *m/pl* [lävä'bōs] 145

washer arandela *f* [ärände'lä] 56

washing line cuerda *f*, soga, lazo *m*

[kōō·er'dä, sō'gä, lä'sō] 144

watch *(noun)* reloj *m* [relō(h)'] 153; **pocket ~** reloj *m* de bolsillo [relō(h)' de bōlsē'lyō] 143; **stop ~** cronómetro *m* [krōnō'metrō] 143; **wrist ~** reloj *m* de pulsera, de pulso [relō(h)' de pōōlse'rä, de pōōl'sō] 153; **~ band** pulsera *f* de reloj [pōōlse'rä de relō(h)'] 143

watchmaker relojero *m* [relōhe'rō] 38

water agua *f* [ä'gōō·ä] 45; **bottled ~** agua *f* purificada [ä'gōō·ä pōōrēfē-kä'dä] 114; **distilled ~** agua *f* destilada [ä'gōō·ä destēlä'dä] 45; **drinking ~** agua *f* potable [ä'gōō·ä pōtä'ble] 144; **fresh ~** agua *f* dulce [ä'gōō·ä dōōl'se] 114; **running ~** agua *f* corriente ä'gōō·ä kōrryen'te 82; **~ skiing** esquí *m* acuático [eskē' akōō·ä'-tēkō] 185; **~ temperature** temperatura *f* del agua [temperätōō'rä del ä'gōō·ä] 186

waterfall cascada *f*, salto *m* de agua, caída *f* de agua [käskä'dä, säl'tō de ä'gōō·ä, kä·ē'dä de ä'gōō·ä] 123

wave ola *f* [ō'lä] 186

weather tiempo *m* [tyem'pō] 25, **~ prediction** pronóstico *m* [prōnōs'tēkō] 27; **~ report** parte *m* meteorológico [pär'te mete·ōrōlō'hēkō] 25

wedding boda *f* [bō'dä] 123

Wednesday miércoles *m* [myer'kōles] 33

week semana *f* [semä'nä] 32; **this coming ~** la semana *f* que viene [lä semä'nä ke vye'ne] 32; **a ~ from now** de hoy en ocho días [de oi en ō'tshō dē'äs] 31; **two ~s from now** de hoy en quince días [de oi en kēn'se dē'äs] 31

weekly cada semana [kä'dä semä'nä] 32

welcome *(greeting)* ¡bienvenido! [byenbenē'dō] 12

welcome (noun) acogida f [äkōhē'dä] 12; **you're ~** de nada [de nä'dä] 21

well bien [byen] 12; **get ~ soon** que se mejore, te mejores (fam) [ke se mehō're, te mehō'res] 20; **~ done** bien hecho, bien asado, bien cocido [byen e'tshō, byen äsä'dō, byen kōsē'dō] 102

wet mojado [mōhä'dō] 155

what? ¿qué? [ke] 18; **~ for?** ¿para qué? [pä'rä ke] 18

wheel rueda f [rōo·e'dä] 56

when? ¿cuándo? [kōo·än'dō] 18

where? ¿dónde? [dōn'de] 18; **~ from?** ¿de dónde? [de dōn'de] 18; **~ to?** ¿adónde? [ädōn'de] 18; **~ is...?** ¿dónde está...? [dōn'de estä'] 19

which? ¿cuál? [kōo·äl'] 18

whisk(e)y whisk(e)y m [ōo·ēs'kē] 114

white blanco [bläng'kō] 194

who? ¿quién? [kyen] 18

wholesaler mayorista m + f [mäyōrēs'-tä] 38

whom (to ~) ¿a quién? [ä kyen] 18

whom (with ~) ¿con quién? [kōn kyen] 18

whose? ¿de quién? [de kyen] 18

why? ¿por qué? [pōr ke] 18

wide ancho [än'tshō] 127

widowed viudo [vyōo'dō (-ä)] 79

wife esposa f, mujer f [espō'sä, mōoher'] 35

wig peluca f [pelōo'kä] 158

win ganar [gänär'] 188

wind viento m [vyen'tō] 27; **north (east) ~** viento m del norte (este) [vyen'tō del nōr'te, (es'te)] 27; **south (west) ~** viento m del sur (oeste) [vyen'tō del sōor, (ō·es'te)] 27

windbreaker cazadora f [käsädō'rä] 135

winding road camino m sinuoso [kämē'nō sēnōo·ō'sō] 43

window ventana f [ventä'nä] 94; **~**

pane vidrio m, cristal m (Sp) [vē'-drē·ō, krēstäl'] 94; **~ seat** asiento m de ventanilla [äsyen'to de ventänē'lyä] 67

windshield parabrisas m [päräbrē'säs] 56; **~ washer** lavaparabrisas m [läväpäräbrē'säs] 56; **~ wiper** limpiaparabrisas m [lēmpyäpäräbrē'säs] 56

wine vino m [vē'nō] 113; **dry ~** vino m seco [vē'nō se'kō] 113; **house ~** vino m de la casa [vē'nō de lä kä'sä] 113; **new ~** vino m nuevo [vē'nō nōo·-e'vō] 113; **red ~** vino m tinto [vē'nō tēn'tō] 113; **rosé ~** vino m rosado [vē'nō rōsä'dō] 113; **sweet ~** vino m dulce [vē'nō dōol'se] 113; **vintage ~** vino m añejo [vē'nō añe'hō] 113; **white ~** vino m blanco [vē'nō bläng'-kō] 113

wing ala f [ä'lä] 71

winter invierno m [ēmbyer'nō] 33

wire (tool) alambre m [äläm'bre] 57

wire telegrama m [telegrä'mä] 147

withdraw retirar [retērär'] 152

within dentro [den'trō] 32

witness testigo m [testē'gō] 49

wood carvings tallas f/pl de madera [tä'lyäs de mäde'rä] 144

wool lana f [lä'nä] 137; **pure ~** lana f pura [lä'nä pōo'rä] 137; **pure virgin ~** pura lana f virgen [pōo'rä lä'nä vēr'hen] 137

words palabras f/pl [pälä'bräs] 147

work (noun) obra f [ō'brä] 178

worker obrero m [ōbre'rō] 38

worsted estambre m [estäm'bre] 137

wound herida f [erē'dä] 172; **~ salve** ungüento m [ōongōo·en'tō] 161

wrapping paper papel m de envolver, de embalar (Sp) [päpel' de envölver', de embälär'] 138

wrench llave f inglesa [lyä've ēngle'sä] 57

wrestle luchar [lo͞otshär'] 190
wrestler luchador *m* [lo͞otshädōr'] 190
wrestling lucha *f* [lo͞ot'shä] 190
wrist muñeca *f* [mo͞onye'kä] 168
write escribir [eskrēbēr'] 24
writer escritor *m* [eskrētōr'] 38
writing paper papel *m* de carta [päpel'
de kär'tä] 138

X

x-ray *(noun)* radiografía *f*, rayos *m/pl*
equis [rädyōgräfē'ä, rä'yōs e'kēs]
173
x-ray *(verb)* hacer una radiografía
[äser' o͞o'nä rädyōgräfē'ä] 173

Y

yacht yate *m* [yä'te] 77
yard *(approx.)* metro *m* [me'trō] 126
year año *m* [ä'nyō] 32; **happy new ~**
próspero año nuevo [prōs'perō

ä'nyō no͞o·e'vō] 23
yellow amarillo [ämärē'lyō] 194
yes sí [sē] 21
yesterday ayer [äyer'] 31; **day before ~**
anteayer [änte·äyer'] 31
you usted [o͞oste'] 12
young joven [hō'ven] 35
younger más joven [mäs hō'ven] 35
your su [so͞o] 13
youth group grupo *m* juvenil [gro͞o'pō
ho͞ovenēl'] 97

Z

zebra crossing paso *m* de peatones,
paso *m* cebra [pä'sō de pe·ätō'nes,
pä'sō se'brä] 43
zero cero [se'rō] 28
zipper cierre *m*, cremallera *f* [sye're,
kremälyer'ä] 136
zoo jardín *m* zoológico [hardēn sō·ō-
lō'hēkō] 123
zoology zoología *f* [sō'ōlōhē'ä] 39